1492

DISCOVERY, INVASION, ENCOUNTER

Sources and Interpretations

1492

DISCOVERY, INVASION, ENCOUNTER

Sources and Interpretations

Edited, with introductions and an essay, by
MARVIN LUNENFELD
State University of New York, College at Fredonia

D.C. HEATH AND COMPANY
Lexington, Massachusetts   Toronto

Acquisitions Editor: James Miller
Production Editor: Tina V. Beazer
Designer: Cornelia Boynton
Production Coordinator: Charles Dutton
Text Permissions Editor: Margaret Roll
Cover: (*from top*) Compass medallion, detail from a fifteenth century French mariner's map of South America (The British Library); The stern of a caravel, German woodcut, 1486 (The Granger Collection); Detail of a painting depicting the sinking of his fleet by Cortés (Museo de America, Madrid); Aztec painting depicting encounter with Spaniards (Bibliothèque Nationale).

For permission to use copyrighted photographs, grateful acknowledgment is made to the copyright holders listed on page 355, hereby considered an extension of this copyright page.

Published simultaneously in Canada.

Printed in the United States of America.

International Standard Book Number: 0-669-21115-x

Library of Congress Catalog Number: 90-80531

10 9 8 7 6 5 4 3 2 1

To Harold and James

CONTENTS

PREFACE

Christopher Columbus alone had the monomaniacal passion to renew the transatlantic voyaging abandoned long before by the Norsemen. Notwithstanding our society's tendency to overemphasize the uniqueness of the single individual, it is important to recall how much difference he made. But this book does not aim to provide a biography of Columbus nor to offer a narrative tracing his voyages. There are a number of thorough volumes available on these subjects, and many more will roll off the presses in the Quincentenary Jubilee of 1992.

There is a distinct usefulness, however, in focusing on the epochal first voyage. The familiar story of moving out into the dark of the "Ocean Sea" can still call up the wonder of the initial contact with people living in what appeared to be a Garden of Eden. Yet this book should lure its readers beyond this often retraced path into unfamiliar areas.

How does one even describe what happened when Columbus made his first landfalls in the Western Hemisphere? A discovery? Columbus boasted that Ferdinand and Isabella had ennobled him and given him command of "all the islands and continents that I should discover and gain in the Ocean Sea." But half a millennium later, most westerners feel uncomfortable with so bold and ethnocentric an assertion that Columbus "found" two vast landmasses, already inhabited by peoples ranging from the most unassuming to the highly sophisticated. However, the word *discovery* is by now so inseparable from the events of 1492 that it is better to use the term, with an explanation, than to abandon it altogether. If indeed there was any *discovery* made, it was mutual, between peoples alien to one another.

The verb *discover* in fact took a long time to establish itself in English as "a search for the unknown." Who in the fifteenth century was so foolish as to wish to look for anything totally unknown? European navigators were searching for usable maritime routes to the wealthy East. Attitudes took time to change. The explorers had directed their energies toward finding a profitable route to a known destination; it took time for them to begin dreaming of searching out new lands. The geographer Richard Hakluyt wrote in 1589 of "This voyage intended for the discoverie of Cathay [China] and divers other regions, dominions, islands unknown."

Invasion might be a better term to use for the events under study, except that the European newcomers often found willing allies among local inhabitants, who were anxious to use the bearded men from across the ocean to conquer nearby enemies. Sensitive to verbal nuances, the Spanish grappled conscientiously with the problem of finding proper terminology to describe their actions. After prolonged debate, a general royal ordinance promulgated by Philip II in 1573 decreed that, "Discoveries are not to be called conquests. Since we wish them to be carried out peacefully and charitably, we do not want the use of the term conquest to offer any excuse for the employment of force or the causing of injury to the Indians. . . ."

The neutral word *encounter* has recently come into general scholarly use. *Encounter* seems friendly enough, evoking the idea of social gatherings. There is, after all, not that much difference in traveling over a sea, a mountain, or a desert to get the encounter started. If all that happened in 1492 was that Columbus "encountered" the Amerindians, the historian would successfully escape the ethnocentric connotations of a *discovery* and the violent implications of an *invasion*. The derivation of *encounter* from the Latin should, however, put us on guard. The word comes from the fusion of *in* ("in") + *contra* ("against"), so it is not as neutral as it appears.

The question of labeling Columbus's "Great Enterprise" generates controversy because choosing only one of the three descriptive terms—*discovery*, *invasion*, or *encounter*—predetermines one's interpretation. In this book, we use not just one of the three words, but all of them. The primary documents and scholarly readings in the book thus have been set in conflict. History of the best kind challenges conventional wisdom and is not meant to provide comfort. Despite the divergence of views, we have striven to provide thoughtful readers with enough information to determine the meanings of 1492 for themselves.

Part One, *Discovery*, offers a variety of viewpoints on why Columbus set sail, how he managed to reach the Western Hemisphere, what he thought he found once arrived, and how others viewed him and his achievement. He has always had his detractors as well as his supporters.

The next part, *Invasion*, deals with the impact of the voyage, on the residents of both the New World and the Old. After a look at Columbus's skirmishes, the readings go on to describe the extraordinary assaults on the vast empires of the Aztecs and the Incas. Since these astonishing Spanish victories raised the expectations of the English and the French, these other Europeans' responses also merit brief examination. Passing from pitched battles to pulpits, lecture halls, and courts, we examine the bitter arguments over the justification of the conquests and the ill treatment meted out to the native peoples.

Encounter, the last part, offers a number of views held by Amerindians of whites, and vice versa. Some readings focus on a group's initial thoughts about the other's way of dress (or undress), appetites, technologies, and sexual practices. Some selections describe how mutually incompatible civilizations attempted to understand one another, borrow ideas and techniques and, on the most intimate level, interact religiously and sexually. Next come observations on the causes of the natives' death toll and the transfer of diseases between continents. Finally, we consider the massive exchange of plants, animals, and humans between the hemispheres.

To steal a person's name is to take his or her identity. Words such as "savage," "barbarian," and "heathen," which whites once freely applied to native Americans, were intended to show which was the superior people.

Columbus, convinced that he was in the Asian waters of the "Indies," named the islanders *los Indios*. The English version, "Indian," all too often calls up a vision of a mounted plains brave in feathered war bonnet, the cliché of every Western movie. Roger Williams, founder of the colony of Rhode Island, noted the aborigines' puzzlement over the name when he wrote in 1643—"They have often asked mee why wee call them *Indians*." A European child still reads books about "red Indians," a distant echo of misconceptions concerning the decorative use of body paint.

Native peoples use their traditional tribal names among themselves. Where appropriate, this book follows that understandable preference. Writing about the Western Hemisphere's peoples collectively, the introductions use either "native," "aborigine," or the relatively new "Amerindian," preferred by ethnohistorians because it is less tainted than any other term by unfortunate past associations.

Some of the selections are primary sources that were written at the time, or near the time, of the events described. Other selections are secondary sources, that is, descriptions or interpretations produced by later writers. The introductions point out which sources are primary and which are secondary because it is necessary to be aware of the difference. Primary source documents of an official nature are sometimes propagandistic accounts written by leaders, soldiers, or clerics in the heat of the moment. The recent secondary source accounts usually attempt an acceptable scholarly level of neutral balance. This is not always easy to accomplish, however, because the history of the New World is replete with genocide, economic and political conflict, and desperate cultural struggles that continue to engender strong emotions.

ACKNOWLEDGMENTS

It was my good fortune to be selected as a fellow for the 1987 Newberry Library Summer Institute on Transatlantic Encounters, and to be invited to subsequent institutes to offer workshops. The varied viewpoints freely expressed by the staff, fellows, and faculty at these sessions helped to determine what selections would be in this book. The participants in the 1989 National Endowment for the Humanities Summer Institute on "The Encounter of Cultures: Sixteenth-Century Mexico," sponsored by the University of Maryland and held in Mexico City and Oaxaca, were equally generous with advice and suggestions. Invaluable assistance in locating written and visual sources was rendered by librarians at The Newberry Library, the University of Chicago, Fredonia College, and Buffalo State College. At D. C. Heath, Tina Beazer, Cia Boynton, Rosemary Jaffe, James Miller, and Margaret Roll all assisted in seeing the book through the production process.

I also thank the following scholars who reviewed the manuscript at various stages: Kenneth Andrien, Ohio State University; J. Patrick Donnelly, Marquette University; Marc Gilbert, North Georgia College; De Lamar Jensen, Brigham Young University; David LaFrance, Oregon State University; Murdo MacLeod, University of Florida; and Duane Osheim, University of Virginia.

M. L.

The World in 1492

In 1492 the world beyond Europe was not a sleeping beauty waiting to be awakened. The "ocean blue" into which Christopher Columbus's small craft sailed seethed with activity. The Caribbean Taínos paddled canoes from island to island. Polynesians skillfully navigated catamarans from speck to speck, travelling hundreds of miles across the Pacific. A host of cargo-laden Arabian ships flew before the monsoons in the Indian Ocean. Imperial couriers on horseback traversed the road atop the Great Wall of China. Inca runners hurried along Peru's long Highway of the Sun.

All this movement was taking place in the fragmented world whose widely separated regions lived largely or completely isolated from each other. Columbus's early medieval predecessors as Atlantic voyagers, the Norse, had reached the Western Hemisphere long before the Spanish, yet they had left there no permanent mark. But Columbus's voyages would have a far different outcome. For reasons to be examined, he had the more lasting impact on a Europe that was ready, by his time, to capitalize on his trip. With his voyages, the unification of the globe into a single human community began.

The overview that follows of the lands around the globe in 1492, which were on the verge of being brought together for the first time, focuses on the more developed societies, showing their significant differences and similarities.

Different methods of agriculture shaped these societies in various ways; we will examine the impact of three staples: wheat, rice and corn. We will also consider the interchange of plants and animals between the hemispheres and the disastrous transmission of European diseases to the Americas.

Our look at the world in 1492 will conclude by considering why Europeans were especially expansionistic, compared to people of other cultures. Here we will investigate how Europe used commerce, ship technology, and firepower to forge ahead with exploration. In particular, we will contrast Europe with China, the richest and most powerful empire on earth in the fifteenth century, to learn why China seemingly dropped out of competition with Europe to explore. We will also consider the conflict between the competing faiths of Christianity and Islam, of which the latter had far more adherents by 1492.

The Imagined World

The realization that the earth is a globe did not originate with any Iberian or Italian sailor. Christian Europe had inherited this idea from classical Greece, along with remarkably correct knowledge about the earth's size.

There is no foundation for the tenacious belief that Columbus, wise beyond the knowledge of his day, had to contend with ignorant flat-earth proponents. At the beginning of the fifteenth century, Pierre d'Ailly, a French cardinal, summarized the view held by the educated: "Although the Earth is carved into mountains and valleys, which are the cause of its imperfect roundness, it may be considered round, and this explains why lunar eclipses caused by the Earth's projected shadow appear round, for this reason we say that the Earth is round."

Europeans believed that the globe was arranged in parallel belts of climate zones, from the frigid poles to the torrid equator—the latter supposedly too hot for human life. (Only actual experience corrected this misapprehension. In the sixteenth century, Father José Acosta wrote of his experience in Panama: "I confess that I laughed and made sport of Aristotle's meteors and his [ancient Greek] philosophy seeing that at the time and place where, according to his rules, everything had to burn and be made of fire, I and my companions were cold.")

But when Columbus set sail in 1492, people in the Eastern Hemisphere knew only the tripartite division of Europe, Asia, and Africa. These three continents constituted a great land mass surrounded by the world ocean, which was strewn with islands, both known and assumed. The Greeks had called this vast inhabited area the *ecumene*. Moreover, ancient writers had speculated that a natural harmony called for the existence of other populated continents—one in the Eastern Hemisphere and two in the Western Hemisphere—to balance the *ecumene's* known continents. In the first century A.D., the Roman poet Seneca had predicted in his drama *Medea:*

The years run slow, but yet shall come
A time when Ocean frees our bonds,
When vast new worlds shall stand revealed,
Iceland [Thule] shall not be the last of lands.

The Norse Voyages

Centuries before Columbus, during a global warming trend, the Norse boldly ventured forth, sailing from Scandinavia to Iceland and then to Greenland. Sometime after 1,000 A.D., Leif Ericsson landed in rich country, which he dubbed "Vinland" because it bloomed with self-pollinating wheat (*vin*). His, and later expeditions, brought along women and children to brave the seas together with their men. For a few years all went well between the Norse and the local inhabitants, but in time conflict broke out. With false bravado, the *Saga of Erik the Red* sneered at the natives as "small ill-favored men with ugly hair on their heads." These original inhabitants had weapons equal to those of the Norse, however, and drove them off. The saga describes a battle in which all the Norsemen fled. A woman, Freydis, scorned fear and stayed to fight the natives although she had to move slowly because she was pregnant.

> She found a dead man in her path, Thorbrand Snorrason—he had a flat stone sticking out of his head. His sword lay beside him; she picked it up and prepared to defend herself with it. The Skraelings [natives] were approaching her. She pulled out her breasts from under her shift and slapped the sword on them, at which the Skraelings took fright, and ran off to their boats and rowed away.

Although Freydis fought for the colonies, the Norse in general became less drawn to these lands in constant conflict. They had few commercial impulses encouraging them to cling to Vinland as a trading post, nor were they intent on spreading a religion, having been only recently, and partially, Christianized. They went there to farm, and when that seemed too difficult they left. (We will soon discuss how different economic, technological, and religious conditions caused later Europeans to prevail in new lands.)

Late medieval climatic change made the Norse retreat permanently, as the "Little Ice Age" closed in and caused the abandonment of even the colonies on Greenland. By the fifteenth century, all contact with the far west had faded into the mists of mythology; only in the twentieth century have the settlements in Newfoundland been excavated. Some scholars speculate, however, that Columbus may have visited Iceland and learned of sagas narrating Norse voyages to the west. It is known that Danes shared information with the Portuguese as early as the 1420s; and during 1470–1473 a joint Danish-Portuguese expedition failed to find a northwest passage to Asia—if indeed that was the voyage's purpose. While Columbus resided at Lisbon he may have heard details at court of the voyage. Ultimately, the fact that the Norse rather than Columbus could claim the title of "first" European in the Western Hemisphere meant little; Columbus's voyage alone proved to be the lasting contact, the one that forever changed human consciousness.

How the World View Changed

Columbus's voyage and subsequent ventures showed that the globe was not just a single *ecumene* surrounded by a vast sea. As the later explorer Amerigo Vespucci told his sponsor: "Rationally, let it be said in a whisper, experience is certainly worth more than theory." But navigation around this globe of alternating water and land did not come quickly. Giovanni da Verrazzano, looking for a northern route to the fabled East, complained: "My intention . . . was to reach Cathay [China] and the extreme eastern coast of Asia, but I did not expect to find such an obstacle of New Land as I have found." Only the circumnavigation of the world (1519–1521) by Ferdinand Magellan's few surviving crew members conclusively demonstrated that ships could move from ocean to ocean in a continuous passage. Robert

Thorne, writing to Henry VIII of England in 1527, summarized the view: "So I judge, there is no land unhabitable, nor sea innavigable."

There were many countries for explorers to visit, so let us briefly examine some of the major ones around the newly-opened globe. In the spirit of Jules Verne's 1872 story about a mad race across the globe, *Around the World in Eighty Days*, we will in the next few sections make a grand tour from Europe to Africa to Asia to America. Along the way we take quick glances at governments and people.

The Grand Tour: Europe

The world of 1492, soon to be connected into a global system, comprised a host of disparate societies with leaders of varying abilities. Europe swarmed with small states, some of which were coalescing into larger units. In what is today Spain, Ferdinand of Aragón and Isabella of Castile saw their dynamic marriage yield the beginning of a united peninsula when Granada, the last Muslim kingdom in Iberia, fell after a ten-year campaign. It was not mere accident that Ferdinand and Isabella, to whom Pope Alexander VI granted the title Catholic Sovereigns, sponsored Columbus within months of that conquest. Their lands were at the forefront of an aggressive Christendom and were prime markets for expanding Italian commercial activities. Castile's active maritime force competed directly with Portugal's, and in the 1470s the two kingdoms had gone to war over possession of Atlantic islands. Between 1488 and 1495, a period of dynastic struggles and domestic problems, John II's Portugal experienced a lull in exploration. The Spanish rulers took advantage of this critical opportunity.

Ferdinand and Isabella availed themselves of Italian financial backing in launching their program of exploration. In 1492 Amerigo Vespucci arrived in Seville as the agent of Lorenzo de Medici, the ruler of Florence, whose family had risen to power through wealth acquired in banking. That year was also a fateful one in Florence as the fiery Dominican preacher Girolamo Savonarola revealed during his Advent sermon that he had seen a hand in the heavens brandishing a sword surrounded by the blazing words "the sword of God is about to strike the earth." In a sense his prophecy came true upon the death that very year of Lorenzo de Medici. Lorenzo's foresight as a politician had maintained a balance of power among the small states comprising the Italian peninsula. But the collapse of Italian alliances upon Lorenzo's death encouraged Charles VIII of France to invade the peninsula, ushering in two generations of struggle in Italy between the Spanish and the French. The struggle ended in two centuries of Spanish domination, giving Spain even greater access to Italian resources and control over the papacy.

In Rome in 1492, Alexander VI, the notorious Borgia pope from Aragón, was beginning his reign. "Of all the pontiffs who have ever reigned," the diplomat and political theorist Niccolò Machiavelli was to write, "Alexander best showed how a pope might prevail both by money and force." Spain and Portugal would come to this pope the next year to partition the newly investigated portion of the globe—an act that soon inspired a French king to remark sarcastically: "I should very much like to see the passage in Adam's will that divides the New World. . . ." Spain's share of America's wealth added greatly to its power; the gold of Mexico and the silver of Peru would aid Ferdinand and Isabella's heirs when they strove for what their enemies called "universal domination" in Europe's heartland. In time, however, this same dependence upon wealth transported across the Atlantic would encourage monarchs to undertake ruinous military burdens that, by the early seventeenth century, would undermine Spain's domestic economy.

At the other end of Europe, momentous change was also under way in 1492. The Grand Duke of Moscovy ruled the core of what was then becoming Russia. There, Ivan III the Great, grandfather of the famous Ivan the Terrible, was the first of his dynasty to shake loose from the grip of the Golden Horde, as the Mongol rulers of Russia were known. His claim to ruler "of all the Russians" was recognized in 1492 by the prince of Lithuania. Ivan had married Zoë, niece of the last Byzantine emperor, and in 1492 the Orthodox Metropolitan (bishop) of Moscow proclaimed Moscow the "Third Rome," the rightful successor to the Roman and Byzantine empires as the center of Orthodox Christendom. At the same time, the ruler of Muscovy assumed the title czar (derived from *Caesar*), beginning a fitful territorial expansion that would continue until the twentieth century.

Other countries dominated the rest of northern and eastern Europe in 1492. Sweden, Denmark, and Norway were united in the Kolmar Union under Sten Sture I, the Elder. Casimir IV, king of Poland and grand duke of Lithuania, died in 1492, having expanded his two realms to their maximum territorial extent. In Hungary, Laszlo II fought desperately against encroaching Ottoman Turks, the greatest power in eastern Europe. With the acquiescence of eastern European monarchs, the nobility was forcing free peasants into serfdom on vast consolidated farms that grew grain for western Europe. The descendants of these eastern European peasants would not recover their freedom for centuries.

The Grand Tour: Turkey to Africa

The Ottoman Sultan Bayezid II's vast Muslim domains stretched across North Africa, and from Persia to Serbia and the southern Ukraine. In 1453 the establishment of the Ottoman capital at Istanbul, formerly the Christian city of Constantinople, had ended the Byzantine Empire, last remnant of the ancient Roman Empire. Istanbul, "the place that is like Paradise" according to a poet, was the largest metropolis in the Mediterranean basin. Its population, over 100,000 in 1492, would rise to 700,000 a century later. The sultan's major military activity in 1492 (912/913 in the Islamic calendar) was one in a series of lunges at Hungary, a country that the Turks would eventually conquer in 1526. By the beginning of 1492 Turks and other Islamic peoples dominated a great swath of land from the south of Spain across North Africa and down into Africa as far as Mozambique. After the first Muslims spread into the Holy Land and Persia from Arabia, they extended their dominion from India through southeast Asia and penetrated into China and the Philippines. Christianity lagged far behind, entirely confined within the fragments of what once had been the ancient Roman Empire. The one gain Catholics saw in centuries was at Granada, which in 1492 fell to Ferdinand and Isabella. Hardly suffering from this loss, Islam remained the only religion established throughout the length of the *ecumene*. A visitor from another solar system would likely have concluded in 1492 that the future belonged to the Muslims.

Columbus proved to be the savior of Christianity by handing the Western Hemisphere over to the Spanish, who were bitter foes of Islam. Father Bernardino de Sahagún's sixteenth-century *General History of the Things of New Spain* acknowledged that the Catholic Church's constant retreat ended only in America:

> The Church left Palestine and now the Muslims live, reign and hold dominion in Palestine. From there it went to Asia in which there are nothing but Turks and Muslims. It went to Europe where, in the greater part thereof [due to the Protestant Reformation], the Church is not obeyed. Where it now has more tranquil seat is in Italy and Spain, whence crossing the ocean, it has arrived in these regions of the Western Indies. . . .

The Church's powerful influence in Latin America—both as the traditional bastion of upper-class status and as the contemporary advocate of the masses—can be traced back to the protected status that it gained from Columbus. Muslims and Jews had no place in his plan for the lands he chanced upon.

During 1492 (5252/5253 of the Hebrew calendar), Spain, which had the largest Jewish community in Europe, expelled its Jews. Spanish Jews unwilling to accept baptism were granted four months to put their affairs in order before departing. Even a bitterly antisemitic priest acknowledged that he was moved by the pathetic sight of the people of Israel leaving "as if from the captivity of Egypt, tired, hungry, and beset by robbers." Improvised armadas gathered to ferry out the exiles; Columbus noted in his logbook that he was delayed by crowding at harborside. Leaving Palos, his ships swung into the Sáltes and passed La Rábada, where his three vessels turned west, and a single accompanying craft, carrying the last of the Jews, turned east. Muslim territories proved to be a haven for the refugees. Many of the 180,000 refugees ended up in the Turkish possessions. The Sultan said that he "marveled greatly at expelling the Jews from Spain, since this was to expel their wealth."

North Africa lay wholly in Turkish hands, although Egypt, under Sultan

Qu'it Bay, clashed with its Turkish overlords. Several powerful black empires controlled large parts of sub-Sahara Africa. The Sudanese people lived south of Timbuktu united in the short-lived, brilliant Songhai empire that spread the Muslim faith all through western Africa. This Bantu-speaking empire disintegrated shortly after the death of Ali Ber in 1492. The kingdom of Kongo, based upon a craft-village economy, dominated a region south of the Congo (Zaire) River more than half the size of England. Its ruler, Nzinga a Knuwu, had taken the name João I (John I) when he converted to Christianity ten years earlier. Eventually, however, he abandoned the faith and his new name because giving up polygamy had cost him alliances, and he felt that Christ had never delivered compensating military victories. In Christian Ethiopia, Eskender (Alexander), styled the Lion of the Tribe of Judah and King of Kings, welcomed his first Portuguese visitor. His mother, the Empress Eléni, was instrumental in accepting Portuguese offers to aid in the fight against Muslims. Travel and trade across the Indian Ocean made Ethiopia an important information post, where soon the Portuguese would discover how to travel on to the Indian subcontinent.

The Grand Tour: South Asia

In 1492 most of India was under Muslim domination, except for the Hindu kingdom of Vijayanagar in the south. The Muslim sultan, Sikandar Lodi, resided at Delhi. His regime would soon be swept aside by invaders from central Asia, much as the early Delhi sultans, themselves of central Asian descent, had once swept over the wealthy kingdom on the plains. The Indian subcontinent was accustomed to marauders and visitors. Perhaps accordingly, its people had become adept at absorbing new cultures into the mainstream of their culture and new peoples into the highly compartmentalized social system that Portuguese visitors called *castes*. This next wave of invaders, the Mughals, had a government that was to be the envy of contemporary European rulers. Their liberal religious policy was two hundred years in advance of the later "enlightened" societies of the West: Indian courts were open not only to orthodox Muslims and Hindu Brahmans, but to Parsi priests, Jain saints, and later to Christian missionaries. In Tibet, Dönyö Dorje, its nominal ruler, was subordinate to its spiritual leader, the Dalai Lama (Grand Monk).

In the countries of southeast Asia, the people were Theravada (the "lesser wheel") Buddhists, who venerated their leaders as gods. Despite their exalted status, the rulers did not persecute those of other faiths, due to the humane doctrines of their tolerant religion. In Thailand, Rama Thibadi II, a ruler from the Ayuthia Dynasty, would be the first in his line to give trading privileges to the Portuguese. On the Indochinese mainland, the tiny realm of Vietnam had slowly extended its conquests southward as far as Binh Dinh. Although rebuffed earlier by the Chinese, Vietnam could not be stopped. (Nearly five centuries later France and the United States would learn the same costly lesson.)

Meanwhile, Islam had made great advances in the Malay Archipelago, where Sultan Mahmud was the seventh (and last) of the native rulers. His port, Malacca, was perhaps the greatest in all the world. "No trading port as large as Malacca is known," wrote the Portuguese Tomé Pires, in *The Account of the East* (1517), "nor anywhere do they deal in such fine and highly-prized merchandise. Goods from all over the East are found here; goods from all over the West are sold here." Under Malacca's patronage, Islam spread to the Javanese trading ports and the "Spice Islands," today part of Indonesia. These islands were the ultimate goal in the competition between the Portuguese and the Spanish. When Columbus found land in 1492 (which he misidentified as part of Asia), the Spanish thought victory was theirs. They were soon proven wrong. In 1513—the same year Vasco Núñez de Balboa would first see the dauntingly vast Pacific at Darien, Panama—the Portuguese would finally reach the "Spice Island" chain.

The Grand Tour: China and Japan

Shortly after the completion of his book, Tomé Pires became Portugal's first ambassador to China. China was under the paternal rule of the most venerated of its Ming Emperors, Xiao-zong (Hsiao-tsung). In 1492 (the years 4189/4190 in the Chinese calendar) the emperor was locked in a struggle with the Confucian bureaucracy. In the eyes of the governing elite, he relied too much on a foreign-born minister and favored his wife's relatives too much.

Fifteenth-century China had the potential to expand greatly its geographical horizons. Xiao-zong's chief minister asked to see the records of the earlier Zheng he (Cheng Ho) expeditions, which had traversed the Indian Ocean from 1405 to 1433. These seven expeditions, some involving as many as 62 ships and 32,000 troops, contacted 30 countries and reached as far as the east coast of Africa! A stone tablet erected there poetically commemorates the voyages:

> We have traversed immense water spaces and have beheld huge waves like mountains rising sky-high, and we have set eyes on barbarian regions far away hidden in a blue transparency of light vapors, while our sails loftily unfurled like clouds day and night continued their course. . . .

Zheng he, "the three-Jeweled Eunuch," brought back with him as prisoners the king of Ceylon and the prince of Sumatra. He also brought tribute gifts from sixteen rulers—one such gift was an African giraffe.

Despite this ample booty, the Jewel-Ship voyages were not resumed after 1433. The reason is hidden in the records of the Foreign Office. At the request of Xiao-zong's chief minister, the president of the War Office looked up the background and discovered that a minor official had hidden or destroyed the data. The official kept silent through three days of beatings, until he finally confessed:

> The expeditions of Zheng he to the Western Ocean wasted tens of thousands in money and grain, and moreover the people who met their deaths on these expeditions are countless. Although he returned with wonderful precious things, what benefit was it to the state? This was merely an action of bad government of which ministers should severely disapprove. Even if the old archives were still preserved they should be destroyed in order to suppress a repetition of these things at the root.

The president rose and said to him, "Your hidden virtue, sir, is not small—surely my seat [office] will shortly be yours."

Both of these men understood that Zheng he had been a Muslim counterweight used by a previous emperor to thwart his civil service. The elite resented the drain on the treasury merely, as they saw it, to bring back expensive goods for the harem. The Confucian bureaucrats made sure that naval exploration would not be resumed. They were successful because China lacked several of the elements that encouraged European naval ventures. China did not have a missionary religion that it wished to spread by force of arms. In addition, the scholarly elite distrusted the military. Warships were considered an extravagance; no threat loomed from the sea in 1492. Commanders were expected to focus on the immediate threat from land invasion to the north, and rulers spent their money finishing the Great Wall—the top priority at the time.

The Chinese lumped merchants along with soldiers as parasites. The scholarly elite venerated agriculture and scorned commerce. Chinese culture disdained the mere amassing of wealth, emphasizing instead social harmony and order. An ancient text counselled that emperors "should consider the Empire as if it formed a single household." A prosperous economy and sophisticated technology gave Chinese officials little inclination to look beyond their boundaries.

In the sixteenth century, Chinese merchants would be forbidden to travel abroad. Extensive trade routes covered all regions along the China Sea and the Indian Ocean, as well as nearby islands in the Pacific (possibly excepting the continent of Australia), but as mainland China would turn inward, this traffic would fall to its expatriate community. Thus, because Ming China lacked incentive to round Africa and directly contact Europe, the dwarf kingdoms would visit the giant, not the reverse.

To the east, Japan remained independent of Chinese domination. In the thirteenth century, during Marco Polo's visit to China, the latter's emperor had attempted, but failed, to occupy Japan. Polo's *Travels*, overstating the wealth of the kingdom, fired the European imagination:

> I will tell you a wonderful thing about the palace of the Lord of that island. You must know that he has a great palace which is entirely roofed with gold. Just as

our churches are roofed with lead, insomuch it would scarcely be possible to estimate its value.

In the Japan that Columbus hoped to visit, not only was there no Great Lord (the emperor Tsuchi-Mikado was a retiring figurehead under the control of the Ashikaga shogunate) but the ruling clan was also dissolving. In 1493 warlords drove Shogun Yoshitane from his capital. Sparse verse by the Japanese poet, Sogi, captures the melancholy of this troubled time:

To live in the world
Is sad enough without this rain
Pounding on my shelter.

Would anything in the capital of Kyoto have satisfied Columbus? The three-story Golden Pavillion of Kitayama, a Zen temple, with its roof sheathed in the pure yellow metal, might have passed the test. The explorer would, however, never see it, for where he expected to find Japan, he blundered instead upon lands of which he had never dreamed.

The Grand Tour: The Western Hemisphere

In 1492 the Reverend Speaker Ahuitzotl, eighth leader of the Aztecs, was extending the confederation of the Triple Alliance through Mesoamerica. He was not much of an organizer and less of a conciliator, relying instead on economic incentive and terror to keep his allies and his conquests in line. Only Venice rivaled his capital, a splendid city built in an aquatic environment. Within a generation, the Spanish conquistadores would be dazzled by their first sight of the city of México-Tenochtitlán. Bernal Díaz wrote:

> And when we saw all those cities and villages built in the water, and other great towns on dry land, and that straight and level causeway leading to México, we were astounded. These great towns and temples and buildings rising from the water, all made of stone, seemed like an enchanted vision . . ., indeed, some of our soldiers asked whether it was not all a dream.

But despite their inland-boating skills, the Aztec remained essentially a land-bound society with little interest in maritime navigation.

The ancient Mayan civilization, which long predated the Aztecs, had no centralized authority in 1492. A half century earlier, the city of Mayapan ruled over the northern Yucatán peninsula, but in 1492 this city of 12,000 was only one of 16 communities that shared its area. The very disunity of the interior tribes prevented the Spanish from conquering a broad area and prolonged the Mayan resistance until 1700.

The destruction of Mayan culture prevents us from learning of their society's intellectual accomplishments. Only four Mayan books would survive at the hands of Spanish conquerors and priests. But from other sources, one can surmise that the Mayas had one of the most artistic and refined societies on the globe. Their calendrical system, based upon careful astronomical observations, was far in advance of any European system and was rivaled only by that of China.

Seacoast Mayas, the Putum, engaged in heavy trade and so were unfazed by foreigners. They were friendly to Columbus in 1502, but not curious about him. These Mayas had a complex long-distance trading network, centered on Cozumel Island, for waterborne bulk goods, such as salt, cacao, cotton, and ceramics. The Putum's reach incorporated the Aztecs to the east and Panamas to the south. Some Mayan goods even found their way to Peru.

The Incas, much as did the Aztecs, underwent an explosive expansion toward the end of the fifteenth century. Under the rule of Tupac Inca Yupanqui, who succeeded his father Pachacuti in 1471, they consolidated a unified empire from the present Columbia-Ecuador border to central Chile—a coastal distance of over 2,500 miles. This expansion was accomplished in a mere thirty years. A superb transport system of 7,000 miles of imperial roads tied the empire together. The section of the *Capac Nan* (Beautiful Road), which snakes through central Ecuador from the high-altitude city of Quito, opened immediately after the Inca's death. On these roads couriers ran postal service messages, travelling up to 150 miles per day to speed communication in a land that had no large beasts of burden.

Having little mainland left to conquer, the Inca himself, or a delegated commander, set out on a naval expedition to the bleak Galápagos Islands but turned back empty-handed. He died in 1493, considering himself master of the known world. But despite their naval prowess, the Peruvians, Mayas, and Aztecs never crossed the Atlantic, so far as records show. With justifiable, if ethnocentric, pride, Dionyse Settie, the first Englishman to publish a personal account of what Europeans called the "New World," exalted: "Consider also that Christians have discovered these countries and peoples, which so long have lain unknown, and they not us." The varied areas of the globe uncovered in the course of exploration would be found to have vastly different customs, yet grew only a few basic staple foods: primarily wheat, rice, or corn (maize).

The Staff of Life

By 1492 the planet had already reached the end of the long warming trend that had encouraged the Norse exploration half a millennium before. Expanded food resources were beginning to strain under the weight of multiplying populations, for fully 70 percent of humanity depended upon merely 7 percent of land under cultivation. Each of three vast land areas depended upon a different staple: wheat in western Eurasia, rice in eastern Eurasia, and corn in the Americas. The basic staple of each area profoundly influenced the way in which its society developed.

As cultivated in Europe, wheat (along with barley, oats, and rye) was a low-yield crop grown on individual plots that required the cooperative labor of humans and animals to turn the soil. Beasts also provided the manure required for the intense fertilization of wheat. The heavy plow used in northern Europe brought men into the fields, partially displacing women who had been predominant in planting. This strenuous effort at cultivation was worthwhile because wheat's high nutritional value made for a hardy populace. The abundance of beasts in Europe also meant relatively high per capita meat consumption (although this was falling by the late fifteenth century).

Wheat requires large amounts of land because a half or two-thirds of the land under cultivation must lay fallow during any year. Peasants could, and did, constantly attempt to move out to frontier areas where they might bring fertile new land under cultivation. Feudal law attempted to keep them in place, but this was often in vain because empires founded in the post-Roman period never held together long or saw their will enforced with regularity. Peasants were kept so busy by farming that they had little time free to be mobilized by rulers for massive public works projects on the scale of Mesoamerica's ceremonial centers.

Europeans developed into aggressive individuals. Their life was always insecure because the yield per seed was very low, and their crops constantly were at the mercy of the weather or the caprices of long-distance transportation. Thus famine alternated with plenty. The annual killing of field animals that were unlikely to survive winter inured Europe's peasants to bloodletting on a massive scale. Drawing on this toughness, rulers mobilized their subjects' fighting prowess to improve their personal status at the expense of their neighbors and, eventually, at the expense of the world.

Of all the staples, rice demands the most centralized political organization for effective cultivation and leads to the largest population concentrations. It is feasible to reap two crops, or even three, a year from the same rice paddy. Since rice provides more food per acre than any other staple, huge numbers of people could live crowded together and still have enough food. But these multitudes crowded into small spaces had to develop ritualized deferential behavior to survive daily contact and live in peace.

Reliable irrigation and a mobilized army of male and female laborers were essential before dry or wet rice paddies would yield their rich crop. Building waterproof dikes, equipped with sluices and channels, around the wet plots required much bureaucratic planning—and endless hand labor, summed up in a traditional Chinese proverb: "Work when the sun rises, rest when the sun sets. The emperor is far away." Farmers could neither leave the land nor stray far from their incessant duties, so distant governments were always assured of regular tax collection. Such conditions made for compliant subjects and durable regimes. Although its central government was subject to cyclical rise and fall, imperial China was by far the most prosperous area of the world in 1492, with a consistently well-fed population.

Compared to the growing of other staples, corn demands relatively little effort from the peasantry. Corn grows quickly and is even edible before it ripens. It can be cultivated on dry land cleared by the slash-and-burn method, planted along the shores of Mexican lakes, or set into Andean terraces. Since relatively little time had to be spent on cultivation, the Mesoamerican and Peruvian elites appropriated much of the corn-growing peasantry's potential free time to build vast pyramid-temple-palace complexes, roads, and hydraulic works.

Since corn grows everywhere, merchants had little incentive to organize long distance transmission of bulk agricultural goods. Corn has a low nutritional value, but when combined with beans and squash, it can support large populations. In corn-growing societies, women retained their importance in agriculture. They used digging sticks to make the holes for hand planting seeds, a job that required no great strength. In the Andean regions, the potato took over wherever corn could not be grown. Animal protein would have been a great help in supplementing this barely adequate diet, but the Western Hemisphere lacked large beasts to domesticate and use for protein.

Due to the intensive cultivation of the three staple foods, at the end of the fifteenth century, China, the Mediterranean community, and the Americas accounted for three-quarters of the globe's population. Estimates of China's population at this time run to over 100 million. (The Chinese population had decreased when a wave of disease struck in the thirteenth century.) The Mediterranean area, with 60 to 70 million people, was slowly rebounding from plague outbreaks that followed upon the fourteenth-century Black Death's destruction of one-quarter to one-third of the population. Meanwhile the Americas, untouched as yet by major epidemics, may have had as many as 80 million inhabitants.

Hitherto completely separate, the Eastern and Western Hemispheres suddenly came into contact with each other in 1492. Thus began a drastic shift in the relationship between populations, with both beneficial and fatal results. European crops and livestock were carried across the ocean, providing new sources of food. Indigenous American plants were pushed aside by such invaders as wheat, bluegrass, daisies, and dandelions, while native animals and the Amerindians themselves were crowded by imported horses, dogs, pigs, and steers that ran wild in vast herds and encountered few natural enemies.

The introduction of Western Hemisphere crops to the rest of the globe encouraged explosive population growth and long-range improvement in human diet. Today 60 percent of the food eaten by the world's people is of American origin. It would be difficult to imagine Italy without tomatoes, Ireland without white potatoes, Hungary without paprika, China without sweet potatoes and peanuts, Africa without manioc (tapioca), or East India and Southeast Asia without hot peppers and cayenne. All these ingredients, as well as chocolate and tobacco, spread throughout the world as a consequence of Columbus's voyage.

For the peoples of the Western Hemisphere, however, contact brought disaster. As Mark Twain wrote: "It was wonderful to find America, but it would have been more wonderful to miss it." Soon after Columbus's arrival, Amerindians suffered the greatest population collapse known to history. Between three-quarters and nine-tenths of the native population died during the next century as they contracted newly-introduced diseases. Consequently, the pandemics that emptied North and South America by the seventeenth century left Columbus's misnamed "Indies" to be refilled by multitudes from Europe, Africa, and ultimately everywhere on the globe. In the Americas the varied civilizations of the world of 1492 were to merge.

The Great Traditions

Four major forms of civilization flourished in the broad landmass of Eurasia. While Islam continually expanded its boundaries by creating a succession of "gunpowder empires," the Hindu population of south Asia relied upon its increasingly elaborate caste structure for stability during the subsequent years of Mughal decline, and China remained focused upon a familial form of governmental organization. Europe emphasized elaborating feudal kingdoms within its limited territorial area. It alone among the four societies developed a tradition of self-governing mercantile urban republics, but by 1492 merely a handful of northern Italian city-states retained their independence.

All four great centers of civilization had elaborate bureaucratic structures, significant cities, iron implements, writing, and a high technology. These characteristics created stable societies which, even if they might be overthrown, would prove difficult for outsiders to change. From the thirteenth to the fifteenth century, successive waves of aggressive Turks and Mongols had pressed their way into China, India, North Africa, and northeastern Europe. Soon these outsiders began to learn local customs and to be absorbed into the major cultures. But effective firearms and improved fortifications would eventually put an end to the easy movement of nomads.

Elsewhere—in southeast Asia, in the African empires, and in the great civilizations of the Americas—"high" culture was confined to temple-palace complexes standing amidst peasant villages. These kingdoms, coalitions, and empires were fragile and rapid-changing. They rose and fell with the fortunes of an individual leader, a family line, a climate change, a decline in the economy, or a sudden invasion. Hunter-gatherer groups and stable agrarian tribes occupied Australia, much of the Americas, the interior of Africa, the Pacific islands, and the Arctic coastline. Although these people were insulated from contact with the other societies, they led hard lives, and the future of their ways of life was to prove bleak. The established folkways of agrarian peoples around the world was transcended in the more prosperous civilizations that released artists and intellectuals from the pressure to conform to tradition.

The Creative Impulse

Around the globe, creative individuals expanded the confines of their cultural inheritance to serve the needs—and reflect the interests—of their elites. Antonío de Nebrija presented Queen Isabella with a Castilian grammar in 1492, the first such compilation for any Latin-derived vernacular. "Language," he declared to her, "is the ideal weapon of empire." Diego de San Pedro completed *A Prison of Love*, an influential romance of chivalry soon translated into many languages. Also in 1492, the female humanist Cassandra Fedele delivered several eloquent Latin orations in Venice; so highly esteemed was she that the year before, the Venetian Senate had denied her permission to accept Queen Isabella's invitation to join the Spanish court.

In Milan, Leonardo da Vinci was building his model of an enormous equestrian statue for Duke Ludovico Sforza and jotting into his secret notebooks scientific observations and a sketch of a bat-wing flying machine. In the same city-state in 1492, Bramante was painting frescos in the Sforza castle and beginning to build the choir and cupola of the church of Santa Maria della Grazie. Dominico Ghirlandaio in Florence painted scenes from the lives of the Virgin and Saint John. In the city's Medici gardens, the seventeen-year-old Michelangelo worked on imitations of the ancient statues in Lorenzo de Medici's collection. And in German territory, Martin Behain, acting on orders from the Nuremberg city council, constructed the first surviving terrestrial globe.

An Egyptian, Suyúti, universal historian and compiler, was becoming the most prolific Arabic author of all time, with more than 500 books to his credit. In China Wang Shuo-ren strove for the unity of knowledge, insisting that Confucianism, Taoism, and Buddhism were equally valid paths to self-fulfillment. Wang Yang-ming, a Confucian scholar-official, wrote guides to behavior much influenced by Buddhism. His most famous aphorism—"Knowledge is the beginning of conduct; conduct is the completion of knowledge"—is still quoted in Asia. The young scholar Wen Zheng-ming (Wen Cheng-ming) was beginning his cycle of popular bandit-hero stories, which would become rallying points for opposition to despotism. Zhen-chou (Chen-ch'ou) set his hand to drawing the most perfect of persimmons, while the finest painter Japan has produced, Sesshū, prepared ink landscape scrolls. As a result of contact, commerce, the creation of public museums, and the spread of printing, these cultural contributions—and a knowledge of the doings of all humanity—have become available to the whole world in the aftermath of the European voyages of exploration.

The European Challenge

How did the Europeans pull ahead of their rivals? There are answers to this question that do not involve ugly racist claims of superiority. People everywhere come up with approximately the same solutions for problems, depending upon natural resources available in their area. Complex civilizations have developed in a half dozen places—Mesopotamia, Egypt, the Indus Valley, China, Mesoamerica, and the Andies. The larger the cultural area each civilization had to draw upon, and the longer contiguous high cultures survived, the more inventions and advances there were to be passed around and perfected. Thus it happened, for example, that realization of gunpowder's explosive power occurred almost simultaneously to metallurgists at either end of Eurasia. The earliest drawings of guns date from 1326 in Europe and from 1332 in China. Both drawings show a vase-shaped container armed with a single oversized arrow; this similarity suggests rapid transmission of the innovation, wherever it was first invented.

By maintaining contact with each other, societies in the *ecumene* enjoyed an enormous head start over portions of the world that were relatively isolated. Western Europe made better use of these contacts than did any other part of Eurasia. This was due to the historical developments in western Europe that fused intense local rivalries to an aggressive form of commerce and an expansionistic religion.

The Portuguese (rather than the Spanish) ruling house made the first moves in the early 1400s to break out of Europe's isolation. When Columbus joined the naval service of the king of Portugal, he put himself directly in the mainstream of Europe's effort to push past its boundaries. Slowly, Portuguese navigators traced their way along the west coast of Africa, setting up forts, trading communities, and churches. They found their way to India, where they became a part of the local trade patterns. João de Castro, a Portuguese official, decried what he saw as the unfortunate domination of commerce over religion: "The Portuguese entered India with the sword in one hand and the Crucifix in the other; finding much gold, they laid the Crucifix aside to fill their pockets."

But in his moralizing, Castro missed the point that the southern and western Europeans were motivated to undertake exploration by an early form of capitalism today often called "commercial capitalism" to distinguish it from later industrial capitalism. Concentrating on commerce, Europeans pushed outward in search of markets and in pursuit of resources to combine and accumulate. The principal element in this story is the long-distance trade that was primarily in luxury goods. Merchants were backed by powerful princes who adhered to the economic philosophy of mercantilism for more energetic trade, and often sponsored their own voyages. Monarchs, in turn, looked to these merchants for economic backing to counterbalance the power of their landed aristocrats. The growth of banking, insurance, and early forms of joint-stock ventures created a solid economic base to finance expeditions. Traders gradually accumulated geographic knowledge and a unique understanding of other cultures—essential information for the success of their ventures.

All these commercial factors were closely allied with an expansionistic Christianity that cast a spiritual veil over the mundane financial details. Bernal Díaz, untroubled by the mixed motives of his fellow conquerors of Mexico, celebrated with an easy conscience those who "died in the service of God and of His Majesty, and to give light to those who sat in darkness— and also to acquire that wealth which most men covet."

Through commerce and war, European kingdoms improved their shipping and gained an ultimate advantage over the rest of the world. In 1400 European ships were still entirely dependent on fair breezes and rarely attempted to make headway against an adverse wind. But by 1492 a technological spurt had fused Mediterranean-style ships with Atlantic-style ships to produce the heavy carrack that was good for trade and the lighter caravel that was good for exploration. "The best ships in the world and able to sail anywhere," wrote the Venetian Cadamosto. These vessels could make speed in rough seas with their broad square-rigged sails, yet maneuver in unknown harbors by means of smaller triangular sails.

Columbus's own experience testified to the virtues of the new sailing craft. The *Niña* and the *Pinta* were agile caravels; the *Santa María*, a lumbering carrack, hit a reef and sank on Christmas eve in 1492. Nothing accurate was known about these ships until 1986, when a bundle of documents from Seville's Archive of the Indies was first published, including papers concerning the *Niña*, Columbus's favorite ship. She proves to have been sixty-seven feet long, with a beam of twenty-one feet, and a draft of just under seven feet. The ship had four masts, perhaps the result of refitting from three in 1498. For weapons, she carried ten breech–loaded bombards.

Although European naval technology was sufficiently advanced in 1492 to allow sailors to move out into unknown waters, it was still by no means the best in the world. The Chinese, the Indians, and the Arabs had long been innovators in ship technology, having developed such instruments as the marine compass, astrolab, windrose, astronomical tables, and heavy brass cannon. The Incas had balsa wood rafts whose enormous size astonished the first Spanish observers.

Why then did western ships become increasingly seaworthy and develop an ever-greater carrying and fighting capacity than those of any rival? Europe's advantage lay in the systematic application of scientific advances to technology. For example, this interplay constantly forced the pace of substituting machines for muscle power in propulsion and warfare. As an

Italian resident at the court of Ferdinand and Isabella observed: "Enough for us that the hidden half of the globe is brought to light. . . . Thus shores unknown will soon become accessible—for one in emulation of another sets forth in labors and mighty perils."

Improvements in cannonry, spurred by the constant bickering of European kingdoms, led to the creation of powerful gunships that forced their way into other lands. Small crews manning these ships could master a remarkable amount of power, enabling them to sail rapidly and wreak unparalleled destruction. Westerners were also willing to push military developments to extremes not thought of by more inhibited societies. In Macao, China, for example, Jesuit priests, angry with the Dominican monks, used their shooting prowess to blow up the monastery of Saint Dominic! A passage from a local chronicler at Ceylon (today Sri Lanka) shows terror and surprise at the first arrival of the Portuguese:

> There were in the harbor a race of very beautiful people who wore boots and hats of iron and never stop in any place. They eat a sort of white stone [bread] and drink blood [wine]. . . . They have guns with a noise like thunder and a ball travelling from one of them, after traversing a league, will break a castle of marble.

By the end of the sixteenth century, Portuguese and Spanish gunships were being supplanted by the even more formidable fleets of Dutch and English men-of-war. The great naval expeditions not only initiated new contacts between countries, but also brought peoples of the world face to face with each other for the first time. Juan Luis Vives, born in 1492, enthused: "Truly, the globe has been opened up to the human race." The results, unfortunately, have not been all good. Often the encounters between black and white, occidental and Asian, or Amerindian and European, brought misunderstanding and conflict.

Human beings never needed an excuse to be intolerant; history records endless struggles over language, territory, and religion. This latent hostility becomes most apparent in colonialism, imperialism, and slavery. In 1525 the Spaniard Friar Tomás Ortiz urged that Amerindians be enslaved and universally condemned the native peoples he had met: "They were like donkeys, dumb, crazy, and without sense. . . . They did not have the makings or skills of men." Similarly, the cultivated Chinese elite sneered at Europeans as "long-nosed barbarians"—unsanitary, smelly people who rarely washed. Huo Ru-xia (Huo Ju-hsia), a seventeenth-century official, thought he knew how to deal with the outsiders:

> Once we have branded them as bandits we are obliged to exterminate them— only to see more of them come. Is this policy wise? [Instead] build cities for them and govern them with Chinese officials. From then on they will be subject to Chinese law. This is the way barbarians have been transformed into Chinese.

Europeans were no less intolerant. Cotton Mather, an eighteenth-century Puritan minister in New England, assailed the Amerindians: "These doleful creatures are the veriest ruins of mankind which are to be found anywhere upon the face of the earth." He condemned their constant washing and attacked their sweat lodges as "heathen superstition." Even in the twentieth century a Crow chief, Plenty-Coups, felt bewildered by the differences between his people and whites: "We kept the laws we made and lived our religion. We have never been able to understand the white man, who fools nobody but himself." The world, it is clear, still carries the burdens of racial and religious intolerance that came to light during the great age of contact.

That first wave of voyages sought out inhabited lands. In addition to Columbus's, these expeditions include Bartolomeu Díaz's rounding Africa, Vasco da Gama's reaching India, Sebastian Cabot's voyage to North America, and Ferdinand Magellan's crews and Sir Francis Drake's separate circumnavigations of the globe. This era of discovery closed with the death of Captain James Cook in 1779 in Hawaii; a second, more abstract and "scientific," phase of exploration opened when human beings started searching out uninhabited areas. This new search has run the course from Robert Peary's 1902 expedition to the North Pole to landings on the moon.

In 1992 the Columbus Space Sail Cup will call upon design teams in the Americas, Europe, and Asia to develop three solar-powered spacecraft. The first to reach Mars will win. No one expects friendly natives to row out to greet these crafts. Space probes have already informed earthlings that no life appears to exist in the solar system, outside our blue-green globe. Upon close inspection of television images, scientists have found all planets and moons to be frozen or boiling, poisoned wildernesses. Unless a startling technological breakthrough releases us from the boundaries of our solar system, the only animate matter we may ever encounter is on our own planet. In all its amazing diversity, this life is ours to save or destroy.

López de Gómara began the dedication of his *General History of the Indies* with understandably exaggerated pride: "The greatest event since the creation of the world, excluding the Incarnation [God becoming man] and death of the Creator, is the discovery of the Indies, and so you call them the New World." Christopher Columbus broke the ancient seal of ignorance that earlier societies had set upon the Ocean Sea. His venture gave him a significant role in the coming together of humanity. To this adventurer belongs much of the glory, and some of the shame, for the events that followed.

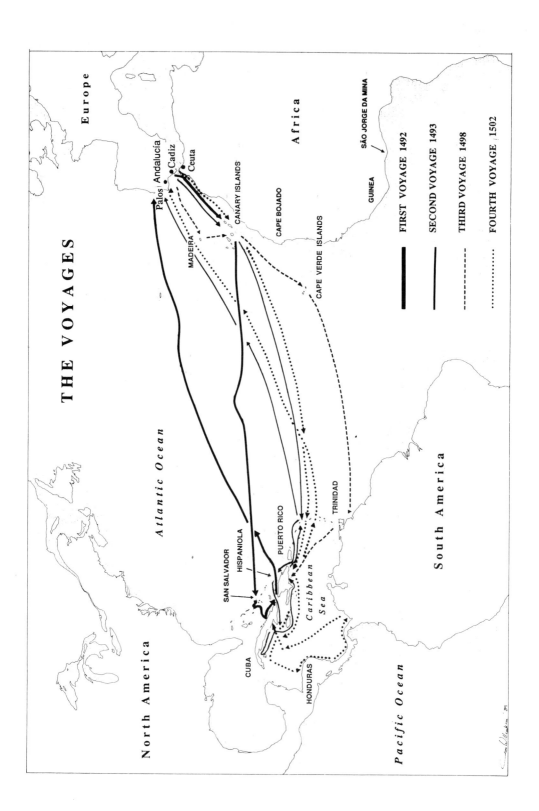

THE VOYAGES

Europe

Africa

North America

Atlantic Ocean

South America

Pacific Ocean

Caribbean Sea

Palos
Andalucía
Cadiz
Ceuta

CANARY ISLANDS

MADEIRA

CAPE BOJADO

CAPE VERDE ISLANDS

GUINEA

SÃO JORGE DA MINA

SAN SALVADOR
HISPANIOLA
PUERTO RICO
TRINIDAD
CUBA
HONDURAS

FIRST VOYAGE 1492

SECOND VOYAGE 1493

THIRD VOYAGE 1498

FOURTH VOYAGE 1502

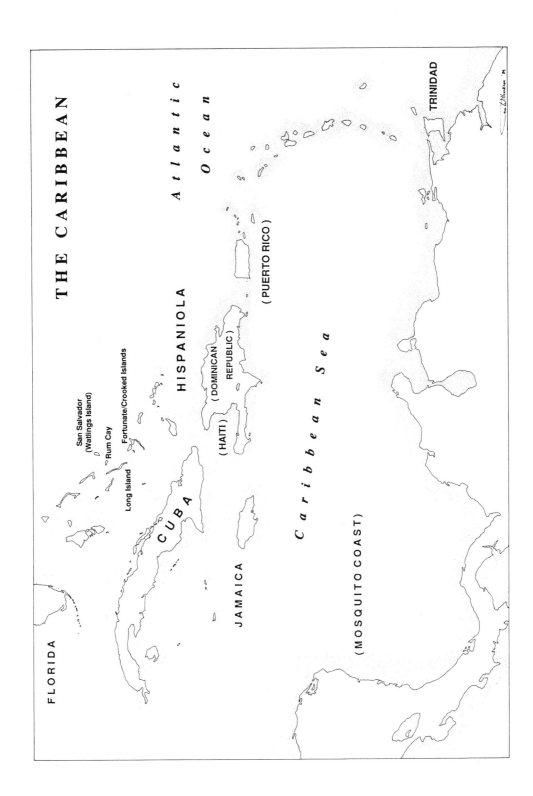

THE CARIBBEAN

FLORIDA

San Salvador
(Watlings Island)

Rum Cay

Long Island

Fortunate/Crooked Islands

Atlantic Ocean

HISPANIOLA

(DOMINICAN REPUBLIC)

(HAITI)

(PUERTO RICO)

CUBA

JAMAICA

Caribbean Sea

(MOSQUITO COAST)

TRINIDAD

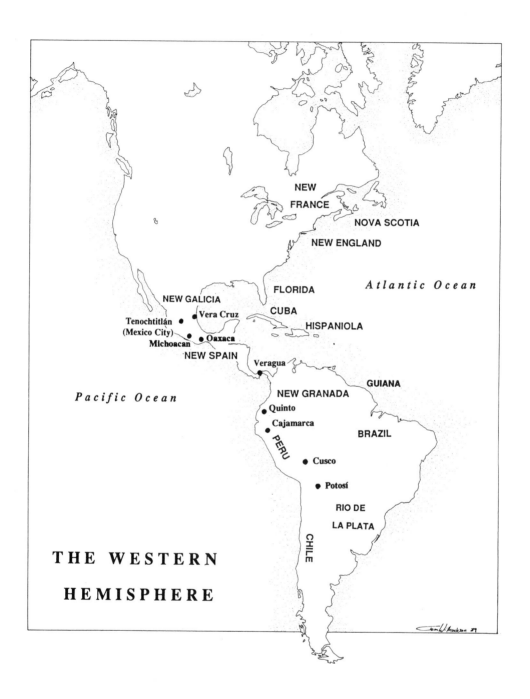

NEW
FRANCE

NOVA SCOTIA

NEW ENGLAND

FLORIDA

Atlantic Ocean

NEW GALICIA

CUBA

● Vera Cruz

Tenochtitlán ●
(Mexico City)

HISPANIOLA

● Oaxaca

Michoacan ●

NEW SPAIN

Veragua
●

GUIANA

NEW GRANADA

Pacific Ocean

● Quinto

● Cajamarca

BRAZIL

PERU

● Cusco

● Potosí

RIO DE

LA PLATA

CHILE

THE WESTERN

HEMISPHERE

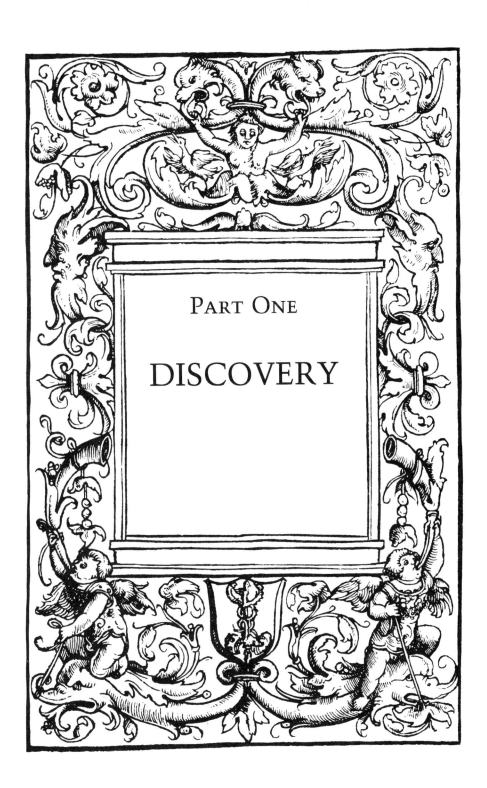

PART ONE

DISCOVERY

Columbus's First Voyage

Andrés Bernáldez, curate of Los Palacios, near Seville, Spain, was the grandson of a humble notary public. His grandmother, hearing Andrés, at age twelve, read a register belonging to her husband, said, "Child, why do you not so write the events of the present time, as they are? For to do so would be no idle task. If you write of the good things that come to pass in your days, those who come after will know of them and, marveling as they read of them, will give thanks to God." His accounts, celebrating the reign of Ferdinand and Isabella, present all the great events from the viewpoint of a small-town, Old Christian cleric. The writing style is straightforward, for he narrates events with little comment. From these pages, it is possible to recapture the impression the first voyage made on an ordinary man of unsophisticated mind.

> *"with the help of God, they would strike land."*

Columbus stayed at Bernáldez's house shortly after he arrived from Portugal. They were such good friends that these selections read like the dinner talk of the Admiral, retelling tales about his remarkable voyage. Simple as this narrative is, some details are not found elsewhere because the writer took some of his information from "certain papers," now lost, that Columbus had left in safekeeping with him.

I n the name of God Almighty: there was a man of the land of Genoa, a seller of printed books, who carried on his trade in this land of Andalusia, whom they called Christopher Columbus, a man of great intelligence, though with little book learning, very skilled in the art of cosmography and the mapping of the world. From that which he had read in Ptolemy and in other books, and by his own natural ingenuity, he formed an opinion as to how and in what way this world, in which we were born and in which we live, is fixed in the arc of heaven, so that in no part does it reach to the skies, nor is there anything firm to which it is joined, but there is only land and water, formed in a circle, amid the space of the heavens. And he

SOURCE Andrés Bernáldez, *History of the Two Catholic Sovereigns, Don Fernando and Doña Isabella*, Ch. 118ff., trans. Cecil Jane, *The Voyages of Christopher Columbus . . .* (London: The Argonaut Press, 1930), Appendix One, pp. 309–314.

conceived of a way in which a land, rich in gold, might be attained, and he had the opinion that, as this world and the firmament of land and water can be traversed round about by land and water, as John Mandeville [Document 6] relates, it followed that one who had such ships as were suitable and who was ready to persevere through sea and land, of a surety would be able to go and to pass by the westward, to the right of St. Vincent, and to go by way of Jerusalem, and to Rome and to Seville, which would be to compass all the earth and the roundness of the world. And his ingenuity enabled him to make a mappemonde [world map], and he studied much in it, and he formed an idea as to what part of the Ocean Sea it was needful to go through and traverse, so that one could not fail to strike land, and he conceived of the land of much gold which would be reached, as clearly as if he had seen it. And delighted with his idea, knowing that discovery greatly pleased King John [II] of Portugal, he went to apply to him, and told him of the fruit of his imagination, and he was not given credence, for the King of Portugal had many old and very skilled navigators, who held him to be of no account and who fancied that in the world there could be no greater discoverers than themselves.

So it was that Christopher Columbus came to the court of King Don Ferdinand and of Queen Doña Isabella, and made to them a statement of his ideas, to which for a while they did not give much credence; and he pleaded with them, and asserted that which he told them to be certainly true and he showed them his mappemonde, so that in the end he inspired them with a desire to know of those lands. And dismissing him from their presence, they summoned learned men, astrologers and astronomers, and men about the court, learned in cosmography, from whom they took information, and the opinion of the major part of them, when they had heard the argument of Christopher Columbus, was that he spoke the truth, with the result that the king and queen came to an agreement with him, and commanded that three ships should be given him in Seville, fitted out, for the time for which he asked, with men and food, and sent him forth, in the name of God, our Lord, and of Our Lady, to discover. And he departed from Palos in the month of September 1492, and pursued his voyage through the sea, beyond the Cape Verde Islands, and thence always to the westward, having his prow pointed over to where we see the sun set in the month of March, in which direction all mariners believed that it was impossible to strike land, and many times had the kings of Portugal sent out in that direction to discover land, since the opinion of many was that in that direction they might find lands very rich in gold, and never were they able to reach or to discover any land, and they returned always with their labour lost; and in accordance with the good fortune of the king and queen and in accord with their deserving, God will that in their days and under their reign these lands should be reached and discovered.

In one of the ships, moreover, went as captain, Martín Alonso Pinzón, a native of Palos, a great sailor, and a man of excellent knowledge in matters of the sea. And from the island of Cape Verde, they went towards the direction which Columbus, the captain of the fleet, believed should be sought, and they sailed thirty and two days, before they struck land. And in the last days of this voyage, seeing that they had gone more than a thousand leagues and had not discovered land, the opinions of the sailors were divided, for some of them said that there was no reason in going further, for then they would go to their doom without hope of rescue, and that it would be marvellous were they to be assured of their safe return, and of this opinion were most of them; and Columbus and the other captains, with gentle words, persuaded them to go further and said that they might be sure that, with the help of God, they would strike land. And Christopher Columbus looked one day up at the sky, and saw birds flying very high, from one direction to another, and he showed them to his companions, saying to them, "Good news!" And half a day after that they sighted land and, coming to it, they lost the largest ship of the three which they had, in Española [Hispaniola], for it ran aground there, but not a single man was lost. And on the first island they landed, and Columbus took formal possession of it in the name of the king and queen, with flag and standard unfurled, and he gave it the name of San Salvador [Watlings Island?], and the people of it called it Guanahaní, and those who lived there, like all the people of those lands, went about as naked as when they were born, men and women alike; and there, although the natives fled from our men, they were able to have speech with some of these Indians, and they gave to them of the things which they had brought, with which they were reassured. And to the second island which he reached, he gave the name Santa María [Rum Cay], in honour of Our Lady.

To the third island which he reached, he gave the name Fernandina [Long Island], in memory of King Don Ferdinand: to the fourth island which he reached, he gave the name Isabella [Fortunate/Crooked Islands], in memory of Queen Doña Isabella; to the fifth island which he reached, he gave the name Juana [Cuba], in memory of Prince Don Juan, and so each island, of those which they reached, they named with a new name. And they followed the coast of this island of Juana westwards, and they found it to be so great that they thought that it must be a continent, and as they found in it no towns or villages on the coast of the sea, but only small clusters of houses, with the people of which they could not have speech, since they fled as soon as they saw them, they put into an excellent harbour. And thence Christopher Columbus sent two men inland to learn if there was there a king or if there were great cities, and these men went three days' journey and found a vast number of villages of wood and straw, all with an innumerable number of people, but nothing of importance, and they accordingly returned. And the Indians, whom they had already taken, told them by signs that it was not the mainland but an island.

And following the coast of it eastwards for about a hundred and seven leagues, they there came to the end of it in a certain cape, and thence they saw another island, distant from this eastwards eighteen leagues, to which Christopher Columbus gave the name Española, and they went thither; and following the north coast, as they had done in the case of Juana, they saw it, like all the other islands, to be very lovely beyond words, and this Española to be far finer than all the rest, for in it there are many very notable ports of the sea, beyond comparison as good and better than any that are in the land of the Christians; and many rivers of marvellous size. The land is lofty and in it there are very high sierras and very lofty mountains, lovely and of a thousand forms, all accessible and full of trees, of a thousand different shapes and kinds, very tall, so that they seem to touch the sky, and I believe that they never lose their leaves, as appears from the fact that it was then the time when it is winter here, when all trees lose their leaves, and in that land the trees were as trees are here in the month of May; and some of them were flowering, and on some of them were fruits and seeds. And there in the trees sang nightingales and other birds, in the morning, in the month of November, as here they do in May. In that land there are six or seven species of palm, which are a wonder to see, owing to the diversity between them; as for the fruits, trees and plants, which grow there, they are marvellous. There are in the island groves of pine trees, pasture lands and plains, very great. The trees and fruits are not like those here.

There are in the island mines of gold, which is not there regarded at its true value. It appeared to Christopher Columbus and to the others who were with him, that, having regard to the richness and beauty of the land, there should be great profit to be gained from tilling the soil, planting it, and cultivating crops and keeping stock, imported from Spain. They saw in this island of Española many great rivers and of very sweet water, and they found that there was much gold in their sand. They found that the mountain trees there differ from those of Spain. They saw and learned from the Indians that in this island there are great mines of fine gold and of other metals.

The people of these islands, and of the others already mentioned, all go naked, men and women alike, as when they were born, with as little bashfulness and as little shame as do Castilians when fully dressed. Some women wear a kind of small skirt, hanging at the back and held by a cord round their waists and running between their legs, which does not further hide their nakedness. Others conceal their nakedness with a leaf of a tree, which is large and suitable for this purpose. Others wear a cloak made of woven cotton, which covers the hips and which reaches down to the middle of the thigh; and I believe that they wear this when they are with child.

They have no iron or steel, nor arms, nor anything which is made from such materials, nor have they any other metal, except gold. They were very frightened by our people, so that three men with arms could put a thousand to flight, and they had no weapons, except canes and sticks, without iron, somewhat sharp at the end, which could hardly wound our men. And although they possess such arms, they do not know how to use them, or to make use of stones, which are useful weapons, for their heart fails them. On this voyage, it happened that Christopher Columbus sent two or three men from the ship to a certain town to have speech with those people, and an innumerable crowd of people came out, and when they saw our men come near, they all fled, and not one remained behind; and afterwards some were reassured and lost their fear, and they proved to be very gentle and very cheerful, and they delighted in talking with our men. They were all people without craft and without malice, generous and very amiable, sharing what they had with each other, and they offered to give what they had without stint.

After they had lost their fear, they came to the ships, showing our men very great love and affection, and in return for everything which was given them from the things in the ships, they gave many thanks and received them with much pleasure and as valuables, and they gave to our men whatever they had. It happened that a sailor, in return for a small needle, was given a piece of gold equal to two and a half castellanos, and to others, in exchange for trifles of equally small value, much more was given; and for new blancas they gave two pieces of gold equal to three castellanos, and an arroba and two of woven cotton, of which there is much in those lands.

Christopher Columbus, and those who were on this voyage, did not learn the belief and creed of these peoples. They pointed to the sky, indicating that they believed that there lay all strength and holiness, and they thought and believed that our men with this fleet who had come there, were come from the heavens and were people of another world, and with this idea, when they had lost their fear, they showed all respect and reverence for our men in every way. And this was not because they were so innocent and of so very small understanding, for these people are very subtle and possess a very quick intelligence, and they are men who navigate all those seas, of which they give an account that is marvellous, but it is because they never saw people wearing clothes, or ships of similar size to ours, nor have they heard any account of such.

As soon as Christopher Columbus arrived in the Indies with his fleet, in the first island, he took some Indians by force in order to obtain information concerning that country, and so it was that, speaking by signs and speaking in words, the people of the ships very soon came to understand the natives, and the latter were very useful on the voyage, for wherever the ships came our men let some go and sent them out, and they went on land crying out, "Come! come to see people who have come from heaven." And those who heard, when they had made sure of what was said, went to tell it to the rest from village to village and town to town, telling all to come and see this wonderful people who came from heaven; and so all, men and women, came to see so great a marvel, and after they had lost their fear, and when their minds had been set at rest, all went without terror to the men of the fleet, and brought them abundance to eat and drink, of such things as they had.

In all those islands, they had certain ships in which they navigated, which they call canoes, which are and were of the length of our fustas, some of them being large and some small, but all narrow, for they are each of them no more than a trunk of a tree, and they hollow them out with very sharp flints. In point of size, they are like an eight-banked fusta, but a fusta cannot compare with them in its rowing, for they travel so quickly that it is incredible. In these canoes, the people of those islands navigate all the seas there, and carry on trade with each other. There are some canoes which will hold and convey sixty men, and others carry more, having crews of eighty men to navigate them. Each one has an oar in his hand, and in all these islands they have not seen any diversity in the build and customs of these peoples, nor in their language, but they all have large foreheads and faces, round heads, as narrow from temple to temple as from the forehead to the neck: they have straight black hair, bodies of medium size; their colour is ruddy, and nearer to white than black.

It appeared that they all understood one another and were of the same language, which is wonderful in so many islands; they had no diversity in language, and this may be the result of navigation, for they were masters of the sea, and it was because they had no means of navigation that in the Canaries they did not understand one another and each island had its own language. I have already said that Columbus went along the island which he called Juana, in his ship, for a hundred and seven leagues along the coast in a straight line, so that this island appears to be larger than England and Scotland taken together. In the western part of the island of Juana there remained two provinces to which Columbus did not go, to one of which the Indians gave the name Naan, where they say that men are born with a tail, but I do not believe that it is there, as is indicated in the mappemonde, in which I have read, and if it be there, it will not be long before it is visited, with God's help. These islands and provinces, according to what the Indians say, are each fifty or sixty leagues in length.

The island of Española [Hispaniola, today divided between Haiti and the Dominican Republic], which the Indians call Haiti, is, in comparison with the others already mentioned, as gold to silver; it is very large and very lovely, with trees and rivers, mountains and plains, and with very beautiful seas and harbours. Its circumference [greatly exaggerated here] is equal to that of all Spain from Colibre, which is in Cataluna, near Perpignan, by the coast of the Spanish sea, round Granada and Portugal and Galicia and Vizcaya, to Fuenterrabia, which is the end of Vizcaya. They went a hundred and eighty-eight leagues of four miles each, in a straight line from west to east, and from this the greatness of this Española is obvious, for it is very large and is situated most conveniently and nearest the mines of gold and for all trade alike from the mainland on this side and the mainland on that. Christopher Columbus formed a settlement there in Española, Haiti as the Indians call it, in a town to which he gave the name of the town of la Navidad, and left there forty men with artillery and arms and food, beginning to build a fort; and he left master workmen to make it, and left them enough to eat

8

for a certain time. And he left there picked men, from those whom he had with him, men of good understanding and capacity for everything.

And he was forced, as it would appear, to leave them, since, as he had lost a ship, there was no way in which they could depart, and this was concealed here, and it was said that they were left only to begin the work of colonisation. Columbus made friends with a king of that district where he left the people, and they made promises to each other as friends and brothers, and Columbus recommended to him those men whom he had left there. The ship which was lost [the Santa María] was wrecked in Española near where he left those forty men.

There are there, at the entrance of the Indies, certain islands, which the Indians of the islands already mentioned call *Caribs*, which are inhabited by certain people whom they regard as very ferocious, and of whom they are much afraid, because they eat human flesh. They have many canoes with which they go about all the neighbouring islands and steal whatever they can, and take and carry away captive such men and women as they can, and kill them and eat them, a matter for great wonder and amazement. They are more ill formed than the others only in the fact that they have this evil custom; they are a very powerful race and have many arms, for they use arrows and bows of cane, and they set a sharp flint in the arrow head, or fish bones, in place of iron, which they do not possess. They wear their hair long like women, and are dreaded as ferocious by the people of the islands already mentioned, and this is because the other people are very cowardly and very domesticated and without malice, and not because the Caribs are strong or because our men have to take more account of them than of the others.

And in the islands of the Caribs, and in the other islands mentioned, there is gold beyond measure, and an infinite amount of cotton; there are especially spices, such as pepper, which burns more and has four times as much strength as that which we use in Spain, and is regarded by all the people of these islands as very useful and very medicinal. There are bushes of flax, aloe, gum-mastic and rhubarb, and many other good things, as it seemed to the said Columbus. There are no four-footed beasts, or any animals such as there are with us to be seen in such of the islands as were discovered, except some small curs, and in the fields some very large mice, which they call *hutias* and which they eat and which are very savoury, and they eat them as rabbits are eaten here and they regard them as of the same value. There are many birds, all different from those here, and especially many parrots.

When the above-mentioned land had been discovered by Columbus, he returned to Castile, and arrived at Palos on the three-and-twentieth day of March, in the year 1493, and entered Seville with much honour on the thirty-first day of March, Palm Sunday, having fully realised his object, and there was very well received. He brought ten Indians, of whom he left four in Seville, and went to Barcelona to present six to the king and queen. There he was very well received, and the king and queen gave him great credence, and commanded him to prepare another fleet and go with it, and they gave him the title of "High Admiral of the Ocean Sea of the Indies," and they commanded that he should be styled Don Christopher Columbus, for the honour of his dignity. . . .

QUESTIONS

1. What opinion does the author have of Columbus?
2. Why did Columbus succeed when the alleged westward expeditions of the king of Portugal failed?
3. How did Columbus "take possession" of islands?
4. What valuable items did Columbus think he had found?
5. Why was the colony of Natividad founded?
6. What were Columbus's rewards for the expedition?

BERIAN INITIATIVES

2

Portugal

At Christopher Columbus's birth, the outline of a European's view of the world was dramatically smaller than it had been in the thirteenth century, when the new Mongol empire provided security on the trading roads in a vast area from China to the Black Sea. Marco Polo's visit of 1271–1295 is the most famous only because he wrote of his travels (Document 11). Colonies of Italian merchants, mostly Genoese, were established at the southwestern terminals of the "silk roads" to Tabriz [Afghanistan], Samarkand [Turkestan], and Ormuz [Iran], and thence to China or the spice-producing regions of Southeast Asia. Malacca became an enormous international port, with shipping of spices to China and the Malabar cities of India.

> *"the logic of its geohistory dictated Atlantic expansion."*

Displacement of the Mongols in the fourteenth century by the isolationist native Ming Dynasty closed up the roads and, along with increased Islamic hostility toward Christians, reduced European trade through Alexandria [Egypt] to a minimum. Payment at Alexandria for Asian luxury goods was required in gold or silver, and this stimulated a search for precious metals. The nearest gold mines were in the Niger region of Africa, and Italian merchants, such as the Genoese Malfante, tried to reach these sources directly by traveling across the dangerous Sahara Desert. The merchants had more success when they allied Italian finance to Portuguese navigation in a methodical search along Africa's west coast for a reliable contact with gold traders via ship.

Other motives besides a search for gold impelled the elite and the seamen of Portugal to look to the coast of Africa for new wealth. These included shortages at home of grain and fish, and, unfortunately, a search for slave labor to work sugar plantations. Many other European kingdoms considered a seafaring solution to their internal problems, but only Portugal was ready, for reasons discussed in this selection, to put in the consistent effort that was required.

hy was Portugal, of all the polities of Europe, most able to conduct the initial thrust? One obvious answer is found on any map. Portugal is located on the Atlantic, right next to Africa. In terms of the

SOURCE From *The Modern World-System, Capitalist Agriculture and the Origins of the European World-Economy in the Sixteenth Century*, pp. 49–52 by Immanuel Wallerstein, 1974. Reprinted with permission of Academic Press.

colonization of Atlantic islands and the exploration of the western coast of Africa, it was obviously closest. Furthermore, the oceanic currents are such that it was easiest, especially given the technology of the time, to set forth from Portuguese ports (as well as those of southwest Spain).

In addition, Portugal already had much experience with long-distance trade. Here, if Portugal cannot match the Venetians or the Genoese, recent research had demonstrated that their background was significant and probably the match of the cities of northern Europe.

A third factor was the availability of capital. The Genoese, the great rivals of the Venetians, decided early on to invest in Iberian commercial enterprise and to encourage their efforts at overseas expansion. By the end of the fifteenth century, the Genoese would prefer the Spaniards to the Portuguese, but that is largely because the latter could by then afford to divest themselves of Genoese sponsorship, tutelage, and cut in the profit. Verlinden calls Italy "the only really colonizing nation during the middle ages." In the twelfth century when Genoese and Pisans first appear in Catalonia, in the thirteenth century when they first reach Portugal, this is part of the efforts of the Italians to draw the Iberian peoples into the international trade of the time. But once there, the Italians would proceed to play an initiating role in Iberian colonization efforts because, by having come so early, "they were able to conquer the key positions of the Iberian peninsula itself." As of 1317, according to Virginia Rau, "the city and the port of Lisbon would be the great centre of Genoese trade. . . ." To be sure, in the late fourteenth and early fifteenth centuries, Portuguese merchants began to complain about the "undue intervention [of the Indians] in the *retail* trade of the realm, which threatened the dominant position of national merchants in that branch of trade." The solution was simple, and to some extent classic. The Italians were absorbed by marriage and became landed aristocrats both in Portugal and on Madeira.

There was one other aspect of the commercial economy that contributed to Portugal's venturesomeness, compared to say France or England. It was ironical that it was least absorbed in the zone that would become the European world-economy, but rather tied in a significant degree to the Islamic Mediterranean zone. As a consequence, her economy was relatively more monetized, her population relatively more urbanized.

It was not geography nor mercantile strength alone, however, that accounted for Portugal's edge. It was also the strength of its state machinery. Portugal was in this regard very different from other west European states, different that is during the fifteenth century. She knew peace when they knew internal warfare. The stability of the state was important not only because it created the climate in which entrepreneurs could flourish but because it encouraged nobility to find outlets for their energies other than in internal or inter-European warfare. The stability of the state was crucial also because it itself was in many ways the chief entrepreneur. When the state was stable, it could devote its energies to profitable commercial ventures. For Portugal, as we have seen, the logic of its geohistory dictated Atlantic expansion as the most sensible commercial venture for the state.

Why Portugal? Because she alone of the European states maximized will and possibility. Europe needed a larger land base to support the expansion of its economy, one which could compensate for the critical decline in seigniorial revenues and which could cut short the nascent and potentially very violent class war which the crisis of feudalism implied. Europe needed many things: bullion, staples, proteins, means of preserving protein, foods, wood, materials to process textiles. And it needed a more tractable labor force.

But "Europe" must not be reified. There was no central agency which acted in terms of these long-range objectives. The real decisions were taken by groups of men acting in terms of their immediate interests. In the case of Portugal, there seemed to be advantage in the "discovery business" for many groups—for the state, for the nobility, for the commercial bourgeoisie (indigenous and foreign), even for the semiproletariat of the towns.

For the state, a *small* state, the advantage was obvious. Expansion was the most likely route to the expansion of revenue and the accumulation of glory. And the Portuguese state, almost alone among the states of Europe of the time, was not distracted by internal conflict. It had achieved moderate political stability at least a century earlier than Spain, France, and England.

It was precisely this stability which created the impulse for the nobility. Faced with the same financial squeeze as European nobles elsewhere, they were deprived of the soporific and financial potential (if they won) of internecine warfare. Nor could they hope to recoup their financial position by internal colonization. Portugal lacked the land. So they were sympathetic to the concept of oceanic expansion and they offered their "younger sons" to provide the necessary leadership for the expeditions.

The interests of the bourgeoisie for once did not conflict with those of the nobility. Prepared for modern capitalism by a long apprenticeship in long-distance trading and by the experience of living in one of the most highly monetized areas of Europe (because of the economic involvement with the Islamic Mediterranean world), the bourgeoisie too sought to escape the confines of the small Portuguese market. To the extent that they lacked the capital, they found it readily available from the Genoese who, for reasons of their own having to do with their rivalry with Venice, were ready to finance the Portuguese. And the potential conflict of the indigenous and foreign bourgeoisie was muted by the willingness of the Genoese to assimilate into Portuguese culture over time.

Finally, exploration and the consequent trade currents provided job outlets for the urban semiproletariat, many of whom had fled to the towns because of the increased exploitation consequent upon the seigniorial crisis. Once again, a potential for internal disorder was minimized by the external expansion.

And if these conjunctures of will and possibility were not enough, Portugal was blessed by the best possible geographic location for the enterprise, best possible both because of its jutting out into the Atlantic and toward the south but also because of the convergence of favorable oceanic currents. It does not seem surprising thus, in retrospect, that Portugal made the plunge.

3

Round Africa to India

The Portuguese gained a toehold in Muslim North Africa with King John I's conquest of Ceuta in 1415. His son Henry ("the navigator," as he was labeled in the nineteenth century) withdrew from court after an unsuccessful attempt to capture Tangiers so that he might direct expeditions along the west coast of Africa, where Muslims held no sway. Although the contemporary chronicler Gomes Eannes de Azura, whose work is excerpted below, presents the prince's motives in a way appropriate to the time in which he writes, modern historians point out that Henry was likely interested principally in increasing his income from fishing and maritime activities. Also, he was not the only patron of exploration, since during his lifetime two-thirds of the trips were sponsored by the king, aristocrats, or merchants.

> *"no mariners or merchants would ever dare to attempt it."*

Contrary to early historical speculation, Henry appears to have had no master plan to explore the coastline, much less to try to reach India. Because he gathered together a "think tank" of geographers and navigators in the far south of Portugal at Sagres, however, he set the pattern of systematic exploration that would guide the royal house thereafter. His principal achievement was to support many tries, at last successful in 1434, to round Cape Bojado ("Bulging Cape"). Today the cape is a mere bump on the part of Africa then called Guinea, but it was an actual and psychological barrier blocking entry to the fabled "Sea of Darkness." By Henry's death in 1460, a fleet had reached as far as Sierra Leone.

King John II was the first Portuguese monarch to put into play a comprehensive plan of systematic discovery. He founded a series of trading colonies supported by forts, of which the principal was São Jorge da Mina ("the Mine") at the Gulf of Guinea. By 1482 his ships reached the mouth of the Congo River.

Christopher Columbus tried his luck in Portugal because the Genoese had a well-established trading and banking presence there. Possibly he was a commercial agent for a firm interested in Portugal's commerce with Africa. Whether or not he ever took an actual navigational role in a voyage has not been established, but he did learn enough about the sea to offer a plan for a great oceangoing "enterprise" to King John II in 1483 or 1484.

When Columbus presented his proposal to the court to sail west to the riches of the Orient, he drastically underestimated the size of the globe. The men appointed by the king to review the proposal rejected it on the sensible grounds that the estimate of distance was impossibly small. His wishful belief that only 2,500 miles lay between the Azores and Japan mistakenly placed the latter kingdom approximately on the longitude of the Virgin Islands—a shortfall of 8,000 miles. It is difficult to tell, in view of the committee's rejection, if King John II would have had any sensible reason to act in the underhanded manner about which Columbus's son reports in the second selection.

The final blow to the foreigner's hopes came when Bartolomew Dias rounded the Cape of Good Hope, returning in 1488 with news that an eastern passage to India was feasible. There was nothing for Columbus to do but look for another patron. When Castile took up the challenge and gave Columbus his three ships, the race for Asia was on in earnest. During the reign of King Manuel I, appropriately nicknamed "the Fortunate," his servant Vasco da Gama returned to Lisbon from India in 1499. In the final selection, the king of Portugal cheerfully, but diplomatically, informs Ferdinand and Isabella of this feat and, coincidentally, sets out Portugal's legal claims to a monopoly in trade in the area.

Henry "the Navigator" and the Exploration of the Coast of Africa, 1451–1460

In which five reasons appear why the Lord Infant [Henry] was moved to command the search for the lands of Guinea [Africa].

We imagine that we know a matter when we are acquainted with the doer of it and the end for which he did it. And since in former chapters we have set forth the Lord Infant as the chief actor in these things, giving as clear an understanding of him as we could, it is meet that in this present chapter we should know his purpose in doing them. And you should note well that the noble spirit of this Prince [Henry], by a sort of natural constraint, was ever urging him both to begin and to carry out very great deeds. For which reason, after the taking of Ceuta [1415] he always kept ships well armed against the Infidel [Muslims], both for war, and be-

SOURCE Gomes Eannes de Azura, *Chronicle of the Discovery and Conquest of Guinea*, ed. and trans. C. R. Beazley and Edgar Prestage, 2 vols. (London: Hakluyt Society, 1896–1898), pp. 27–30.

17

cause he had also a wish to know the land that lay beyond the isles of Canary and that Cape called Bojador ["Bulging"], for that up to his time, neither by writings, nor by the memory of man, was known with any certainty the nature of the land beyond that Cape. Some said indeed that Saint Brandan [legendary Irish explorer] had passed that way; and there was another tale of two galleys rounding the Cape, which never returned. But this doth not appear at all likely to be true, for it is not to be presumed that if the said galleys went there, some other ships would not have endeavoured to learn what voyage they had made. And because the said Lord Infant wished to know the truth of this,—since it seemed to him that if he or some other lord did not endeavour to gain that knowledge, no mariners or merchants would ever dare to attempt it—(for it is clear that none of them ever trouble themselves to sail to a place where there is not a sure and certain hope of profit)—and seeing also that no other prince took any pains in this matter, he sent out his own ships against those parts, to have manifest certainty of them all. And to this he was stirred up by his zeal for the service of God and of the King Edward his Lord and brother, who then reigned. And this was the first reason of his action. . . .

The second reason was that if there chanced to be in those lands some population of Christians, or some havens, into which it would be possible to sail without peril, many kinds of merchandise might be brought to this realm, which would find a ready market, and reasonably so, because no other people of these parts traded with them, nor yet people of any other that were known; and also the products of this realm might be taken there, which traffic would bring great profit to our countrymen.

The third reason was that, as it was said that the power of the Moors [Muslims] in that land of Africa was very much greater than was commonly supposed, and that there were no Christians among them, nor any other race of men; and because every wise man is obliged by natural prudence to wish for a knowledge of the power of his enemy; therefore the said Lord Infant exerted himself to cause this to be fully discovered, and to make it known determinately how far the power of those infidels extended.

The fourth reason was because during the one and thirty years that he had warred against the Moors, he had never found a Christian king, nor a lord outside this land, who for the love of our Lord Jesus Christ would aid him in the said war. Therefore he sought to know if there were in those parts any Christian princes, in whom the charity and the love of Christ was so ingrained that they would aid him against those enemies of the faith.

The fifth reason was his great desire to make increase in the faith of our Lord Jesus Christ and to bring to him all the souls that should be saved,—understanding that all the mystery of the Incarnation, Death, and Passion of our Lord Jesus Christ was for this sole end—namely the salvation of lost souls—whom the said Lord Infant by his travail and spending would fain bring into the true path. . . .

But over and above these five reasons I have a sixth that would seem to be the root from which all the others proceeded: and this is the inclination of the heavenly wheels [astrology]. For, as I wrote not many days ago in a letter I sent to the Lord King, that although it be written that the wise man shall be Lord of the stars, and that the courses of the planets (according to the true estimate of the holy doctors) cannot cause the good man to stumble; yet it is manifest that they are bodies ordained in the secret counsels of our Lord God and run by a fixed measure, appointed to different ends, which are revealed to men by his grace, through whose influence bodies of the lower order are inclined to certain passions. . . . And that was because his ascendent was Aries, which is the house of Mars and exaltation of the sun, and his lord in the XIth house, in company of the sun. And because the said Mars was in Aquarius, which is the house of Saturn, and in the mansion of hope, it signified that this Lord should toil at high and mighty conquests, especially in seeking out things that were hidden from other men and secret, according to the nature of Saturn, in whose house he is. And the fact of his being accompanied by the sun, as I said, and the sun being in the house of Jupiter, signified that all his dealings and his conquests would be loyally carried out, according to the good pleasure of his king and lord.

Why ships had not hitherto dared to pass beyond Cape Bojador.

So the Infant, moved by these reasons, which you have already heard, began to make ready his ships and his people, as the needs of the case required; but this much you may learn, that although he sent out many times, not only ordinary men, but such as by their experience in great deeds of war were of foremost name in the profession of arms, yet there was not one who dared to pass that Cape of Bojador [in West Africa] and learn about the land beyond it, as the Infant wished. And to say the truth this was not from cowardice or want of good will, but from the novelty of the thing and the wide-spread and ancient rumour about this Cape, that had been cherished by the mariners of Spain from generation to generation. And although this proved to be deceitful, yet since the hazarding of this attempt seemed to threaten the last evil of all, there was great doubt as to who would be the first to risk his life in such a venture. How are we, men said, to pass the bounds that our fathers set up, or what profit can result to the Infant from the perdition [loss] of our souls as well as of our bodies—for of a truth by daring any further we shall become wilful murderers of ourselves? Have there not been in Spain other princes and lords as covetous perchance of this honour as the Infant? For certainly it cannot be presumed that among so many noble men who did such great and lofty deeds for the glory of their memory, there had not been one to dare this deed. But being satisfied of the peril, and seeing no hope of honour or profit, they left off the attempt. For, said the mariners, this much is clear, that beyond this Cape there is no race of men nor place of inhabitants: nor is the land less sandy than the deserts of Libya, where there is no water, no tree, no green herb—and the sea so shallow that a whole league from land it is only a fathom deep, while the currents are so terrible that no ship having once passed the Cape, will ever be able to return.

Therefore our forefathers never attempted to pass it: and of a surety their knowledge of the lands beyond was not a little dark, as they knew not how to set them down on the charts, by which man controls all the seas that can be navigated. . . .

Columbus in Portugal,
1477–1485

Finding himself near Lisbon, and knowing that many of his Genoese countrymen lived in that city, he [Columbus] went there as soon as he could. When they learned who he was, they gave him such a warm welcome that he made his home in that city and married there.

As he behaved very honorably and was a man of handsome presence and one who never turned from the path of honesty, a lady named Doña Felipa Moniz, of noble birth and superior of the Convent of the Saints, where the Admiral [Columbus] used to attend Mass, had such conversation and friendship with him that she became his wife. His father-in-law, Pedro Moniz Perestrello, being dead, they went to live with his widow, who, observing the Admiral's great interest in geography, told him the said Perestrello, her husband, had been a notable seafarer; and she told how he and two other captains had gone with license from the King of Portugal to discover new lands, agreeing to divide all they discovered into three parts and cast lots for the share that should fall to each. Sailing to the southwest, they discovered the islands of Madeira and Pôrto Santo [in 1418]. Since the island of Madeira was the larger of the two, they made two parts of it, the third being the island of Pôrto Santo, which fell to the share of the Admiral's father-in-law, Perestrello, who governed it till his death.

Seeing that her stories of these voyages gave the Admiral much pleasure, she gave him the writings and sea-charts left by her husband. These things excited the Admiral still more; and he informed himself of the other voyages and navigations that the Portuguese were then making to [São Jorge da] Mina and down the coast of Guinea, and greatly enjoyed speaking with the men who sailed in those regions. To tell the truth, I do not know if it was during this marriage that the Admiral went to Mina or Guinea, but it seems reasonable that he did so. Be that as it may, one thing leading to another and starting a train of thought, the Admiral while in Portugal began to speculate that if the Portuguese could sail so far south, it should be possible to sail as far westward, and that it was logical to expect to find land in that direction. . . .

In due time, the Admiral, convinced of the soundness of his plan, proposed to put it into effect and sail over the Western Ocean in search of new

SOURCE From *The Life of the Admiral Christopher Columbus by His Son Ferdinand*, trans. and annotated by Benjamin Keen, 1959, pp. 14–36, passim. Reprinted by permission of the translator.

lands. But he knew that his enterprise required the cooperation and assistance of some prince; and since he resided in Portugal, he decided to offer it to the king of that country. Although King João [John II] listened attentively to the Admiral, he appeared cool toward the project, because the discovery and conquest of the west coast of Africa, called Guinea, had put the prince to great expense and trouble without the least return. At that time the Portuguese had not yet sailed beyond the Cape of Good Hope [in 1488], which name according to some was given that cape in place of its proper one, Agesingua, because it marked the end of those fine hopes of conquest and discovery; others claim it got that name because it gave promise of the discovery of richer lands and of more prosperous voyages.

Be that as it may, the King was very little inclined to spend more money on discovery; and if he paid some attention to the Admiral, it was because of the strong arguments that the latter advanced. These arguments so impressed the King that the launching of the enterprise waited only upon his acceptance of the conditions laid down by the Admiral. The latter, being a man of noble and lofty ambitions, would not covenant save on such terms as would bring him great honor and advantage, in order that he might leave a title and estate befitting the grandeur of his works and his merits.

So the King, counseled by a Doctor Calzadilla in whom he placed much trust, decided to send a caravel secretly to attempt what the Admiral had offered to do, thinking that if those lands were discovered in this way, he would not have to give the Admiral the great rewards he demanded. With all speed and secrecy, then, the King outfitted a caravel on the pretext of sending provisions and reinforcements to the Cape Verde, and dispatched it whither the Admiral had proposed to go. But because the people he sent lacked the knowledge, steadfastness, and ability of the Admiral, they wandered about on the sea for many days and returned to the Cape Verde and thence to Lisbon, making fun of the enterprise and declaring that no land could be found in those waters.

When he learned of this, the Admiral, whose wife had meantime died, formed such a hatred for that city and nation that he resolved to depart for Castile with his little son Diego—who after his father's death succeeded to his estate.

Letter from Manuel I
to Ferdinand and Isabella, 1499

Most high and excellent Prince and Princess, most potent Lord and Lady!

Your Highnesses already know that we had ordered Vasco da Gama, a nobleman of our household, and his brother Paulo da Gama, with

SOURCE *A Journal of the First Voyage of Vasco da Gama*, ed. and trans. E. G. Ravenstein (London: Hakluyt Society, 1898), pp. 77–79.

four vessels to make discoveries by sea, and that two years have now elapsed since their departure. And as the principal motive of this enterprise has been with our predecessors, the service of God our Lord, and our own advantage, it pleased Him in His mercy to speed them on their route. From a message which has now been brought to this city by one of the captains, we learn that they did reach and discover India and other kingdoms and lordships bordering upon it; that they entered and navigated its sea, finding large cities, large edifices and rivers, and great populations among whom is carried on all the trade in spices and precious stones, which are forwarded in ships (which these same explorers saw and met with in good numbers and of great size) to Mecca, and thence to Cairo, whence they are dispersed throughout the world. Of these [spices, etc.] they have brought a quantity including cinnamon, cloves, ginger, nutmeg, and pepper, as well as other kinds, together with the boughs and leaves of the same; also many fine stones of all sorts, such as rubies and others. And they also came to a country in which there are mines of gold, of which [gold], as of the spices and precious stones, they did not bring as much as they could have done, for they took no merchandise with them.

As we are aware that your Highnesses will hear of these things with much pleasure and satisfaction, we thought well to give this information. And your Highnesses may believe, in accordance with what we have learnt concerning the Christian people whom these explorers reached, that it will be possible notwithstanding that they are not as yet strong in the faith or possessed of a thorough knowledge of it, to do much in the service of God and the exaltation of the Holy Faith, once they shall have been converted and fully fortified in it. And when they shall have thus been fortified in the faith, there will be an opportunity for destroying the Moors [Muslims] of those parts. Moreover, we hope, with the help of God, that the great trade which now enriches the Moors of those parts, through whose hands it passes without the intervention of other persons or peoples, shall, in consequence of our regulations, be diverted to the natives and ships of our own kingdom, so that henceforth all Christendom, in this part of Europe, shall be able in a large measure to provide itself with these spices and precious stones.

QUESTIONS

1. Why was Portugal, of all the European kingdoms, the most likely candidate for expansion?
2. What were the principal factors that pushed a small European state into exploration and colonization?
3. What social groups in Portugal were the most interested in the push to expand?
4. What five reasons does the chronicler of the exploits of Henry "the Navigator" give for Henry's desire to explore the west coast of Africa?
5. In what ways does the list of motivations set out for Henry "the Navigator" (from Question 4) differ from those enumerated by a modern historian (Document 2)?

6. Why had European sailors not passed beyond the Cape of Bojador?
7. Why did Columbus decide to remain in Portugal?
8. Why was Columbus's plan to sail west rejected by the king of Portugal?
9. List the advantages to Portugal, and to all Christians, that Manuel I saw in the successful voyage to India.

4

Spain During the Reconquest

In 711 A.D., Muslims from North Africa landed on the Iberian Peninsula. Generals Tariq and Musa proceeded to conquer its Visigothic Christian leadership within seven years. Quickly enough, the bulk of the population converted.

In the least productive lands to the far north, at small rural areas in the Asturian mountains, tiny Christian realms survived as heirs to the half-forgotten tradition of Visigothic sovereignty. From these remnants, grew the kingdoms of León, Castile, Aragón, and Portugal. During an early stage of the conflict, Christians came to believe the apostle St. James the Younger, on his white horse, took part in the fighting. A belief that God was on their side endured.

> *"a society organized for war, . . ."*

The process of "reconquering" land that once belonged to Christians was complex because much of the fighting on the borders was undertaken by aristocrats operating on their own, with royal approval after the fact. This set a pattern for the conquest of the New World, where independent conquistadores, sometimes with and often without specific authorization from the crown, put into practice the negotiating and fighting techniques their ancestors evolved over centuries. Islands of the Caribbean, the plains of Mexico, and the heights of the Andes would resound with the crusading war cry of the Reconquest: "St. James and at them!"

It is hardly surprising that a process lasting seven centuries should have given rise to innumerable differences of interpretation, especially since terms like Reconquest, Holy War and Crusades have been used with considerable ambivalence, since some periods have been but little studied and since source material is generally patchy. However, it is

SOURCE *The Reconquest of Spain,* pp. 173–178, by D. W. Lomax. Reprinted by permission of The Peters Fraser & Dunlop Group Ltd.

already possible to indicate the main lines of development and some of the problems yet to be solved.

If one defines the Reconquest as the transfer of political power over the Peninsula from Muslim to Christian hands, then it is clear that this really occurred between 718 and 1492. What is also clear is that most of the characteristics of this transfer already existed by the time of Alfonso III [866–911], rather than being inventions of the eleventh century. The chronicles of his reign show that the policy of reconquering the whole of Spain had already been formulated and adopted, that one motive for this policy was the desire to recover the heritage which the Muslims had allegedly usurped from the rightful successors of the Visigothic [Germanic tribal] monarchy, and that the other motives included religious hatred of the enemy: the Christians were already fighting against the Muslims, not only as "usurpers" but also as "infidels." On the other hand, there is simply no earlier evidence for deciding how far this religious motivation and the adoption of this policy preceded their formulation in the texts of Alfonso III's reign. There is a similar lack of evidence about such questions for 910–1035; and in both periods the safest course is to suspend judgment rather than to argue from the silence of our scanty texts. In contrast, the whole tradition of Frankish [Germanic tribal] military involvement is fairly well documented from Charlemagne down to the reconquest of Granada; it was by no means a novelty in the age of Alfonso VI [1065–1109].

What then was new in the eleventh century? With the collapse of the caliphate, there ended any chance of a powerful independent monarchy among the Spanish Muslims, and the balance of political power tipped decisively away from them and towards the Christians, although the reasons for this decisive change are still obscure. On the Christian side, there now appeared for the first time, not foreign expeditionaries nor the concept of the Holy War—both had existed for centuries—but the idea of the Crusade, that is, a Holy War entered into for religious motives (among others, no doubt), authorized by the Church and conferring on its participants a specific juridical status, no matter whether they were French, English or Spanish. And, of course, Frankish expeditions increased in frequency, size, recruiting-areas and effectiveness ... most of them went to the Ebro valley and provided essential assistance in its reconquest. ...

One must discount the view that the peaceful co-existence of the ordinary people was occasionally disturbed by warfare provoked by the religious and political establishment; it would be truer to say that the kings made occasional ineffectual attempts to limit the endless warfare enjoyed by their subjects. This was natural enough: as in medieval Russia, though to a lesser extent, the ease with which peasants could acquire land and freedom on an open frontier meant that it was difficult for the civil and military authorities to control them. Consequently, they were left within the framework of frontier townships and militias to do very much as they liked, and what they liked was plundering Muslim villages. The concepts of Reconquest and

Crusade may have originated among the leaders of Christendom; the practice of permanent warfare against the Muslims was a creation of the people. And, despite the gaps in our evidence, it seems clear that even these concepts of Reconquest, Holy War and Crusade became widely diffused and accepted among the lower levels of society. . . .

Even with what is known now, however, it ought to be possible to reach some tentative conclusions. The Reconquest was a lengthy process and a continuous one in the sense that fighting rarely stopped for long, but it was not, as is often implied, a slow, steady and gradual one. The Christians did not advance steadily, step-by-step; they took great leaps forward, to the Duero [River], the Tagus [River], the Guadalquivir [River] and the south coast, and after each leap they waited for centuries to consolidate their position before making the next one. Rather than gradual, the Reconquest was spasmodic; it proceeded not by townships but by great regions such as Aragón, New Castile or Andalusia, and one of its results was to emphasize the importance of such regions as the basic units of Spanish national life.

Other results have aroused more polemical discussion. Sánchez Albornoz has argued that the Muslim Conquest diverted Spain from its natural development as a European country and that though the Reconquest corrected this diversion, its slowness placed Spain several centuries behind Europe on the path of progress. Though this theory does not define Europe or progress, it implicitly identifies both with France, and on its own terms is unanswerable. Not even Spain, where most things are possible, can be as French as France—but this is not the fault of Tariq [Muslim general] or Pelayo [Germanic Christian warrior].

Other historians argue that Spanish civilization reached its zenith in the tenth century and then declined because its Muslim rulers were replaced by Christians; but this is hardly supported by the history of civilization in neighbouring Morocco, where no Reconquest occurred. The case of Spain is more complex and unusual than, for example, the decline of Italy in the seventeenth century or the rise of England in the nineteenth; for between 1050 and 1250 Spain *transferred* from one culture, the Islamic, which was passing its zenith, to another, western Christendom, which was rising. Her exceptional case cannot therefore be measured by the simpler standards of Morocco or France, for unlike them she has mixed two cultures, the Islamic and the Latin Christian, in a process which has here been called the Muslim Conquest and the Reconquest.

The mixture was strongest between 1000 and 1250 when political forces reinforced nobler motives making for religious toleration. Spain was then a land of several religions, and not until 1492 did it adopt the European pattern of religious uniformity which before 1250 would have been as disastrous for the Christians as it proved for the Almoravids and Almohads [North African Muslim groups]. Under a regime of religious pluralism this society was intellectually very productive: The science of ancient Greece and medieval Persia and India was translated into Arabic in Syria, imported into Spain by the scholars of Ummayad Córdoba, augmented by Spanish scholars like Averroes and then translated into Latin by Christian scholars who spread the knowledge to the rest of Europe. Astronomy, physics, medicine, optics, mathematics, alchemy and magic suddenly burst upon a world which had known little beyond Bede and Isidore [of Seville]. So too did stories from Asian bazaars, new types of mysticism, new legends about the after-life and new philosophical theories. Thanks to the translators, both Spanish and foreign, doctors throughout Europe learned new cures for diseases, merchants and administrators could calculate accounts with positioned Hindu numbers and overseas discoverers could rely on tables of the stars for the voyages to Africa, Asia and America. It was the Reconquest which provided suitable conditions for these translations, for only in reconquered territory did Christians have the opportunity and interest to make them. None were made in Muslim Africa, where all educated men read Arabic, and even in Sicily such translations were fewer and dependent on capricious royal patronage.

In Spain these translations crowned a political, economic, social and cultural revolution as profound as any in medieval Europe. This had been achieved because the Christians had learnt several lessons in the twelfth century. The first and most important was the value of unity: realizing that their former quarrels had led to defeat at the hands of the Almohads, the Christians collaborated with each other after 1224 and, in their turn, exploited Muslim disunity. Secondly, recognizing the ineffectiveness of foreign crusaders and of the international military Orders, they learned to rely on themselves alone and to create their own Orders of Santiago, Calatrava and Alcántara. Thirdly, the resettlement of the south with Christians ensured that the next African invasion would face not merely Christian garrisons in a Muslim country but a solid line of Christian cities, prosperous and belligerent, with their own militias and castles. The social revolution which this implied led briefly to a wide distribution of property in Andalusia; but this did not last. Emigration from north to south probably impoverished the northern nobles, driving them into rebellion, whilst southern land was so cheap that noble families could buy up farms and amass great estates, and whenever the monarchy was weak they enriched themselves, and rewarded their vassals, at the expense of crown, Church and cities.

Indeed, they were almost forced to do so by the nature of Spanish society. For though capable leaders' unity, self-reliance and resettlement all helped to achieve the Reconquest, the most important factor was probably the willingness of Christian Spaniards to transform their society for this purpose. This transformation was extremely thorough. Late medieval Castile became essentially a society organized for war, a dynamic military machine which would fuction well so long as it had more lands to conquer. It might be disconcerted by military defeats, but it could survive them. What threw it into complete confusion was the end of the attempt at conquest, and when the kings stopped leading their armies against Granada they implicitly invited their barons to find a new role which could only be that of fighting each other. Just as the English barons of Edward III or Henry V united to plunder the French, so the Castilian barons would unite under Alfonso XI [1312–1350] to plunder Granada, the France of Castile; but, just as peace with France led to civil wars within England under Richard II and Henry VI, so peace with the Muslims led to civil wars within Castile under Fernando IV [1295–1312] and Juan II [1406–1454]. Fernando and Isabel [Ferdinand and Isabella] could cure one crisis in 1481 simply by setting the war-machine to work once more, to conquer Granada; but after 1492, there was no more Muslim territory to be conquered inside Spain. The machine was running out of land, and more crises loomed ahead.

It might of course have been sent against the Maghrib [in North Africa], and raids were made on Melilla (1497), Oran (1509) and Algiers (1510), and perhaps it might have conquered Morocco. Or it might have been turned back against northern Europe, with incalculable effects on the sixteenth-century religious wars. However, in thanksgiving for the fall of Granada, Isabel equipped Columbus's exploratory expedition and in 1492 his discovery of America opened up a virtually limitless stretch of conquerable territory. Castilian society rose to the occasion. Within fifty years it conquered most areas from Texas to Argentina and established the framework of political, religious, social and economic life within which they would henceforth live.

No other European society could have done this at that date. Explorers from England, for example, discovered Nova Scotia in 1497, but no permanent English settlement was made in America until the seventeenth century. Only Spain was able to conquer, administer, Christianize and Europeanize the populous areas of the New World precisely because during the previous seven centuries her society had been constructed for the purpose of conquering, administering, Christianizing and Europeanizing the inhabitants of al-Andalus [Muslim Spain]. Thus if the Reconquest is important in Old World history because it is the primary example of the reversal of an Islamic conquest and because it fostered the transfer of Greek and Asian culture to western Europe, in the general sweep of world history it is vital because it prepared the rapid conquest and Europeanization of Latin America and thereby spared it most of the religious and imperialist wars which would henceforth afflict almost all the rest of mankind.

5

Conquest of the Canary Islands

The logical progress of the Christian southward sweep across the Iberian Peninsula would, by the sixteenth century, have taken their war across the narrow stretch of water separating the Spanish kingdoms from Muslim North Africa. Instead, Castile followed the example of Portugal, which settled the Azores and Madeira, far out in the Atlantic.

To head off the Portuguese, Ferdinand and Isabella launched a preemptive strike on the little-known island of Gran Canaria, arriving just before their Portuguese rivals. The use of sword, cannon, musket, horse, and dog to subdue the unclothed Stone Age Canary islanders was copied by Columbus during his Caribbean assault. It should be noted that Felipe Fernández-Armesto, author of this selection, refers to all native populations as "savages," an unfortunate bit of outdated terminology.

> *"the crucial similarity between the Canarians and Indians."*

The Iberian islands formed stepping-stones for exploration in the midst of what one scholar has called the "Atlantic Mediterranean." Fortunately for Columbus, the Canaries (which take their name not from birds, but from the Spanish for the dogs found there) sit in the southern wind zone of westerlies, which made his first voyage feasible.

I n the Treaty of Alcaçovas of 1479, Ferdinand and Isabella expressly reserved to Castile the conquest of the stretch of coast opposite the Canary Islands, where their subjects established a garrison at Santa Cruz de la Mar Pequeña, and continued to make raids and attempts at conquest in a sporadic and individual fashion. In 1492 the monarchs commissioned the conquistador Alonso de Lugo to organize these efforts, but the vastness of the area and the strength of resistance confined him to raiding and the maintenance of coastal footholds. The fall of Granada in 1492 released energies for assaults elsewhere on the mainland. In 1495 the Pope confirmed Castile's rights—for although these had long been assumed, pontifical clarification was useful in the face of conflicting Portuguese claims—and in 1497 a major and successful expedition, which conserved many elements of organization and personnel from the time of the Granada

SOURCE *Ferdinand and Isabella*, pp. 146–161, passim, by Felipe Fernández-Armesto, 1975. Taplinger Publishing Co. Inc.

war, seized Melilla for the monarchs. But the same years saw the rise of the Barbary corsairs and, correspondingly, the difficulties of making more than local North African conquests increased. In that area of expansion Ferdinand and Isabella were limited to a coastal, military presence and could not establish settled colonies.

But already before the completion of the Reconquest, when Castilian expansion overseas could be launched in earnest like the ships that bore it, settlers from Andalucia had begun the colonization of the Canary Islands. . . .

The decisive phase came with the reign of Ferdinand and Isabella, who completed the conquest of the Canary Islands, encouraged their "peopling" with colonists by means of fiscal exemptions, and imposed a policy of land- and water-sharing, which encouraged sugar production. Madeiran and Valencian personnel were deliberately introduced to run the irrigation and refining industries. Genoese capitalists were brought in with sufficient money concentrations to set up the waterways and mills, and Negro slaves imported to supplement the indigenous and colonial labour-force. As well as sugar, corn was cultivated on dry lands by poorer settlers; and other Spanish crops like grapes, quince and saffron were introduced and nurtured in a garden economy of the Andalucian type, which grew up in the hinterlands of the growing townships. Cattle, pigs and sheep were imported to supplement the goats, while Castilian co-operative pastoral methods were promoted. The indices of the rapidity and extent of change are clear. Before the monarchs' reign, sugar was unknown on Gran Canaria; but within a few years Bernáldez could call it "a land of many canes." A clergyman who visited La Laguna in 1497, within a year of its foundation, found "only two or three shanties"—but by the end of the reign it had some 6,000 inhabitants. To a great extent, the architect of the new kind of colonial economy was Alonso Fernández de Lugo, who had served in the conquest of Gran Canaria and took command for the wards in Tenerife and La Palma: he seems to have realized that because of the distribution of rainfall in the archipelago, the western islands could be adapted for sugar-farming in a way that had not been possible in the earlier conquests. He introduced the sugarcane in 1484, as soon as the conquest of Gran Canaria was completed, and risked controversy and unpopularity during his governorship of Tenerife by favouring foreign technicians and capitalists. . . .

For the monarchs particularly desired that the soil of the Indies should be divided among the colonists, and a new agronomy introduced, just as was being effected by their command at the same time in the Canary Islands. They repeated the same policy, based on land grants and fiscal exemptions, for encouraging immigration, as had been used in the Canaries. Lastly, the elements of the new agronomy were not to be cultivated to the exclusion of the pastoral sector, which the monarchs were determined to favour in their new as in their old realms. Within a few years, as in the Canaries, the labour force of the new colonies was expanded by the importation of Negroes, though the paganism and indiscipline of black slaves so perturbed the early governors, and the Portuguese monopoly of the trade was so strong, that the supply was only intermittent under the Catholic monarchs. Isabella was personally opposed to the employment of Negroes because she was afraid that their pagan practices would impede Spanish efforts to evangelize the Indians. Even though after her death Ferdinand removed all restrictions on the trade in blacks, the labour force of the New World colonies remained far more heavily dependent on indigenous sources than did that of the Canary Islands; as Columbus insisted, "The Indians are the wealth of Hispaniola— for they perform all labour of men and beasts." . . .

To exacerbate the efforts of their relative remoteness, the methods of finance employed in the conquests of the Canaries and the New World displayed ominous features for the future of royal government there. In the Canary Islands from 1477, the monarchs had placed the burden of financing the conquest on the royal exchequer [treasury], and indeed the first expeditions relied heavily on public finance: the methods of finance and recruiting of these early days were largely borrowed from the *Reconquista* [Reconquest]. But as the conquest wore on and more expeditions were dispatched, private sources of finance and means of recruiting tended increasingly to displace public ones. Instead of wages, the *conquistadores* would receive the promise of *repartimiento* or a share of the soil; instead of the yield from the sale of indulgences or the direct use of the royal fifth to meet the expenses of war, fifths yet uncollected were pledged as rewards to conquerers who could raise the necessary finance elsewhere. In other words, the conquest of the islands was begun with the financial arrangements of the *Reconquista*, and terminated with those of the conquest of the New World. . . .

In many ways the crucial similarity between the Canarians and Indians was that they were naked: that was the first fact Columbus noticed about the Indians and the first which Europeans had observed about the Canarians; indeed for every European observer of primitive peoples till well into the sixteenth century, clothes were the measure of difference between primitivism and civilization; conformity of dress was a sign of conformity of manners. The promotion of European *couture* was a major preoccupation of the proselytizers of the Moors and the Spanish settlers among the Indians. Beatriz de Bobadilla, heiress of the isle of Gomera and enslaver of its people, argued before Ferdinand and Isabella that the Gomerans could not be considered truly Christian on the ground that "they go about naked." Hieronymus Münzer at about the same time displayed the same state of mind when he wrote of the Canarians. "They all used to go naked, but now use clothes like us." Then he added, very characteristically of his epoch, "Oh, what doctrine and diligence can do, that can turn beasts in human shape into civilized men!" But in terms of the two cultural traditions of which men in the late Middle Ages disposed—that of Christianity and that of classical antiquity— social nakedness had a profound significance: it evoked in the context of the first idea of primitive innocence, in that of the second, the legend of the age of gold.

Both these concepts were of great importance in the formation of European ideas about the Canary Islanders and Indians. Accounts of the Canary Islanders influenced notions of the age of gold; Peter Martyr and his correspondents thought the Indians a model of sylvan innocence. Of both peoples, it was thought that their uncorrupt state peculiarly fitted them to hear the gospel and helped to create the widespread impression that the existing and often harsh juridical norms for the treatment of pagans were unsuited to them. . . .

In 1477, however, a new factor intervened which acted as a catalyst around which the prevailing doctrine on savages' rights was altered. In October of that year, Ferdinand and Isabella took the conquest of the three still unsubdued Canary Islands under their own wing, out of the hands of the local seigneurs and private adventurers, whose efforts had been so unproductive in the preceding years. On the question of whether the islanders should be enslaved, the Catholic monarchs upheld the cautious doctrines of Pope Eugenius and the missionaries. In 1477, their liberation of "certain Canarians who are Christians and others who are on the road to conversion" on the grounds that "it would be a source of bad example and give cause why none should wish to be converted," may be compared with the aim expressed by Eugenius forty-three years previously when he spoke of the danger of pagans being deterred from joining the faith. No doubt the monarchs' attitude was not uncoloured by the exigencies of power: enslavement would have involved a change in the natives' status from royal vassals to personal chattels, whereas the monachs' aim was as far as possible to exclude intermediate lordship from the institutions by which they ruled their monarchy (or at least to limit it where it existed already). In this respect, their ordinances against enslavement of the Canary Islanders were motivated in a way akin to those by which they protected the Indians of the New World. Columbus's first plans for enslaving the Indians aroused the monarchs' immediate disapproval. "What does he think he is doing with my vassals?" Isabella is traditionally said to have asked. They commissioned a "junta of theologians" to examine the proposed enslavement, and when they pronounced unfavourably, ordered Fonseca to have the slaves liberated and their owners compensated. This was almost a re-enactment of their reaction to the enslavement of the Gomerans in 1489.

It was equally in the interests of extending their own power that the monarchs insisted on their right to make war against the savages. This was made clear by their attitude to the bulls of indulgence for the conversion of the Canarians, promulgated by Sixtus IV in 1478. The Pope, continuing the traditions of peaceful evangelization and apparently sharing the common opinion that to make war on the islanders was unlawful, designated the funds expressly for the conversion of the natives and the erection of religious houses. By an insidious abuse of language, however, the monarchs' writs on this subject described the bulls as "for the said conversion and conquest" or with equivalent phrases. Antonio Rumeu de Armas has recently shown that this early case of "double-think" caused a rift between the monarchs and some of their clergy, in which opponents of the use of violence actually attempted to suspend the collection of funds. At the end of the day, the success of the monarchs' policy brought their expansionist and evangelistic aims into perfect harmony: it would be but a short step now to Alexander VI's bulls [Document 27] on the New World, where the duty of evangelization would be seen as making the Castilian conquest just. This was an important moment in the elaboration of the canonistic doctrine of just war: conversion had never in itself been generally considered a sufficient pretext (though it had been advocated by individuals) up to that time.

In the remainder of the monarchs' reign one final development was still to come. Most clerics and religious continued to espouse exclusively peaceful methods of conversion. And Ferdinand and Isabella were not ill-disposed towards attempts along those lines, provided obedience to themselves was among the objects to which the missionaries sought to persuade their congregations: for instance, the mission of Fray Antón de Quesada, whom the monarchs dispatched to Tenerife in 1485, involved a brief both to convert the natives and reduce them to royal authority. Meanwhile, peaceful conversion revived in peninsular Spain when Granada was conquered and proselytization of the new community began. The tenacity of the pacific point of view about conversion during these wars led to the separation in doctrine of a war of conversion from a war waged in order to subject the heathen and so render by peaceful means possible conversion. This was not a point contrary to existing doctrines but merely a question which earlier jurists had left in doubt. Under this new doctrinal distinction, Ferdinand and Isabella were free to make war on the Indians and Canarians as on rebel subjects, theoretically without prejudice to the question of peaceful conversion. . . .

QUESTIONS

1. How did the Spanish shape their society around war?
2. What were the main aspects of the Christian Reconquest and Crusade against Iberia's Muslims?
3. Which lessons in conquest did the Christian kingdoms of Iberia learn in the twelfth century?
4. Sometimes it is maintained that Castile stumbled by luck into supporting Columbus. Why was Spain, based upon its history and location, a good candidate to carve out an overseas empire?
5. Locate the Canary Islands on a map.
6. What similarities would Columbus have noted between the islanders in the Canaries and in the Caribbean?
7. Why were black slaves brought to both the Canaries and the Caribbean?
8. What were the key elements in the varying policies of the monarchs toward the native peoples in each location?

OTIVATING FACTORS

6

Wonders of the Ocean Sea

Stories of the marvels and wonders to be found in distant parts of the world have always had an audience. This immensely popular travel guide was created by attaching a fanciful collection of tales about distant realms, culled from many sources, to a reasonably accurate account of a trip to the Holy Land. The vision of a world that one could circumnavigate given enough time certainly had its appeal to Columbus. Ordinary readers were more attracted by outrageous tales of life on Asian islands, like those of one-legged men who screen the sun by means of their broad foot (which might be a distorted memory of East Indians carrying parasols), or one-eyed giants taken right out of Homer's *Odyssey*.

> *"diverse folks, . . . of diverse manners and laws . . ."*

Sir John presents to his readers a magical world where anything is possible. The harassed European, encouraged to be chaste, limited to one marriage partner, kept in poverty by private property, and likely to regard women as subordinate to men, could find here less deprived lands. To his credulous audience, Sir John carried as much authority as Marco Polo (Document 11).

Despite the real wonder, after 1492, of an entire hemisphere being newly uncovered, people continued to look for tales like Sir John's. In Carlo Ginzburg's *The Cheese and the Worms: The Cosmos of a 16th Century Miller* (1980), old Menocchio talks about the intellectual ferment stirred in his acute mind by "having read that book of Mandeville about many kinds of races and different laws that sorely troubled me" (p. 42).

The first European arrivals in the New World spent time chasing after phantoms, such as the Golden Man *(El Dorado)*, who was coated afresh every day with gold dust by his subjects. Columbus hoped to find the wealthy Seven Cities of Cíbola (allegedly founded by a Spanish monk who fled the Muslims) or at least locate the island of the Amazons, as evidenced in the second selection. He eagerly misinterprets gestures and half-understood words in the expectation that what he wants is around the next bend. The islanders were probably happy to tell Columbus anything to send him on his way. He alternated between belief and skepticism. An entry in his logbook, dated 9 January 1493, relates how he convinced himself that he saw three mermaids *(sirenas)* standing high out of the water: "They had faces something similar to those of human beings, but were not so handsome as it was customary to represent them." He had likely encountered manatees, tame sea cows that feed on herbs near shore.

Mandeville, *The Travels*

I John Mandeville, Knight although I be not worthy, that was born in England, in the town of St. Albans, and passed the sea in the year of our Lord Jesus Christ, 1322, in the day of St. Michael; and hitherto have been long time over the sea, and have seen and gone through many diverse lands, and many provinces and kingdoms and isles and have passed throughout Turkey, Armenia the little and the great; through Tartary, Persia, Syria, Arabia, Egypt the high and the low; through Lybia, Chaldea, and a great part of Ethiopia; through Amazonia, India the less and the more, a great part; and throughout many other Isles, that be about India; where dwell many diverse folks, and of diverse manners and laws, and of diverse shapes of men. . . .

Beside the land of Chaldea [Babylonia] is the land of Amazonia, that is the land of women. And in that realm is all women and no man; not, as some men say, that men may not live there, but for because that the women will not suffer no men among them to be their sovereigns. . . . And then they have loves that use them; and they dwell with them an eight days or ten, and then go home again. And if they have any male child they keep it a certain time, and then send it to the father when he can go alone and eat by himself; or else they slay it. And if it be a female they do away with one breast with an hot iron. And if it be a woman of great lineage they do away the left breast that they may the better bear a shield. And if it be a woman on foot they do away the right breast for to shoot with bow turkeys: for they shoot well with bows.

In that land they have a queen that governs all that land, and all they be obedient to her. And always they make her queen by election that is most worthy in arms; for they be right good warriors and brave, and wise, noble and worthy. And they go oftentime in soldiering to help other kings in their wars, for gold and silver as other soldiers do; and they maintain themselves right vigourously. This land of Amazonia is an isle, all surrounded with the sea save in two places, where be two entries. And beyond that water dwell the men that be their paramours and their loves, where they go to solace them when they will. . . .

There is another land, that is full great, that men call Lamary [Sumatra]. In that land is full great heat. And the custom there is such, that men and women go all naked. And they scorn when they see any strange folk going clothed. And they say, that God made Adam and Eve all naked, and that no man should be ashamed to show himself such as God made him, for nothing is foul that is of human nature. And they say that they that be clothed be folk of another world, or they be folk that believe not in God. And they say,

SOURCE From *The Travels of Sir John Mandeville* (1499 edition, from 1725 text), ed. A. W. Pollard (London: Macmillan & Co., 1900; reprinted New York: Dover Publications, Inc., 1964), pp. 5–131, passim. Text modernized. Reprinted by permission of Dover Publications, Inc.

that they believe in God that formed the world, and that made Adam and Eve and all other things. And they wed there no wives, for all the women there be common and they forsake no man. And they say they sin if they refuse any man; and so God commanded to Adam and Eve and to all that come of him, when he said, "Be fruitful and multiply and replenish the earth." And therefore may no man in that country say, This is my wife; nor no woman may say, This my husband. And when they have children, they may give them to what man they will that has companied with them. And also all the land is common; for all that a man holds one year, another man has it another year; and every man takes what part that he likes. And also all goods of the land be common, grains and all other things: for nothing there is kept in close, nor nothing there is under lock, and every man there takes what he will without any contradiction, and as rich is one man there as is another. . . .

But in that country there is a cursed custom, for they eat more gladly man's flesh than any other flesh; and yet is that country abundant of flesh, of fish, of grains, of gold and silver, and of all other goods. There go merchants and bring with them children to sell to them of the country, and they buy them. And if they be lean they feed them till they be fat, and then they eat them. And they say, that it is the best flesh and the sweetest of all the world. . . .

I say securely that a man might go all the world about, both above and beneath, and come again to his own country, so that he had his health, good shipping and good company, as I said before. And always he should find men, lands, isles and cities and towns, as are in their countries. For you know well that those men that dwell even under the Pole Antartic are foot against foot, to those that dwell even under the Pole Artic, as well as we and those men that dwell against us are foot against foot; and right so it is of other parts of the world. For that a part of the earth and of the sea has his contrary of things which are even against him. And you shall understand that, as I conjecture, the land of Prester John [see Document 9], emperor of India, is even under us. For if a man shall go from Scotland or England unto Jerusalem, he shall go always upward. For our land is the lowest part of the west and the land of Prester John is in the lowest part of the east. And they have day when we have night, and night when we have day. And, so much as a man ascends upward out of our countries to Jerusalem, so much shall he go downward to the land of Prester John; and the cause is for the earth and the sea are round.

For it is the common word that Jerusalem is in midst of the earth; and that may well be proved thus. For, and a man there take a spear and set it even in the earth at midday, when the day and the night are both alike long, it makes no shadow. And David also bears witness thereof, when he says, "God our king before the beginning of the word wrought health in midst of the earth." And therefore they that go out of our countries of the west toward Jerusalem, so many journeys as they make to go there upward, so

MACROBIUS, GLOBAL MAP (1483) *This is an example of "deductive" map making. A fifth-century Greek grammarian living in Rome created a model of what the earth should look like. He emphasized the need to keep to a theoretical symmetry by placing a landmass in the north and south of each hemisphere. Only the Eastern Hemisphere is shown because the other half of the map was dropped over the centuries. We still divide the globe as he did into two frigid, two temperate, and one hot equatorial zone, and continue to place north at the top. Columbus relied on the map for arguments in favor of his voyage. It seemed to demonstrate that it was possible to use the world ocean to pass from area to area, and that he was likely to find populated landmasses.*

many journeys shall they make to go into the land of Prester John downward from Jerusalem. And so he may go into those isles going round all the roundness of the earth and of the sea till he come even under us.

And therefore I have oft-times thought on a tale that I heard, when I was young, how a worthy man of our country went on a time for to see the world; and he passed India and many isles beyond India, where are more than five thousand isles, and he went so long by land and by sea, going round the world, that he found an isle where he heard men speak his own language. For he heard one drive beasts, saying to them such words as he heard men say to oxen in his own country going at the plough; of which he had great marvel, for he knew not how it might be. But I suppose he had so long went on land and on sea, going round the world, that he was come in to his own marches; and, if he had passed furthermore he should have come even to his own country.

Columbus's Letter About the First Voyage

I n these islands I have so far found no human monstrosities, as many expected, but on the contrary the whole population is very well formed, nor are they negroes as in Guinea [Africa], but their hair is flowing and they are not born where there is intense force in the rays of the sun. . . .

As I have found no monsters, so I have had no report of any, except in an island "Quaris," which is the second at the coming into the Indies, and which is inhabited by a people who are regarded in all the islands as very fierce and who eat human flesh. They have many canoes with which they range through all the islands of India and pillage and take whatever they can. They are no more malformed than are the others, except that they have the custom of wearing their hair long like women, and they use bows and arrows of the same cane stems, with a small piece of wood at the end, owing to their lack of iron which they do not possess. They are ferocious among these other people who are cowardly to an excessive degree, but I make no more account of them than of the rest. These are they who have intercourse with the women of "Martinio," which is the first island met on the way from Spain to the Indies, in which there is not a man. These women engage in no feminine occupation, but use bows and arrows of cane, like those already mentioned, and they arm and protect themselves with plates of copper, of which they have much.

SOURCE Columbus's Letter to the Sovereigns on His First Voyage, 15 February–4 March 1493 in *Journals and Other Documents on the Life and Voyages of Christopher Columbus*, trans. and ed. S. E. Morison (New York: The Heritage Press, 1963), pp. 182–186, passim.

In another island, which they assure me is larger than Española [Hispaniola], the people have no hair. In it there is gold incalculable, and from it and from the other islands I bring with me Indians as evidence.

QUESTIONS

1. Why would an author make up a pseudo-travelbook filled with wild tales, and what would keep Europeans believing these stories for two centuries?
2. In what ways would the stories about the people of "Lamory" fulfil the deepest hopes of the common people and the greatest fears of the aristocratic and clerical elite?
3. Why would Columbus, having found no "monsters" in his first voyage, still expect to locate Amazons, cannibals, and hairless men on other islands?

7

The Craze for Spices

Spices once had many uses that are now unnecessary or forgotten. Today they hardly seem worth the effort once invested in crossing deserts by caravan or in spending months in leaky ships. Yet from a medical standpoint, they once performed an invaluable role similar to today's chemical drugs. Small amounts of the more exotic varieties, like opium, balm of mithridate, or lemnian earth, could cost a fortune, thus providing a powerful economic motive to get to the sources.

> "the West sacrificed its precious metals for them [spices]."

During an age when fresh food was available only in the summer, spices preserved. They also enlivened dried foods and dreary "brewetts" of creamy sauced meat, poultry, or fish. Since starchy ingredients reduce the intensity of salt or spice, a large quantity was required. Cooks also threw handfuls of black pepper into dishes because that was the rage. Readers addicted to hot sauces for their tacos will understand.

Columbus was aware that the Portuguese had located a profitable pepper substitute called *malaguetta* in Africa. He hoped to use Castilian resources to beat the Portuguese to Asian spice islands for the real thing. The promise of gaining direct access to spice sources controlled by Arab intermediaries was a powerful argument that Columbus used during his negotiations with Ferdinand and Isabella. Over and over in his logbook, he mentions gold and spices as though they were of equal value. He brought along samples of spices, which he constantly and anxiously compared with whatever he culled from the islands. Upon his return, his enemies at court made much of his failure to bring back the expensive spices he had boasted that he would locate. Since the New World blocked Columbus's way to the Orient, Portugal won the race.

Culinary and Medicinal Uses

Pepper occupies a peculiar position in the history of food. An ordinary seasoning we are far from considering indispensable today, it was for many centuries associated with spice, the primary object of trade with the Levant. Everything depended on it, even the dreams of the fifteenth-century explorers. "As dear as pepper" was a common saying.

Europe had had a very old passion for pepper and spices—cinnamon, cloves, nutmeg and ginger. We must not be too quick to call it a mania. Islam, China and India shared the taste, and every society has its crazes for particular foods that become almost indispensable. They express the need to break the monotony of diet. A Hindu writer said: "When the palate revolts against the insipidness of rice boiled with no other ingredients, we dream of fat, salt and spices."

It is a fact that the poorest and most monotonous diets in underdeveloped countries today are those which most readily resort to spices. By spices we mean all types of seasoning in use in our period (including pimento, which came from America under many names) and not merely the glorious spices of the Levant. There were spices on the tables of the poor in Europe in the middle ages: thyme, marjoram, bay leaves, savory, aniseed, coriander and particularly garlic, which Arnaud de Villeneuve, a famous thirteenth-century doctor, called the peasants' theriac [snake bite antidote]. The only luxury product amongst these local spices was saffron. . . .

The West inherited spices and pepper from Rome. It is probable that both were later in short supply, in Charlemagne's time, when the Mediterranean was all but closed to Christianity. But compensation followed rapidly. In the twelfth century the craze for spices was in full swing. The West sacrificed its precious metals for them and engaged in the difficult Levant trade which meant travelling half-way round the world. The passion was so great that along with black and white pepper (both genuine peppers, the colour depending on whether or not the dark coating was left on) Westerners bought "long pepper," also from India, and a substitute product like the bogus pepper or *malaguetta* which came from the Guinea coast from the fifteenth century onwards. Ferdinand of Spain tried in vain to prevent the importing of cinnamon and pepper from Portugal (it meant letting silver out of the country in return) arguing that *"buena especia es el ajo"*—garlic is a perfectly good spice.

Cookery books show that the mania for spices affected everything: meat, fish, jam, soup, luxury drinks. Who would dare cook game without using "hot pepper," as Douet d'Arcy counselled as early as the beginning of the fourteenth century? The advice of *Le Ménagier de Paris* (1393) was to "put in the spices as late as possible." Its recipe for black pudding ran as follows: "take ginger, clove and a little pepper and crush together." In this booklet, *oille*, "a dish brought back from Spain" and consisting of a mixture of various meats, duck, partridge, pigeon, quail and chicken (to all appearances the popular *olla podrida* of today), also becomes a mixture of spices, "aromatic drugs," eastern or otherwise, nutmeg, pepper, thyme, ginger and basil. Spices were also consumed in the form of preserved fruits and elaborate powders to treat any disease medicine might diagnose. They were all reputed "to drive off wind" and "favour the seed." In the West Indies, black pepper was often replaced by red pepper, "axi or chili," which was so liberally sprinkled over meat that new arrivals could not swallow a mouthful.

In fact there was nothing in common between this spice-orgy and the late and moderate consumption known to the Roman world. It is true that the Romans ate little meat (even in Cicero's time it was the object of sumptuary laws). The medieval West, on the other hand, was carnivorous. We might assume that the badly preserved and not always tender meat cried out for the seasoning of strong peppers and spicy sauces, which disguised its poor quality. Some doctors argue today that the sense of smell has some curious psychological features. They claim that there is a sort of mutual exclusion between the taste for seasonings "with a bitter smell, like garlic and onion . . . and the taste for more delicate seasonings with sweet and aromatic smells, reminiscent of the scent of flowers." In the middle ages, the former may have predominated.

Things were probably not so simple. In any case consumption of spice increased in the sixteenth century (until then, it had been a great luxury) with the sharp rise in deliveries following Vasco da Gama's voyage. The increase was particularly marked in the north, where purchases of spices far exceeded those in the Mediterranean regions. The spice-market shifted from Venice and its *Fondaco dei Tedeschi* [a center for German merchants] to Antwerp (with a short sojourn at Lisbon) and then to Amsterdam, so the trade was not governed by simple considerations of commerce and navigation. Luther, who exaggerated, claimed that there was more spice than grain in Germany. The large consumers were in the north and east. In Holland, in 1697, it was thought that after coin, the best merchandise "for cold countries" was spice, consumed "in prodigious quantities" in Russia and Poland. Perhaps pepper and spices were more sought after in places where they had been late arrivals and were still a new luxury. When Abbé Mably reached Cracow he was served with wine from Hungary and "a very plentiful meal which might have been very good if the Russians and the Confederates had destroyed all those aromatic herbs used in such quantities here, like the cinnamon and nutmeg that poison travellers in Germany." It would seem therefore that in eastern Europe the taste for strong seasoning and spices was still medieval in style at that date, while the ancient culinary customs were to some extent disappearing in the West. But this is conjecture and not fact.

It seems at any rate that when spices began to fall in price and to appear on all tables, so that they were no longer a symbol of wealth and luxury, they were used less and their prestige declined. Or so a cookery book of 1651 (by François-Pierre de La Varenne) would suggest, as does Boileau's satire (1665) ridiculing the misuse of spices.

As soon as the Dutch reached the Indian Ocean and the Indian Archipelago they did their utmost to restore and then maintain for their own profit the monopoly in pepper and spices against the Portuguese (whose trade was gradually eliminated) and soon against English competition and later French and Danish. They also tried to control supplies to China, Japan, Bengal and Persia, and were able to compensate for a slack period in Europe by a sharp rise in their trade with Asia. The quantities of pepper reaching Europe via Amsterdam (and outside its market) probably increased, at least until the middle of the seventeenth century, and then were maintained at a high level. Annual arrivals in about 1600 before the Dutch success were possibly of the order of 20,000 present-day quintals [one quintal = 101.42 pounds], hence an annual quota of 20 grams per inhabitant for 100 million Europeans. Consumption may well have been of the order of 50,000 quintals in about 1680, more than double the figure at the time of the Portuguese monopoly. The sales of the *Oost Indische Companie* [a Dutch East India Company] from 1715 to 1732 suggest that a limit was reached. What is certain is that pepper ceased being the dominant spice-trade commodity it was in the days of Priuli and Sanudo and the undisputed supremacy of Venice. Pepper still held first place in the trade of the Company in Amsterdam in 1648–1650 (33% of the total). It fell to fourth in 1778–1780 (11%) after textiles (silk and cotton, 32.66%), spices (24.43%) and tea and coffee (22.92%). Was this a typical case of the ending of a luxury consumption and the beginning of a general one? Or the decline of excessive use?

For this decline the popularity of new luxuries—coffee, chocolate, alcohol and tobacco—can legitimately be blamed; perhaps also the spread of new vegetables which gradually began to vary Western diet (asparagus, spinach, lettuce, artichokes, peas, green beans, cauliflower, tomatoes, pimentoes, melons). These vegetables were mostly the product of European, and especially Italian, gardens. (Charles VIII brought the melon back from Italy.) Some, like the cantaloupe, came from Armenia, others, like the tomato, haricot bean and potato, from America.

One last but rather unconvincing explanation remains. A general decrease in meat consumption took place after 1600 or even earlier, which meant a break with former diet. Concurrently the rich adopted a simpler style of cooking, in France at least. German and Polish cooking may have been behindhand and have also had better supplies of meat and therefore a

43

greater need for pepper and spices. But this explanation is only conjectural and those given before will have to satisfy us until fuller information is available.

Columbus's Logbook, 1492

Friday 19 October 1492

It is an island [Crooked Island] of many very green and very large trees. And this land is higher than the other islands found, and there are on it some small heights; not that they can be called mountains, but they are things that beautify the rest; and it seems to have much water. There in the middle of the island, from this part northeast, it forms a great bight [cove] and there are many wooded places, very thick and of very large extent. I tried to go there to anchor in it so as to go ashore and see so much beauty; but the bottom was shoal and I could not anchor except far from land and the wind was very good for going to this cape where I am anchored now, to which I gave the name Cabo Hermoso, because such it is. And so I did not anchor in that bight and also because I saw this cape from there, so green and so beautiful; and likewise are all the other things and lands of these islands, so that I do not know where to go first; nor do my eyes grow tired of seeing such beautiful verdure and so different from ours. And I even believe that there are among them many plants and many trees which in Spain are valued for dyes and for medicinal spices; but I am not acquainted with them, which gives me much sorrow. And when I arrived here at this cape the smell of the flowers or trees that came from land was so good and soft that it was the sweetest thing in the world. . . .

Sunday 21 October 1492

. . . Here there are some big lakes and over and around them the groves are marvelous. And here and in all of the island the groves are all green and the verdure like that in April in Andalusia [the south of Spain]. And the singing of the small birds [is so marvelous] that it seems that a man would never want to leave this place. And [there are] flocks of parrots that obscure the sun; and birds of so many kinds and sizes, and so different from ours, that it is a marvel. And also there are trees of a thousand kinds and all [with] their own kinds of fruit and all smell so that it is a marvel. I am the most sorrowful man in the world, not being acquainted with them. Because I am quite certain that all of them are things of value; and I am bringing samples of them, and likewise of the plants. . . .

Source *The Diario of Christopher Columbus's First Voyage to America 1492–1493*. abstr. Fray Bartolomé de Las Casas, trans. Oliver Dunn and J. E. Kelley, Jr. (Norman: University of Oklahoma Press, 1989), pp. 99–111, passim. Footnotes removed. Reprinted by permission.

Tuesday 23 October 1492

I should like to leave today for the island of Cuba, which I believe must be Cipango [Japan] according to the indications that these people give of its size and wealth, and I will not delay here any longer nor . . . around this island in order to go to the town, as I had decided [to do], in order to talk to this king or lord. [This] is so as not to delay much, since I see that here there is no gold mine, and that to go around these islands there is need of many kinds of wind, and the wind does not blow just as men would wish. And since one should go where there is large-scale commerce, I say that there is no reason to delay but [reason] to go forward and investigate much territory until we encounter a very profitable land; although my understanding is that this land may be very profitable in spices. But that I do not recognize them burdens me with the greatest sorrow in the world; for I see a thousand kinds of trees, each of which has its own kind of fruit, and they are green now as in Spain in the months of May and June; and there are a thousand kinds of plants, and the same with flowers and of everything. Nothing was recognized except this aloe, of which today I also ordered a lot brought to the ship to take to Your Highnesses. . . .

8

Searching for Gold

Europe faced a constant drain of its precious metals through the luxury trade with Asia, via a host of middlemen. Rulers did what they could to keep a supply on hand for internal trade, but the draw of eastern goods was too great. As economies slowly recovered during the fifteenth century, the pressure grew to find new sources of the metals. The silver mines of Central Europe flourished from 1470–1540, while some gold was drawn by panning rivers. Portuguese voyages to West Africa managed to get directly into coastal contact with the caravan trade to the Bambus, the gold-mining center of the Sudan. Silver circulates in a slow-moving economy; gold is the currency for an expanding economy. As population increased and trade expanded, Europe experienced a gold famine.

> *"who has gold has a treasure with which he gets what he wants"*

Columbus had to justify his expeditions by locating valuable goods, in particular gold. A theory of the day postulated a relationship between the closeness of the sun and the location of deposits. This fixed idea drove Columbus ever southward toward the equator on his voyages. In 1492 he could not locate the enormous mines he was sure were close at hand, or at least on the next island. Beginning with his second voyage in 1493, he set islanders to panning grains of gold from their rivers. Every three months, each native fourteen years or older had to bring to the forts a small bell filled with gold dust. In exchange, they had hung around their necks a copper token, stamped with the date. Anyone caught without an updated token had his or her hands cut off as punishment.

In the first selection, a letter discussing his fourth voyage (1502–1504), an aged and exhausted Columbus rambles in a deluded way that the mines of Veragua (today's Panama) are those of the biblical King Solomon. His reference to bringing souls to paradise refers to Catholic doctrine, which claims that the charitable purchase of a certificate of indulgence shortens the time a tormented soul is delayed in purgatory, an unpleasant stopping point before entering heaven.

The author of the second selection, José de Acosta, was a Spanish Jesuit missionary who saw the gold mines of Mexico and the mountain of silver at Potosí, Bolivia, which is still being worked. His discussion exemplifies the fanciful view of the day concerning where precious metals were to be found, along with a reasonable description of how the extraction process worked. Imbedded in the writing is his sense of the deep fascination gold had, and has, for Europeans.

Amerindians were confused about this passion for gold as an object of desire in itself, since it was not their medium of exchange. An Aztec sneered: "as if they were monkeys, the Spanish lifted up the gold banners and gold necklaces. . . . Like hungry pigs they craved that gold, swinging the banners of gold from side to side."

Columbus's Letter About the Fourth Voyage, 1502–1504

When I discovered the Indies, I said they were the world's wealthiest realm. I spoke of gold, pearls, precious stones, spices and of the markets and fairs. But, because not everything turned up at once, I was vilified. . . .

The Genoese, the Venetians and everyone who has pearls, precious stones and other things of value, they all carry them to the ends of the earth to barter and convert into gold. O, most excellent gold! Who has gold has a treasure with which he gets what he wants, imposes his will on the world, and even helps souls to paradise. When the lords of these lands in the region of Veragua [Panama] die, they bury their gold with the corpse, so they say.

SOURCE Columbus's *Lettera Rarissima* to the Sovereigns, 7 July 1503 in *Journals and Other Documents on the Life and Voyages of Christopher Columbus*, trans. and ed. S. E. Morison (New York: The Heritage Press, 1963), pp. 382–383, passim. Reprinted by permission.

On one voyage 674 quintals [one quintal = 101.42 lbs] of gold were brought to Solomon, besides what the merchants and mariners took, and what was paid in Arabia. From this gold he made 200 lances and 300 shields, and he made the canopy which was to be above them of gold plates embellished by precious stones. He made many other objects out of gold, and many huge vessels richly embellished with precious stones. Josephus [ancient Jewish author] mentions this in his history, *de Antiquitatibus*. The matter is also described in Chronicles and in the Book of Kings [Bible]. Josephus says that this gold was obtained in Aurea [in East Africa]. If so, I declare that those mines of the Aurea are but a part of these in Veragua, which extend westward 20 days' journey and are at the same distance from the pole and the equator. Solomon bought all that gold, precious stones and silver; and you can give orders to collect it if you see fit.

Acosta

Gold, silver, and metals grow naturally in land that is barren and unfruitful. And we see, that in lands of good temperature, the which are fertile with grass and fruits, there are seldom found any mines; for that Nature is contented to give them vigor to bring forth fruits more necessary for the preservation and maintenance of the life of beasts and men. And contrariwise to lands that are very rough, dry, and barren (as in the highest mountains and inaccessible rocks of a rough temper) they find mines of silver, of quick-silver, and of gold; and all those riches (which come into Spain since the West Indies were discovered) have been drawn out of such places which are rough and full, bare and fruitless: yet the taste of this money makes these places pleasing and agreeable, well inhabited with numbers of people. . . .

We find not that the Indians in former times used gold, silver, or any other metal for money, and for the price of things, but only for ornament, . . . whereof there was great quantity in their temples, palaces, and tombs, with a thousand kinds of vessels of gold and silver, which they had. They used no gold nor silver to traffic or buy but did change and sell one thing for another, as Homer and Pliny report of the Ancients. They had some other things of greater esteem which went current amongst them for price, and instead of coins; and unto this day this custom continues amongst the Indians, as in the Provinces of Mexico, instead of money they use cacao, which is a small fruit, and therewith buy what they will. In Peru they use coca to the same end, the which is a leaf the Indians esteem much, as in Paraguay, they have stamps of iron for coin, and cotton woven in Santa Cruz de la Sierra. Finally, the manner of the Indians traffic, and their buying and selling, was to

SOURCE José de Acosta, *The Natural and Moral History of the Indies* [1590], trans. Edward Grimston (London, 1604). Book IV, Chs. 3–4. English modernized.

exchange, and give things for things: and although there were great marts and famous fairs, yet had they no need of money, nor of brokers, for that every one had learned what he was to give in exchange for every kind of merchandise. . . .

Gold amongst other metals has been always held the most excellent, and with reason, being the most durable and incorruptible of all others; for fire which consumes and diminishes the rest amends it, and brings it to perfection. Gold which has often passed through the fire, keeps his color, and is most fine and pure. . . . And although his substance and body be firm and solid, yet does it yield and bow wonderfully; the beaters and drawers of gold know well the force it has to be drawn out without breaking. All which things well considered, with other excellent properties, will give men of Judgment to understand, wherefor the Holy Scripture do compare Charity to

TAKING REVENGE *This woodcut illustrates a book of travels to the New World by an Italian adventurer. In one passage of his history, he gleefully recounts how a group of mainland natives, driven to distraction by the pressure on them to find gold for the Spanish, wreaked vengeance on their tormentors by pouring molten gold down their throats. The story is probably too fine an example of poetic justice to be true. The illustration is of ethnographic interest, however, because it accurately shows an aspect of male costume.*

gold. To conclude, there is little need to relate the excellencies thereof to make it more desirable. For the greatest excellency it has, is to be known, as it is, amongst men, for the supreme power and greatness of the world.

Coming therefore to our subject; at the Indies there is great abundance of this metal, and it is well known by approved histories that the Incas of Peru did not content themselves with great and small vessels of gold, as pots, cups, goblets, and flagons; with bowls or great vessels, but they had chairs also and litters of massive gold, and in their temples they had set up many Images of pure gold, whereof they find some yet at Mexico, but not such store as when the first Conquerors came into the one and the other kingdom, who found great treasure, and without doubt there was much more hidden in the earth by the Indians. It would seem ridiculous to report that they have made their horse shoes of silver for want of iron, and that they have paid three hundred crowns for a bottle of wine, and other strange things; and yet in truth this has come to pass, yes and greater matters. They draw gold in those parts after three sorts, or at the least, I have seen all three used. For either they find gold in grains, in powder, or in stone. They do call gold in grains, small morsels of gold, which they find whole, without mixture of any other metal, which hath no need of melting or refining in the fire: and they call them pippins, for that commonly they are like pippins, or seeds of melons. . . . There is another kind which the Indians call *papas* [potatoes] and sometimes they find pieces very fine and pure, like to small round roots, the which is rare in that metal, but usual in gold. They find little of this gold in pippin, in respect of the other kinds. Gold in stone is a vein of gold that grows or ingendereth within the stone or flint, as I have seen in the mines of Saruma, within the government of Salinas [Ecuador], very great stones pierced and intermixed with gold; others that were half gold, and half stone. The gold which grow in this manner is found in pits or mines, which have veins like silver mines, but it is very hard to draw it forth . . . .

The most famous gold is that of Carabaya in Peru, and of Valdivia in Chile, for that it rise with his alloy and perfection, which is twenty-three carats and a half, and sometimes more. They make account likewise of the gold of Veragua [Panama] to be very fine. They bring much gold to Mexico from the Philippines, and China, but commonly it is weak, and of base alloy. Gold is commonly found mixed with silver or with copper, but that which is mixed with silver is commonly of fewer carats than that which is mixed with copper. If there be a fifth part of silver . . . it is then properly called Electrum, which has the property to shine more at the light of the fire than fine gold or fine silver. That which is incorporated with copper, is commonly of a higher value. They refine powdered gold in basins, washing it in many waters until the sand falls from it, and the gold, as most heavy, remains in the bottom. They refine it likewise with quick-silver and strong water, for . . . this water has the virtue to separate gold from dross, or from other metals. After it is purified and molten, they make bricks or small bars to carry it to Spain for being in powder they cannot transport it from the Indies, for they can neither custom it, mark it, nor take assay, until it is melted down. . . .

Today the great treasure of Spain comes from the Indies, because God has appointed the one realm to serve the other by giving up its wealth so as to be under good governance, thus mutually enjoying one another's goods and privileges.

QUESTIONS

1. What roles did spices play in the lives of Europeans during the Medieval and Renaissance eras?
2. What made spices so expensive by the time they reached the user?
3. How many unlabeled spices can you recognize out of their containers?
4. Columbus seemed to be confused by the vegetation he found on the islands. What could he have expected to see if he were really in Asia?
5. Why were Europeans so anxious to find gold?
6. In what type of terrain did sixteenth-century explorers expect to find precious metals?
7. Why, according to Acosta, does Spain have the right and the duty to take all the gold and silver from the New World?
8. Where, according to Columbus, did the biblical King Solomon get his gold?

9

Help in the Struggle Against Islam

The constant advance of Muslim power in the fifteenth century made Europeans fearful. The Ottoman Turks held the Balkans, Greece, the Ionian Islands and, from 1480–1481, even Otranto on the Italian peninsula. The extent of the menace did not prevent the kingdoms and city-states of Europe from indulging in constant, bitter warfare. Dreams about renewed crusades or "holy leagues" against the Muslims came crashing to earth before the reality of Christian disharmony.

"we have the highest crown on earth . . ."

Salvation from the Muslim threat would have to come from outside, perhaps from the fictitious Christian ruler, Prester John. He was believed to be both a king and a priest (presbyter) who ruled "India." Where exactly his "India" might be found was a matter for learned speculation. Likely candidates were (1) Africa, (2) what we today label the Indian subcontinent, and (3) the extreme of Asia.

Prester John represented to credulous medieval Europeans a faint hope of help against Islam from a powerful outside source. When people are desperate, they create their own saviors. The selection below is from a letter, forged in France, that was purported to be from this great and powerful king/priest.

Most civilizations would not have acted on so faint a hope, but driven by maritime prowess, commercial ambition, and missionary religious impulse, the Portuguese went to find him. As it turned out, remarkably enough, there actually was in Abyssinia (today's Ethiopia) a line of black Christian kings. In 1493, João Pero da Covilhã arrived at the court of Alexander, Lion of the Tribe of Judah and King of Kings. After the monarch gave his visitor a wife, he forced him to stay, but Covilhã did manage to get word back to Lisbon.

P rester John, by the Grace of God most powerful king over all Christian kings, greetings to the Emperor of Rome and the King of France, our friends. We wish you to learn about us, our position, the government of our land, and our people and beasts. And since you say that our Greeks, or men of Grecian race, do not pray to God the way you do in your country, we let you know that we worship and believe in Father, Son, and the Holy Ghost, three persons in one Deity and one true God only. We attest and inform you by our letter, sealed with our seal, of the condition and character of our land and men. And if you desire something that we can do for you, ask us, for we shall do it gladly. In case you wish to come hither to our country, we shall make you on account of your good reputation our successors and we shall grant you vast lands, manors, and mansions.

Let it be known to you that we have the highest crown on earth as well as gold, silver, precious stones and strong fortresses, cities, towns, castles, and boroughs. We have under our sway forty-two kings who all are mighty and good Christians. . . .

Our land is divided into four parts, for there are so many Indias. In Greater India lies the body of the Apostle Saint Thomas for whom our Lord has wrought more miracles than for the [other] saints who are in heaven. And this India is toward the East, for it is near the deserted Babylon and also near the tower called Babel. . . .

Know also that in our country there grows wild pepper amidst trees and serpents. When it becomes ripe, we send our people to gather it. They put the woods on fire and everything burns, but when the fire has died out, they make great heaps of pepper and serpents and they put the pepper together and carry it later to a barn, wash it in two or three waters, and let it dry in the sun. In this way it becomes black, hard, and biting. . . .

SOURCE *Prester John: The Letter and the Legend*, pp. 6–78, passim. Trans. Vsevolod Slessarev. Copyright © 1959 University of Minnesota. Renewed 1987 Helga Slessarev. Reprinted courtesy of the University of Minnesota Press.

Let it be known to you that we have swift horses which can carry a knight in full armor for three or four days without taking food.

And whenever we go to war, we let fourteen kings, clad in garments of gold and silver, carry in front of us fourteen ensigns adorned with sundry precious stones. Other kings who come behind carry richly decorated banners of silk.

Know that in front of us there march forty thousand clerics and an equal number of knights, then come two hundred thousand men on foot, not counting the wagons with provisions or the elephants and camels which carry arms and ammunition. . . .

Know that I had been blessed before I was born, for God has sent an angel to my father who told him to build a palace full of God's grace and a chamber of paradise for the child to come, who was to be the greatest king on earth and to live for a long time. And whoever stays in the palace will never suffer hunger, thirst, or death. When my father had woke up from his slumber, he was overly joyful and he began to build the palace which you will see.

First of all, its walls are of crystal, the ceiling above is of precious stones and it is adorned with stars similar to those of the sky, and its floor is also of crystal. There are no windows or doors in this palace and inside it has twenty-four columns of gold and various precious stones. We stay there during the big holidays of the year and in the midst of it St. Thomas [an apostle of Christ who allegedly traveled to India] preaches to the people. And inside our palace there is [water] and the best wine on earth, and whoever drinks of it has no desire for worldly things, and nobody knows where the [water] goes or whence it comes.

There is still another great marvel in our palace, for no food is served in it except on a tray, grill, or trencher that hangs from a column, so that when we sit at the table and wish to eat, the food is placed before us by the grace of the Holy Spirit.

Know that all the scribes on earth could not report or describe the riches of our palace and our chapel. Everything we have written to you is as true as there is God, and for nothing in the world would we lie, since God and St. Thomas would confound us and deprive us of our title.

Columbus's Vision

Historians increasingly tend to emphasize the mystical side of Columbus over his practical concerns, as is demonstrated by the first selection. Columbus was hardly unusual in believing that all his petty tribulations and mighty successes were due to God's direct intervention. This was the belief of the age, held alike by popes, the Protestant reformers, and every conquistador.

"a thoroughly medieval combination of apocalyptic . . . spirituality and imperial ideology."

Spain was an appropriate place for Columbus to go, for after the trials of the wars against the Muslims, the establishment of the Inquisition, and the expulsion of the Jews, it was filled with individuals who believed they would be called upon to do sacred missions. Columbus always received his greatest support from Spanish clerics, for clearly he was in agreement with them. His overt piety is confirmed by all existing sources, which together lead to the conclusion that he was something of a mystic. Often he expressed his belief that he was "a man sent from God," which commended him to the monarchs. "The Holy Trinity moved me," he wrote, "to come with this message into your royal presence."

God supposedly wanted him to open up to the Gospel that part of the world that was unknown. The land must be inhabited—it would be absurd for God to send him to a barren place. Columbus headed ever southward on each successive voyage, perhaps because he was searching for the Garden of Eden, thought to be in the tropics. The second selection, from a letter describing his third voyage, details his remarkable view about the "real" shape of that part of the world, which indicates to him that he has reached the earthly paradise, from which Adam and Eve were long ago expelled. The heavy flow of fresh water from the delta of the Oronoco River into the Gulf of Paria, near the island of Trinidad, convinced Columbus that he was at the source of all the great rivers of the world. The belief at that time was that these rivers had their source in an earthly paradise.

If no one had ever crossed the Atlantic before Columbus, this was not because it could not be done, but because God hid its mysteries until His chosen one was sent out to reveal all. Columbus's confidence that he would succeed was always based less on practical considerations than on the Almighty's intention that he would succeed. In time of stress, as in the third selection, which dates from the difficult voyage of 1502–1504, the tired old man heard voices and saw visions. The message the Deity gave him was, as always, a positive one.

The Approach of the End of Time

C hristopher Columbus has usually been depicted in both scholarly and popular histories as an eminently rational geographer and courageous explorer who overcame the scientific ignorance and prevailing religious superstition of his day in convincing Ferdinand and Isabella to underwrite his initial voyage of discovery. This image of the discovery of America has little to do, I suggest, with the genesis of Columbus's "Enterprise of the Indies" or with his own understanding of the historical implications of his discoveries once they were made. Nor does it explain the thoughts and actions of the *conquistadores* and the mendicant religious orders, Columbus's immediate successors in the New World. There is a considerable body of evidence that suggests that Columbus and his successors were motivated to make their voyages of conquest and conversion by a thoroughly medieval combination of apocalyptic [the violent struggle when God will bring the world to an end] spirituality and imperial ideology. The stimulus for these men was of the profoundest cultural sort; it was the ritual of taking possession of the New World, that is, fitting it into the cosmic framework of the Old.

The ritual of taking possession was not always (or even usually) performed in a rational manner, but rather was marked by a highly energized, sometimes almost frantic acting out of Old World hopes and fears in a land whose existence had been unimagined for centuries. There was little objective interest in that New World and its inhabitants; it and they represented the primordial Chaos that lay outside the Christian cosmos and had somehow to be incorporated into it.

It is not clear precisely when Columbus conceived of his "Enterprise of the Indies"—his plan to reach the Far East, the home of the Grand Khan, more rapidly and efficiently by sailing west rather than traveling overland to the east as Marco Polo [Document 11] and others had done. But it does seem certain that his plan was based on his reading of a variety of well-known ancient and medieval sources and that his general conceptions of geography and cosmography were traditional in nature. Columbus's sources included Aristotle, Pliny the Elder, Solinus, and Marco Polo, but paramount among them were two others, Pierre D'Ailly and Paolo Toscanelli.

Pierre D'Ailly, the prominent French cardinal and conciliarist, active in the first quarter of the fifteenth century, was the author of a variety of works on history, cosmology, geography, and theology. An incunabulum [books

SOURCE P. M. Watts, "Columbus: Crusader and Mystic," *Humanities*, vol. 6, no. 6 (December 1985), pp. 15–17. Reprinted with permission of *Humanities* magazine, National Endowment for the Humanities.

printed before 1500 A.D.] consisting of a collection of D'Ailly's works came into Columbus's hands sometime prior to his initial voyage of discovery and was read and annotated by him. A work entitled *Imago mundi* [Document 12], a compendium of medieval geography and cosmology, appears to have especially interested Columbus. He annotated it copiously, particularly the eighth chapter, "On the size of the inhabitable earth," wherein D'Ailly (borrowing freely from the thirteenth-century philosopher Roger Bacon) argued that the western ocean was not very wide. Conclusive proof for D'Ailly and for Columbus was provided in the apocryphal [biblical] Esdras 6:42, wherein it is written that only one-seventh of the world is covered by water. In the letter describing his fourth voyage to the New World, Columbus stated that his discoveries had verified Esdras 6:42, as well as other parts of *Imago mundi*.

The second major stimulus for Columbus's "Enterprise of the Indies" is supposed to have come from the famous Renaissance mathematician and astronomer, Paolo Toscanelli [Document 11]. It is tempting to think that the great Toscanelli directly inspired Columbus to undertake his voyages of discovery, but no conclusive proof that Columbus and Toscanelli actually corresponded has emerged. What is certain is that Columbus read a letter that Toscanelli addressed to Alfonso V of Portugal in 1474. In that letter Toscanelli also argued that the size of the western ocean was smaller than generally believed and that the East could be reached more quickly by sailing west. In other words, the contents of the letter did not fundamentally differ from other sources available to Columbus. There is no documentation to indicate that Columbus thought that his voyage would significantly revise the cosmography contained in these sources, only that he intended to substantiate the claims of Aristotle, D'Ailly, Toscanelli, and others regarding the facility of navigating the western ocean.

Historical evidence does indicate however, that Columbus's proposed voyage was part of a much larger plan. Moreover, it may well have been the attraction of this larger plan that led Ferdinand and Isabella to decide to support Columbus when they did. In Columbus's mind, the "Enterprise of the Indies" was nothing less than the first step in a crusade in which he believed that he, Ferdinand, and Isabella had been divinely preordained to restore the Holy Land to the Christian faith. It was a vision to which he referred throughout his correspondence with the monarchs and which he intended to elaborate at length in an uncompleted work that he called *The Book of Prophecies*.

Until recently *The Book of Prophecies* has received relatively little scholarly attention, probably because of the continuing emphasis on the rational side of Columbus at the expense of his spiritual side. The book consists of a very important prefatory letter addressed by Columbus to Ferdinand and Isabella, along with excerpts from a wide range of ancient and medieval authors. It appears that Columbus and his collaborator, a Carthusian monk named Gaspar Gorricio, selected these excerpts in order to illustrate a number of interrelated themes. The most important of these are the aforementioned recovery of the Holy Land, prophesied in numerous biblical passages, and the final conversion of all the peoples of the world to Christianity, prophesied in John 10:16, the Apocalypse, and elsewhere.

Columbus's reading of a number of short works by D'Ailly, contained in the same incunabulum as *Imago mundi*, led him to believe that this final conversion was imminent. In the prefatory letter he went so far as to assert that only 155 years remained before the appearance of the Antichrist and the eve of the end of time. Columbus appears to have been convinced that Ferdinand and Isabella had been divinely designated to play a special role in the denouement of history. The proof of this calling, he believed, was their victory over the Moors at Granada early in 1492 (thus completing the *Reconquista* [Reconquest] begun almost three centuries earlier) and their expulsion of the Jews from their kingdom. He believed that he had provided the Spanish monarchs with efficient access to the riches of the East through the sea route opened up by his voyage. These riches would be used to finance an expedition to the Holy Land. Columbus himself was prepared to play an active role in this crusade, as he indicated in the letter describing the fourth voyage.

Columbus was not alone in interpreting the events of 1492 as signs of the approach of the end of time, nor in believing Ferdinand and Isabella to be the Messiah-Emperor whose coming had been foretold in a number of widely circulated medieval prophecies and histories. Not coincidentally, the decades immediately preceding 1492 saw a revival of interest in the writings of the twelfth-century Calabrian abbot Joachim of Fiore, perhaps the most important and influential apocalyptic thinker of the Middle Ages. Basing his position on the concordances that he saw between the Old and New Testaments, Joachim attempted to discern the patterns of history, to prophesy the events that would mark the advent of the Antichrist. Aspects of Columbus's vision of history can surely be traced back to Joachim as well as to Pierre D'Ailly (himself a conduit for Joachim's ideas as well as those of others). Several prophecies contained in the *Book of Prophecies* are explicitly attributed to Joachim, including the prediction that he who will reconquer Jerusalem for the Christians will come from Spain. And there is reason to believe that there are lost sections of the *Book of Prophecies* that contained other Joachite materials.

The Franciscans provide another probable link between Columbus and Joachism. The ties between that order and the ideas of Joachim were early and strong, and the Franciscans were at the heart of the Joachite revival in late fifteenth-century Spain. Several important early biographies of Columbus indicate that he was associated with the Franciscan Tertiaries, the branch of the order open to laymen. One account relates that a penitent Columbus walked the streets of Seville dressed in the robes of a Franciscan. Columbus's son Diego tells us that his father was buried in the robes of a Franciscan Tertiary.

It might seem likely that the discovery of a new world would quickly rupture both the cosmography and the eschatology [the study of final things] of the medieval world picture. The extraordinary truth is not only that the discoveries [did] not interrupt the continuity of the medieval world picture but that throughout the sixteenth century at least the ritual of taking possession was enacted almost entirely within a centuries-old framework. This ritual of absorbing the New World into the cosmos of the Old begins with Columbus's first landfall. As his journals indicate, he was obsessed with naming and claiming the coastal regions that he explored for Ferdinand and Isabella and for Christianity. Almost always, the names he selected for the New World were drawn from the religious and political ideology of the Old. He died feeling certain that his voyages had set the stage for the final conversion of all races to Christianity. How could the discovery of so many heretofore unknown peoples not be proof that the fulfillment of John 10:16 was at hand?

Certainly that expectation fired the first several generations of Franciscan missionaries who traveled from Spain to the New World. Girolamo Mendieta, whose *História de las Indias* is one of the most important sixteenth-century chronicles of the evangelization of the New World, described Columbus as having opened the door through which the mendicant friars could enter and convert the heathen natives. But it was Hernán Cortés [Document 25], not Columbus, whom Mendieta made the central figure in his story.

Cortés was of noble Roman descent (or so Mendieta claimed) and somehow the grandeur of that imperial culture accrued to him. More important, Mendieta compared Cortés with Moses, saying that he had led the Indians from idolatry to Christianity just as Moses had led his people from Egypt to the Promised Land. Finally, Mendieta (and at least one other Franciscan, Diego Valadés) compared Cortés with Martin Luther. Mendieta believed (incorrectly) that the two had the same birthdate and that their historical destinies were therefore somehow interwoven. Mendieta damned Luther for having splintered the Church at a crucial moment in its prophetic history. Cortés, on the other hand, was a true Christian soldier for the part he played in aiding the Franciscans in the mass conversion of the Indians. These gains in the New World would presumably outweigh the losses to the Protestants in the Old.

The stakes in the evangelization of the New World were enormous: the capture of lost souls before the End and the effort to counteract the terrifying split caused by the Reformation. This undoubtedly accounts for the fierce, relentless nature of the early Franciscan missionary work in the New World. Indigenous religious art was systematically destroyed as part of this "spiritual conquest." Thousands of natives were quickly baptized with little or no instruction in the Christian faith. Missionary and Indian alike participated in ritual dramas of dominance and submission. Gradually, as significant numbers of the mendicants lived in the new environment for significant periods of time, they began to regard the natives on their own terms and even, as in the famous example of the Dominican Bartolomé de Las Casas, to admire and defend native cultures per se. Only then did the Old World cosmos begin to disintegrate and a new one start to emerge.

Columbus Nears the Earthly Paradise, 1498

I have always read that the world, land and water, was spherical, and authoritative accounts and the experiments which Ptolemy [ancient Greek geographer] and all the others have recorded concerning this matter, so describe it and hold it to be, by the eclipses of the moon and by other demonstrations made from east to west, as well as from the elevation of the pole star from north to south. Now, as I have already said, I have seen so great irregularity that, as a result, I have been led to hold this concerning the world, and I find that it is not round as they describe it, but that it is the shape of a pear which is everywhere very round except where the stalk is, for there it is very prominent, or that it is like a very round ball, and on one part of it is placed something like a woman's nipple, and that this part, where this protuberance is found, is the highest and nearest to the sky, and it is beneath the equinoctial line and in this Ocean sea at the end of the East. I call that "the end of the East," where end all the land and islands. . . .

Holy Scripture testifies that Our Lord made the earthly paradise and in it placed the tree of life, and from it issues a fountain from which flow four of the chief rivers of this world, the Ganges in India, the Tigris and Euphrates in . . . , which cut through a mountain range and form Mesopotamia and flow into Persia, and the Nile which rises in Ethiopia and enters the sea at Alexandria.

I do not find and I have never found any writing of the Romans or of the Greeks which gives definitely the position in the world of the earthly paradise, nor have I seen it in any world map, placed with authority based upon proof. Some placed it there where are the sources of the Nile in Ethiopia, but others traversed all these lands and found no similarity to it in the climate or in elevation towards the sky, to make it comprehensible that it was there, nor that the rising waters of the deluge had reached that place, &c [etc.]. Some Gentiles wished to show by arguments that it was in the Fortunate islands, which are the Canaries, &c. St. Isidore [of Seville] and Bede and [Walafridus] Strabo and the Master of Scholastic History [Petrus Comestor] and St. Ambrose and [Duns] Scotus and all the learned theologians agree that the earthly paradise is in the East, &c.

SOURCE *The Four Voyages of Columbus*, trans. and ed. Cecil Jane, 2 vols. (London: Hakluyt Society, 1929, 1932; reprinted New York: Dover Publications, 1988), vol. 2, pp. 28–36, passim. Reprinted by permission.

I have already said that which I hold concerning this hemisphere and its shape, and I believe that if I were to pass beneath the equinoctial line, then, arriving there at the highest point, I should find an even more temperate climate and difference in the stars and waters. Not that I believe that to the summit of the extreme point is navigable, or water, or that it is possible to ascend there, for I believe that the earthly paradise is there and to it, save by the will of God, no man can come. . . .

Columbus's Dream, 1503

In the month of January [1503], the mouth of the river [Río Belén in Panama] silted up. In April, the ships were all worm-eaten, and it was impossible to keep them above water. At this time, the river made a channel, by which with difficulty I brought out three empty. The boats went back into the river for salt and water. The sea became high and rough and did not allow them to come out. The Indians were many and gathered together and attacked them, and in the end they slew them. My brother and all the rest of the people were in a ship which remained inside. I was outside on so dangerous a coast, utterly alone, in a high fever and in a state of great exhaustion. Hope of escape was dead.

I toiled up to the highest point of the ship, calling in a trembling voice, with fast-falling tears, to the war captains of your highnesses, at every point of the compass, for succour, but never did they answer me. Exhausted, I fell asleep, groaning. I heard a very compassionate voice, saying: "O fool and slow to believe and to serve thy God, the God of all! What more did He for Moses or for His servant David? Since thou wast born, ever has He had thee in His most watchful care. When he saw thee of an age with which He was content, He caused thy name to sound marvellously in the land. The Indies, which are so rich a part of the world, He gave thee for thine own; thou hast divided them as it pleased thee, and He enabled thee to do this. Of the barriers of the Ocean sea, which were closed with such mighty chains, He gave thee the keys; and thou wast obeyed in many lands and among Christians thou hast gained an honourable fame. What did He more for the people of Israel when He brought them out of Egypt? Or for David, whom from a shepherd He made to be king in Judaea?

"Turn thyself to Him, and know now thine error; His mercy is infinite; thine old age shall not prevent thee from achieving all great things; He has many heritages very great. Abraham had passed a hundred years when he begat Isaac, and Sarah was no girl. Thou criest for help, doubting. Answer, who has afflicted thee so greatly and so often, God or the world? The re-

SOURCE Columbus's letter to the Sovereigns (1503) in *Select Documents Illustrating the Four Voyages of Columbus*, trans. and ed. Cecil Jane, 2 vols. (London: Hakluyt Society, 1930–1933), vol. 2, pp. 28–36, 85–86 passim. Reprinted with permission.

wards and promises which He gives, He does not bring to nothing, nor does He say after He has received service, that His intention was not such and that it is to be differently regarded, nor does He inflict suffering in order to display His power. Not one jot of His word fails; all that He promises, He performs with interest; is this the manner of men? I have said that which thy Creator has done for thee and does for all men. Now in part He shows thee the reward for the anguish and danger which thou hast endured in the service of others."

I heard all this as if I were in a trance, but I had no answers to give to words so true, but could only weep for my errors. He, whoever he was, who spoke to me, ended saying: "Fear not; have trust; all these tribulations are written upon marble and are not without cause."

I arose when I was able, and at the end of nine days came fine weather, but not such as allowed the ships to be brought out of the river.

QUESTIONS

1. Why did Christians fear Muslims?
2. Where was the "India" that Prester John was thought to rule?
3. Why did it not occur to credulous Europeans that if Prester John really wanted to contact them, he would have done so?
4. What was the point of giving so fabulous a description of Prester John's wealth?
5. Where did Columbus's "Enterprise of the Indies" fit into his cosmic musings about the future of the universe?
6. Which spiritual aspects of Columbus's ideas were common to the writings of the twelfth-century Joachim of Fiore and the sixteenth-century Franciscan missionaries?
7. What was the "earthly paradise," and why does Columbus expect to find it off the coast of South America (which he mistakenly identifies as "the end of the East")?
8. During his exhausted sleep, what did Columbus believe God said that bolstered his sagging confidence in his mission of exploration?

THE SHORT ROUTE TO ASIA

The Search for Japan

The Polos were an important merchant dynasty in Venice, where commerce was compatible with aristocratic status, unlike the rest of Europe. Marco's father Niccolò, and uncle Maffeo, left him home while they traveled to the court of the Mongol emperor of Cathay (China). After returning with a letter from the great Khan to the pope asking that holy men be sent to teach the Mongols about Christianity, they set out again during 1271 in the company of friars. Marco, who was fifteen at the time, would not be able to return for twenty-three years. Shortly after his homecoming, Marco was caught in the crossfire of a war between Venice and Genoa. While in a Genoese jail for three years, he met a literary man to whom he dictated from memory an accurate account of his astonishing travels, which are excerpted in the first selection.

> *"Cipangu is an island in the eastern ocean."*

The Mongol dominions, formed shortly before the Polos set out, stretched from the China Sea to the Crimea. This made it possible for merchants to travel long distances safely. Although Marco never visited Cipangu, it loomed large when he was at the imperial court, because Kublai, the emperor, made two attempts to conquer it. *Cipangu* or *Zipangu* were European adaptations of the Chinese *Jin-pen-kwé*, derived in turn from the islanders' *Nippon* ("land of the rising sun"). Possibly *Japan* is our variant of the Malay form, *Japún*.

By the time Columbus read the *Travels* in one of the first printed copies, the Mongol empire had long since disintegrated. This was not known to him or to anyone else in Europe. His trust in the book as a guide was rather like consulting the original Bell telephone directory to look up someone in Los Angeles.

Paolo Toscanelli was at the center of a group of Florentine humanist scholars deeply interested in geographic investigation. They commissioned maps, on which they speculated that far to the west of Ireland lay uncharted islands, which they denominated the Antilles, after a classical reference. Toscanelli accepted Marco Polo's estimate that the Asian mainland extended much farther east than previously thought, and that Japan lay another 1,500 miles out to sea. At that time, the circumference of the globe was believed to be 25,000 miles. By deciding that the globe's circumference was approximately 20,000 miles (a less accurate figure) Toscanelli concluded that only 2,500 miles of Atlantic sailing would take a ship from Spain to Japan.

Much is known about Toscanelli, but every aspect of his presumed correspondence with Columbus, reprinted in its entirety as the second selection, has been called into question. One view is that Columbus wrote to the old scholar, who was willing to help him but did not bother to draw up a fresh letter, and so sent along a copy of an earlier one he had prepared for Fernam Martins to transmit to the king of Portugal. Both Columbus and Toscanelli were knowledgeable about the spice trade, the former as an associate of Genoese groups, and the latter as a member of his family's firm. A second possibility is that Columbus found the detailed letter, and perhaps a sea chart, in the king's files, made a copy to further his ambitions in Castile, and concocted the rest of the correspondence to explain how he came into possession of the information. The third possibility is that all the material was forged by an unknown person for unclear reasons.

This is the sort of fascinating problem that may never be solved, but every biographer feels an urge to try it. If the letters are not fabrications, the material they incorporate from Marco Polo, their encouragement to sail west, and the chart showing islands in the Ocean Sea (possibly the one mentioned in his logbook, Document 15) help to explain Columbus's ability to sway influential persons whom he took into his confidence.

When news of the first voyage reached Italy, knowledgeable observers in Florence and Genoa decided Columbus had done little more than reach mid-Atlantic islands. Columbus had no doubt, however, that he was in eastern waters, a delusion that can be noted in the third selection, which is drawn from entries in his logbook.

Marco Polo

Cipangu [Japan] is an island in the eastern ocean . . . of considerable size; its inhabitants have fair complexions, are well made, and are civilized in their manners. Their religion is the worship of idols. They are independent of every foreign power, and governed only by their own kings. They have gold in the greatest abundance, its sources being inexhaustible, but as the king does not allow of its being exported, few merchants visit the country, nor is it frequented by much shipping from other parts. To this circumstance we are to attribute the extraordinary richness of the sovereign's palace, according to what we are told by those who have access to the place. The entire roof is covered with a plating of gold, in the same manner as we cover houses, or more properly churches, with lead. The ceilings of the halls are of the same precious metal; many of the apartments have small tables of pure gold, of considerable thickness; and the windows also have golden ornaments. So vast, indeed, are the riches of the palace, that it is impossible to convey an idea of them. In this island there

SOURCE *The Travels of Marco Polo the Venetian,* ed. Thomas Wright (London: Henry G. Bohn, 1854), pp. 350–353, passim.

are pearls also, in large quantities, of a red (pink) colour, round in shape, and of great size, equal in value to, or even exceeding that of the white pearls. . . .

The reader should, however, be informed that the idolatrous inhabitants of these islands, when they seize the person of an enemy, who has not the means of effecting his ransom for money, invite to their house all their relations and friends, and putting their prisoner to death, dress and eat the body, in a convivial manner, asserting that human flesh surpasses every other in the excellence of its flavour. . . .

It is to be understood that the sea in which the island of Cipangu is situated is called the Sea of Chin [China Sea], and so extensive is this eastern sea, that according to the report of experienced pilots and mariners who frequent it, and to whom the truth must be known, it contains no fewer than seven thousand four hundred and forty islands, mostly inhabited. It is said that of the trees which grow in them, there are none that do not yield a fragrant smell. They produce many spices and drugs, particularly lignum-aloes and pepper, in great abundance, both white and black. It is impossible to estimate the value of the gold and other articles found in the islands; but their distance from the continent is so great, and the navigation attended with so much trouble and inconvenience, that the vessels engaged in the trade, from the ports of Zaiton and Quinsay, do not reap large profits, being obliged to consume a whole year in their voyage, sailing in the winter and returning in the summer. For in these regions only two winds prevail; one of them during the winter, and the other during the summer season; so that they must avail themselves of the one for the outward, and of the other for the homeward-bound voyage. These countries are far remote from the continent of India. In terming this sea the Sea of Chin, we must understand it, nevertheless, to be a part of the ocean; for as we speak of the English Sea, or of the Aegean Sea, so do the eastern people of the Sea of Chin and of the Indian Sea; whilst all of them are comprehended under the general term of the ocean. We shall here cease to treat further of these countries and islands, as well on account of their lying so far out of the way, as of my not having visited them personally, and of their not being under the dominion of the Grand Khan. . . .

The Toscanelli Letters

To Christopher Columbus, [from] Paul, the physician, health:
    I notice the splendid and lofty desire thou hast to journey whither grow the spices, and as answer to thy letter I send thee a copy of another letter I wrote some time back to a friend and servant of the Most Serene King of Portugal, before the wars of Castile, in reply to another which

SOURCE Spanish version in Las Casas, *História de las Indias*, vol. I, book 1, ch. 12, pp. 92–93; trans. Henry Vignaud, in *Toscanelli and Columbus* (London: Sands & Co., 1902), pp. 305–321, passim.

by command of H.H. [His Highness], he wrote me on the said matter, and I send thee another such chart for navigating as is the one I sent him, by which thou shalt be satisfied of thy request; which copy is the one following.

To Fernam Martins, Canon of Lisbon, Paul the physician sends greetings.

I have had pleasure in learning of the favour and condescension which you enjoy from your most liberal and most magnificent King, and though I have other ofttimes spoken of the very short route which there is hence to the Indies where the spices grow—a shorter sea-route than that which you take for Guinea [Africa]—you tell me that His Highness now demands of me a statement and ocular demonstration in order that the said route be understood and taken; and though I, for my part, know that I can show it him in the form of a globe (such as the world is), I have resolved—it being a simpler task and of easier comprehension—to show the said route on a map such as those made for navigating, and thus I send it to H.M. [Alfonso V] made and drawn by my hand: whereon is given all the extremity of the west, starting from Ireland southwards to the end of Guinea, with all the islands that are on this route, opposite which [islands] due west is the beginning of the Indies with the islands and places whither you can deviate by the equinoctial line, and for what distance—that is to say, in how many leagues you can reach those places most rich in all manner of spice, and of jewels, and of precious stones; and be not amazed if I call west [the place] where the spice grows, for it is commonly said that it grows in the east, yet who so steers west will always find the said parts in the west, and who so goes east overland will find the same parts in the east. . . .

The straight lines which are lengthwise on the said map show the distance that there is from west to east; the others which are crosswise show the distance from north to south. I have also given on the said map many places in the extent of India, whither one might go should there befall some mischance of storm or of head winds or any other hap that betided unforeseen, and also in order that all these parts may be well known, whereof you should much delight.

Know likewise that in all those islands there live and traffic none but merchants, bearing in mind that there is there as great an assemblage of vessels, sailors, merchants, and merchandise as in all the rest of the world, and in particular at a most superb port named Zaiton, where 100 huge vessels of pepper load and unload yearly, besides the other numerous vessels carrying the other spices.

This land is very populous, and in it are many provinces and many kingdoms and cities out of number beneath the sway of a Prince called [the] Great Khan [Mongol ruler of China], which name, in our vernacular, means King of Kings; whose abode is for the most time in the province of Cathay [China]. His predecessors wished greatly to hold intercourse and converse

66

with Christians, and some two hundred years ago they sent to the Holy Father [praying] that he would send them many wise men and doctors who might teach them our faith, but those whom he sent returned on the road, because of obstacle[s]; and likewise to Pope Eugenius came an ambassador who related unto him the great friendship that they bear to Christians, and I have talked much with him of many things . . . .

And from the city of Lisbon, straight to the west, in the said map are 26 spaces, and in each one of them there are 250 miles as far as the most superb and mighty city of Quinsay, which has a circumference of 100 miles, which are 25 leagues, wherein are ten bridges of marble. The name of which city in our vernacular means City of Heaven; whereof are related marvels manifold concerning the dimensions of its manufactures and revenues (this space is almost the third part of the globe), which city is in the province of Mango, close to the city of Cathay, wherein the King mostly dwells, and from the island of Antilia—that which you call Seven Cities—whereof we have information, to the most superb city of Cipango [Japan], there are ten spaces, which are 2500 miles, that is to say 625 leagues, which island is exceeding rich in gold and pearls and precious stones.

Know that they cover the temples and royal dwellings with pure gold; thus the route being unknown, all these things are hidden, and one may go thither very safely. Many other things might be said, but as I have already spoken to you by word of mouth and you are of excellent thoughtfulness, I know that there is naught left for you to understand, and in so much I expatiate no more. And may this satisfy your demands so far as the shortness of time and my pursuits allow; and thus I remain most ready to satisfy and serve His Highness to such extent as he may command.

Done in the city of Florence on the 25 of June of the year 1474.

Columbus's Logbook, 1492

Sunday 21 October

. . . And afterwards I will leave for another very large island that I believe must be Cipango [Japan] according to the indications that these Indians that I have give me, and which they call Colba. In it they say there are many and very large ships and many traders. And from this island [I will go to] another which they call Bohío, which also they say is very big. And the others which are in between I will also see on the way; and, depending on whether I find a quantity of gold or spices, I will decide what I am to do. But I have already decided to go to the mainland and to the city of Quinsay [in Asia] and to give Your Highnesses' letters to the Grand Khan [Mongol ruler of China] and to ask for, and to come with, a reply.

SOURCE *The Diario of Christopher Columbus's First Voyage to America 1492–1493*, abstr. Fray Bartolomé de Las Casas, trans. Oliver Dunn and J. E. Kelley, Jr. (Norman: University of Oklahoma Press, 1989), pp. 109–129, passim. Footnotes removed. Reprinted by permission.

Wednesday 24 October

Tonight at midnight I weighed anchors from the island of Isabela [Fortunate/Crooked Islands], from the Cabo del Isleo, which is in the northern part, where I was staying, to go to the island of Cuba, which I heard from these people was very large and of great commerce and that there were there gold and spices and great ships and merchants; and they showed me that [sailing] to the west-southwest I would go to it. And I believe so, because I believe that it is so according to the signs that all the Indians of these islands and those that I have with me make (because I do not understand them through speech) [and] that it is the island of Cipango of which marvelous things are told. And in the spheres that I saw and in world maps it is in this region.

Friday 26 October

He went from the southern part of the said islands five or six leagues. It was all shoal. He anchored there. The Indians that he brought said that from the islands to Cuba was a journey of a day and a half in their dugouts, which are small vessels made of a single timber which do not carry sails. These are canoes. He left from there for Cuba, because from the signs that the Indians gave him of its size and of its gold and pearls he thought it must be it, that is, Cipango.

Sunday 28 October

While he was going toward land with the ships, two dugouts or canoes came out. And when they saw that the sailors were getting into the launch and were rowing to go look at the depth of the river in order to know where they should anchor, the canoes fled. The Indians said that in that island there were gold mines and pearls, and the Admiral saw a likely place for pearls and clams, which are a sign of them. And the Admiral understood that large ships from the Grand Khan came there and that from there to *tierra firme* [the mainland] was a journey of ten days. The Admiral named that river and harbor San Salvador.

Tuesday 30 October

He went out of the Rio de Mares to the northwest and, after he had gone 15 leagues, saw a cape full of palms and named it Cabo de Palmas. The Indians in the caravel *Pinta* said that behind that cape there was a river and that from the river to Cuba was a four-day journey. And the captain of the *Pinta* said that he understood that this Cuba was a city and that that land was a very big landmass that went far to the north, and that the king of that land was at war with the Grand Khan, whom they call *cami*, and his land or city, Faba, and many other names. The Admiral decided to go to that river and to send a present to the king of the land and to send him the letter of the sovereigns. And for this purpose he had a sailor who had gone on the same kind of mission in Guinea, and certain Indians from Guanahaní wished to go with him so that afterward they would be returned to their own land. In the opinion of the Admiral he was distant from the equinoctial line 42 degrees toward the northern side (if the text from which I took this is not corrupt). And he says that he must strive to go to the Grand Khan, whom he thought was somewhere around there, or to the city of Cathay [China], which belongs to the Grand Khan. For he says that it is very large, according to what he was told before he left Spain. All this land, he says, is low and beautiful, and the sea deep.

Thursday 1 November

. . . They all speak the same language and all are friends and I believe that all of these islanders are friends and that they wage war with the Grand Khan, whom they call *cavila* and the province, Basan. And they also go naked like the others. The Admiral [Columbus] says this. The river, he says, is very deep; and in the mouth, ships can be laid alongside the shore. Fresh water is short a league of reaching the mouth, and it is very fresh. And it is certain, the Admiral says, that this is *tierra firme* and that I am, he says, off Zayto [Zaiton, an Asian city] and Quinsay a hundred leagues more or less from the one and from the other; and well this is shown by the sea, which comes in a way other than the way it has until now. And yesterday when I was going to the northwest I found that it was cold.

12

Land Beyond Ireland

Pierre d'Ailly (Petrus Ailliacus), Cardinal of Cambrai, France, who wrote the *Imago Mundi (The Picture of the World)* in about 1414, intended his book to be a careful review of the academic geography known in his day. This is a very difficult selection to read because it refers to so many ancient authors, all tumbled together. He incorporated into his book an updated version of Ptolemy's *Geographia*, translated from the ancient Greek by the Arabs and thence into Latin. Ptolemy, writing about 130 A.D., had rejected the excellent estimate for the circumference of the globe made earlier, deciding instead upon a size about one-sixth too small. Further, he stretched China out far beyond its eastern limit.

> "the east and the west are near by, since a small sea separates them."

Reading the *Imago Mundi* encouraged Columbus to calculate the space from the Canary Islands to Japan at one-quarter the actual distance. Columbus's personal copy is heavily annotated, although scholars are uncertain if most of the notes date from before the first voyage, or after, when he was anxious to find information to bolster his belief that he had actually reached the Orient.

Columbus did not spend all his time in libraries looking for literary verification that the world was small and the distance to the Indies short. He spent time at wharves in Lisbon, and on the docks of Madeira and the Azores. The Portuguese sailors went far out into the sea to catch favorable winds for sailing to the coast of Africa, and to fish. They were familiar with the Sargasso Sea and its mid-Atlantic area of doldrums. Bold English fishermen were already working the vast schools near Newfoundland.

In the sixteenth century, when the Spanish crown was engaged in a lengthy lawsuit contesting the inheritance of the Admiral's family, a story useful to the crown's advocates surfaced about an unknown pilot who was blown off course, discovered the New World, and told Columbus about it just before he died. Ferdinand Columbus was anxious to discredit this story. In the biography he wrote, excerpted for the second selection, he presented his father's memories of hearing sailors' personal accounts and some secondhand stories told in taverns.

Imago Mundi

The investigation into the quantity of the habitable earth demands that we should consider "habitability" from two angles. One has respect to the heaven; that is, how much of it can be inhabited on account of the Sun, and how much cannot. On this sufficient was said previously in a general way. From another angle it must be considered with respect to the water, i.e., how far the water is in the way. To this we now turn, and on it there are various opinions among the wise men. Ptolemy in his book *The Arrangement of the Sphere (Dispositione Spere)* would have almost a sixth part of the earth habitable because of the water. So also his *Algamestus*, in Book II, says that there is no known habitation except on one fourth of the earth, i.e., where we live; and that it extends lengthwise from east to west, the equator being in the middle. Its breadth is from the equator to the pole; and it is a fourth of the colurus [sphere]. Aristotle, however, in the close of his book on *The Heaven and the Earth* would have it that more than a fourth is inhabited. Averroes confirms this. Aristotle says that a small sea lies between the confines of Spain on the western side and the beginnings of India on the eastern side. He is not speaking of Hither Spain *(certeriori)* which in these times is commonly known as Spain, but of Farther Spain *(ulteriori)* which is now called Africa. On this topic certain authors have spoken, such as Pliny, Orosius, and Isidore. Moreover Seneca in the fifth book of the *Naturalium* holds that the sea is navigable in a few days if the wind is favorable. Pliny in the *Naturalibus* Book II informs us

SOURCE Petrus Ailliacus, *Imago Mundi*, trans. E. F. Keever (Wilmington, N.C., 1948).

that it has been navigated from the Arabian Sea to the Pillars of Hercules in rather a short time. From these and many other reckonings, on which I shall expand when I speak of the ocean, some apparently conclude that the sea is not so great that it can cover three quarters of the earth. Add to this the judgment of Esdras in his IV Book [Bible] where he says that six parts of the earth are inhabited and the seventh is covered with water. The authority of this book the Saints have held in reverence and by it have established sacred truths. . . .

There ought to be an abundance of water toward the poles of the earth because those regions are cold on account of their distance from the sun; and the cold accumulates moisture. Therefore the water runs down from one pole toward the other into the body of the sea and spreads out between the confines of Spain and the beginning of India, of no great width, in such a way that the beginning of India can be beyond the middle of the equinoctial circle and approach beneath the earth quite close to the coast of Spain. Likewise Aristotle and his commentator in the *Libro Coeli et Mundi* came to the same conclusion because there are so many elephants in those regions. Says Pliny: "Around Mt. Atlas elephants abound." So also in India and even in ulterior Spain there are great herds of elephants. But, reasons Aristotle, the elephants in both those places ought to show similar characteristics; if widely separated they would not have the same characteristics. Therefore he concludes those countries are close neighbors and that a small sea intervenes; and moreover that the sea covers three-quarters of the earth; that the beginnings of the east and the west are near by, since a small sea separates them.

Old Sailors' Tales

The Admiral [Columbus] . . . was impressed by the many fables and stories which he heard from various persons and sailors who traded to the western islands and seas of the Azores and Madeira. Since these stories served his design, he was careful to file them away in his memory. I shall tell them here in order to satisfy those who take delight in such curiosities.

A pilot of the Portuguese King, Martín Vicente by name, told him that on one occasion, finding himself four hundred and fifty leagues west of Cape St. Vincent, he fished out of the sea a piece of wood ingeniously carved, but not with iron. For this reason and because for many days the winds had blown from the west, he concluded this wood came from some islands to the west.

SOURCE From *The Life of the Admiral Christopher Columbus by His Son Ferdinand.* trans. and annotated by Benjamin Keen, 1959, pp. 24–27, passim. Reprinted by permission of the translator.

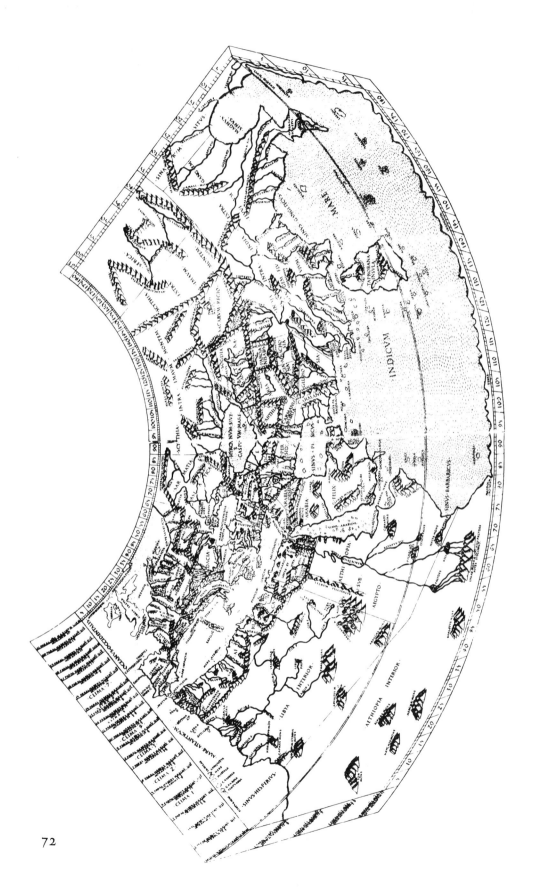

Pedro Correa, who was married to a sister of the Admiral's wife, told him that on the island of Pôrto Santo he had seen another piece of wood brought by the same wind, carved as well as the aforementioned one, and that canes had also drifted in, so thick that one joint held nine decanters of wine. He said that in conversation with the Portuguese King he had told him the same thing and had shown him the canes. Since such canes do not grow anywhere in our lands, he was sure that the wind had blown them from some neighboring islands or perhaps from India. Ptolemy [ancient Greek writer] in the first book of his *Geography,* Chapter 17, writes that such canes are found in the eastern parts of the Indies. Some persons in the Azores also told him that after the wind had blown for a long time from the west, the sea cast on the shores of those islands (especially of Graciosa and Fayal) pine trees that do not grow on those islands or anywhere in that region. On the island of Flores, which is one of the Azores, the sea flung ashore two dead bodies with broad faces and different in appearance from the Christians.

The Admiral also tells that in 1484 an inhabitant of the island of Madeira came to Portugal to ask the King for a caravel in order to discover some land which he swore he saw every year and always in the same situation; his story agreed with that of others who claimed to have seen it from an island of the Azores. On the basis of such stories, the charts and maps of ancient days showed certain islands in that region. . . .

One Diogo de Teive also went in search of that island. His pilot, Pedro de Velasco by name, a native of Palos de Moguer, told the Admiral in Santa María de la Rábida that they had departed from Fayal and sailed more than one hundred and fifty leagues to the southwest. On their return they discovered the island of Flores, to which they were guided by the many birds they saw flying in that direction; as they knew them to be land and not marine birds, they decided they must be flying to some resting place. Then they steered northeast until they reached Cape Clear at the western end of Ireland. Although they encountered very high westerly winds in this region, the sea remained calm. They decided this must be due to the fact that the sea was sheltered by some land on the west; but since it was already August and they feared the onset of winter, they gave up the search for that island. This happened forty years before the discovery of our Indies.

PTOLEMY, MAP OF KNOWN WORLD (1478) *Columbus owned and carefully studied this map (left) originally created by a Greek scholar who lived in the second century* A.D. *It uses an innovative grid pattern to locate the inhabited area known to the ancient world. Even today the Earth is measured, as on this map, in 360° of longitude. This second printed version of the map did not take into account Portuguese voyages that proved the Indian Sea was not landlocked. East India is small, whereas the island of "Taprobana" (probably Sri Lanka) is very large. Indochina is roughly sketched, with China extending eastward beyond a "Great Gulf." Columbus was encouraged by this distortion to believe that Asia occupied vastly more of the globe than, in fact, it does.*

This story was confirmed to the Admiral by a one-eyed sailor in the port of Santa María, who told him that on a voyage he had made to Ireland he saw that land, which at the time he supposed to be a part of Tartary; that it turned westward (it must have been what is now called the Land of Cod); and that foul weather prevented them from approaching it. The Admiral says that this account agrees with one given him by Pedro de Velasco, a Galician, who told him in the city of Murcia in Castile that on a voyage to Ireland they sailed so far northwest that they saw land to the west of Ireland; this land, the Admiral thought, was the same that a certain Fernão Dulmo tried to discover. I relate this just as I found it told in my father's writings, that it may be known how from small matters some draw substance for great deeds.

QUESTIONS

1. What would make the island of Cipangu (Japan) worth visiting?
2. In what ways does the account of the kingdom of Cipangu fit the description offered by Prester John (Document 9) of his dominions?
3. What similarities are there between the account of customs in Cipangu and the description of "Lamory" by Sir John Mandeville (Document 6)?
4. How would Toscanelli's correspondence have enlightened Columbus?
5. How much knowledge of Marco Polo's book does Toscanelli demonstrate?
6. How did reading *Imago Mundi* encourage Columbus that by sailing west, he would reach Asia?
7. According to the ancient experts cited in the cardinal's book, what percentage of the earth might Columbus expect to be covered with water?
8. Analyze the common points in stories Columbus heard from sailors he met while in Portugal and its possessions.

THE FIRST CROSSING

13

The Capitulations of Santa Fe

Once the Catholic sovereigns agreed to back Columbus's project, they issued authorizations in April 1492 to procure vessels. Crews were recruited from the ports at the Odiel-Rio Tinto estuary to staff two caravels and a small square-rigged merchant ship. Before Columbus was able to take advantage of this commitment, he had to come to an agreement with the rulers concerning a statement of his purposes and the reward he would be given, if he were successful. Iberian kings had drawn up many such agreements with navigators, and would sign many more after this one.

> *"it is right and reasonable that you should be rewarded."*

The *Contract*, dated April 17, set the terms of what Columbus was expected to accomplish and what would be his financial reward. His offices and hereditary titles, which are repeated in the *Title*, are remarkably extensive for a foreigner who had little more to offer (as can be seen in the veiled wording) than a vague proposal to find something, somewhere.

In the society of the day, the grant by the crown of an honorific *Don* preceding a man's name denoted admission to the nobility, which carried many privileges. During his lifetime Columbus was deprived of his titles of viceroy and governor, due to inept rule. When later monarchs came to believe that too much had been promised in the way of financial reward by Ferdinand and Isabella, royal lawyers spent decades struggling with heirs to reduce the scope of the favors.

These documents refer to him as Cristóbal Colón or Cristoval Colon, which are the Spanish versions of the Italian, Cristoforo Colombo. North Americans refer to Columbus by the Latinized form. He never signed his name in any of these styles, preferring instead a pyramid-shaped assortment of letters that has not been deciphered to every expert's satisfaction.

The Contract

Don Fernando [Ferdinand] and Doña Ysabel [Isabella] by the Grace of God King and Queen of Castille, León, Aragón, etc.,

Whereas you, Cristóbal Colón, are setting out by Our command with certain of Our ships and people to discover and acquire certain

SOURCE *Christopher Columbus His Own Book of Privileges*, ed. B. F. Stevens (London, 1893), pp. 42–45.

islands and mainland in the Ocean Sea; and whereas it is hoped, with the help of God, that some of the said islands and mainland in the said Ocean Sea will be found and acquired through your effort and diligence; and whereas you are thus exposing yourself to danger in Our service; it is right and reasonable that you should be rewarded. Desiring to honor you and do you favor for the reasons aforesaid, We declare Our will and pleasure that when you have discovered and acquired the said islands and mainland in the said Ocean Sea, or any of them, you Cristóbal Colón shall be Our Admiral of the said islands and mainland so discovered by you, and shall be Our Viceroy and Governor therein, and shall be entitled to style yourself Don Cristóbal Colón. Your sons and successors in the said office and duty shall likewise be entitled to call themselves Don and Admiral, Viceroy and Governor thereof. You may exercise and enjoy the rights of Admiralty together with the office of Viceroy and Governor of the said islands and mainland that you shall discover and acquire, in person or by deputy. You may hear and determine all causes, civil or criminal, belonging to the jurisdiction of Admiralty and of Viceroy and Governor, according to the law and as the Admirals of Our Kingdoms are accustomed to do. You shall have power to punish offenders. You may exercise the said offices of Admiral, Viceroy, and Governor, in person or through your deputies, in all matters pertaining to the said offices or any one of them. You are to receive the fees and stipends belonging to and arising from the said offices, in like manner as Our High Admiral in the Admiralty of Our Kingdoms uses to levy them. . . . [T]hat after your discovery and acquisition of the said islands and mainland in the said Sea, the administration of the oath and the performance, by you or your deputy, of the ceremonies required on such occasions, they [our officials] shall hold and acknowledge you throughout your life, and your son and successor, and successor after successor forever, as Our Admiral of the said Ocean Sea and as Viceroy and Governor of the islands and mainland that you, the said Don Cristóbal Colón, shall discover and acquire. They shall accord you, and your deputies in the said offices of Admiral, Viceroy, and Governor, all the honors, graces, favors, pre-eminences, exemptions, immunities, and other things belonging thereto. They shall pay you, or cause to be paid, all fees and emoluments accruing to or arising from the said offices. . . .

Given in Our city of Granada, the 30th day of April, 1492.

I the King.   I the Queen.

I, Johan de Coloma, Secretary to the King and Queen our Sovereigns, caused this to be written by Their command.

The Title

T he following are the favors which, on the petition of Don Cristóbal Colón, Your Highnesses grant him as reward for his discoveries in the Ocean Seas and for the voyage that with God's help he is now about to make in Your Highnesses' service.

First, Your Highnesses, as Sovereigns of the said Ocean Seas, appoint the said Cristóbal Colón, now and henceforth, their Admiral in all islands and mainlands that shall be discovered by his effort and diligence in the said Ocean Seas, for the duration of his life, and after his death, his heirs and successors in perpetuity, with all the rights and privileges belonging to that office, in like manner that Don Alonso Enriques, Your High Admiral of Castille, and his predecessors in that office, held it in their jurisdictions.

It so pleases Their Highnesses,
    Johan de Coloma

Your Highnesses also appoint the said Don Cristóbal their Viceroy and Governor-General in all islands and mainlands that, as has been stated, he may discover and acquire in the said Seas. For the government of each of them, he may nominate three candidates for each office, and Your Highnesses shall select the man best qualified for their service, so that the lands that Our Lord permits him to discover and acquire in Your Highnesses' service may be the better governed.

Your Highnesses grant to the said Don Cristóbal Colón one tenth of all merchandise, whether pearls, gems, gold, silver, spices, or goods of any kind, that may be acquired by purchase, barter, or any other means, within the boundaries of the said Admiralty jurisdiction. After all expenses have been deducted, of what remains he may take and keep the tenth part and dispose of it as he pleases, the other nine parts to accrue to Your Highnesses.

In any suit over goods that he may import from the said islands and lands to be discovered, or goods obtained in exchange for merchandise exported by other merchants from here, which may arise in the place where the said transaction took place, it is Your Highnesses' will that the Admiral or his representative, and no other magistrate, shall sit in judgment over the said suit, if the jurisdiction pertains to him by virtue of the superiority of the Admiral's office; and so it is hereby provided.

It so pleases Their Highnesses, since it pertains to the said office of Admiral which the said Admiral Don Alonso Enriques and his predecessors held in their jurisdictions, and if it be just.

In all vessels fitted out for the said trade at any time, the said Don

SOURCE *Raccolta di Documenti e Studi* . . . (Rome, 1892–1894), trans. J. H. Parry and R. G. Keith, 5 vols., *New Iberian World* (New York: Times Books, 1984), vol. I, pp. 18–19. Reprinted by permission.

Cristóbal Colón may, if he wishes, invest one eighth of the total cost of the fitting-out, and may keep for himself one eighth of the profit of such venture.

Executed and dispatched, with Your Highnesses' replies at the end of each clause. In the town of Santa Fe de la Vega de Granada, 17th day of April 1492.

I the King.   I the Queen.

14

The Navigator

The first selection presents Columbus as he wanted himself to be seen at court. The accuracy of this account by a friend and admirer, Father Las Casas, is open to some question. Columbus liked to pose as an expert in celestial navigation, which was an impressive mystery to the uninitiated, but his way of assessing wave and wind were not much different from the methods employed by the ancient Greeks. He was, to give him full credit, a master of the difficult art of getting from one place to another across the trackless waters. S. E. Morison, in the second selection, assesses exactly how much Columbus did know about more advanced navigational techniques. Morison was an expert on this subject, since he was a member of the United States Navy and himself sailed all of Columbus's routes.

"I began sailing at an early age and haven't stopped yet."

Las Casas

As a child, his [Columbus's] parents made him learn to read and write, and he learned such calligraphy—I saw his writing many times—that he could have made a living by it. He also studied arithmetic and drawing with the same skill and degree of excellence. He studied Latin in Pavia—the *Historia portuguesa* praises him as a good Latinist—which must have given him an unusual insight into human and divine affairs. Since God had endowed him with good judgment, a sound memory and eagerness to learn, he sought the company of learned men and applied himself to his studies with great intensity, acquiring proficiency in

SOURCE Bartolomé de Las Casas, *História de Las Indias*, trans. and ed. Andrée Collard (Harper Torchbook, 1971), pp. 16–17, passim. Reprinted by permission.

geometry, geography, cosmography, astrology or astronomy, and seamanship. This is clear from his writings about the Indies and from some letters I saw that he wrote to King Ferdinand and Queen Isabella. Surely, as a God-fearing man and considering the fact that he was writing to a King, he must have avoided exaggeration. I transcribe a few passages from these letters because I think they are documents of value.

> Your Highnesses: I began sailing at an early age and haven't stopped yet. The art of navigation inspires the navigator to want to know the secrets of this world. I have practiced this art for over forty years, sailing all waters known today. I have known many scholars, churchmen and laymen alike, Latins and Greeks, Jews and Moors, and many others of many other sects; I found God amenable to my eagerness since He gave me inspiration and intelligence. He made me proficient in navigation, gave me some knowledge of astrology, geometry and arithmetic, and endowed me with the ability to draw the sphere, accurately placing cities, rivers, mountains, islands and harbors. By this time I have studied all the latest writings about cosmography, history, chronicles, philosophy and other arts, so that Our Lord broadened my understanding and gave me the certitude that it was possible to go to the Indies from here; He fired me with the will to do so and it is with this fire that I address myself to Your Highnesses. Everyone laughed at my enterprise and dismissed it as a joke. My knowledge and my quoting of authorities have proved of no help. And now I trust only in Your Highnesses. . . .

These are the words of Christopher Columbus, written in 1501 from Cádiz or Seville, and he had drawn a map of the sphere on the letter. He wrote another letter to the same monarchs in January 1495, from Hispaniola, in which he talks about the craftiness of navigators who act one way instead of another in order to deceive their people, thus endangering the ships sometimes, and he says:

> Once, King Reynel—may God rest his soul—sent me to Tunis [in North Africa] to seize the galley *Fernandina*. We had come to the island of St. Peter in Sardinia, and a watchman told me that with the galleass or galley there were two more vessels and one galleon, which so upset the people on board they refused to continue the voyage, saying they wanted to go back to Marseilles and get another ship and more people. Seeing that I could not prevail upon their fear, I agreed and, changing the compass point, I set sail at sunset, so that at sunrise the next morning we were clear within the Cartagena Bay, and they thought for sure we had been sailing toward Marseilles [in the south of France].

He annotated books, and one of his annotations verifies by experience how the five zones are inhabited. It says:

> In February 1477, I sailed 100 leagues past the island of Tile, whose southern part is 73° away from the equinox, not 63° as some maintain, and it isn't within the line that includes the West, as Ptolemy says, but rather much further West. That island is as large as England. The English go there to trade, especially from Bristol. When I was there, the sea was not frozen but the tides were tremendous. In some parts high tide rose 25 fathoms deep twice a day, and receded likewise.

And it is true that Ptolemy's Tile—modern cosmographers call it Frislanda [Iceland]—is where he says it is. He goes on verifying that the Equator is habitable. "I was below the Equator in Portuguese territory, therefore I know they are wrong when they say the zone is not habitable." . . . Elsewhere he states that he sailed many times from Lisbon to Guinea [Africa] and noted very carefully how its degree corresponds to 56 and two-thirds miles; that he was in the island of Enxion in the Aegean Sea and saw mastic being sapped from certain trees; that he sailed East and West almost without interruption for twenty-five years and saw it all; that "I brought two ships to Puerto Santo and left one there for a day because it was taking water, but I arrived in Lisbon a whole week before that ship because I had stormy southwest winds and she had only the sparse contrary winds from north northwest."

All this proves not only that Christopher Columbus was a skilled seaman and experienced navigator but also that he studied carefully all things pertaining to the sea and knew the basic theories and principles of navigation without which pilots make dreadful mistakes, as can be seen in these Indies, where accuracy is a matter of chance. I think Christopher Columbus was the most outstanding sailor in the world, versed like no other in the art of navigation, for which divine Providence chose him to accomplish the most outstanding feat ever accomplished in the world until now. . . .

A Modern Assessment

The Admiral [Columbus] liked to pose as an expert in celestial navigation, which (he well said) was a mystery to the uninitiated, like prophetic vision. In forty years at sea, off and on (so he wrote in 1501), he had acquired sufficient "astrology" (that is, astronomy), geometry and arithmetic, as well as practical knowledge, for the purposes of maritime discovery. In a postil [marginal note] of uncertain date he talks of "taking the sun" on his Guinea voyage. Yet the testimony of his own journals proves that the simple method of finding latitude from a meridional observation of the sun, long used by Arabs in "camel navigation" of the desert, was unknown to Columbus. Polaris observations for latitude he made not infrequently on his last two voyages, but these observations, though "not too bad," were of no use to his navigation, because he never knew the proper corrections to apply. It has been stated that the invention of the astrolabe enabled Columbus to discover America; but his Journal proves that he was unable to use the astrolabe on his First Voyage, and there is no evidence of his taking such an instrument on any other. The picture books also show Columbus taking solar or stellar altitudes with a cross staff. That simple

SOURCE S. E. Morison, *Admiral of the Ocean Sea: A Life of Christopher Columbus* (Boston: Little, Brown & Co., 1942), one-vol. ed., pp. 183–196, passim; reprinted by permission.

instrument would have been more useful to him than a quadrant for shooting Polaris in low latitudes; but he never had one, and probably never saw one.

The common quadrant (not to be confused with Hadley's quadrant or any other reflecting instrument) was the only instrument of celestial navigation that Columbus ever employed. This was a simple quarter-circle of hardwood, with sights along one edge through which the heavenly body could be lined up, a plummet attached to the apex by a silk cord, and a scale of 90° on the arc, from which the altitude could be read as cut by the cord at the moment when sun or star was lined up through the sights. On a rolling and pitching ship it was very difficult to keep the plane of the quadrant perpendicular and at the same time catch your star through the pin holes. When you did, you hallooed to the other fellow to mark the degree on the arc cut by the cord; but the cord just then might be doing a big swing. Columbus never managed to do any accurate work with his quadrant until he had a whole year ashore at Jamaica. . . .

So many indoor geographers and armchair admirals have adduced Columbus's ignorance of celestial navigation as evidence that he was no seaman that I must rub in two points.

1. Celestial navigation formed no part of the professional pilot's or master's training in Columbus's day, or for long after his death. It was practiced only by men of learning such as mathematicians, astrologers and physicians, or by gentlemen of education like Antonio Pigafetta who accompanied Magellan, or D. João de Castro, who on India voyages in the 1530's and '40's had everyone down to the ship's caulker taking meridional altitudes of the sun. Mathematics was so little taught in common schools of that era, and the existing ephemerides (compiled largely for astrologers) were so complicated, that even the best professional seamen could do nothing with them. So simple an operation as applying declination to altitude and subtracting the result from 90° was quite beyond their powers. The great Portuguese-Jewish mathematician Pero Nunes (Nonnius), who discovered the vernier, wrote some forty-five years after Columbus's discovery, "Why do we put up with these pilots, with their bad language and barbarous manners; they know neither sun, moon nor stars, nor their courses, movements or declinations; or how they rise, how they set and to what part of the horizon they are inclined; neither latitude nor longitude of the places on the globe, nor astrolabes, quadrants, cross staffs or watches, nor years common or bissextile, equinoxes or solstices?"

2. Celestial observations were not used in Columbus's day, even by the Portuguese, to find one's way about the ocean; but to determine latitudes of newly discovered coasts and islands in order to chart them correctly. Vasco da Gama on his great voyage of 1497–1499 to India was far better equipped than Columbus for celestial navigation, but he always disembarked and hung his astrolabe on a tree or a tripod to take the altitude of the sun, as the poet Camoëns describes him doing.

So, in order to determine his daily positions at sea, and trace his course across the unknown stretches of the Western Ocean, Columbus was dependent on *dead-reckoning* (D.R.), which means simply laying down your compass courses and estimated distances on a chart. That is not so easy as it sounds. . . .

Like all good practical navigators Columbus made frequent use of the sounding lead when approaching the coast, or when he thought he was near land. The standard length of lead line for small vessels in those days, and for centuries after, was 40 fathoms; but each of Columbus's fleet carried a dipsey (deep sea) lead line of 100 fathoms, and on one occasion he bent two together to make a 200-fathom sounding. We may smile at his trying to sound in mid-ocean, where the modern chart reports a depth of some 2400 fathoms; but the leadsman reporting "No bottom, sir," after repeated casts through heavy mats of gulfweed was far more reassuring as to the safety of the Sargasso Sea than any amount of speculation. Sounding in a breeze is troublesome, as a vessel has to back some of her sails in order to check her way and give the lead a chance to reach bottom. For that reason this elementary precaution when approaching a coast is often forgotten, and more vessels go ashore through neglect to heave the lead than from any other cause. Columbus was very punctilious about sounding until he found by experience that the outer Bahamas were so steep and the water so clear that you could find no bottom until it was visible. Then he too grew careless, and so lost his flagship on Christmas eve.

Columbus's only aids to navigation, then, were the mariner's compass and dividers, quadrant and lead line, sea chart and ruler, traverse table and ordinary multiplication table, and one of the recent Ephemerides of Johannes Müller (Regiomontanus) designed more for astrologers than for navigators. There is no evidence that he added to this equipment on any later voyage; indeed the astrolabe that he had on the First Voyage and was unable to use seems to have been left behind. Two mariners who were with him on the Third Voyage later testified that he carried "charts, quadrants, tables, sphere, and other things." So, to all intents and purposes, he was a dead-reckoning navigator pure and simple.

This is not to say that Columbus was a poor navigator; far from it. Dead-reckoning was about 99 per cent of the navigator's art in 1492, and in high latitudes there are long periods of overcast or stormy weather when celestial observations are impossible. Dead-reckoning is still the foundation of navigation. . . .

It must be remembered, however, that the modern navigator checks his D.R. daily (if weather permits) by latitude or longitude sights or both, which Columbus never learned to do. And, as an error of half a point in your course will mean an error of about 250 miles in landfall on an ocean crossing, it is evident that Columbus's D.R. was extraordinarily careful and accurate. Possibly he was not much more skillful than his better contemporaries, although the bad guesses of the pilots on the First Voyage home, and their surprise at Columbus's excellent landfall in 1496, would seem to show the contrary. Andrés Bernáldez [Document 1], who had his information directly from the Admiral after that event, wrote, "No one considers himself a good pilot and master who, although he has to pass from one land to another very distant without sighting any other land, makes an error of 10 leagues, even in a crossing of 1000 leagues, unless the force of the tempest forces him and deprives him of the use of his skill." No such dead-reckoning navigators exist today; no man alive, limited to the instruments and means at Columbus's disposal, could obtain anything near the accuracy of his results.

Judged therefore not simply by what he did, but by how he did it, Columbus was a great navigator. He took his fleet to sea not as an amateur possessed of one big idea, but as a captain experienced in *el arte de marear*. He was well, though not superlatively well, equipped with such navigational aids and instruments as the age had produced. Modestly conscious of his own imperfections, he wrote to the Sovereigns before his last voyage predicting that "with the perfecting of instruments and the equipment of vessels, those who are to traffic and trade with the discovered islands will have better knowledge" than was vouchsafed to him. Over and above his amazing competence as a dead-reckoning navigator, he had what a great French seaman, Jean Charcot, recognized and named *le sens marin*, that intangible and unteachable God-given gift of knowing how to direct and plot "the way of a ship in the midst of the sea."

QUESTIONS

1. What royal benefits were Columbus and his descendants to be given if he were successful?
2. List the sources of revenue Columbus might expect should he discover and acquire islands and mainlands in the Ocean Sea.
3. How successful was Columbus's self-education program?
4. In what way was—or was not—Columbus a skillful, up-to-date navigator?
5. What were the principal navigational aids available to professional pilots or masters during Columbus's lifetime?

Selections from Columbus's Logbook

Columbus had the inspiration to keep his journal and record for the sovereigns the contacts he anticipated making. Many other captains of the age did not do the same, to our great loss. Because of its intended use, the journal focuses on what might be pleasing to the monarchs, its intended audience, and therefore is not entirely objective. An additional problem of interpretation is that the original remains lost, so one must rely upon a transcript made of it by Las Casas. At times Las Casas quotes directly, while at other points he summarizes, which accounts for the jumps from "I" to "he" or "the Admiral." Possibly the transcriber also dropped material that did not suit his interests.

> "at two hours after midnight the land appeared, . . ."

The thirty-three-day voyage from the Canary Islands to the first landfall was, as can be read, relatively uneventful. From his experience in the Portuguese service, Columbus anticipated encountering a belt of calm. He did have some further trouble with his crew in late September, when he failed to find the islands they expected at any moment. Unlike the disciplined crews of the *Niña* and the *Pinta* headed by the two Pinzón brothers, who had sailed together before, the *Santa María*'s sailors signed on at the dock and thus lacked cohesion. The crew did some grumbling toward the end of the trip, but despite legend they never undertook a mutiny against their foreign captain.

W hereas, Most Christian and Very Noble and Very Excellent and Very Powerful Princes, King and Queen of the Spains and of the Islands of the Sea, our Lords: This present year of 1492, after Your Highnesses had brought to an end the war with the Moors [Muslims] who ruled in Europe and had concluded the war in the very great city of Granada, where this present year on the second day of the month of January I saw the Royal Standards of Your Highnesses placed by force of arms on the towers of the Alhambra, which is the fortress of the said city; and I saw the Moorish King come out to the gates of the city and kiss the Royal Hands of Your Highnesses and of the Prince my Lord; and later in that same month, because of

SOURCE *The Diario of Christopher Columbus's First Voyage to America 1492–1493*, abstr. Fray Bartolomé de Las Casas; trans. Oliver Dunn and J. E. Kelley, Jr. (Norman: University of Oklahoma Press, 1989), pp. 19–65, passim. Footnotes removed. Reprinted by permission.

the report that I had given to Your Highnesses about the lands of India and about a prince [ruler of China] who is called "Grand Khan," which means in our Spanish language "King of Kings"; how, many times, he and his predecessors had sent to Rome to ask for men learned in our Holy Faith in order that they might instruct him in it and how the Holy Father had never provided them; and thus so many peoples were lost, falling into idolatry and accepting false and harmful religions; and Your Highnesses, as Catholic Christians and Princes, lovers and promoters of the Holy Christian Faith, and enemies of the false doctrine of Mahomet [Mohammed] and of all idolatries and heresies, you thought of sending me, Christóbal Colón [Spanish version], to the said regions of India to see the said princes and the peoples and the lands, and the characteristics of the lands and of everything, and to see how their conversion to our Holy Faith might be undertaken. And you commanded that I should not go to the East by land, by which way it is customary to go, but by the route to the West, by which route we do not know for certain that anyone previously has passed. So, after having expelled all the Jews from all of your Kingdoms and Dominions, in the same month of January Your Highnesses commanded me to go, with a suitable fleet, to the said regions of India. . . .

Friday 3 August

We departed Friday the third day of August of the year 1492 from the bar of Saltés [River] at the eighth hour. We went south with a strong sea breeze 60 miles, which is 15 leagues, until sunset; afterward to the southwest and south by west, which was the route for the Canaries.

Thursday 6 September

He departed that day in the morning from the harbor of Gomera [in the Canary Islands] and he took the course for his voyage. And the Admiral [Columbus] learned from a caravel that was coming from the island of Hierro that three Portuguese caravels were sailing in that vicinity in order to capture him. It must have been from envy that the king [John II] felt because of the Admiral's having gone away to Castile. And he proceeded all that day and night in very light winds and in the morning he found himself between Gomera and Tenerife.

Sunday 16 September

He sailed that day and night on his route west. They made about 39 leagues but he reported only 36. That day he had some storm clouds and it drizzled. Here the Admiral says that today and from then on they found such extremely temperate breezes that the savor of the mornings was a great delight, for nothing was lacking except to hear nightingales, he says; and the

87

weather was like that in April in Andalusia [the south of Spain]. Here they began to see many bunches of very green vegetation which a short time before (so it appeared) had torn loose from land, because of which everyone judged that they were near some island but not near a large landmass, according to the Admiral, who says: Because I think the mainland is farther ahead.

Saturday 22 September

He steered west-northwest more or less, inclining to one side and the other; they made about 30 leagues. They saw scarcely any weed. They saw a few petrels and other birds. The Admiral says here: this contrary wind was very necessary for me, because my people were very worked up thinking that in these seas winds for returning to Spain did not blow. For a portion of the day there was no weed; later it was very thick.

Sunday 23 September

He steered northwest and at times northwest by north and at times on his route, which was west, and they made no more than 27 leagues. They saw a dove and a booby and another small river bird and other white birds. The weed was plentiful and they found crabs in it. Since the sea had been calm and smooth the men complained, saying that since in that region there were no rough seas, it would never blow for a return to Spain. But later the sea rose high and without wind, which astonished them, because of which the Admiral says here that the high sea was very necessary for me, [a sign] which had not appeared except in the time of the Jews when they left Egypt [and complained] against Moses, who took them out of captivity.

Tuesday 25 September

This day there was much calm and later it blew and they went on their way west until night. The Admiral began talking to Martín Alonso Pinzón, captain of the other caravel, *Pinta*, about a chart that he had sent to him on the caravel three days before, on which the Admiral had apparently drawn certain islands in that sea; and Martín Alonso said that they were in that region and the Admiral answered that so it seemed to him, but since they had not encountered them it must have been caused by the currents which always had driven the vessels northeast and that they had not traveled as far as the pilots said. And at this point the Admiral said to send the said chart to him. And it having been sent over by means of some cord, the Admiral began to plot their position on it with his pilot and sailors. At sunset Martín Alonso went up on the poop of his vessel and with much joy called to the Admiral asking him for a reward: that he saw land. And when he heard this said and affirmed, the Admiral says that he threw himself on his knees to give thanks to Our Lord, and Martín Alonso and his men said *Gloria in excelsis deo*. The Admiral's men and those of the *Niña* did the same. They all climbed the masts and into the rigging and all affirmed that it was land, and so it appeared to the Admiral, and that it was about 25 leagues off. Until night everybody continued to affirm it to be land. The Admiral ordered the ships to leave their course, which was west, and for all of them to go southwest where the land had appeared. They had gone that day about four leagues and a half and during the night 17 leagues southeast, which makes 21, although he told the men 13 leagues, because he always pretended to the men that they were making little way so the voyage would not appear long to them. So he wrote that voyage in two ways: the shorter was the pretended; and the longer, the true. The sea became very calm, because of which many sailors went swimming. They saw many *dorados* [dolphins in all likelihood] and other fish.

Wednesday 3 October

He steered his usual course. They made 47 leagues. He told the men 40. Petrels appeared. There was much weed, some very old and other very fresh, and it bore something like fruit. They did not see any birds and the Admiral believed that the islands drawn on his chart lay behind him.

The Admiral says here that he did not want to delay by beating into the wind the past week and on these days when he was seeing so many signs of land, even though he had information about certain islands in that region. [This was] in order not to delay, since his objective was to pass to the Indies; and if he were to delay, he says, it would not make good sense.

Saturday 6 October

He steered on his route to the *vueste* [west] or *gueste*, which is the same thing. They made 40 leagues between day and night. He told the men 33 leagues. Tonight Martín Alonso said that it would be well to steer southwest by west; and to the Admiral it seemed that Martín Alonso said this because of the island of Cipango [Japan]; and the Admiral saw that if they missed it they would not be able to strike land so quickly and that it was better to go at once to the mainland and afterward to the islands.

Wednesday 10 October

He steered west-southwest; they traveled ten miles per hour and at times 12 and for a time seven and between day and night made 59 leagues; he told the men only 44 leagues. Here the men could no longer stand it; they complained of the long voyage. But the Admiral encouraged them as best he could, giving them good hope of the benefits that they would be able to secure. And he added that it was useless to complain since he had come to find the Indies and thus had to continue the voyage until he found them, with the help of Our Lord.

Thursday 11 [and 12] October

He steered west-southwest. They took much water aboard, more than they had taken in the whole voyage. They saw petrels and a green bulrush near the ship. The men of the caravel *Pinta* saw a cane and a stick, and took on board another small stick that appeared to have been worked with iron, and a piece of cane, and other vegetation originating on land, and a small plank. The men of the caravel *Niña* also saw other signs of land and a small stick loaded with barnacles. With these signs everyone breathed more easily and cheered up. On this day, up to sunset, they made 27 leagues.

After sunset he steered on his former course to the west. They made about 12 miles each hour and, until two hours after midnight, made about 90 miles, which is twenty-two leagues and a half. And because the caravel *Pinta* was a better sailer and went ahead of the Admiral it found land and made the signals that the Admiral had ordered. A sailor named Rodrigo de Triana saw this land first, although the Admiral, at the tenth hour of the night, while he was on the sterncastle, saw a light, although it was something so faint that he did not wish to affirm that it was land. But he called Pero Gutiérrez, the steward of the king's dais, and told him that there seemed to be a light, and for him to look: and thus he did and saw it. He also told Rodrigo Sánchez de Segovia, whom the king and queen were sending as *veedor* [recorder of valuables] of the fleet, who saw nothing because he was not in a place where he could see it. After the Admiral said it, it was seen once or twice; and it was like a small wax candle that rose and lifted up, which to few seemed to be an indication of land. But the Admiral was certain that they were near land, because of which when they recited the *Salve* [hymn to the Virgin Mary], which sailors in their own way are accustomed to recite and sing, all being present, the Admiral entreated and admonished them to keep a good lookout on the forecastle and to watch carefully for land; and that to the man who first told him that he saw land he would later give a silk jacket in addition to the other rewards that the sovereigns had promised, which were ten thousand *maravedís* as an annuity to whoever should see it first. At two hours after midnight the land appeared, from which they were about two leagues distant. They hauled down all the sails and kept only the *treo*, which is the mainsail without bonnets, and jogged on and off, passing time until daylight Friday, when they reached an islet of the Lucayas, which was called Guanahaní in the language of the Indians. Soon they saw naked people; and the Admiral went ashore in the armed launch, and Martín Alonso Pinzón and his brother Vicente Anes [Yáñez], who was captain of the *Niña*. The Admiral brought out the royal banner and the captains two flags with the green cross, which the Admiral carried on all the ships as a standard, with an F [for Fernando (Ferdinand)]

and a Y [for Ysabel (Isabella)], and over each letter a crown, one on one side of the **✚** and the other on the other. Thus put ashore they saw very green trees and many ponds and fruits of various kinds. The Admiral called to the two captains and to the others who had jumped ashore and to Rodrigo Descobedo, the *escrivano* [recording agent] of the whole fleet, and to Rodrigo Sánchez de Segovia; and he said that they should be witnesses that, in the presence of all, he would take, as in fact he did take, possession of the said island for the king and for the queen his lords, making the declarations that were required, and which at more length are contained in the testimonials made there in writing. Soon many people of the island gathered there. . . .

16

The Pinzón Version of the Crossing

The exact amount of credit to be allocated among the leaders of the 1492 crossing remains in dispute. Only Columbus is remembered by the general public, but each ship had both a commander and a master. The staffing of the voyage was the responsibility of the Pinzóns from Palos [de la Frontera], save for help from three of the Niños of nearby Moguer, who owned the *Niña*. Martín Alonso Pinzón commanded the *Pinta*, with his younger brother Francisco Martín as master. Vicente Yáñez Pinzón commanded the *Niña*, with a cousin Diego Pinzón as master. Columbus's second in command on the *Santa María* was her owner Juan de la Cosa.

> *"Onwards, onwards . . ."*

Who should have the most credit for the crossing and the actual discovery was exhaustively discussed through the course of a lawsuit brought by Diego Columbus, second Admiral of the Indies, against the Spanish crown. The Columbus family complained that the king was not acknowledging the full extent of the land Christopher Columbus had been the first to visit and so was cutting back on the percentage due the heirs. A compromise that was accepted in 1536 by Luis Columbus gave him an annual pension in lieu of further income from the New World, an estate in Veragua [today's Panama], and titles.

Questions put to witnesses during the course of the lawsuit indicate that there were always doubts about Christopher Columbus being the central figure in the explorations, as is commonly assumed. As early as the first quarter of the sixteenth century, the claim of Martín Alonso Pinzón to nearly an equal share for credit in the first voyage was filed by his family and friends. Columbus more than once sought Martín's advice and, to some degree, deferred to his judgment. In terms of practical navigational skills, the Pinzóns were at least equal to Columbus, and perhaps his superior in some areas.

Columbus did acknowledge that [Martín Alonso] Pinzón had an interest in reaching Japan and in visiting islands in the Atlantic, one that predates their first meeting. During a visit to Rome, Martín may have been shown a document (which has never been located) from the Vatican Library, mentioned in the opening part of the selection, that described a fanciful voyage of the Queen of Sheba to Japan. Encountering Columbus at a low point in Columbus's efforts, Martín might have encouraged him to try again with Queen Isabella.

The town of Palos de la Frontera was obligated, because of "certain things done and committed" to the disservice of the crown, to provide two equipped caravels at the town's expense for one year. García Fernández, steward of the *Pinta*, testified "that without his (Martín) giving the two ships to the Admiral he would not have been where he (Columbus) was, nor would he have found people because nobody knew the said Admiral." With Martín's blessing, the crew members (none of them criminals) were persuaded to sail on the voyage.

The inquest could take no testimony from Martín because he died in 1493. So far as the remaining witnesses were concerned, testimony was taken in various parts of the Spanish empire; answers to a list of questions prepared by the crown were given to notaries without cross-examination. The test is difficult to follow because most of it is in the form of answers to these questions. Readers should also keep in mind that the questions (only four of which are reprinted here) were designed to put Columbus in an unflattering light, since it was in the crown's interest to belittle his contribution.

Testimony to Inquest by Martín Alonso Pinzón's Son

This witness . . . is the son of the said Martín Alonso Pinzón and was residing in Rome with merchandise belonging to his father, and during that year before he went to explore [with Columbus], his father came to Rome; and the said Martín Alonso Pinzón, this witness' father, was in the Pope's library one day, where he often spent time due to his friendship with one of the Pope's clients a great cosmographer who had many long manuscripts that he often showed to this witness and his father

SOURCE *Plietos de Colón* in *Colección de Documentos Inéditos . . . de Ultramar* 2ª Serie 25 vols. (Madrid, 1885–1932), vol. VIII, pp. 127–128, 160–161, 209–210, 228–230; trans. J. H. Parry and R. G. Keith, 5 vols., *New Iberian World* (New York: Times Books, 1984), vol. I, pp. 17, 63–64. Reprinted by permission.

while conversing with them. Thus this witness and his father learned of these lands that were ready to be discovered; and with his industry and the knowledge of the sea that he possessed, he many times told this witness how he would like to equip an expedition of two ships and go to discover these lands; and he knows this because of what he has said, and it happened in this way and he saw it with his own eyes.

. . . [W]hen the witness was in the library of Pope Innocent VIII, he was given a manuscript . . . and the father of this witness took it with him when he returned to Castille from Rome with the intention of going to discover the said land. And he had begun preparing to carry out his plans, which he discussed many times with the witness, when the said Admiral came to this town of Palos with the intention of going to discover those lands, and the father of this witness saw him come with this intention.

Thus when [Columbus] learned of Martín Alonso's intention to go exploring, he thought it well to ask him [for his assistance] and to offer him a share [in the enterprise]. And Martín Alonso told him that his purpose was good and he knew a good deal about it, and that if he had not come so quickly, he would have gone with two caravels to discover those lands himself. And when the said Admiral had seen the above, he became a great friend of the father of this witness and entered into an agreement with him, asking him to go with him; and this witness knows about this because he saw it.

. . . [H]e said because the Admiral [agreed to give] half of the favors (mercedes) granted by Their Highnesses in this case to [Martín Alonso] and the said Martín Alonso showed him the said manuscript, which increased his resolve; and when they made their agreement, the said Martín Alonso gave the Admiral money and sent him to Court along with a friar called Juan Perez, and this witness knows about this because he was present through all of it.

. . . [A]fter the Admiral returned from the Court, he brought an order and funds from Their Highnesses to go with three ships to explore those lands. But when he saw that no one in this town of Palos dared come with him or even less wanted to give them their ships, asking why they should go, since he would never find land; and after he had been in this situation for over two months without finding a way of getting either ships or men, he entreated the said Martín Alonso to come with him, showing him the favors Their Highnesses were granting him if he found the said lands, promising to give him half the said lands, and telling him that if he went with him he would be the principal captain of the said ships, and that as a man with many relatives and friends he could get the expedition equipped and manned, which would be a service to Their Highnesses. And the said Martín Alonso, seeing that the Admiral had no way of equipping the expedition, and considering the share he would receive, as well as the service to Their Highnesses, agreed to go with him, gave him the original document he had brought from Rome and also donated his ships; and, with his relatives and friends, equipped the expedition in one month. And this witness knows about this because he saw it, and also saw them depart on the said voyage.

Questions put to crew members by the Inquest

15.* Item, if they know that on the said voyage Martín Alonso went as one of the principal persons, serving as captain of one of his two ships, and that his brothers were captains of the other two. And that they went from the island of Hierro in the Canaries eight hundred leagues to the west, and when he was two hundred leagues from land, the Admiral was undecided where to go. Since he had found no land where he expected, he went on board the ship of the said Martín Alonso and asked what he thought they should do, since they had already gone two hundred leagues farther than he expected, and should have reached land before now.

16. Item, if they know that Martín Alonso said, "Onwards, onwards (Adelante, adelante), an expedition and embassy dispatched by such Princes as Our Lords the King and Queen of Spain has never failed before, and may it please God that it will not fail because of us. You, sir, may wish to return, but I am determined to go on until I discover the land or never return to Spain." Thus, because of his diligence and recommendation, they continued on.

17. Item, if they know that the Admiral asked him if they should continue on the same course, and Martín Alonso told him no, that he had many times told him that they were not going in the right direction; and that if they turned a quarter to the southwest they would reach land more quickly. And the Admiral answered him, "Well, let us do as you say," and so they promptly altered course, because of the diligence and recommendation of the said Martín Alonso Pinzón, who was at that time very expert in the affairs of the sea.

18. Item, if they know that after they altered course following what the said Martín Alonso Pinzón had recommended, within three or four days they reached land at the island of Guanahaní in the Lucayas [the Bahamas].

Answer of García Fernández, steward of the Pinta, to the Fifteenth Question

He said that what he knew was that the said Martín Alonso shipped as captain of one of his own vessels called the Pinta, in which this witness sailed as steward, and that a brother of Martín Alonso was master of the ship that was called the Pinta, and that the other brother called Vicente Yáñez was master of the ship that was called the Niña, and that all three vessels ran from the island of Ferro 400 leagues, more or less, to the southwest, and

---

* The editor has eliminated the first fourteen questions.

that then Martín Alonso came to the Admiral and said to him, "Sir, let us run southwest by west," and the Admiral said that he congratulated him; and the Admiral encouraged them, speaking firmly to the said Martín Alonso, and to all those in his company who declared that they would never sight land; and they altered their course to the southwest and found a land that was called Guanahaní; and the first people who saw the said island were those in the ship *Pinta* in which this witness was; and the said Martín Alonso ordered lombards to be fired as a signal of joy; which order being executed, the Admiral, who was astern of the ship *Pinta*, came up; and as soon as they saw the land, Martín Alonso shouted to the Admiral Columbus that he should approach, and when he did, the Admiral said, "Martín Alonso, Sir, you have found land!" and that then Martín Alonso said, "Sir, my reward is earned," and that the Admiral then said, "I give you 5,000 *maravedis* as a bonus!" and this witness knows because he saw it.

Answers of Diego Fernández Colmenero

In reply to the sixteenth question, he said he knows about this because the said Martín Alonso Pinzón went as captain of one of the ships, and Vicente Yáñez, his brother, was captain of another, and that another brother of theirs, Francisco Martín, was master of the said Martín Alonso's ship. And following their course they left the Canary Islands, and this witness heard from some of the sailors who returned that the Admiral had asked Martín Alonso what they should do, since they had already sailed the distance he expected to go and should by then have reached land. When asked from whom he heard this, he said from sailors and persons who had gone on the voyage with the abovesaid men, and this is what he knows about this question.

In reply to the seventeenth question, he said he knows about this because he also heard the seamen and others who went on the voyage say that the events mentioned in the question had occurred as stated; and that the said Martín Alonso had replied to the Admiral Christopher Columbus that any man who was leading an embassy from such Princes ought not to turn back nor was it right to do so; and thus they decided to continue on, and he knows this for the reasons he has stated.

In reply to the eighteenth question, he said that he likewise heard tell that, continuing their voyage with the rest of the fleet and following the course that the said Martín Alonso had recommended, they altered course to the southwest, and Martín Alonso did this because he saw, over the sea, birds that roosted on land, and because of his diligence and knowledge, the Admiral followed the course that the said Martín Alonso had recommended, and that the said Martín Alonso was very expert in things of the sea, and was well known for this, not only in this town but elsewhere. Asked how he knows all this, he said because he talked about it with the men on the voyage and remembers it well.

QUESTIONS

1. What were the signs of land that the sailors anticipated seeing?
2. What gave Columbus's crew cause to complain?
3. Why might Columbus have kept two different calculations of the distance the three ships were traveling?
4. What encouraged the Pinzón brothers to continue on the course Columbus set?
5. The logbook entries of 25 September and 3 October mention a (long-lost) seachart of the Atlantic in Columbus's possession. Did this chart prove decisive in his discovery of landfall?
6. What was the meaning of the symbolic acts that took place after thanksgiving at the first landfall?

SSESSING COLUMBUS AND
HIS ACHIEVEMENT

Contemporaries

Ferdinand Columbus was born in 1488 in Cordóba, where his father was awaiting the report of a committee set up by Ferdinand and Isabella to study the proposal for a voyage. His mother was Beatriz Enríques de Araña, a peasant who had become mistress of the thirty-seven-year-old Columbus, a widower who already had a son, Diego. Soon after his father's triumph, Ferdinand entered the service of the court as a page, a significant honor.

His Son: *"very moderate and modest."* Las Casas: *"great spirit and lofty thoughts, . . ."*

The financial results of the early voyages were at first disappointing. Ferdinand recalled how he and his half-brother were followed about by tormentors, who shouted: "There go the sons of the Admiral of the Mosquitoes."

At age thirteen, Ferdinand accompanied his father, from May 1502 to November 1504 on the dangerous fourth voyage. Five years later, after his father's death, he was sent to Hispaniola to erect churches and monasteries, but after a few months he obtained permission to return to Spain. By then, his father's percentage of New World wealth was beginning to yield large sums. He never traveled the ocean again, preferring to live on his wealth in Seville, studying his vast collection of books and manuscripts.

He was kept active in the law courts protecting his family's interests in drawn-out litigation between his family and the crown (see Document 16). During the proceedings, Ferdinand gathered the documents and depositions that help make his father's biography useful and direct, although caution must be used. For example, the University of Pavia's matriculation records do not support the claim that his father studied there.

What little is known about Columbus's early adventures, other than that told by his son, comes from the writings of Bartolomé de Las Casas. The Dominican friar was in close contact with Columbus and recorded his remarks. Although Las Casas was a stern critic of Columbus's treatment of the natives, he was an advocate of the navigator's essential greatness.

His Son

Two things which are important to know about every famous man are his birthplace and family, because men generally accord more honor to those who were born in great cities and of noble parents. Therefore some wished me to tell how the Admiral [Columbus] came of illustrious stock, although misfortune had reduced his parents to great poverty and need . . . .

But I have spared myself such labor, believing that the Admiral was chosen for his great work by Our Lord, who desired him as His true Apostle to follow the example of others of His elect by publishing His name on distant seas and shores, not in cities and palaces, thereby imitating Our Lord himself, who though his descent was from the blood royal of Jerusalem, yet was content to have his parentage from an obscure source. Similarly, the Admiral, although endowed with all the qualities that his great task required, chose to leave in obscurity all that related to his birthplace and family. . . .

The Admiral was a well-built man of more than average stature, the face long, the cheeks somewhat high, his body neither fat nor lean. He had an aquiline nose and light-colored eyes; his complexion too was light and tending to bright red. In youth his hair was blonde, but when he reached the age of thirty, it all turned white. In eating and drinking, and in the adornment of his person, he was very moderate and modest. He was affable in conversation with strangers and very pleasant to the members of his household, though with a certain gravity. He was so strict in matters of religion that for fasting and saying prayers he might have been taken for a member of a religious order. . . .

Leaving his other personal traits and customs for mention at the proper time, let us speak of the sciences to which he most devoted himself. He learned his letters at a tender age and studied enough at the University of Pavia to understand the geographers, of whose teaching he was very fond; for this reason he also gave himself to the study of astronomy and geometry, since these sciences are so closely related that one depends upon the other. And because Ptolemy, in the beginning of his *Geography*, says that one cannot be a good geographer unless one knows how to draw, too, he learned drawing, in order to be able to show the position of countries and form geographic bodies, plane and round. . . .

SOURCE From *The Life of the Admiral Christopher Columbus by His Son Ferdinand.* trans. and annotated by Benjamin Keen, 1959, pp. 3–9, passim. Reprinted by permission of the translator.

POSSIBLE PORTRAIT OF COLUMBUS *There are dozens of supposed portraits of Christopher Columbus, none definitive. Here is the first one published with a modest claim to accuracy. This woodcut engraving by Tobias Stimmer, done at Basil in 1575, is a copy of the lost 1550 "Jovius Portrait," once owned by Paolo Giovvio, Archbishop of Novera. Its subject is dressed in a Spanish tabard, a red cloak then worn by sailors. The frame shows two figures standing on world globes, one a European and the other an Amerindian.*

Las Casas

As concerns his appearance, he was fairly tall, his face long and giving an impression of authority, his nose eaglelike, his eyes blue, his complexion light and tending to bright red. His beard and hair were fair in his youth but very soon turned gray from his labors. He was witty and cheerful in speech and . . . eloquent and boastful in his negotiations. His manner was serious, but not grave; he was affable with strangers and mild and pleasant with members of his household, whom he treated with dignity, and so he easily won the love of those who saw him. In short, he had the appearance of a man of great importance. He was sober and moderate in eating and drinking, in dress and footwear. He would often say, whether jokingly or angrily: "God take you, don't you agree to that?" or "Why did you do that?" In the matter of Christian doctrine he was a devout Catholic. Nearly everything he did or said he began with: "In the name of the Holy Trinity I shall do this" or "—this will come to pass," or "—may this come to pass.". . .

He appeared very grateful for benefits received at the divine hand and it was almost a proverb with him, which he repeated frequently, that God had been especially good to him, as to David. When gold or precious objects were brought to him he would enter his chapel and kneel, asking the bystanders to do the same, saying: "Let us give thanks to the Lord, who made us worthy of discovering such great wealth.". . .

He was a man of great spirit and lofty thoughts, naturally inclined—as appears from his life, deeds, writings, and speech—to undertake great and memorable enterprises; patient and long-suffering . . . quick to forgive injuries, and wishing nothing more than that those who offended him should come to know their error and be reconciled with him. He was most constant and forbearing amid the endless incredible hardships and misfortunes that he had to endure, and always had great faith in the Divine Providence. And as I learned from him, from my own father, who was with him when he returned to settle the island of Hispaniola in 1493, and from other persons who accompanied and served him, he was always most loyal and devoted to the King and Queen.

QUESTIONS

1. Why might Columbus want to hide his background—even from his own children?
2. What might have caused Ferdinand to emphasize his father's devout Catholicism?
3. About what details do Ferdinand Columbus and Las Casas agree?

SOURCE Bartolomé de Las Casas, *História de las Indias,* 3 vols. (Mexico: Fondo de Cultura Economica, 1951), vol. I, ch. 3, pp. 29–30, passim. Editor's translation.

Nineteenth-Century Historians

From 1842 to 1846, Washington Irving was America's minister to Spain. His admiration for things Spanish, combined with his superbly romantic story-telling skills, helped him to write *Tales of the Alhambra* and *Chronicle of the Conquest of Granada*. Irving earned his initial literary success with the massive scholarly biography from which this first selection is taken. It was the result of three years' work in Madrid, where he was fortunate to gain access to the American ambassador's excellent library and to a solid collection of primary sources culled by Don Martín Navarrette from otherwise closed archives. Irving's book did much to revive the reputation of a long-neglected Columbus. Following its publication in 1828, the biography remained standard until the end of the century. The mayor of New York extolled the author in 1859 for his works on Columbus and Washington, "those examples of herioc duty and heroic patriotism."

> "overshadowing, all-controlling destiny shaping events . . ."

George Bancroft's ten-volume *History of the United States* (1834–1876) has left an equally enduring mark upon the way North Americans view the historical record. The narrative version of their past that most Americans learn is of a heroic Columbus who "discovered" two enormous land masses: the northernmost one was sparsely populated by "savages," and the southernmost one was just seeing the start of experiments with civilization in "barbaric" Mexico and Peru. Once the brave conquistadores completed their work, the New World became the arena for struggles between the European powers. The Amerindians quickly faded out of sight, while the black population received little attention until the Civil War.

Bancroft was a leading historian of the Western Hemisphere in the nineteenth century. His contemporaries included William Prescott, student of the conquest of Mexico, and Francis Parkman, the recorder of the battles between France and England in North America. These scholars were superb writers who created models of the past that closely matched the ethnic and class preconceptions of their readers. Notice how neatly Bancroft fits the round peg of a Catholic Columbus into the predestined square hole of a (mostly) Protestant United States.

Irving

His conduct as a discoverer was characterized by the grandeur of his views, and the magnanimity of his spirit. Instead of scouring the newly found countries, like a grasping adventurer eager only for immediate gain, as was too generally the case with contemporary discoverers, he sought to ascertain their soil and productions, their rivers and harbours. He was desirous of colonizing and cultivating them, of conciliating and civilizing the natives, of building cities, introducing the useful arts, subjecting every thing to the control of law, order and religion, and thus of founding regular and prosperous empires. In this glorious plan he was constantly defeated by the dissolute rabble which he was doomed to command; with whom all law was tyranny, and order restraint. They interrupted all useful works by their seditions; provoked the peaceful Indians to hostility; and after they had thus drawn down misery and warfare upon their own heads, and overwhelmed Columbus with the ruins of the edifice he was building, they charged him with being the cause of the confusion.

Well would it have been for Spain had her discoverers who followed in the track of Columbus possessed his sound policy and liberal views. What dark pages would have been spared in her colonial history! The new world, in such case, would have been settled by peaceful colonists, and civilized by enlightened legislators, instead of being overrun by desperate adventurers, and desolated by avaricious conquerors. . . .

It cannot be denied, however, that his piety was mingled with superstition, and darkened by the bigotry of the age. He evidently concurred in the opinion that all nations which did not acknowledge the Christian faith were destitute of natural rights; that the sternest measures might be used for their conversion, and the severest punishments inflicted upon their obstinacy in unbelief. In this spirit of bigotry he considered himself justified in making captives of the Indians, and transporting them to Spain to have them taught the doctrines of Christianity, and in selling them for slaves, if they pretended to resist his invasions. In so doing he sinned against the natural benignity of his character, and against the feelings which he had originally entertained and expressed towards this gentle and hospitable people; but he was goaded on by the mercenary impatience of the crown, and by the sneers of his enemies at the unprofitable result of his enterprizes. . . .

With all the visionary fervour of his imagination, its fondest dreams fell short of the reality. He died in ignorance of the real grandeur of his discovery. Until his last breath, he entertained the idea that he had merely opened a new way to the old resorts of opulent commerce, and had discovered some of the wild regions of the east. He supposed Hispaniola to be the ancient

SOURCE Washington Irving, *The Life and Voyages of Christopher Columbus*, ed. J. H. McElroy, pp. 565–569, passim. Copyright 1981. Reprinted with permission of Twayne Publishers, a division of G. K. Hall & Co., Boston.

Ophir [probably Somaliland in east Africa] which had been visited by the ships of Solomon, and that Cuba and Terra Firma [the mainland] were but remote parts of Asia. What visions of glory would have broken upon his mind could he have known that he had indeed discovered a new continent, equal to the whole of the old world in magnitude, and separated by two vast oceans from all the earth hitherto known by civilized man! And how would his magnanimous spirit have been consoled, amidst the chills of age and cares of penury, the neglect of a fickle public, and the injustice of an ungrateful king, could he have anticipated the splendid empires which were to spread over the beautiful world he had discovered; and the nations, and tongues, and languages which were to fill its lands with his renown, and revere and bless his name to the latest posterity!

Bancroft

Most remarkable in the character of Columbus was the combination of the theoretical and the practical; and most remarkable in his theories was the anomaly that though nearly all of them were false, they led to as grand results as if they had been true. The aperture through which failure creeps into carefully laid schemes is usually some glaring defect of character; and such defect often appears where little suspected, in natures warped by genius, or where one quality is unduly developed at the expense of another quality. We often see men of rare ability wrecked by what would be regarded an act of folly unaccountable in the stupidest person; but we do not often see success resulting from these same defects. The greatest defect in the faculties of Columbus, extravagance of belief, was the primary cause of his success. . . .

Nothing more plainly proves the power that sent him forth than the fact that in scarcely one of his original conceptions was he correct . . . . But what he knew and did, assuredly, was enough, opening the ocean to highways, and finding new continents; enough to fully entitle him to all the glory man can give to man; and as for his errors of judgment, had he been able to map America as accurately as can we to-day, had he been divine instead of, as he claimed, only divinely appointed, with myriads of attendant ministers, his achievement would have been none the greater. . . .

Once born in him the infatuation that he was the divinely appointed instrument for the accomplishment of this work, and frowning monarchs or perilous seas were as straws in his way. We see clearly enough what moved him, these four hundred years after the event, though he who was moved in reality knew little about it. By the pressure of rapidly accumulating ideas we see brought to the front in discovery Christopher Columbus, just as in the

SOURCE H. H. Bancroft, *Collected Works*, 39 vols. (San Francisco: A. L. Bancroft, 1882–1890), vol. VI, pp. 232–237, passim.

reformation of the church Martin Luther is crowded to the front. The German monk was not the Reformation; like the Genoese sailor, he was but an instrument in the hands of a power palpable to all, but called by different persons different names. . . .

. . . [T]here were even in the most unlovable parts of him something to respect, and in his selfishness a self-sacrificing nobleness, a lofty abandonment of self to the idea, which we can but admire. It was not for himself, although it was always most zealously and jealously for himself; the ships, the new lands, the new peoples, his fortunes and his life, all were consecrate; should the adventure prove successful, the gain would be heaven's; if a failure, the loss would fall on him. Surely the Almighty must smile on terms so favorable to himself. And that he did not finally make good his promises with regard to rescuing the holy sepulchre, and building temples, and converting nations, was for the same reason that he did not finally satisfy his worldly pretensions, and secure himself in his rulership. He had not the time. In all his worldly and heavenly ambitions, the glory of God and the glory of himself were blended with the happy consummation of his grand idea. And never did morbid broodings over the unsubstantial and shadowless produce grander results than these incubations of alternate exaltation and despondency that hatched a continent. And in all that was then transpiring, there are few intelligent readers of history who cannot see an overshadowing, all-controlling destiny shaping events throughout the world, so that this then unknown continent should be prepared to fill the grand purpose which even then appeared to be marked out for it.

QUESTIONS

1. How does Irving excuse Columbus from blame in the tragic fate of the Amerindians?
2. How does Irving's American patriotism influence his assessment of Columbus?
3. Who was to blame for Columbus's failures as a colonial administrator?
4. How does Bancroft manage to avoid mentioning that Columbus was Catholic?
5. According to Bancroft, in what ways was Columbus a tool of the "Almighty" in shaping America's "grand purpose"?

Twentieth-Century Reassessments

S. E. Morison's *Admiral of the Ocean Sea* was published in 1942, during the darkest year of World War II, when U.S. marine power had been thoroughly humbled by Imperial Japan. The author provided his country with an authentic naval hero who, if not yet quite an American citizen, could encourage his spiritual heirs. It immediately gained the status of a classic, and has been reissued time and again. Morison, who himself rose to the rank of admiral, has a splendid feel for navigating the deep. He knows thoroughly the waters of the Atlantic and Caribbean. His style combines a hard-edged masculine sensibility with a small boy's romantic enthusiasm for everything connected with sailing.

> *"The standard Columbus Day image of Columbus is false."*

Not many influential scholars attack Columbus, perhaps because the brutal conquistadores and the greedy colonists draw the lightning. The masterful scholarship of A. Ballesteros y Beretta's *Cristóbal Colón y el descubrimiento de América* (1940) is very charitable toward its subject, perhaps because of the glory he brought to Spain. In going against this trend, Carl O. Sauer's *The Early Spanish Main* (1966) presents the Caribbean landfall as the first act of a tragedy. Columbus, in the author's eyes, bears the blame for a number of unfortunate mistakes that set precedents for those who came after him.

Hans Koning's *Columbus: His Enterprise* (1976) incorporates into its brief text a vitriolic series of condemnations of the Great Man theory of history. Operating from a radical viewpoint, possibly influenced by the Vietnam War era, the author presents a Columbus who is an entrepreneur rather than a sailor, the organizer of pirate expeditions rather than altruistic explorations. Koning's emphasis on Columbus's cruelty places his subject squarely within an updated version of the Black Legend (Documents 30–32).

Columbus's ancestry has always been open to debate, because he was secretive about his origins. Salvador de Madariaga's 1942 biography presented the highly controversial opinion that the admiral's distant relatives were Jews who converted to Christianity. The evidence offered by this book, and by more recent authors, is slight. Drawing upon a massive array of documents, Paolo Emilio Taviani's exhaustive commentaries on Columbus's life and achievements make a case for the family's old Genoese origins. Taviani, himself born in Genoa, fought during World War II with the partisans against the Nazi occupation of northern Italy. He also served in parliament, and was professor of economic history at the University of

Genoa. His intense local patriotism suffuses all his writing about Christopher Columbus.

Morison

My main concern is with the Columbus of action, the Discoverer who held the key to the future in his hand, and knew in exactly which of a million possible keyholes it would turn the lock. I am content to leave his "psychology," his "motivation" and all that to others. Yet, as the caravels sail on tropic seas to new and ever more wonderful islands, and to high mountain-crested coasts of terra firma where the long surges of the trade winds eternally break and roar, I cannot forget the eternal faith that sent this man forth, to the benefit of all future ages. . . .

America would eventually have been discovered if the Great Enterprise of Columbus had been rejected; yet who can predict what would have been the outcome? The voyage that took him to "The Indies" and home was no blind chance, but the creation of his own brain and soul, long studied, carefully planned, repeatedly urged on indifferent princes, and carried through by virtue of his courage, sea-knowledge and indomitable will. No later voyage could ever have such spectacular results, and Columbus's fame would have been secure had he retired from the sea in 1493. Yet a lofty ambition to explore further, to organize the territories won for Castile, and to complete the circuit of the globe, sent him thrice more to America. These voyages, even more than the first, proved him to be the greatest navigator of his age, and enabled him to train the captains and pilots who were to display the banners of Spain off every American cape and island between Fifty North and Fifty South [latitudes]. The ease with which he dissipated the unknown terrors of the Ocean, the skill with which he found his way out and home, again and again, led thousands of men from every Western European nation into maritime adventure and exploration. And if Columbus was a failure as a colonial administrator, it was partly because his conception of a colony transcended the desire of his followers to impart, and the capacity of natives to receive, the institutions and culture of Renaissance Europe. . . .

Other discoveries there have been more spectacular than that of this small, flat sandy island that rides out ahead of the American continent, breasting the trade winds. But it was there that the Ocean for the first time "loosed the chains of things" as Seneca had prophesied, gave up the secret that had baffled Europeans since they began to inquire what lay beyond the western horizon's rim. Stranger people than the gentle Taínos, more exotic plants than the green verdure of Guanahaní have been discovered, even by

SOURCE From *Admiral of the Ocean Sea: A Life of Christopher Columbus*, one-vol. ed., pp. 6–671, passim; two-vol. ed., vol. I, p. 236, by Samuel Eliot Morison. Copyright 1942, © 1970 by Samuel Eliot Morison. By permission of Little, Brown and Company.

the Portuguese before Columbus; but the discovery of Africa was but an unfolding of a continent already glimpsed, whilst San Salvador, rising from the sea at the end of a thirty-three-day westward sail, was a clean break with past experience. Every tree, every plant that the Spaniards saw was strange to them, and the natives were not only strange but completely unexpected, speaking an unknown tongue and resembling no race of which even the most educated of the explorers had read in the tales of travelers from Herodotus to Marco Polo. Never again may mortal men hope to recapture the amazement, the wonder, the delight of those October days in 1492 when the New World gracefully yielded her virginity to the conquering Castilians.

Sauer

Columbus gave to Spain a New World the existence of which he never admitted. Seamen of western nations had long been voyaging far out into the Ocean Sea and were familiar with its winds and currents. . . .

Spanish seamen of the Atlantic ports of Andalusia were accustomed to cross a thousand miles of open sea to the Canaries and return. It was they who would provide the navigating skill for the venture of Columbus. He would direct them to sail west from the Canaries through unknown waters. His objective has never been made clear and perhaps was uncertain. In promoting his venture he proposed to sail west to the kingdoms of the Far East, yet having made the crossing he construed a wholly imaginary geography of Asiatic shores that disregarded everything that was known. Repeatedly he said that he was within a few days' sail of a famous city or country of the Orient, but instead of continuing west turned south. The secret of which he spoke as known to him alone led him south along tropical shores that would become known as the West Indies, peopled by simple natives whom he misnamed Indians.

Columbus had a genius for words, not as to their proper meaning but to cast a spell and to persuade. . . . The romantic publicity he gave to the new lands above all was to portray them as lands of infinite gold. All the fabled gold lands of antiquity were relocated in his discoveries or in parts he was about to discover. Columbus was looking for gold mines from the first landing on a coral island to his last days in Veragua. It did not matter that his success was slight. Always and everywhere there was vast promise of gold. The sovereigns and people of Spain became imbued by his obsession, picturesquely and fantastically presented. The course of Spanish empire was first turned to its fateful search for gold by the *idée fixe* [fixed idea] that dominated Columbus. . . .

SOURCE From *Early Spanish Main*, pp. 290–291, by Carl Sauer. Copyright © 1966 The Regents of the University of California.

Spain was confronted suddenly with the discovery of land across the ocean without any thought what should be done with it. Spain was unprepared but not so Columbus. He had secured the incredible contract that vested in him and his heirs in perpetuity the almost absolute rule over whatever he might discover and possess, subject to sharing the profits with the Spanish Crown. The inevitable conflict of interest began to develop immediately and troubled the affairs of the Spanish Indies for years.

Columbus, who is not known ever to have managed any enterprise, began in Española [Hispaniola] with the stupid mistake of building Isabela, which started up the troubles with his Spaniards. He was in trouble with his men most of the time and was engaged in putting down a revolt at the time of his removal. They were his employees, subject to his dictates which considered only his own wishes. The revolt of Roldán broke the control of Columbus who was forced to accept the allotment of native communities (repartimiento) to Spanish grantees (vecinos) and thereby to introduce against his will an institution that was basic to the administration of the Spanish colonies.

His Indian policy was simple, rigid, and unworkable. He found the natives friendly, apt at learning, and timorous. He would put them to work to produce gold, which their caciques [chiefs] would collect on a per capita basis. The impossible demand turned amiability to fear, flight, and retaliation. Many were captured, more died of hunger. Caciques were liquidated, their subjects shipped as slaves. Pacification by terror began thus as an instrument of colonial policy.

The government of Columbus was a continuing series of bad decisions. Always he insisted that he had been right and would have succeeded but for his enemies. Experience taught him nothing. The heritage of his mistakes continued long after him.

Koning

C hristopher Columbus was what a friend of mine calls "a grade-school hero." Every American child in second or third grade learns about the brave sailor, son of a Genoese weaver, who convinced the King and Queen of Spain to let him sail west. Fighting the elements and a crew who thought the earth was flat, he persisted, and with his three little ships discovered America.

After school, only people who are sailing enthusiasts or who are fascinated by geography ever come to grips with this man again. The books written for these people are hardly more critical than those written for

SOURCE From *Columbus: His Enterprise*, pp. 9–121, passim, by Hans Koning. Copyright 1976 by Hans Koning. Reprinted by permission of Monthly Review Foundation.

children. They try to be scientific and unbiased about the facts of navigation and about the ideas Columbus had on geography. They do not much question the traditional approach.

And that approach is of the dashing adventurer, the fearless knight with blazing blue eyes (because American books on Columbus have the interesting habit of describing this son of the Mediterranean as looking like an Englishman or a Scandinavian), or, if you prefer, the Errol Flynn of the late-night television movie. He overcomes the doubts and fears of a stick-in-the-mud, superstitious environment. He is the first Yankee, and what indeed could be more appropriate?

Now this may all seem perfectly harmless. Why worry about a good adventure yarn, especially if its actors lived almost five hundred years ago?

The answer of this book is: the grade-school image of Columbus is not naive, it is false. The standard Columbus Day image of Columbus is false.

This is important, for it did not get that way by chance. It is distorted in the same way that much in United States history is distorted. Our past, our present, and our future are burdened by these distortions. Thus there is nothing spoil-sport in taking a cold and hard look at what Columbus was all about. . . .

Most of what has been written about Columbus's early days at sea is based on speculation by people thinking in retrospect about his days of fame, and how they *should* have been. The discoverer of a great continent must have been a great man; the originator of such a voyage must have been a dashing, brilliant seaman. . . .

It is well to remember, as an antidote to romantic sea tales written in warm libraries, that ships were then floating slums and floating sweatshops. The common fate of crew and officers gave a certain solidarity that would not have been found on land among such disparate men, but they were still masters and servants, and no nonsense. The captain was lord over life and death, and any man who evoked his displeasure could be lashed, locked in irons, keelhauled, or hanged. The food for the crew was vile—though on a normal voyage probably no worse than what they were used to on land. As for their quarters, there weren't any. The men simply had to bunk down for the night wherever they could find a dry spot, which is not easy on a sailing boat; and those who had one change of dry clothes with them were the fortunate ones.

Those were the men who did the work, though. It has been said that the great explorers of Africa were simply the first white men carried around that continent by blacks; likewise, those famous captains were the first men sailed across the oceans by their crews. . . .

It lies within our comfortable liberal tradition that we don't like events to be depicted in stark colors. We like shadings. We particularly don't like things or people to be written up as all bad. Everything has its nuances, we claim. Only fanatics and extremists fail to see that. . . .

Well, fanatical and extreme as it may be, I find it very hard to think of any shadings or nuances in a character portrait of Christopher Columbus.

Grant him the originality and fierce ambition needed to set that western course. But what else is there to say? Here was a man greedy in large ways, and in small ways—to the point where he took for himself the reward for first sighting land from the *Pinta* lookout. Cruel in petty things, as when he set a dying monkey with two paws cut off to fight a wild pig; cruel on a continental scale, as when he set in motion what de Las Casas called "the beginning of the bloody trail of conquest across the Americas.". . .

Perhaps we will come to say that Columbus was not only a man of his time, but that he was a man of his race.

The word "race" may no longer be accepted in science because it cannot properly be defined. That does not prevent us all from knowing quite well what is meant by "the white race"; but let us say then that Columbus was a typical man of the (white) West. And the West has ravaged the world for five hundred years, under the flag of a master-slave theory which in our finest hour of hypocrisy was called "the white man's burden." Perhaps the Master-Race Nazis were different from the rest of us, mostly in the sense that they extended that theory to their fellow whites. (In doing so, they did the subject races of this world a favor. The great white-race civil war which we call World War II weakened Europe and broke its grip on Asia and Africa.) I am not ignoring the cruelties of other races. They were usually less hypocritical, though; they were not, in Marx's phrase, "civilization mongers" as they laid waste to other lands. But they too fill the pages of history with man's inhumanity to man.

Taviani

Despite the allegations of those who call him an adventurer, dishonest or simply lucky, Columbus was a true genius.

The great plan to *buscar el Levante por el Poniente* [search for the East from the West] could not have been conceived without the overweening desire for glory and the decisive, tenacious, almost stubborn character of the man, so typical of the Ligurians [Genoese].

Only a madman, or a man of truly formidable character, renounces family, earnings and all the joys life can offer for eight long years—eight decisive years, from 1485 to 1492—and during that same period renounces his strongest, most vital passion, the sea.

During those years Columbus did not set foot on a ship's bridge, except to travel from Lisbon to Castile; nor did he even catch a glimpse of the sea during his seven years in Spain. But prior to that, in the last months of his

SOURCE P. E. Taviani, *Christopher Columbus. The Grand Design* (London: Orbis Publishing Limited, 1985), pp. 539–540. Reprinted by permission.

stay in Portugal, he was already devoting himself exclusively to his great plan. Columbus was surely no madman. His father Domenico might be accused of megalomania, but not Christopher, who although imaginative and ambitious, displayed exceptional gifts of tenacity and realism.

He carried out the Atlantic venture, revealing himself to be an excellent captain, capable of withstanding the fury of the elements and the rebellious complaints of his crew.

He demonstrated his gifts before the great discovery, dealing, almost as an equal, with the King of Portugal, the rulers of Spain, and the Genoese, Florentine and Jewish bankers. Aware of his own value and of the strength of his ideas, he was not presumptuous, or he would never have won the esteem and affection of Fray Marchena and Fray Pérez. Nor would he have gained so many friends, patrons and admirers at the Spanish Court, and certainly not the understanding of the wise and intelligent Queen Isabella.

He was able to convince that shrewd and experienced captain of Palos, Martín Alonso Pinzón, the man who shares the merit and the glory and who helped Columbus enlist most of his crew; and he subsequently won the admiration and respect of those sailors, compelling obedience in the perilous voyage.

His study and patient research show him to have possessed an extraordinary memory and intelligence. If the earlier postils [marginal notes] in *Il Milione* [Marco Polo's *Travels*, Document 11] are somewhat ingenuous, those to the *Imago Mundi* [Document 12] show the advances he was able to make in a few years, perhaps a few months.

If his Latin contained errors, he deserves all the more praise for the commitment with which he tackled works written in perfect classical style, sometimes, as with Seneca [ancient Roman writer], even abstruse. His powers of memory emerge from the very metric error in transcribing Seneca's verses, because the deduction must be that he often copied down interesting passages entirely from memory.

To imagination, intelligence, daring and willpower, he brought constancy and spiritual strength. His deep, unswerving religious sentiment hardened his resolve and brought him serenity even in the most troubled moments; he was ever aware of being an instrument of Divine Providence.

Christopher Columbus did not become a discoverer by chance. He was a discoverer because he was an inventor, the inventor of a new idea, a new perspective.

He was one of the giants of human history.

QUESTIONS

1. Upon what will Columbus's fame rest, according to Morison?
2. Does Morison present the Castilian assault upon the New World as a "rape" or a "seduction"?

3. Was there anything positive in Columbus's legacy, according to Sauer?
4. In what ways, according to Sauer, did Columbus mismanage the matters to which he was entrusted by the Spanish sovereigns?
5. Why does Koning say it is wrong to think about Columbus as "a grade-school hero"?
6. What does Koning mean by insisting that Columbus was a man of his "race"?
7. In what way does Koning reject the celebrations by Las Casas and Morison of Columbus's skill as a captain?
8. According to Taviani, where does Columbus's true genius lie?

Photograph Portfolio A

Figure A–1
Columbus at Sea

This sixteenth-century engraving offers an allegorical interpretation of Christopher Columbus's first voyage. An allegory is a veiled presentation with symbolic meanings implied, but not expressly stated. Characters are usually types or personifications, rather than realistically drawn persons. There was a vogue during the Renaissance for using images taken from ancient pagan mythology to accompany and glorify contemporary persons. Try to figure out what messages this complex illustration would convey to a reader of that day.

The figure on shipboard can be identified as Columbus because the flag on the mast bears a coat of arms granted to him by Ferdinand and Isabella in 1493. It shows a castle, a lion, anchors, and an inlet with islands. The use of this heraldry was a great privilege for Columbus because the castle and the lion were symbols of Isabella's dominions in Castile and León.

FIGURE A–1

Columbus is wearing armor and carrying a banner showing Christ's crucifixion. A bird with a cross above its head leads the ship. The traditional symbol for the Holy Spirit is a dove, so this is another Christian symbol. Columbus is thus portrayed as the perfect Christian knight bringing the faith to new lands. Does it appear from his costume that he will do so peacefully? What does he see in the distance? Will his passage be smooth, or are the seas troubled? The water is filled with sea creatures. Some are dolphins, but others are the slithery monsters often painted in unknown waters on ancient maps. What does Columbus's attitude toward them say about his bravery?

The sea is also populated by individuals from Greco-Roman mythology, there by virtue of the illustrator's vivid imagination. Why does the illustrator tie something as new as this voyage to ancient themes? Diana the Huntress holds the ship by a rope. She can be identified by her bow and quiver of arrows. The crescent on her head identifies her as the moon goddess; there is also a sliver of moon in the sky. The moon goddess was perpetually virginal. What might this say about the New World, to which she is leading the knight? There are many references in books of the time to the so-called virginal and unfulfilled quality of the New World, which ignored both the existence and rights of the original inhabitants.

Not far from Diana are two sirens, sea nymphs who use their hypnotic song to lure sailors to their death on reefs. These women were a symbol of temptation. What does this indicate about Columbus's difficulties in attempting to be the perfect Christian knight? Off to the other side of the ship is Neptune, crowned king of the sea. He carries a pronged trident and is pulled along on his sea shell by three sea horses. The number 3, although used here in pagan context, would remind Christians of the Holy Trinity (Father, Son, Holy Spirit), which reinforces the theme of Columbus as messenger of Christianity to new shores. Neptune is accompanied by two seamen, the masculine equivalent of mermaids, who blow triumphantly on conch shells. How would this indicate Columbus's status in world history?

Thinking about the illustration as a whole, what would you say was its overall message? What does it tell you about contemporary attitudes toward the man and his mission that would not have been as apparent in a more straightforward illustration of the real Columbus on the real *Niña*?

Figure A–2
Columbus Lands in the New World

This is an imagined series of events concerning 1) the arrival of Columbus's ships at San Salvador, 2) the Europeans taking possession of the land, and 3) the initial encounter with the Taínos. The scenes are symbolic of the first landfall, since the illustrator makes no effort to develop accurately a reconstruction of events or a display of the participants.

Columbus, holding a pike, is dressed as a nobleman, with a Spanish neckruff over his garb and a sword at his side. The natives have the well-muscled physique of classical Greco-Roman statues. Why were sixteenth-century viewers uncritical of inaccuracy? Do Columbus and his two companions give the impression of wanting to make friends with the inhabitants of this island?

The largest of the three ships is of the carrack type, intended to be the *Santa María*. Notice its high forecastle and mounted guns. The other two are lighter caravels, like the *Niña* and *Pinta*. Also observe the square-rigged and triangular lateen sails. How do the natives greet the landing party coming from these ships? Are they coming forward, running away in fear, or, perhaps, dancing?

The actual possession ceremony, as described in the logbook of the voyage, involved Columbus's raising of the royal standard. The other two captains held aloft banners, each embroidered with a green cross and the initials of the king and queen. The royal recorder then took down Columbus's

FIGURE A–2

testimony and notarized all the witnesses. This illustration, by a French-man, shows a cross being planted. Why does he invent this action, but leave out the banners?

Columbus prepares to receive gifts from the natives. How would you describe this moment? What would this act of giving mean to European viewers? The natives are bearing cups, a chest, sculpture, rings, and neck-laces. Are these artifacts Amerindian or European? The necklace in the hand of the person closest to Columbus resembles the gold chains worn by European aristocrats who belonged to chivalric orders. Looking at the illus-tration as a whole, which is the dominant group—Europeans or Amerin-dians? Who is at the center—the most important area?

Figure A–3
Vespucci Awakens America

A German cartographer read a popular book of letters from Amerigo Ves-pucci and decided that Vespucci, not Columbus, was the first to realize that the continent in the southern half of the Western Hemisphere was a "New World," separate from Asia. Since the other continents were already named after mythic women *(Europa, Africa, Asia)*, the map maker feminized the Italian's Christian name by changing the final *o* to an *a*.

Vespucci knew Columbus, and he enjoyed enough confidence at the court of Spain to be named its chief pilot, in charge of coordinating explora-tions. Four voyages are claimed for him between 1497 and 1504, but schol-ars accept only two: one under the command of Alonso de Ojeda in 1499 to Brazil, and another under his own command for Portugal in 1501 along the same coastline.

This engraving makes an allegorical statement, similar in intent to Fig-ure A–1. It shows Vespucci meeting the New World, who is personified by a woman. She wears a headdress of leaves or feathers and is rising from a hammock, which is an Amerindian invention. Does she look Amerindian? Her body type and light hair are typical of European nudes found in paint-ings of the day. How does she respond to Vespucci? Is she startled and fearful, or alert and pleased, or simply rising from slumber? If she was asleep, what would this say about the importance of the arrival of Europeans?

A sword is hidden under Vespucci's cloak. Does his bearing and de-meanor show a peaceful or a warlike attitude? He carries a simplified marine astrolabe, used to assess location by "shooting" the stars or sun. Vespucci proudly mentions his skill with this instrument in his letters. In his other hand, he holds a banner emblazoned with the stars of the "South-ern Cross," which are visible only in the Southern Hemisphere. Consider also the shape of the finial atop the staff. Are these Christian references?

In this allegory, Vespucci symbolizes Europe. How then would you de-

FIGURE A–3

scribe Europe's relationship to the New World? Which figure dominates the picture? Contrasting the astrolabe and the great ships behind Vespucci with the hammock and the small Brazilian war club leaning against the tree beside the woman, what is the illustration implying about the respective technologies of the two hemispheres?

The natural landscape includes a number of animals, most of them drawn incorrectly, that were thought typical of the Western hemisphere: an anteater, an opossum climbing the tree, a sloth, and a horselike tapir. There are also four human figures in the distance. What are they doing? Why would the artist have included cannibals, since they are subordinate to the principal story portrayed in the foreground? Think about the illustration as a whole. What is the overall message conveyed to the viewer?

Figure A–4
The Picture of the World

The first modern atlas in single-sheet format was Abraham Ortelius's *Theatrum Orbis Terrarum*, or The Picture of the World, published in 1579. Previous charts were hung on walls, if they were large, or were rolled up and thus difficult to consult. Ortelius's book consists of fifty-three copperplate maps plus descriptive entries. The initial world view is followed by area

FIGURE A–4

maps for countries and regions. This work is scientific: the compiler acknowledged by name all eighty-seven authors of the maps consulted or copied, thus removing cartography from the realm of the anonymous and the plagiarized. By the time of Ortelius's death in 1598, twenty-eight editions had appeared in many translations. For the first time, one could hold the whole world in one's hands.

This title page presents four women, who represent the four known continents. Starting at the top, the fully clothed figure seated under a grape arbor is *Europa* (Europe). She is crowned, and holds a scepter in one hand and an orb in the other. The orb—a sphere representing the world and capped by a cross—goes back at least as far as the ninth century A.D., to the significant Christian reign of Charlemagne, first Holy Roman Emperor. What does it mean that *Europa* is equipped with this symbolic gear? To either side of her are sketchy world globes, one showing the Asian mainland and the other the Atlantic. How are these two globes related either to her or to the book as a whole?

Two of the figures are standing. *Asia*, richly dressed in silks and jewelry, is not especially Asiatic in face or form. In her hand, she holds an urn of burning incense or spice. Across from her is *Africa*, with fully realized African features, half-draped in flowing cloth. In her hand she carries a flowering branch (perhaps of a type of pepper), and around her head is the blazing sun. How do the attributes of these two figures compare to what a European might actually find in their respective continents?

The reclining figure at the bottom of the page is *America*. Compare her attributes and posture to Figure A–3. You should recognize her headdress, the hammock slung behind her, and the Brazilian war club. In what ways is *America* presented as a savage, warlike, and uncivilized land? She carries a bow and arrows, and holds a severed human head. Next to her is a bust on a pedestal, placed there to balance the pictorial space. This piece of statuary is classical in inspiration, as befits the massive Greco-Roman architectural frame incorporating Doric pillars and a wide pediment ornamented with the skulls of oxen.

Which of the figures is predominant? Why? One woman is seated on a thronelike seat, two are standing, and the fourth is reclining. What does their posture tell you about the importance of the respective continents in this design? Finally, notice the glances. Which is the boldest and most direct? Which is the most reserved and timid? What would this indicate to the observer about the respective status of the inhabitants of each known continent of the day?

Figure A–5
America: The Strangest Continent

Europe's fascination with America increased, if anything, in the seventeenth century, although observers still had mixed emotions about the New

World. An intellectual tradition had developed around the idea that, because America was "new," its plants, its animals, and, especially, its inhabitants were "weak" and far behind the sturdy, "advanced" environment of
the Old World. This illustration was designed by a Dutch portrait artist. He
made the images explicit by means of a poem, which runs along the bottom
of the page:

America is by far the strangest continent;
Here people live as lawless savages.
But the Spanish came to cultivate this land,
And occupy the harbors with their forts.

This the Dutchman saw. He came, looking around the corner,
Watching for his chance, and he found the sweetness.
One by one he ensnares a city or fort,
Which like a barge he pulls in to his profit.

These lands give forth gold, silver, parrots,
All kinds of cattle, tobacco, Brazilian wood.
Campetji-stockfish wood, and ebony all appear;
Sugar abounds, and also Huyden fish and salt.

FIGURE A–5

The inhabitants of this land take each others' lives
And slaughter each other like cattle in an unheard of manner.
Like mindless and innocent animals, they destroy each other,
Then roast the flesh as their usual fare.

The second verse refers to the late-arriving Dutch, who established a worldwide trading empire by wresting lands from prior colonists. For a time, they held Brazil, Guiana, various Caribbean locations, and New Amsterdam on Manhattan Island. The Dutch East India Company, formed in 1602, took over, and held until modern times, the former Portuguese colonies of Ceylon (today's Sri Lanka), Sumatra, Borneo, Java, New Guinea, and the Spice Islands.

The other verses, setting out the artist's opinions, match the visual forms in the engraving. In the foreground of the illustration, a woman is shown riding an imaginary giant armadillo. She carries a bow, arrows, and a war ax. After having reviewed the earlier illustrations, you should be able to identify what she stands for in allegorical terms. Surrounding her are parrots from the New World and fat-tailed sheep and goats *(Capra Indica)* from the Old World. The goats are found in Asia. What does this indicate about Europeans confusing America with the Orient?

The last four lines refer to an action taking place in the far background. Natives with bows and arrows chase an animal. In front of them are cannibals. Why did the illustrator include the cannibals in the picture? Refer to Figure A–3. To one side, a major battle is taking place between Europeans and natives. The aboriginal people are armed with battle axes similar to the one held by *America*. The nationality of the Europeans, equipped with pikes and fire arms, is left vague, since they do not carry standards or flags.

Looking at the illustration and reading the accompanying verse, does the artist portray a favorable or unfavorable attitude toward the New World? How would you summarize his argument in a few words?

Figure A–6
America the Prodigal

This illustration was created by a Dutch engraver as the frontispiece for a seventeenth-century account of the New World. Its atmosphere is in strong contrast to Figure A–5. The topmost figure should be easy, once again, to identify as *America*. What elements of costume and appearance make this an allegorical personification? America is shown prodigally scattering gold coins and precious objects.

The two bearded men supporting her are obviously non-Amerindian. The European prototype of such statuary identifies the female figure with Venus, who rose from the sea on her shell. Recall the virginal moon goddess (in Figure A–1), with the presumed attributes of the New World. What does this tell us about lingering beliefs concerning the Western Hemisphere?

FIGURE A–6

The Amerindians wear varied clothes and headdresses, mostly fantastical. Did the illustrator make distinctions between residents of the New World? The light-skinned and dark-skinned figures present a mix of Aztec, Brazilian, and Floridian peoples, and the llama would refer to Peru. Two individuals in the foreground have baskets filled with produce and products. There is also a fat-tailed sheep, a traditional symbol of abundance. How do these details fit in with the central figure, who dispenses precious objects?

To the rear of the picture is a European-style fortification with cannons. A number of Europeans mingle with the natives. What is the attitude of the two groups toward one another? Do the Europeans threaten the natives, or vice versa? After reviewing the picture, compare its point of view with that expressed in Figure A–5.

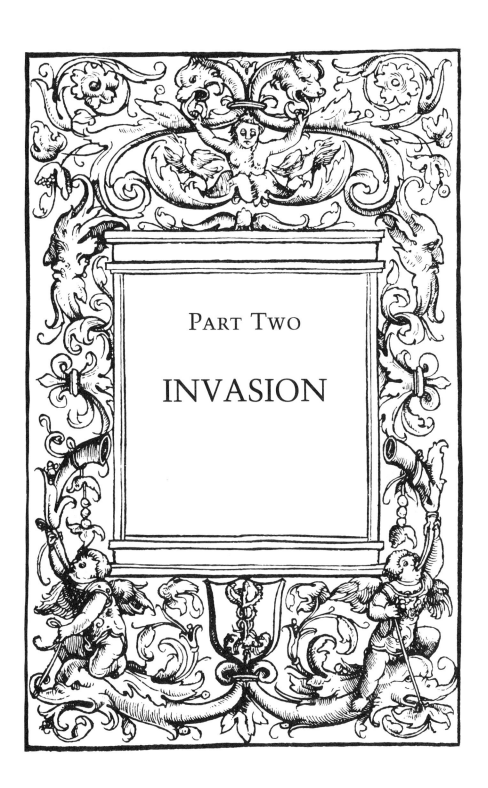

PART TWO

INVASION

NITIAL IMPRESSIONS
IN THE CARIBBEAN

First Voyage

This letter summarizing the first trip and its results, although not directly addressed to Ferdinand and Isabella, was intended for the monarchs to encourage them to fund a second voyage. Columbus characterized all the islanders he encountered in such a way as to convey to the king and queen that conquest would be easy. The size and wealth of the islands is exaggerated to make the most profound impact, although he clearly has not found sufficient sources of wealth to impress scoffers at the court. The letter created much excitement in Spain and the north of Italy, but translations only slowly spread the news to the rest of Europe, which proved at first not all that concerned.

"very many islands, inhabited by numberless people, . . ."

The sensational issue raised in the letter concerning people who did not wear clothes was profoundly interesting to Europeans. The elaborate costume worn by their elite in the sixteenth century was a prime indicator of rank. Not to wear the clothes appropriate to one's social standing—or none at all—indicated to the ruling group an unwillingness to accept subordination. Further, since the moment when Adam and Eve allegedly began to wear garments (or at least leaves), any people who went naked were outside moral law and to be condemned. On the other hand, there was a more favorable view that described people who did not wear clothes as innocent as humankind before the expulsion from the Garden of Eden in the biblical story.

As I know that it will please you that I have carried to completion the duty which I assumed, I decided to write you this letter to advise you of every single event and discovery of this voyage of ours. On the thirty-third day after I left [the Canaries], I reached the Indian Sea, there I found very many islands, inhabited by numberless people, of all of which I took possession without opposition in the name of our most fortunate king by making formal proclamation and raising standards; and to the first of them I gave the name of San Salvador [probably today's Watling's Island], the blessed Savior, through dependence on whose aid we reached both this

SOURCE *Epistola de Insulis Nuper Inventis,* trans. F. E. Robbins (Ann Arbor: University Microfilms, Inc., 1966), pp. 8–18. Reprinted by permission.

and the others. The Indians however call it Guanahaní. I gave each one of the others too a new name; to wit, one Santa María de la Concepción [Rum Cay], another Fernandina [Long Island], another Isabella [Fortunate/Crooked Islands], another Juana [Cuba], and I ordered similar names to be used for the rest.

When we first put in at the island which I have just said was named Juana, I proceeded along its shore westward a little way, and found it so large (for no end to it appeared) that I believed it to be no island but the continental province of Cathay [China]; without seeing, however, any towns or cities situated in its coastal parts except a few villages and rustic farms, with whose inhabitants I could not talk because they took to flight as soon as they saw us.

I went on further, thinking that I would find a city or some farmhouses. Finally, seeing that nothing new turned up, though we had gone far enough, and that this course was carrying us off to the north (a thing which I myself wanted to avoid, for winter prevailed on those lands, and it was my hope to hasten to the south) and since the winds too were favorable to our desires, I concluded that no other means of accomplishment offered, and thus reversing my course I returned to a certain harbor which I had marked and from that point sent ashore two men of our number to find out whether there was a king in that province, or any cities. These men proceeded afoot for three days and found countless people and inhabited places, but all small and without any government; and therefore they returned.

In the meantime I had already learned from some Indians whom I had taken aboard at this same place that this province was in fact an island; and so I went on toward the east, always skirting close to its shores, for 322 miles, where is the extremity of the island. From this point I observed another island to eastward, 54 miles from this island Juana, which I immediately called Hispaniola. I withdrew to it, and set my course along its northern coast, as I had at Juana, to the east for 564 miles.

The before-mentioned island Juana [Cuba] and the other islands of the region, too, are as fertile as they can be. This one is surrounded by harbors, numerous, very safe and broad, and not to be compared with any others that I have seen anywhere; many large, wholesome rivers flow through this land; and there are also many very lofty mountains in it. All these islands are most beautiful and distinguished by various forms; one can travel through them, and they are full of trees of the greatest variety, which brush at the stars; and I believe they never lose their foliage. At any rate, I found them as green and beautiful as they usually are in the month of May in Spain; some of them were in bloom, some loaded with fruit, some flourished in one state, others in the other, each according to its kind; the nightingale was singing and there were countless other birds of many kinds in the month of November when I myself was making my way through them. There are furthermore, in the before-mentioned island Juana, seven or eight kinds of palm trees, which easily surpass ours in height and beauty, as do all the other trees, grasses, and fruits. There are also remarkable pines, vast fields and meadows, many kinds of birds, many kinds of honey, and many kinds of metals, except iron.

There are moreover in that island which I said above was called Hispaniola fine, high mountains, broad stretches of country, forests, and extremely fruitful fields excellently adapted for sowing, grazing, and building dwelling houses. The convenience and superiority of the harbors in this island and its wealth in rivers, joined with wholesomeness for man, is such as to surpass belief unless one has seen them. The trees, coverage, and fruits of this island are very different from those of Juana. Besides, this Hispaniola is rich in various kinds of spice and in gold and in mines, and its inhabitants (and those of all the others which I saw, and of which I have knowledge) of either sex always go as naked as when they were born, except some women who cover their private parts with a leaf or a branch of some sort, or with a skirt of cotton which they themselves prepare for the purpose.

They all of them lack, as I said above, iron of whatever kind, as well as arms, for these are unknown to them; nor are they fitted for weapons, not because of any bodily deformity, for they are well built, but in that they are timid and fearful. However, instead of arms they carry reeds baked in the sun, in the roots of which they fasten a sort of spearhead made of dry wood and sharpened to a point. And they do not dare to use these at close quarters; for it often happened that when I had sent two or three of my men to certain farmhouses to talk with their inhabitants a closely packed body of Indians would come out and when they saw our men approach they would quickly take flight, children deserted by father and vice versa; and that too not that any hurt or injury had been brought upon a single one of them; on the contrary, whenever I approached any of them and whenever I could talk with any of them I was generous in giving them whatever I had, cloth and very many other things, without any return being made to me; but they are naturally fearful and timid.

However when they see that they are safe and all fear has been dispelled they are exceedingly straightforward and trustworthy and most liberal with all that they have; none of them denies to the asker anything that he possesses; on the contrary they themselves invite us to ask for it. They exhibit great affection to all and always give much for little, content with very little or nothing in return. However I forbade such insignificant and valueless things to be given to them, as pieces of platters, dishes, and glass, or again nails and lace points [for clipping hose to garments], though if they could acquire such it seemed to them that they possessed the most beautiful trinkets in the world. For it happened that one sailor got in return for one lace point a weight of gold equivalent to three golden *castellanos*, and similarly others in exchange for other things of slighter value; especially in exchange for brand-new *blancas*, certain gold coins, to secure which they would give whatever the seller asks, for example, an ounce and a half or two ounces of gold, or thirty or forty [pounds] of cotton by weight, which they themselves had spun; likewise they bought pieces of hoops, pots, pitchers, and jars for cotton and gold, like dumb beasts. I forbade this, because it was clearly unjust, and gave them free many pretty and acceptable objects that I had brought with me, in order more easily to win them over to me, and that they might become Christians, and be inclined to love our King and Queen and Prince and all the peoples of Spain, and to make them diligent to seek out and accumulate and exchange with us the articles in which they abound and which we greatly need.

They know nothing of idolatry; on the contrary they confidently believe that all might, all power, all good things, in fact, are in the heavens; they thought that I too had descended thence with these ships and sailors, and in that opinion I was received everywhere after they had rid themselves of fear. Nor are they slow or ignorant; on the contrary, they are of the highest and keenest wit; and the men who navigate that sea give an admirable account of each detail; but they have never seen men wearing clothes, or ships of this sort. As soon as I came to that sea I forcibly seized some Indians from the first island, so that they might learn from us and similarly teach us the things of which they had knowledge in those parts; and it came out just as I had hoped; for we quickly taught them, and then they us, by gestures and signs; finally they understood by means of words, and it paid us well to have them. The ones who now go with me persist in the belief that I leaped down out of the skies, although they have associated with us for a long time and are still doing so today; and they were the first to announce that fact wherever we landed, some of them calling out loudly to the others, "Come, come, and you will see the men from heaven." And so women as well as men, children and grown people, youths and old men, laying aside the fear they had conceived shortly before, vied with each other in coming to look at us, the great crowd of them clogging the road, some bringing food, others drink, with the greatest manifestation of affection and unbelievable good will.

Each island possesses many canoes of solid wood, and though they are narrow, nevertheless in length and shape they are like our double-banked galleys, but faster. They are steered with oars alone. Some of these are large, some small, some of medium size; a considerable number however are larger than the galley which is rowed by eighteen benches. With these they cross to all the islands, which are innumerable, and with them they ply their trade, and commerce is carried out between them. I saw some of these galleys or canoes which carried seventy or eighty oarsmen.

In all the islands there is no difference in the appearance of the people, nor in their habits or language; on the contrary, they all understand each other, which circumstance is most useful to that end which I think our most serene sovereigns especially desire, namely, their conversion to the holy faith of Christ, to which indeed as far as I could see they are readily submissive and inclined.

I have told how I sailed along the island of Juana on a straight course from west to east 322 miles; from this voyage and the length of the course I can say that this Juana is larger than England and Scotland together [an exaggeration]; for beyond the aforesaid 322 miles, in the western part, there are two more provinces which I did not visit, one of which the Indians call Anan, whose inhabitants are born with tails. These provinces extend to a length of 180 miles, as I have found out from these Indians whom I am bringing with me, who are well acquainted with all these islands.

The circumference of Hispaniola, indeed, is more than all Spain from Catalonia to Fuenterrabia. And this is easily proved by this fact, that the one of its four sides which I myself traversed on a straight course from west to east measures 540 miles. We should seek possession of this island and once gained it is not to be thrown away; for although, as I said, I formally took possession of all the others in the name of our invincible King and their sovereignty is entirely committed to that said King, nevertheless in this island I took possession in a special way of a certain large village in a more favorable situation, suitable for all sorts of gain and trade, to which I gave the name Navidad del Señor; and I gave orders to erect a fort there at once. This should by now be built, and in it I left behind the men who seemed necessary with all kinds of arms and suitable food for more than a year; furthermore, one caravel [the wrecked *Santa María*], and for the construction of others men skilled in this art as well as in others; and, besides, an unbelievable goodwill and friendship on the part of the king of that island toward the men. For all those peoples are so gentle and kind that the aforesaid king took pride in my being called his brother. Even if they should change their minds and want to injure the men who stayed in the fort they cannot, since they have no arms, go naked, and are extremely timid; and so if our men only hold the said fort they can hold the whole island, with no hazard on the part of the people to threaten them as long as they do not depart from the laws and government which I gave them.

In all those islands, as I understood it, each man is content with only one wife, except the princes or kings, who may have twenty. The women seem to do more work than the men. I could not clearly make out whether they have private property, for I noted that what an individual had he shared with others, especially food, meats, and the like. I did not find any monsters among them, as many expected, but men of great dignity and kindliness. Nor are they black, like the Negroes; they have long, straight hair; they do not live where the heat of the sun's rays shines forth; for the strength of the sun is very great here, since apparently it is only twenty-six degrees from the equator. On the mountain peaks extreme cold reigns, but this the Indians mitigate both by being used to the region and by the aid of very hot foods upon which they dine often and luxuriously.

And so I did not see any monsters, nor do I have knowledge of them anywhere with the exception of a certain island called Charis [probably today's Puerto Rico], which is the second as you sail from Spain toward India and which a tribe inhabits that is held by its neighbors to be extremely savage. These feed on human flesh. The aforesaid have many kinds of galleys in which they cross to all the Indian islands, rob, and steal all they can. They differ in no respect from the others, except that in feminine fashion they wear their hair long; and they use bows and arrows with shafts of reeds fitted as we said at the thicker end with sharpened arrowheads. On that account they are held to be savage, and the other Indians are afflicted with constant fear of them, but I do not rate them any more highly than the rest. These are the ones who cohabit with certain women who are the only inhabitants of the island of Mateunin [Martinique], which is the first encountered in the passage from Spain toward India. These women moreover, do not occupy themselves with any of the work that properly belongs to their sex, for they use bows and arrows just as I related of their husbands; they protect themselves with copper plates of which there is an ample supply in their land. They assure me that there is another island larger than the above-mentioned Hispaniola; its inhabitants are hairless, and it abounds in gold more than all the others. I am bringing with me men from this island and the others that I saw who bear testimony to what I have said.

Finally, to compress into a few words the advantage and profit of our journey hence and our speedy return, I make this promise, that supported by only small aid from them I will give our invincible sovereigns as much gold as they need, as much spices, cotton, and the mastic, which is found only in Chios [a Genoese possession], as much of the wood of the aloe, as many slaves to serve as sailors as their Majesties wish to demand; furthermore, rhubarb and other kinds of spices which I suppose those whom I left in the before-mentioned fort have already discovered and will discover, since indeed I lingered nowhere longer than the winds compelled, except at the village of Navidad while I took care to establish the fort and to make all safe. Though these things are great and unheard of, nevertheless they would have been much greater if the ships had served me as they reasonably should.

Indeed this outcome was manifold and marvelous, and fitting not to my own claims to merit, but rather to the holy Christian faith and the piety and religion of our sovereigns, for what the human mind could not comprehend, that the divine mind has granted to men. For God is accustomed to listen to his servants, and to those who love his commands, even in impossible circumstances, as has happened to us in the present instance, for we have succeeded in that to which hitherto mortal powers have in no wise attained. For if others have written or spoken of these islands, they have all done so by indirection and guesses; no one claims to have seen them, whence it seemed to be almost a fable. Therefore let the King and Queen, the Prince, their happy realms, and all other provinces of Christendom give thanks to the Savior, our Lord Jesus Christ, who has granted us so great a victory and reward; let processions be celebrated; let solemn holy rites be performed; and let the churches be decked with festival branches; let Christ rejoice on earth as He does in heaven when He foresees that so many souls of peoples hitherto lost are to be saved. Let us too rejoice, both for the exaltation of our faith and for the increase in temporal goods in which not only Spain but all

Christendom together are to share. As these things were done, so have they been briefly narrated. Farewell.

21

Columbus Observes the Islanders

The author of this selection is an exile from Eastern Europe, whose *The Conquest of America: The Question of the Other* was published in France in 1982. He is concerned with giving the language used by the conquerors, from Columbus to Cortés, an intensive reading. His book is not so much a study of history as it is a meditation on the relations between cultures alien to one another, mediated by communication. Todorov develops the concept that the discursive practices of the invaders permitted them to prevail; that is, by losing control of communications, the Amerindians were condemned to their fate. In taking this stance, he has been criticized for subtly underplaying the impact of advanced technology and superior military tactics. Todorov cannot be faulted, however, for demonstrating that a microscopic reading of texts can yield stimulating results.

> *"a part of the landscape."*

The author has an easily discernible stance regarding the treatment Columbus accorded the peoples he encountered, although the issue of making value judgments in history is perhaps cloudier than it appears to Todorov. Columbus decided, for example, that a quick profit might be earned by enslaving the "Caribs," whom he labeled "idolaters" suitable for captivity. On the second voyage, he shipped men and women, of which the majority died, to the slave market in Seville. However ugly this matter (and it is) to modern sensibilities, one could argue that Columbus, in his actions and attitudes, was a man of his day, no worse than others who left their homes to make their fortune across the sea.

Columbus speaks about the men he sees only because they too, after all, constitute a part of the landscape. His allusions to the inhabitants of the islands always occur amid his notations concerning nature, somewhere between birds and trees. "In the interior of the lands, there are many mines of metal and countless inhabitants." "Hitherto,

SOURCE Tzvetan Todorov, *The Conquest of America. The Question of the Other* (New York: Harper & Row, 1984), pp. 34–48, passim. Most citations eliminated. Reprinted by permission.

137

things had gone better and better for him, in that he had discovered so many lands as well as woods, plants, fruits and flowers as well as the people." "The roots of this place are as thick as a man's legs, and all the people, he says, were strong and brave." [W]e readily see how the inhabitants are introduced, by means of a comparison necessary to describe the roots. "Here, they observed that the married women wore clouts of cotton, but the wenches nothing, save for a few who were already eighteen years old. There were also dogs, mastiffs and terriers. They found as well a man who had in his nose a gold stud the size of half a *castellano*": this allusion to the dogs among the remarks on the women and the men indicates nicely the scale on which the latter will be assessed. . . .

Two features of the Indians seem, at first sight, less predictable than the rest: their "generosity" and their "cowardice"; but as we read on in Columbus's descriptions, we perceive that these assertions tell us more about Columbus than about the Indians. Lacking words, Indians and Spaniards exchange, at the first meeting, various small objects; and Columbus unceasingly praises the generosity of the Indians, who give everything for nothing; it sometimes borders, he decides, on stupidity: why do they value a piece of glass quite as much as a coin, and a worthless piece of small change as much as a gold piece? "I have given," he writes, "many other things of slight value from which they took great pleasure." "All that they have they give for any trifle we offer them, so that they take in exchange pieces of crockery and fragments of glass goblets." "For anything at all we give them, without ever saying it is too little, they immediately give whatever they possess." "Whether it is a thing of value or a thing of little cost, whatever the object then given them in exchange and whatever it is worth, they are pleased." Nor more than in the case of languages does Columbus understand that values are conventional, that gold is not more precious than glass "in itself," but only in the European system of exchange. Hence, when he concludes this description of the exchanges by saying: "Even bits of broken cask-hoops they took in exchange for whatever they had, like beasts!" we have the impression that in this case it is Columbus who is worthy of the comparison: a different system of exchange is for him equivalent to the absence of system, from which he infers the bestial character of the Indians.

The feeling of superiority engenders a protectionist behavior: Columbus tells us that he forbids his sailors to make a swap he regards as scandalous. Yet we see Columbus himself offering preposterous presents, which are associated in our mind today with "savages," but which Columbus is the first to have taught them to admire and demand. "I sent for him and gave him a red cap, some little green glass beads which I attached to his arm, and two hawk's bells which I hung from his ears." "I gave him a very fine amber necklace which I was wearing round my neck, a pair of red slippers and a bottle of orange-flower water. He was so pleased with this that it was a wonder." . . . "The lord now wore a shirt and gloves which the Admiral had given him." We understand that Columbus is shocked by the other's nakedness, but are the gloves, the red hat, and the slippers, in these circumstances, presents really more useful than the broken glass goblets? The Indian chiefs, in any case, can henceforth pay him a visit dressed. Subsequently we see that the Indians find other uses for the Spanish gifts, without their utility being demonstrated for all that. "Since they had no clothes, the people wondered what the needles could be used for, but the Spaniards satisfied their ingenuous curiosity, for they showed by signs that the needles serve to remove the thorns and splinters which often penetrate their skin, or else to pick their teeth; hence they began to prize them highly" (Peter Martyr, I, 8).

On the basis of these observations and these exchanges Columbus will declare the Indians the most generous people in the world, thereby making an important contribution to the myth of the noble savage. "They are without covetousness of another man's goods." "They are to such a degree lacking in artifice and so generous with what they possess, that no man would believe it unless he had seen such a thing." "And let it not be said, the Admiral said, that they give liberally only because what they gave was of little worth, for those who gave pieces of gold and those who gave a water calabash acted in the same way and just as liberally. And it is an easy thing," he adds, "to know, when a thing is given, that it is given with a free heart." . . .

The thing is in fact less easy than it appears. Columbus has a presentiment of this when, in his letter to Santangel, he recapitulates his experience: "I could not learn if they possess private property, but I seemed to discern that all owned a share of what one of them owned, and particularly with regard to victuals." . . . Would a different relation to private property provide an explanation of this "generous" behavior? His son Fernando testifies as much, in relating an episode of the second voyage. "Certain Indies which the Admiral had brought from Isabella went into those cabins [which belonged to the local Indians] and made use of whatever they pleased; the owners gave no sign of displeasure, as if everything they owned were common property. The people, believing that we had the same custom, went at first among the Christians and took whatever they pleased; but they swiftly discovered their mistake." Columbus thus forgets his own perception, and soon after declares that the Indians, far from being generous, are all thieves (a reversal parallel to the one that transforms them from the best men in the world into violent savages); thereby he imposes cruel punishments upon them, the same then in effect in Spain: "As on that voyage I made to Cibao, when it happened that some Indian stole something or other, if you discover that some among them steal, you must punish them by cutting off nose and ears, for those are the parts of the body which cannot be concealed." . . .

Columbus's attitude with regard to the Indians is based on his perception of them. We can distinguish here two component parts, which we shall find again in the following century and, in practice, down to our own day in every colonist in his relations to the colonized; we have already observed these two attitudes in germ in Columbus's report concerning the other's language. Either he conceives the Indians (though without using these words) as human beings altogether, having the same rights as himself; but then he sees them not only as equals but also as identical, and this behavior leads to assimilationism, the projection of his own values on the others. Or else he starts from the difference, but the latter is immediately translated into terms of superiority and inferiority (in his case, obviously, it is the Indians who are inferior). What is denied is the existence of a human substance truly other, something capable of being not merely an imperfect state of oneself. These two elementary figures of the experience of alterity are both grounded in egocentrism, in the identification of our own values with values in general, of our *I* with the universe—in the conviction that the world is one.

On one hand, then, Columbus wants the Indians to be like himself, and like the Spaniards. He is an assimilationist in an unconscious and naive fashion; his sympathy for the Indians is "naturally" translated into the desire to see them adopt his own customs. He decides to take several Indians back to Spain in order that "upon their return they might be the interpreters of the Christians and might adopt our customs and our faith." . . . They are disposed, he also says, "to be made to build cities, to be taught to wear clothes, and to adopt our customs." . . . "Your Highnesses may have great joy of them, for soon you will have made them into Christians and will have instructed them in the good manners of your kingdoms." . . . There is never a justification of this desire to make the Indians adopt the Spanish customs; its rightness is self-evident. . . .

"My desire," Columbus writes during the first voyage, "was to pass by no single island without taking possession of it." [O]n occasion, he even offers an island here and there to one of his companions. At the beginning, the Indians must not have understood much about the ceremonies Columbus and his notaries were performing. But when it became apparent what they were doing, the Indians did not seem to be especially enthusiastic. In the course of the fourth voyage, the following episode occurs: "I built here a village and gave many presents to the *quibian*—for so they call the lord of this land—[gloves? a red hat? Columbus does not tell us] but I knew well that this peace would not last. These are, indeed, very wild people [we may translate: unwilling to submit to the Spaniards], and my men are very importunate; finally I took possession of lands belonging to this *quibian* [second half of the exchange: one gives gloves, one takes lands]. As soon as he saw the houses we had built and a lively trade going on, he determined to burn everything and to kill us all." The sequel of this story is even more sinister. The Spaniards manage to capture the *quibian*'s family as hostages; several of the Indians succeed in escaping nonetheless. "The remaining prisoners were seized with despair, for they had not escaped with their comrades, and it was discovered the next morning that they had hanged themselves from the bridge-poles, with some ropes they had managed to find there, bending their knees to do so, for otherwise there was not enough room for them to hang themselves properly." Ferdinand, Columbus's son, who reports this episode, was present at it; he was only fourteen years old at the time, and we may imagine that the reaction which follows was at least as much his father's as his own: "For those of us who were on board our ship, their death was not a great loss, but it seriously aggravated the situation of our men on land; the *quibian* would have been delighted to make peace in exchange for his children, but now that we had no hostages remaining, there was every reason to fear that he would wage war even more cruelly against our village."

Whereupon war replaces peace; but we may assume that Columbus had never entirely overlooked this means of expansion, since from the first voyage he nurses a special project: "I set out this morning," he notes on October 14, 1492, "in search of a place where a fortress might be built." "Because there is a rocky cape on rather high ground, one might well build a fortress here." We know that he will fulfill this dream after his ship is wrecked, and that he will leave his men here. But is not the fortress, even if it proves rather ineffectual, already one step toward war, hence toward submission and inequality?

Thus, by gradual stages, Columbus will shift from assimilationism, which implied an equality of principle, to an ideology of enslavement, and hence to the assertion of the Indians' inferiority. We could already guess this from several summary judgments appearing in the first contacts. "They would make good and industrious servants." "They are fit to be ruled." In order to remain consistent, Columbus establishes subtle distinctions between innocent, potentially Christian Indians and idolatrous Indians, practicing cannibalism; and between pacific Indians (submitting to his power) and bellicose Indians who thereby deserve to be punished; but the important thing is that those who are not already Christians can only be slaves: there is no middle path. Hence he foresees that the ships that transport herds of cattle from Europe to America will be loaded with slaves on the return journey, in order to keep them from remaining empty and until gold is found in sufficient quantities, the equivalence implicitly established between beasts and men not being gratuitous, of course. "The conveyors could be paid in cannibal slaves, fierce but well-made fellows of good understanding, which men, wrested from their inhumanity, will be, we believe, the best slaves that ever were."

The Spanish sovereigns do not accept this suggestion of Columbus's; they prefer to have vassals, not slaves—subjects capable of paying taxes rather than belonging to a third party; but Columbus nonetheless does not abandon his project, and writes again in September 1498: "From here one might send, in the name of the Holy Trinity, as many slaves as could be sold, as well as a quantity of Brazil [timber]. If the information I have is correct, it appears that we could sell four thousand slaves, who might be worth twenty millions and more." The displacements might raise some problems at the beginning, but these will quickly be solved. "It is true that many of them die now; but this will not always be so. The Negroes and the Canarians had begun in the same fashion." This is indeed the meaning of his government of the island of Hispaniola, and another letter to the sovereigns, dated October 1498, is summarized thus by Las Casas: "In all that he says, there seems to emerge the fact that the profit he sought to bestow upon the Spaniards who were to be left in the place consisted in the slaves he would give them to be sold in Castile." In Columbus's mind, the propagation of the faith and the submission to slavery are indissolubly linked.

Michele de Cuneo, a member of the second expedition, has left one of the rare accounts describing in detail how the slave trade functioned at its inception; his narrative permits us no illusions as to how the Indians were perceived. "When our caravels . . . were to leave for Spain, we gathered in our settlement one thousand six hundred male and female persons of these Indians, and of these we embarked in our caravels on February 17, 1495, five hundred fifty souls among the healthiest males and females. For those who remained, we let it be known in the vicinity that anyone who wanted to take some of them could do so, to the amount desired; which was done. And when each man was thus provided with slaves, there still remained about four hundred, to whom permission was granted to go where they wished. Among them were many women with children still at suck. Since they were afraid that we might return to capture them once again, and in order to escape us the better, they left their children anywhere on the ground and began to flee like desperate creatures; and some fled so far that they found themselves at seven or eight days' distance from our community at Isabella, beyond the mountains and across enormous rivers; consequently they will henceforth be captured only with great difficulty." Such is the beginning of the operation; here now is the conclusion: "But when we reached the waters off Spain, around two hundred of these Indians died, I believe because of the unaccustomed air, which is colder than theirs. We cast them into the sea. . . . We disembarked all the slaves, half of whom were sick."

QUESTIONS

1. In what ways does Columbus admire the peoples he encountered? What does he dislike about them?
2. How can Columbus be so confident about the customs and beliefs of the natives when he has so imperfect a grasp of their languages?
3. Where does Columbus say the profit will be to the monarchs, since he found only bits of gold, unknown spices, no merchants, and no rich cities?
4. What does Todorov mean when he writes that the inhabitants "constitute a part of the landscape" to Columbus?
5. Was the exchange of gifts between the islanders and the Europeans done on an equal basis?
6. Why did Columbus decide to enslave the islanders?

22

Myths from the Islands

After Columbus made his fateful decision, in February 1494, to become a slaver, the Taínos of eastern Cuba realized that friendship and passivity were no longer appropriate responses. A month later, they attacked the Magdalena settlement and then Fort St. Thomas. Routing the islanders in March after a fierce combat at the Vega Real, Columbus decided he would have to learn more about the population if he were to control them. He asked one of the five clerics who had come along on the second voyage, the Catalan missionary Ramón Pané, to look into their belief structure. The recognition on Columbus's part that the islanders did indeed have a religion differs considerably from the view he expressed immediately after his first voyage (Document 20).

> *"so much water came from that gourd that it covered the whole earth . . ."*

Pané had a sufficient grasp of the language that, with the help of a young native convert, he felt he comprehended at least some of the subtler points of the religion after two years of conversations. Since the humble friar had no scholarly pretensions, there is a certain objectivity in his *Relación* not to be found in confident narratives by later observers who never felt the need to visit the New World. His refreshing modesty in the face of the unknown led him to write at one point, "I think I am putting first what should be last, and the last first."

The core of the islanders' religion centered on the cult of *cemies*, figures in animal and human form or in three-pointed shapes, formed from stone, wood, clay, and cotton. The objects contained spiritual power, which worshippers believed they could draw on with the figures' aid. The unhappy consequences of a lack of mutual understanding by the Christians and the islanders of each other's religious principles is evident in an incident that would be richly comic save for the results. When the Spanish gave the Taínos crucifixes and statues of the Virgin, the Taínos added these objects to their store of *cemies*. In keeping with their agrarian cult of fertility, they urinated on the sacred objects and buried them in fields to ensure bountiful crops. The Spanish thought this blasphemy and so executed the offenders.

A selection of myths from Pané's investigations are presented here in poetic form and compared to counterparts in other religions. The complexity of these myths require that they be read several times before their meaning can be grasped.

The Creation Story

The Banishment of Yayael

There was a man called Yaya, SPIRIT OF SPIRITS,
  and no one knew his name.
His son was named Yayael, [which means,] "Son of Yaya."
This Yayael was banished for wanting to kill his father.
Thus he was banished for four months.
Afterwards his father killed him, put his bones in a gourd
  and hung it from the roof of his house
  where it hung for some time.
It came to pass that one day, desiring to see his son,
  Yaya said to his wife, "I want to see our son Yayael."
This made her happy, and taking down the gourd, she turned
  it over to see the bones of their son.
From it gushed forth many fish, big and small.
Seeing that these bones had been turned into fishes,
  they decided to eat them.

T he Taíno name of the Supreme Being is "Yaya," which Arrom has translated as "Spirit of Spirits." This would appear to be a form of the superlative, indicating an exceptional quality for Yaya. But when [Father Ramón] Pané adds "no one knew his name," he indicates that the proper name is also a description of the spirit's preeminence in Taíno religion. The inability to "know the name" is equivalent to stating omnipotence. Similar reasoning has been employed in world religions. For example, because the name revealed to Moses (Ex. 3:13) was translated as "I Am Who Am," the scholastic theologians of the Judeo-Christian tradition gave the name of the biblical Yahweh a metaphysical interpretation. For these theologians, the attribution of an unknown name became metaphysical language. To belong only to oneself, they said, was equivalent to the omnipotence of a spirit not subject to the control of any other reality: in short, the Supreme Being. If the same metaphysical interpretation is lent to the opening verses of the Taíno creation story, they are at once the simplest and the most profound of the mythological statements of Taíno religion.

The opening comments by Pané on the Taíno concept of the Supreme Being echo medieval theology. The friar notes that the Taínos believe god "is in heaven and is immortal and that no one can see it and that it has a mother, but no beginning." . . .

SOURCE *Cave of the Jagua. The Mythological World of the Tainos*, pp. 88–176, passim by A. M. Stevens-Arroyo, copyright © 1988. Reprinted with permission of University of New Mexico Press.

The "High God"

Interpreting Pané's account from the perspective of Comparative Religions, I conclude that the Taínos believed one spiritual being ranked above all others. Yaya was superior to all other beings and knowable principally in his attribute of superlativeness. Whether or not he was also invisible, his power dominated all spiritual forces. In the language of Comparative Religions, Yaya is a "high god." . . .

The gourd and fish in the myth both have dual meanings to dramatize the primordial distance between a primitive state of nature and the acquired human gifts of religious understanding. But the complex social and ecological realities in the myth also have an emotional or psychological application. Indeed, the gourd and fish acquire multiple meanings because of the emotions of Yaya and his wife. In the first instance, the parents desire to see their dead son, a taboo; in the second, they have a natural desire to eat the fish they discover in the gourd. These impulses are parallel to the wishes of Yayael, who first wanted to supplant his father in a competition for natural resources and second, to return to Yaya's house in violation of the banishment taboo. Whether preceding or following the violation of a taboo, the Taínos seem to recognize that emotion accompanies human behavior. Sin accordingly admits of psychological shadings, and guilt varies in degree. Clearly, the Taíno myth invites examination with the Freudian notion that parricide [murder of a parent] and cannibalism represent aggression.

But the emotional or psychic dimension of the myth is not restricted to the anthropomorphic personages of father and son. The Taínos also had an affective link to the fish. Anyone who has ever fished knows that a catch should not be taken for granted. Fish often "outsmart" fishermen. These creatures move instinctively in accordance with time, tide, and weather, while human beings can only hope to learn about such things with much patience and experience. In a sense, fish can think. For religious believers like the Taínos, this uncanny ability of such creatures was a manifestation of the numinous. The search for fish, their capture and ingestion, would thus represent a form of communion with the source of all life. Indeed, the Aztecs personified maize [corn] in somewhat the same way, perceiving its harvest and consumption as a human repetition of numinous [divine] order.

Now that the symbols of this Taíno myth have been individually examined, my interpretation may be summarized. I believe the myth explains the religious dimensions of tribal fissure, a social phenomenon that is intimately wedded to the migration of the Taínos from the Orinoco basin and throughout the Caribbean islands. The fissure of the group is necessary to prevent a fatal competition for scant resources between members of the same people. Yayael's attempt to kill his father describes a paradigmatic symbol for the refusal to migrate. Banishment is the social control utilized by the father in order to force his son to bring about fissure. Since the return of Yayael is met with his execution, the message of the myth would seem to be that no matter how long one stays away, once banished, any returning exile is met with the most drastic punishment.

A second level of meaning is a political one. The father represents *cacical* authority; the son, the *naboria*. Since the harvesting economy of the Taínos brought increased importance to certain chiefdoms and an emerging tribal–tributory system, Yaya also represents the prerogatives of a major *cacique* over lesser chiefs, symbolized in Yayael.

Finally, one must examine the subjective and emotional content of the myth. Yayael's aggressive feelings against his father are based on jealousy over rights of farming and fishing. The son's conspiracy against human authority results in banishment; the banishment in turn brings apostasy from religious authority; the return from exile ends in death. The mounting psychic rebelliousness of Yayael builds into hatred and destruction. His sins are lack of love and devotion.

At first glance, the punishment of the parents—their desire to eat the fish, or their transformed son—may seem a minor inconvenience when compared to the mandated execution of Yayael. While the son paid with his life for his indiscretion, the parents seem to get off rather lightly. But if the desire to eat fish is a symbol for cannibalism, collective self-destruction by overpopulation and decimation of the food chain, the punishment of the parents is strikingly severe.

The desires of Yaya and his wife to see the son again describe the negative effects of fissure upon those who are left behind. Even though the banishment and eventual punishment are necessary, they still produce conflicting feelings in the father and mother. Their desire to see the banished or slain child militates against the absoluteness of ostracism. Their "sins" parallel those of Yayael. The son is driven by antagonism to seek to replace his father; the parents are drawn by love to be reunited with their son. In both cases, the society cannot bear such naked emotion. . . .

The Origin of the Sea

Deminán and the Great Flood

[It is said that] one day, when Yaya had gone to his *conucos*,
    [which means,] "the lands that were his inheritance,"
    four sons came forth from one woman,
    who is named Itiba Cahubaba, THE BLEEDING ANCIENT ONE.
All came from the one womb and all were twins.
After dying in childbirth, the woman was cut open
    and they took out these four children.
The first taken out was *caracaracol*,
    [which means,] "The Scabby One."
Caracaracol had "Deminán" for his name;
    the others did not have a name.

And while they were eating, they sensed that Yaya
    was returning from his lands.
While trying in their haste to hang up the gourd,
    they did not put it up securely,
    so that it fell to the ground and broke apart.
[It is said that] so much water came from that gourd that it
    covered the whole earth and from it came many fish.
[It is said that] this is how the sea took its origin.

Relation to the First Genesis Myth

The symbols of the fish and gourd bind this version of creation to the previous one. But there are significant differences. Only Yaya with his house and hanging gourd are the same: the woman is never identified as his wife, as in the first version. Correspondingly, the four children are not said to be Yaya's sons. Perhaps because some of the elements concerning the fish and gourd paralleled the description in the first version of creation, Pané omitted details of what the twins were eating and how they came across the gourd. . . .

Pané affirms the importance of the flood that is produced by the broken gourd when he states that "This is how the sea took its origin." As in the first account, fish appear with the broken gourd, but their destination is clearly stated here as the sea that covers the whole earth. But this flood is not planned; it just "happens." Impersonal forces, resulting from carelessness in hanging up the gourd, rather than conscious human motivation produces it. The uncontrollable flood sweeps the brothers away from the lands of Yaya's inheritance and toward new shores. Not only are the brothers carried along, so too is the broken gourd and the fish who were inside. . . .

I suggest that the broken gourd becomes two flooded canoes, bringing the brothers on a journey from Yaya's spirit home to earth. In this journey they follow the fish, much as would be expected of fishermen. This flood links the food-chain theme to the fate of the brothers. In the first myth, fish intelligence was caused by generation from Yayael's bones. Here, the innocent backwardness of the four brothers puts them into a situation where they must imitate fish to survive. As children without kin, little more could be expected from them. Fortunately, their remaining travels help them attain the gifts of culture. . . . There is a symmetry between what happens to fish at one end of the food chain and to humans at the other. The circle of life energy established in the first Taíno genesis myth is closed by this second account. Fish took their origins from the same mythic home of Yaya as humans; now the two are inseparably bound together on the earth and its seas. The second myth tells us that because of the flood, the distance between origins and ordinary human experience has grown. Intuitive communication with fish is no longer natural, and must be learned like the skills of riding a canoe and catching fish. Fortunately, the flood has removed the fish from the territorial claim of Yaya. Although the four twin brothers are on their own, the fish companions may be eaten because they no longer would be stolen from kin. The fish supplant direct communication with the numinous, because, in fact, they are symbols for the preordained circle of life forces. But as living creatures swimming in the sea, the fish are a step removed from the bones in the gourd. Before the origin (as Yayael's bones) can be ritually evoked, the art of fishing must be mastered. . . .

Seasonal Fertility and Women

In Europe, there is a noticeable change in the seasons through the progression of winter, fall, summer, and spring, and often the telluric [proceeding from the earth] principle of life was believed to disappear. The ancient Greeks developed a myth concerning the separation of Demeter from her daughter Persophone, who was whisked away to the underworld. The myth literally sent feminine fertility "to hell" until the springtime. In Egypt, Isis [ancient mother goddess] had to await the annual regeneration of the Nile in order to reacquire her fertility.

The Taínos shared these notions of femininity and its correspondence with natural processes. But the Caribbean basin knows only slight temperature changes throughout the year, so that telluric fertility cannot be said to "die" in quite the same way as in Europe. Although the earth of the Caribbean islands is always receptive to planting because of climatic warmth, however, there is a need to observe periodic sowing and harvests if the soil is not to be depleted. Thus, Taíno mythology can be expected to explain both fertility and periodicity.

The following episode from Pané's account links seasonal fertility and femininity. The mastery of natural rhythms is placed within the domain of the hero, Guahayona. It is an attainable skill, rather than a birthright, since, unlike Deminán to whom all things were given, Guayahona must create his own opportunities. To achieve his wisdom, the hero exploits cleverness, half-truth, deception, and betrayal.

The Flight of the Güeyo Women

He said to the women, "Leave behind your husbands and let us go
    to other lands and carry off much *güeyo*.
Leave your children and let us take only the herb with us and
    later on we shall return for them."
Guahayona, OUR PRIDE, left with all the women and he went
    searching for other lands.
He came to Matininó, NO FATHERS,
    where he soon left the women behind,
    and he went off to another region called Guanín.
He had left the small children near a brook.

Later, when they began to suffer hunger pains, [it is said that]
     they wept and cried out for their mothers who had gone off.
The fathers were not able to help their children who cried out in
     hunger for their mothers, saying, "mama" trying to speak, but
     really asking for the breast.
Thus they cried out, saying *"toa, toa"* asking to be nursed,
and while they behaved as someone asking for things with deep
     desire and in a great voice, they were transformed into
     small, froglike animals, [called] *"tona"* because they had
     cried out for nursing.
THE CHILDREN WERE TURNED INTO FROGS,
AND FROM THAT TIME ON THE FROG WAS HELD TO BE
     THE VOICE OF SPRINGTIME.
In this way all the men were left without women.

Guahayona tempts the women to steal *güeyo* [salty-tasting ashes from a species of algae], thus preventing its mixture with green chewing tobacco. Without *güeyo*, the tobacco loses some of its shamanistic [magical healing] qualities. . . . The myth establishes a logical link between tobacco without *güeyo* and the separation of the sexes. Men and women belong together in order to achieve fertility, just as *güeyo* and tobacco must be joined to produce the shamanistic *guanguayo*. . . . In this episode, several levels of meaning are kept in rigorously logical parallel, so that the myth simultaneously explains several important phenomena and joins nature and human behavior into an organic totality. . . .

Two islands provide loci for the mythological events. Matininó, where the women find refuge, represents the separation of the sexes; Guanín is the site of reencounter and subsequent fruitfulness. Arrom shows that "Ma-iti-nino," meaning "Without Fathers," is the probable etymological source for the first island. . . . Guanín is presented here as a place, yet it is also the word used to describe the golden alloy prized by the Taínos. The island received this name because it was considered its source, but as explained above, the place is almost certainly mythical. When they are related to the myth, the places keep these meanings. They underscore the situation of the sexes, so that to mention Matininó is to emphasize that women are alone; to speak of Guanín is to suggest sexual union. . . .

As has been suggested, the mythological functions of this episode are focused upon periodic infertility in the tropics which is made analogous with a woman's sexuality. The myth argues that yucca planting cannot occur unless there is rain, just as a husband cannot use his wife for sexual pleasure until her task of nursing the child is completed. Perhaps the nighttime sounds of the frog further identified the woman's fertility as belonging especially to the darkness. Thus, the myth affirms that while both the earth and the woman may appear to be fertile at all times, in fact they are not. Special knowledge of the moon's phases—of time—is required in order to tell the difference. . . .

The Creation of Women

The Tale of Inriri

[It is said that] one day the men went to bathe and while they
    were in the water, it rained a great deal.
They were very anxious to have women, and on many occasions while
    it rained, they had sought to find traces of their women, but
    they were not able to find any news [of them].
But that day when they washed, [it is said that] they saw fall
    from some trees, coming down through the branches a certain
    kind of persons, who were neither men nor women, nor had the
    sexual parts of either male or female.
When the men went to seize them, they escaped as if they
    were eels.
And since the men could not catch them, they called
    two or three men under orders from their *cacique*, so that
    they would see how many there were, and should seek for
    each one a man who was a *caracaracol*, [so called because
    they had rough hands and could thus hold them fast].
They told the *cacique* that there were four CREATURES, and so they
    brought four men who were *caracaracol*.
[This is a disease like scabs that makes the body rough.]
After they had captured the CREATURES, they took counsel about
    how they could make them women, since they did not have the
    sexual parts of male or female.
They sought a bird whose name is Inriri, and which in ancient
    times was called Inriri Cahubabayael, THE SON OF THE
    ANCIENT ONE.
This bird bores holes in trees,
[and in our language is called a woodpecker.]
Likewise they took the women without the sexual parts of male or
    female and they tied their hands and feet.
Then they took this bird and tied it to the bodies.
Thinking that the CREATURES were logs, the bird began to do the
    work to which it was accustomed, boring open and pecking away
    at the place where the female's private is usually found.
[It is said that] in this way, the Indians had women [as the eldest
    tell the tale].

The opening lines of this episode repeat the identification of the rainy
season with the approach of a woman's sexual receptiveness. Here the creatures have never been mothers, however. Their receptiveness to sexual relations is a first-time experience, and, like South American myths, . . .
probably refers to girls before puberty.

Since there is no allusion to Guahayona in the references to the *caciques*,
it seems likely that this is not a direct part of the Hero Myth but a mythic
explanation of puberty rites. It has been included here because its theme is
related to the tale of remote women. Another familiar reference is to the
"*caracaracol*" of the Deminán Creation Myth. The desire for women is

related to water, not only in bathing but especially in the increase of rainfall. Likewise, the myth reintroduces the bird Cahubabael, characterized as a reluctant shaman [medicine man]. . . .

The central reason for interpreting this myth as a description of the puberty rite is the manner in which the shaman mediates the encounter of men and women. The role assigned to the frog in the account of the Güeyo Women is occupied here by the *caracaracoles* with their rough hands. Pané probably misinterprets the reason for their power over the creatures when he says that roughness was what made it possible for the *caracaracoles* to hold onto them . . . [T]he survivors of venereal disease are born with scabby skin, and were considered among the Taínos to have special shamanistic proclivities. The victory over syphilis, which left the skin rough with scabs, was viewed as a manifestation of the numinous. Moreover, because the disease was contracted sexually by the mother, the shamanistic power was directly related to sexuality.

I believe that this myth describes a puberty rite in which the shaman takes a central role, and the reappearance of the bird, Cahubabayel, strengthens this interpretation. . . . Originally punished because he revealed secrets of his profession to the uninitiated, he still makes mistakes. Here, he does not realize that he is boring holes in living creatures; instead, he believes them to be logs of wood. His foolishness contrasts markedly with the wisdom of the *caracaracoles* and the *cacique*.

23

Sacred Entertainments

Investigation into the culture of the natives indicates that they had far more complex social patterns than Columbus could possibly have comprehended, given his hurried and superficial assessment of what he could observe of the most ordinary aspect of their lives. The area that he explored involved a wide variety of peoples in the Greater Antilles (Cuba; Jamaica; Puerto Rico; and the island of Hispaniola, which today contains Haiti and the Dominican Republic), the Lesser Antilles (including the Virgin Islands and the Windward and Leeward Islands), plus the circum-Caribbean (lower Central America, including Panama and Costa Rica, and the northern portion of Colombia).

"they sing their history, . . ."

The first people he encountered were the Taínos (once called Island Arawak) who lived on Hispaniola and Puerto Rico. The Taínos' language has been assigned to a branch of the Arawakan, which can be traced back to the mid-Amazon basin somewhere between

400 B.C. to 1,000 A.D., when the seed speakers moved from the coast of Guiana to the West Indies.

These people had no name for themselves, since *taíno* means "good" or "noble," a word they used when pressed by Europeans to contrast themselves with their enemies, who were thus by definition bad or ignoble. The Taínos were the most sophisticated of the islanders, an experienced trading people who took part in a long-distance network. They lived in villages dominated by chiefs. Columbus discounted their agriculture and their manufacture of cotton and darts, and overlooked their ceremonial plazas, ball courts, and cult figures. Visitors and historians were much more interested than he in making a record of their culture, especially because the people were dying out so fast. Gonzalo Fernández de Oviedo incorporated the analysis in the next document into a five-volume history of the peoples of the Indies [issued in the Sixteenth Century].

T hese people [on Hispaniola] had an excellent way of remembering past events through their songs and dances, which they call *areitos* and we would call singing dances. Livy [ancient Roman author] says that the first dancers came from Etruria to Rome, and that they performed their songs by coordinating their voices with their bodily movements. This was done to forget the deaths caused by the plague the year that Camelo died and must have been like the *areitos* or songs of the Indians. An *areito* was performed in the following manner: when they wanted to celebrate a special holiday or simply to enjoy themselves, many of them would gather, sometimes with the men or the women by themselves, and sometimes mixing, for general celebrations to honor a victory over their enemies or the marriage of the *cacique* or king of the province, or for any other occasion for the common pleasure of them all. To further enjoy themselves, they would hold hands, linking their arms and forming a line or a circle. One of them would be the leader (man or woman), and he would step forward and backward, as in the *contrapas,* and everyone else would imitate, singing the notes he intoned whether they were high or low, and following his movements, measuring every step and word. The leader would then remain silent, though without interrupting his *contrapas,* while the rest responded. After the response, which repeated exactly what the leader said, the leader would continue with another verse that was also repeated by everyone. This lasted three or four hours or more without interruption, until the leader of the dance finished his history; and sometimes it lasted from one day to the next.

SOURCE Gonzalo Fernández de Oviedo, *Historia General y Natural de las Indias,* ed. Juan Pérez de Tudela Bueso, 5 vols. (Madrid: Biblioteca de Autores Españoles 121–171, 1959), vol. I, pp. 112–124; trans. J. H. Parry and R. G. Keith, *New Iberian World* (New York: Times Books, 1984), vol. II, pp. 10–12. Reprinted by permission.

Sometimes along with the singing they play a drum *(atambor)*, which is made of a round piece of wood, hollowed out so that it is concave and more or less as thick as a man's body, depending on how they make it. Its sound is similar to the muffled drums made by the blacks. They put no skin over it, only making some holes and stretching strings across the hollow part, so that it makes an ugly sound. Thus, with or without this unpleasant instrument, they sing their history, relating how their *caciques* died, who and how many they were, and other things that they do not want to forget. Sometimes, the leader of the dance changes the tone and the steps, continuing the story or telling another one (if the first one has finished), with or without the same rhythm.

This dance is similar to those done by the peasants of some parts in Spain, when men and women enjoy themselves with tambourines during the summer. Also I have seen this type of dance in Flanders where men and women dance in many circles, responding to one who leads them in singing in the manner I have described above.

When the *Comendador* Frey Nicholas de Ovando was governor of the island, Anacaona, the wife of the *cacique* Caonabo and a great lady, performed an *areito* in front of him. More than three hundred maidens, all her ladies in waiting and unmarried, participated in the dance, because she did not want any man, married woman, or woman who had known a man to take part in the *areito*.

Returning to our subject, this type of singing on this and the other islands (and in many parts of the continent) is an image of their history or way of recollecting the past and of war and peace, because when they perform those songs, they do not forget their heroic deeds. These songs remain in their memory rather than in books; and this way they recite the genealogies of the *caciques*, kings, and lords they have had, their deeds, and the bad or good times they had, as well as things they want the adults and children to remember. And for this purpose they perform the *areitos*, so they do not forget these things, especially their victories in battle. Other things will be said about these *areitos* later on, when I discuss the continent, because the *areitos* of this island, which I saw in the year 1515, did not seem as notable as the ones I saw on the continent and have seen in other parts.

The reader should not think that this is all savagery, since the same things are done in Italy and Spain and in most of the Christian world, and also among the pagans. What else are the ballads and songs that are based on fact but ways of remembering past history among those who do not read? . . .

During the time these songs and dances last, other Indians give drinks to the dancers and nobody stops, continuing to move their feet while swallowing what they are given to drink, which are certain beverages that are used among them. Thus when the party is over, most of them are drunk and unconscious, stretched out on the ground for many hours. And when someone gets drunk, he is taken out of the dance and the others continue on, so that this intoxication itself puts an end to the *areito*. This happens when it is a solemn *areito,* performed at weddings, funerals, or to commemorate a battle or a famous victory, because other *areitos* are done very often without people getting drunk. Thus they all know this form of narration, either from this vice [of drunkenness] or because they want to learn this type of music, and sometimes similar songs and dances are invented by people who are considered among the Indians to be talented in this art. . . .

Among their other vices, the Indians of this island had one very bad one, which was the inhaling of the smoke of something they call tobacco until they became unconscious. They did this with the smoke of a certain herb that, according to what I understand, has the quality of the henbane *(beleño),* though it does not have the same shape, because this herb has a length of about four of five palms or less with broad and thick leaves, which are soft, fuzzy, and green, being similar to the leaves of ox's tongue or bugloss, as the herbists and doctors call it. This herb I am talking about is similar to the henbane, and they took it in the following way: the *caciques* or principal men had some hollow tubes, smaller than a *jeme* [the distance between the tip of the thumb and index finger] and as thick as one's little finger. These canes had two tubes . . . and they would put these in their nostrils, and the other end in the smoke and the herb that was burning; and these [pipes] were very smooth and well-carved. Then they burned the leaves of that herb wrapped up the way the pages at court did when making smoke; and they would inhale the smoke one, two, three times or more, as often as they could, until they became unconscious for a long time, stretched out on the ground, inebriated or heavily asleep. The Indians who did not have these pipes would take the smoke with canes or reed-grass, and it is the instrument or reeds with which they took the smoke that the Indians call tobacco, rather than the herb itself (as some people thought).

The Indians held this herb in great esteem, growing it in their gardens and fields for the purpose described; and they believed that taking that herb was not only healthy but holy. When the principal *cacique* fell on the ground, his wives (of whom there were many) would put him on his bed or hammock, if he ordered this before he fell down; but if he did not say anything beforehand, he wanted to be left on the ground until his inebriation or drowsiness had gone.

I cannot think of what pleasure they get from that act except for the gluttony of drinking, since they do this before they inhale the smoke or tobacco. Some of them drink so much of a certain wine that they get drunk before they smoke; but when they feel full they look for the smoke. Many of them, even without drinking too much, take the tobacco and do what has been said, until they fall flat on their backs or on their sides on the ground as if they were sleeping. I know that some Christians use this tobacco already, especially those who are sick with syphilis, because they say it alleviates the pain of their disease, but I do not think that this accomplishes anything more than to be dead in life, which I think is worse than the pain they avoid, since they do not get a cure from it.

At the present, many blacks of this city (Santo Domingo) and all the island have adopted this custom, growing this herb on the farms and *haciendas* of their masters for the purpose described; because they say that when they stop working and take the tobacco they lose their tiredness. . . .

QUESTIONS

1. What basic questions about human existence did the islanders try to answer with their myths?
2. What connection can be made between the myths of the islanders and the stories from the ancient Near East, some of which have parallels in the Bible?
3. Did dancing serve any special purpose in the cultural life of the islanders?
4. Was there any social or cultural meaning in drinking and smoking to excess, beyond the recreational aspect?
5. What judgments does Oviedo express about the islanders' customs?

THE USE OF FORCE

24

Coming into Conflict

The accidental sinking of the *Santa María* on Christmas eve, coupled with Columbus's growing fear that the Pinzón brothers would claim a share of his glory, caused him to rush back to Castile to claim his reward. Stopping at a tiny island near the mouth of Samaná Bay in Hispaniola to stock up with yams for the trip, the landing party encountered the first Amerindians they had seen carrying bows and arrows. Columbus guessed that they were the "Caribs" he had heard about, but they could just as well have been Taínos of a more bellicose disposition than those he and his crew had already met. Both the *Niña* and the *Pinta* were leaking, but despite Columbus's bravado in the first selection, drawn from his logbook, it seemed too dangerous to beach the ships for repairs. The ships weighed anchor and set out directly for Spain.

> *"Their appearance, arms, and actions showed them to be a daring and courageous people."*

Because he was short one ship, Columbus left about a third of the crew at Navidad ("Nativity"). Upon his return in 1493, he slowly uncovered the details presented in the second selection. All the facts concerning the fate of the colony never did come to light.

The first accurate and comprehensive accounts of the exploration of the New World were drawn up by Peter Martyr of Anghiera (Anglería). He left Italy in 1497 to attend the court of Ferdinand and Isabella as resident scholar of the humanities, and due to their favor was eventually named Bishop of Jamaica. He realized from the first that unprecedented events were taking place on the other side of the Atlantic. His intelligent dispatches to various Italian aristocrats were collected and printed in 1516. The writing is cool and dispassionate, for although he reported what he was told, or overheard, he wrote in a spirit of disinterested inquiry. Peter Martyr was skeptical of Columbus's claim that he had reached Asia, downplayed reports of marvels and monsters, and discounted rumors of fabulous gold mines. The third selection, drawn from his account, deals with Columbus's activities in Hispaniola during 1495.

Skirmish on the First Voyage

Sunday, January 13th [1493], being off Cabo Enamorado in Samaná Bay on the island of Española [Hispaniola], the Admiral [Columbus] sent ashore a party which encountered some Indians of ferocious aspect, armed with bows and arrows as if ready for war. Their faces showed anger and surprise, but our men, after striking up a conversation with them, managed to buy two of their bows and some arrows. With great difficulty they prevailed on one to come aboard the caravel to speak with the Admiral. Truly, their speech matched their appearance, which was fiercer than that of any other Indians they had seen. The faces of these Indians were stained with charcoal, for all those people have the custom of painting themselves, some black, some red, and others white; some one way and some another. They wore their hair long and gathered behind the head into nets of parrot's feathers.

One of them, standing before the Admiral as naked as the day his mother bore him, said in a haughty voice that all the people in those parts went about in that manner. The Admiral, thinking he was a Carib, and that the bay separated that people from Española, asked him where the Caribs lived. Pointing with his finger, he indicated that they lived farther to the east, on islands where were found pieces of *guanín* [gold] as large as half the caravel's stern. He also related that the island of Matininó [Martinique] was inhabited only by women, with whom the Caribs slept at certain times of the year; if these women [imagined "Amazons"] bore any sons, they gave them to their fathers to raise. After he had answered all the questions put to him, partly with signs and partly with the help of the Indian interpreters from San Salvador, who knew a little of his speech, the Admiral ordered him fed and given some trifles, such as glass beads and pieces of green and red cloth. Then he sent him ashore to induce the others to bring gold, if they had any.

When the ship's boat landed, the Christians encountered fifty-five Indians among the trees on the beach. These Indians were all naked, wore their hair long as do the women of Castile, and had plumes of parrot's feathers or feathers of other birds tied to the backs of their heads. The Indian who had visited the ship persuaded the others to lay down their bows and arrows and the large cudgels which they use as swords, for they have no iron. The Christians began to buy swords and arrows as the Admiral had instructed them to do, but after the Indians had sold two of their bows they disdainfully refused to sell any more; instead they ran toward the place where they had deposited their weapons, with the design of picking them up and also of getting cords with which to tie our men's hands. But the Christians were prepared for their attack, and though only seven in number, fell

SOURCE *The Life of the Admiral Christopher Columbus by His Son Ferdinand*, trans. and annot. by Benjamin Keen, 1959, pp. 117–120 passim. Reprinted by permission of the translator.

upon the Indians with so much spirit that they gave one Indian a slash on the buttocks with a sword and wounded another in the breast with an arrow. Terrified by the valor of our men and the wounds inflicted by our arms, the Indians turned and fled, leaving behind most of the bows and arrows. Many would certainly have been killed had not the pilot of the caravel, who was in charge of the landing party, restrained our men.

The Admiral was not displeased by this incident; for he was convinced these were the Caribs whom the other Indians feared so greatly, or if not Caribs, at least their neighbors. Their appearance, arms, and actions showed them to be a daring and courageous people. The Admiral hoped that when the islanders learned what seven Spaniards had done against fifty-five ferocious Indians, they would feel more respect for the men left behind in the town of Navidad and would not dare annoy them. Later that afternoon the Indians made bonfires on the beach to demonstrate their courage, and a boat was sent to see what they wanted; but nothing our men could do would make the Indians show their faces, so the boat returned.

Their bows are made of yew [wood] and are as large as English and French bows; their arrows are stems of cane, very strong and straight, about an arm and a half long. The arrowhead is a small fire-hardened piece of wood about twelve inches long; in this head they insert a fish tooth or bone and coat it with poison. . . .

The Destruction of the First Colony on Hispaniola

Friday, November 22d [1493], the Admiral [Columbus] reached the northern shore of Española [Hispaniola]. At Samaná Bay he sent ashore one of the Indians that he had taken to Castile. He was a native of the province of Española who had been converted to our holy faith and had offered to persuade all the Indians to serve the Christians and be at peace with them. The Admiral continued on his course toward the town of Navidad; at Cape Angel some Indians came aboard to trade with the Christians. After they had come to anchor in the harbor of Monte Cristi, a shore party discovered two dead men on the banks of a river. One seemed young; the other, who seemed older, had a rope of esparto grass tied about his neck, his arms extended, and his hands tied to a piece of wood in the form of a cross. The party could not be certain if they were Christians or Indians, but regarded it as an evil omen.

Next day, November 26th, the Admiral again sent men ashore at various places. The Indians came to speak with the Christians in a friendly and

SOURCE *The Life of the Admiral Christopher Columbus by His Son Ferdinand*, trans. and annot. Benjamin Keen (New Brunswick, N.J.: Rutgers University, 1959), pp. 117–120. Footnotes eliminated. Reprinted by permission of the translator.

fearless manner; touching our men's shirts and doublets, they would say "shirt, doublet," as if to show they knew the names for those things. This allayed the suspicion that the discovery of the dead men had aroused in the Admiral, for he reasoned that the Indians would not be coming aboard so fearlessly if they had harmed the Christians he left there. Next day, past midnight, when they were off the mouth of Navidad harbor, a canoe approached from the shore and the paddlers asked for the Admiral. They were told to come aboard, that he was there; but they would not come until they had seen and recognized him, so the Admiral must come to the ship's side to speak with them. Then two Indians came aboard, each with a mask over his face, and presented those masks to the Admiral in the name of the *cacique* Guacanagarí, who sent friendly greetings. The Admiral asked about the Christians he had left there and was told that some had died of sickness, some had separated from the rest, and still others had departed for other lands; all had four or five wives apiece. From their words the Admiral gathered that all or most of the Christians must be dead, but since there was nothing he could do for the present, he sent the Indians ashore that night with presents of metal basins and other things for Guacanagarí and his family.

Thursday, November 28th, at the hour of vespers, the Admiral moved his fleet in front of the town of Navidad and found it burned to the ground. That day they saw nobody in the vicinity of the town. Next morning the Admiral went ashore and felt much grief at the sight of the ruins of the houses and the fort. Nothing remained of the houses except some smashed chests and such other wreckage as one sees in a land that has been devastated and put to the sack.

As there was no one in the vicinity whom the Admiral could question, he went with some boats up a river that is nearby. He left orders to clean out the well of the fort during his absence; for at the time of his departure for Castile, fearing some untoward event, he had directed all the gold that was found to be thrown into the well. But the well was empty. Going upstream with the boats, the Admiral did not see a single Indian, because all had fled from their huts into the woods. All he found was some clothing that had belonged to the Christians. Returning to Navidad, the Admiral found the bodies of eight Christians; in the fields near the town were three more who were recognized to be Christians by their clothing; these men seemed to have been dead for about a month.

While the Christians were looking around for papers or other traces of the dead men, a brother of the *cacique* Guacanagarí, accompanied by some other Indians, came to speak to the Admiral. They could say some words in Spanish and knew the names of all the Christians who had been left there. They said that soon after the Admiral's departure those men began to quarrel among themselves, each taking as many women and as much gold as he could. As a result Pedro Gutiérrez and Escobedo slew one Jácome; then, ganging up with nine others, they left with their women for the country of a *cacique* named Caonabó, who was lord of the mines. Caonabó killed them, and some days later marched with a strong force against Navidad, which was held only by Diego de Arana and ten other men who were willing to remain and guard the fortress, all the others having dispersed to various places on the island. Arriving at the town by night, Caonabó set fire to the houses in which the Christians lived with their women, forcing them to flee in fright to the sea, where eight of them drowned; three others, whom these Indians could not identify, were killed ashore. They also said that Guacanagarí fought against Caonabó in defense of the Christians, but was wounded and had to flee.

This story checked with that told by some Christians whom the Admiral sent ashore to gather information and who visited the principal village. They found Guacanagarí suffering from a wound which he said had kept him from calling on the Admiral and reporting to him what had happened to the Christians. He related that as soon as the Admiral left for Castile they began to quarrel among themselves, each seeking to get gold by barter for himself, and as many women as he could; that they would not be satisfied with what he, Guacanagarí, gave them but instead split up into many gangs, some going in one direction and some in another; and that a band of Biscayans went off to a place where they were all killed. He said they should tell this to the Admiral as the true story of what had happened, and that he should come to visit him, for the *cacique* was too ill to leave his house.

Violence and Depopulation
After the Second Voyage

The *caciques* of the island [Hispaniola] had always been contented with little, for they lived a peaceful and tranquil life. When they saw the Spaniards establishing themselves upon their native soil, they were considerably troubled, and desired above all things either to expel the newcomers or to destroy them so completely that not even their memory should remain. It is a fact that the people who accompanied the Admiral [Columbus] in his second voyage were for the most part undisciplined, unscrupulous vagabonds, who only employed their ingenuity in gratifying their appetites. Incapable of moderation in their acts of injustice, they carried off the women of the islanders under the very eyes of their brothers and their husbands; given over to violence and thieving, they had profoundly vexed the natives. It had happened in many places that when our men were surprised by the natives, the latter strangled them and offered them as sacrifices to their gods. . . .

. . . [T]he Admiral resolved to march throughout the whole island. He

SOURCE *De Orbe Novo. The Eight Decades of Peter Martyr D'Anghera*, trans. F. A. MacNutt (New York: G. P. Putnam's Sons, 1912), pp. 105–111, passim.

163

was informed that the natives suffered from such a severe famine that more than 50,000 men had already perished, and that people continued to die daily as do cattle in time of plague.

This calamity was the consequence of their own folly; for when they saw that the Spaniards wished to settle in their island, they thought they might expel them by creating a scarcity of food. They, therefore, decided not only to plant no more crops, but also to destroy and tear up all the various kinds of cereals used for bread which had already been sown, and which I have mentioned in the first book. This was to be done by the people in each district, and especially in the mountainous region of Cipangu [confusion with Japan] and Cibao; that was the country where gold was found in abundance, and the natives were aware that the principal attraction which kept the Spaniards in Hispaniola was gold. At that time the Admiral sent an officer with a troop of armed men to reconnoitre the southern coast of the island, and this officer reported that the regions he had visited had suffered to such an extent from the famine, that during six days he and his men had eaten nothing but the roots of herbs and small plants, or such fruit as grow on the trees. . . .

The Admiral was perfectly aware of the alarm and disturbance that prevailed amongst the islanders, but he was unable to prevent the violence and rapacity of his men, whenever they came into contact with the natives. A number of the principal *caciques* of the frontier regions assembled to beg Columbus to forbid the Spaniards to wander about the island because, under the pretext of hunting for gold or other local products, they left nothing uninjured or undefiled. Moreover, all the natives between the ages of fourteen and seventy years bound themselves to pay him tribute in the products of the country at so much per head, promising to fulfil their engagement. Some of the conditions of this agreement were as follows: The mountaineers of Cibao were to bring to the town every three months a specified measure filled with gold. They reckon by the moon and call the months moons. The islanders who cultivated the lands which spontaneously produced spices and cotton, were pledged to pay a fixed sum per head. This pact suited both parties, and it would have been observed by both sides as had been agreed, save that the famine nullified their resolutions. The natives had hardly strength to hunt food in the forests and for a long time they contented themselves with roots, herbs, and wild fruits. Nevertheless the majority of the *caciques,* aided by their followers, did bring part of the established tribute. They begged as a favour of the Admiral to have pity on their misery, and to exempt them till such time as the island might recover its former prosperity. They bound themselves then to pay double what was for the moment failing.

QUESTIONS

1. How threatening to the Spanish were the armed natives they encountered?
2. Why were the men who were left behind at the fort of Navidad allegedly murdered?

3. What was the cause of the depopulation and upheaval on Hispaniola?
4. Is Columbus's attitude toward the islanders in these varied incidents always the same?
5. Who were the aggressors in these tests of strength?

25

The Assault on Mexico

When Hernán Cortés heard during 1519 that within the interior of Mexico there was a powerful ruler, he marched from Vera Cruz with about 600 men, a few horses, even fewer pieces of artillery, and some guides with the intention of taking over that empire in the name of his sovereigns. His audacious scheme to enter the capital was accomplished within nine months, and the fall of the Triple Alliance within two years.

> *"we could no longer endure the stench of the dead bodies . . ."*

Cortés was commanding his expedition on behalf of the governor of Cuba, who in turn was a deputy of the hereditary Admiral of the Indies. He had permission to explore and trade, but not to colonize, so he and his followers ran a grave risk by going against orders. The charge of disloyalty could be overcome only by success in gaining new riches and by direct appeal to the king himself, which is the reason for the letters excerpted in the following documents. Since they are self-serving propaganda, they should be approached with some caution.

Cortés was a remarkable general and a clever statesman. Like so many of the conquistadores, he came from a poverty-stricken province of Spain where prospects were limited. Neither he nor his companions were trained soldiers, but they were steeped in the traditions of the Reconquest of Iberia from the Muslims (Document 4). They felt that right was on their side when they encountered the brutal religious practices of the Aztecs, and so saw themselves freeing souls from darkness by bringing to them the light of the Gospel.

Bernal Díaz (Document 43), a fighting man in the ranks, thought the capital of Tenochtitlán a second Venice: "And when we saw all those cities and villages built in the water, and other great towns on dry land, and that straight and level causeway leading to Mexico (Tenochtitlán), we were astonished. Those great towns and temples and buildings rising from the water, all made of stone, seemed like an enchanted vision. . . ."

After entering the city, the Spanish seized and imprisoned the vacillating leader of the confederation, Moctezuma (Documents 38 and 39). Cortés was then forced to leave to deal with a Spanish force who had landed on the coast to deprive him of command. Upon his return, he found the population in revolt because of a massacre perpetrated by one of his captains in his absence. The Spanish fled under cover of night, abandoning their loot and suffering heavy losses.

Their astonishing success in returning to conquer can be understood by placing their victories in the context of a general revolt against Aztec hegemony. The Aztecs arrived in the Valley of Mexico in the middle of the thirteenth century and, after suffering much persecution, became independent in 1428. In less than a hundred years, they won contol over the vast central and southern areas of their land by creating a militaristic society to terrify their neighbors. Rival groups, especially the Tlaxcala, chafing under heavy exactions of tribute and sacrificial victims, saw in the coming of the bearded Spanish men their opportunity.

With Cortés supplying tactical leadership, cannons, pack horses, and ships, thousands of allied fighting men under their own commanders provided the overpowering force to besiege Tenochtitlán. The second selection provides an eyewitness account compiled by a missionary from Aztec [sources] about the fall of their city on the day One-Serpent of the Year Three-House, or the thirteenth of August 1521.

The Account by Cortés

T hey [the Aztecs] have a most horrid and abominable custom which truly ought to be punished and which until now we have seen in no other part, and this is that, whenever they wish to ask something of the idols, in order that their plea may find more acceptance, they take many girls and boys and even adults, and in the presence of the idols they open their chests while they are still alive and take out their hearts and entrails and burn them before the idols, offering the smoke as sacrifice. Some of us have seen this, and they say it is the most terrible and frightful thing they have ever witnessed.

This these Indians do so frequently that, as we have been informed, and, in part, have seen from our own experience during the short while we have been here, not one year passes in which they do not kill and sacrifice some fifty persons in each temple; and this is done and held as customary from the island of Cozumel to this land where we now have settled. Your Majesties [King and Queen of Spain and the Roman Empire] may be most certain that, as this land seems to us to be very large, and to have many temples in it, not one year has passed, as far as we have been able to discover, in which three or four thousand souls have not been sacrificed in this manner. . . .

SOURCE Hernán Cortés, *Letters from Mexico*, trans. and ed. A. R. Pagden (London: Oxford University Press, 1972), Letter Two to the Emperor Charles V, pp. 35–253, passim. Footnotes removed. Reprinted by permission.

Afer we had crossed [a] bridge, Moctezuma came to greet us and with him some two hundred lords, all barefoot and dressed in a different costume, but also very rich in their way and more so than the others. They came in two columns, pressed very close to the walls of the street, which is very wide and beautiful and so straight that you can see from one end to the other. It is two-thirds of a league long and had on both sides very good and big houses, both dwellings and temples.

Moctezuma came down the middle of this street with two chiefs, one on his right hand and the other on his left. One of these was that great chief who had come on a litter to speak with me, and the other was Moctezuma's brother, chief of the city of Yztapalapa, which I had left that day. And they were all dressed alike except that Moctezuma wore sandals whereas the others went barefoot; and they held his arm on either side. When we met I dismounted and stepped forward to embrace him, but the two lords who were with him stopped me with their hands so that I should not touch him; and they likewise all performed the ceremony of kissing the earth. When this was over Moctezuma requested his brother to remain with me and to take me by the arm while he went a little way ahead with the other; and after he had spoken to me all the others in the two columns came and spoke with me, one after another, and then each returned to his column.

When at last I came to speak to Moctezuma himself I took off a necklace of pearls and cut glass that I was wearing and placed it round his neck; after we had walked a little way up the street a servant of his came with two necklaces, wrapped in a cloth, made from red snails' shells, which they hold in great esteem; and from each necklace hung eight shrimps of refined gold almost a span in length. When they had been brought he turned to me and placed them about my neck, and then continued up the street in the manner already described until we reached a very large and beautiful house which had been very well prepared to accommodate us. . . .

Most Invincible Lord, six days having passed since we first entered this great city of Tenochtitlán, during which time I had seen something of it, though little compared with how much there is to see and record, I decided from what I had seen that it would benefit Your Royal service and our safety if Moctezuma were in my power and not in complete liberty, in order that he should not retreat from the willingness he showed to serve Your Majesty; but chiefly because we Spaniards are rather obstinate and persistent, and should we annoy him he might, as he is so powerful, obliterate all memory of us. Furthermore, by having him with me, all those other lands which were subject to him would come more swiftly to the recognition and service of Your Majesty, as later happened. I resolved, therefore, to take him and keep him in the quarters where I was, which were very strong. . . .

There are, in all districts of this great city, many temples or houses for their idols. They are all very beautiful buildings, and in the important ones there are priests of their sect who live there permanently; and, in addition to the houses for the idols, they also have very good lodgings. . . .

The most important of these idols, and the ones in whom they have most faith, I had taken from their places and thrown down the steps; and I had those chapels where they were cleaned, for they were full of the blood of sacrifices; and I had images of Our Lady and of other saints put there, which caused Moctezuma and the other natives some sorrow. First they asked me not to do it, for when the communities learnt of it they would rise against

THE SPANISH LANDING IN MEXICO *Father Sahagún used native painters to illustrate his sixteenth-century history of Mexico. What caught the illustrator's attention in this naïve view of Cortés's landing at Vera Cruz in 1519 were the horses and the European livestock, new to his world. A conquistador writes down what he is being told by an Aztec nobleman, whose words are translated into Spanish by Malinche, the renowned native woman who traveled with Cortés. Something like a rainbow frames the scene, which appears to be a peaceful visit rather than an invasion.*

me, for they believed that those idols gave them all their worldly goods, and that if they were allowed to be ill treated, they would become angry and give them nothing and take the fruit from the earth leaving the people to die of hunger. I made them understand through the interpreters how deceived they were in placing their trust in those idols which they had made with their hands from unclean things. They must know that there was only one God, Lord of all things, who had created heaven and earth and all else and who made all of us; and He was without beginning or end, and they must adore and worship only Him, not any other creature or thing. And I told them all I knew about this to dissuade them from their idolatry and bring them to the knowledge of God our Saviour. All of them, especially Moctezuma, replied that they had already told me how they were not natives of this land, and that as it was many years since their forefathers had come here, they well knew that they might have erred somewhat in what they believed, for they had left their native land so long ago; and as I had only recently arrived from there, I would better know the things they should believe, and should explain to them and make them understand, for they would do as I said was best. Moctezuma and many of the chieftains of the city were with me until the idols were removed, the chapel cleaned and the images set up, and I urged them not to sacrifice living creatures to the idols, as they were accustomed, for, as well as being most abhorrent to God, Your Sacred Majesty's laws forbade it and ordered that he who kills shall be killed. And from then on they ceased to do it, and in all the time I stayed in that city I did not see a living creature killed or sacrificed. . . .

. . . Moctezuma, who together with one of his sons and many other chiefs who had been captured previously was still a prisoner, asked to be taken out onto the roof of the fortress where he might speak to the captains of his people and tell them to end the fighting. I had him taken out, and when he reached a breastwork which ran out beyond the fortress, and was about to speak to them, he received a blow on his head from a stone; and the injury was so serious that he died three days later. I told two of the Indians who were captive to carry him out on their shoulders to the people. What they did with him I do not know; only the war did not stop because of it, but grew more fierce and pitiless each day. . . .

We already knew that the Indians in the city [Tenochtitlán] were very scared, and we now learnt from two wretched creatures who had escaped from the city and come to our camp by night that they were dying of hunger and used to come out at night to fish in the canals between the houses, and wandered through the places we had won in search of firewood, and herbs and roots to eat. And because we had already filled in many of the canals, and leveled out many of the dangerous stretches, I resolved to enter the next morning shortly before dawn and do all the harm we could. The brigantines [boats] departed before daylight, and I with twelve or fifteen horsemen and some foot soldiers and Indians entered suddenly and stationed several spies who, as soon as it was light, called us from where we lay in ambush, and we fell on a huge number of people. As these were some of the most wretched people and had come in search of food, they were nearly all unarmed, and women and children in the main. We did them so much harm through all the streets in the city that we could reach, that the dead and the prisoners numbered more than eight hundred; the brigantines also took many people and canoes which were out fishing, and the destruction was very great. When the captains and lords of the city saw us attack at such an unaccustomed hour, they were as frightened as they had been by the recent ambush, and none of them dared come out and fight; so we returned with much booty and food for our allies. . . .

On leaving my camp, I had commanded Gonzalo de Sandoval to sail the brigantines in between the houses in the other quarter in which the Indians were resisting, so that we should have them surrounded, but not to attack until he saw that we were engaged. In this way they would be surrounded and so hard pressed that they would have no place to move save over the bodies of their dead or along the roof tops. They no longer had nor could find any arrows, javelins or stones with which to attack us; and our allies fighting with us were armed with swords and bucklers, and slaughtered so many of them on land and in the water that more than forty thousand were killed or taken that day. So loud was the wailing of the women and children that there was not one man amongst us whose heart did not bleed at the sound; and indeed we had more trouble in preventing our allies from killing with such cruelty than we had in fighting the enemy. For no race, however savage, has ever practiced such fierce and unnatural cruelty as the natives of these parts. Our allies also took many spoils that day, which we were unable to prevent, as they numbered more than 150,000 and we Spaniards were only some nine hundred. Neither our precautions nor our warnings could stop their looting, though we did all we could. One of the reasons why I had avoided entering the city in force during the past days was the fear that if we attempted to storm them they would throw all they possessed into the water, and, even if they did not, our allies would take all they could find. For this reason I was much afraid that Your Majesty would receive only a small part of the great wealth this city once had, in comparison with all that I once held for Your Highness. Because it was now late, we could no longer endure the stench of the dead bodies that had lain in those streets for many days, which was the most loathsome thing in all the world, we returned to our camps.

The Aztec Account

And already Moctezuma met them [the Spanish] there in Uitzillan. Thereupon he gave gifts to the commandant, the commander of soldiers; he gave him flowers, he bejeweled him with necklaces, he hung garlands about him, he covered him with flowers, he wreathed his head with flowers. Thereupon he had the golden necklaces laid before him—all the kinds of gifts of greeting, with which the meeting was concluded. On some he hung necklaces.

Then [Cortés] said to Moctezuma: "Is this not thou? Art thou not he? Art thou Moctezuma?"

Moctezuma replied: "Indeed yes; I am he."

Thereupon he arose; he arose to meet him face to face. He inclined his body deeply. He drew him close. He arose firmly.

Thus he besought him: he said to him: "O our lord, thou hast suffered fatigue, thou hast endured weariness. Thou hast come to arrive on earth. Thou hast come to govern thy city of Mexico [Tenochtitlán]; thou hast come to descend upon thy mat, upon thy seat, which for a moment I have watched for thee, which I have guarded for thee. For thy governors are departed—the rulers Itzcoatl, Moctezuma the Elder, Axayacatl, Tizoc, Auitzotl, who yet a very short time ago had come to stand guard for thee, who had come to govern the city of Mexico. Under their protection thy common folk came. Do they yet perchance know it in their absence? O that one of them might witness, might marvel at what to me now hath befallen, at what I see quite in the absence of our lords. I by no means merely dream, I do not merely see in a dream, I do not see in my sleep; I do not merely dream that I see thee, that I look into thy face. I have been afflicted for some time. I have gazed at the unknown place whence thou hast come—from among the clouds, from among the mists. And so this. The rulers departed maintaining that thou wouldst come to visit thy city, that thou wouldst come to descend upon thy mat, upon thy seat. And now it hath been fulfilled; thou hast come; thou hast endured fatigue, thou hast endured weariness. Peace be with thee. Rest thyself. Visit thy palace. Rest thy body. May peace be with our lords." . . .

And when Moctezuma's address which he directed to the Marquis [Cortés] was ended, Marina [Malinche, a native woman working for the Spanish] then interpreted it, she translated it to him. And when the Marquis had heard Moctezuma's words, he spoke to Marina; he spoke to them in a barbarous tongue; he said in his barbarous tongue:

SOURCE Bernardino de Sahagún, *Florentine Codex: General History of the Things of New Spain*, trans. A. J. O. Anderson and C. E. Dibble (Salt Lake City: School of American Research and University of Utah, 1950–1982), *Book XII: The Conquest of Mexico*, Chaps. XVI, XVII, XXIII, pp. 44–66, passim. Reprinted by permission.

"Let Moctezuma put his heart at ease; let him not be frightened. We love him much. Now our hearts are indeed satisfied, for we know him, we hear him. For a long time we have wished to see him, to look upon his face. And this we have seen. Already we have come to his home in Mexico. At his leisure he will hear our words."

Thereupon [the Spaniards] grasped [Moctezuma] by the hand. Already they went leading him by it. They caressed him with their hands to make their love known to him. . . .

And when they had gone to arrive in the palace, when they had gone to enter it, at once they firmly seized Moctezuma. They continually kept him closely under observation; they never let him from their sight. With him was Itzquauhtzin. But the others just came forth [unimpeded].

And when this had come to pass, then each of the guns shot off. As if in confusion there was going off to one side, there was scattering from one's sight, a jumping in all directions. It was as if one had lost one's breath; it was as if for the time there was stupefaction, as if one were affected by mushrooms, as if something unknown were shown one. Fear prevailed. It was as if everyone had swallowed his heart. Even before it had grown dark, there was terror, there was astonishment, there was apprehension, there was a stunning of the people.

And when it dawned, thereupon were proclaimed all the things which [the Spaniards] required: white tortillas, roasted turkey hens, eggs, fresh water, wood, firewood, charcoal, earthen bowls, polished vessels, water jars, large water pitchers, cooking vessels, all manner of clay articles. This had Moctezuma indeed commanded.

But when he summoned forth the noblemen, no longer did they obey him. They only grew angry. No longer did they come to him, no longer did they go to him. No longer was he heeded. But nevertheless he was not therefore neglected; he was given all that he required—food, drink, and water [and] fodder for the deer [horses].

And when [the Spaniards] were well settled, they thereupon inquired of Moctezuma as to all the city's treasure—the devices, the shields. Much did they importune him; with great zeal they sought gold. And Moctezuma thereupon went leading the Spaniards. They went surrounding him, scattered about him; he went among them, he went in their lead; they went each holding him, each grasping him. And when they reached the storehouse, a place called Teocalco, thereupon were brought forth all the brilliant things; the quetzal feather head fan, the devices, the shields, the golden discs, the devils' necklaces, the golden nose crescents, the golden leg bands, the golden arm bands, the golden forehead bands.

Thereupon was detached the gold which was on the shields and which was on all the devices. And as all the gold was detached, at once they ignited, set fire to, applied fire to all the various precious things [which remained]. They all burned. And the gold the Spaniards formed into separate bars. . . .

And four days after they had been hurled from the [pyramid] temple, [the Spaniards] came to cast away [the bodies of] Moctezuma and Itzquauhtzin, who had died, at the water's edge at a place called Teoaloc. For at that place there was the image of a turtle carved of stone; the stone had an appearance like that of a turtle.

And when they were seen, when they were known to be Moctezuma and Itzquauhtzin, then they quickly took up Moctezuma in their arms. They carried him there to a place called Copulco. Thereupon they placed him on a pile of wood; thereupon they kindled it, they set fire to it. Thereupon the fire crackled, seeming to flare up, to send up many tongues of flame; many tongues of flame, many sprigs of flame seemed to arise. And Moctezuma's body seemed to lie sizzling, and it smelled foul as it burned.

And as it burned, only with fury, no longer with much of the people's good will, some chid him; they said: "This blockhead! He terrorized the world; there was dread in the world, there was terror before him in the world, there was astonishment. This man! If anyone offended him only a little, he at once disposed of him. Many he punished for imagined [faults] which were not real, which were only a fabrication of words." And still many who chid him groaned, cried out, shook their heads in disapproval. . . .

. . . There arose a tearful cry [upon evacuating Tenochtitlán]. Some went rejoicing, each one; some went content, each one, as they went joining the road. And those who had boats, all who owned boats, went forth only at night, but yet, even by day, they went forth. It was as if [the boats] struck against one another as they went.

And everywhere on the roads the Spaniards robbed the people. They sought gold. They despised the green stone, the precious feathers, and the turquoise. [The gold] was everywhere in the bosoms, in the skirts of the poor women. And as for us who were men: it was everywhere in their breech clouts, in their mouths.

And [the Spaniards] seized, they selected the women—the pretty ones, those whose bodies were yellow: the yellow [light-skinned] ones. And some women, when they were to be taken from the people, muddied their faces, and clothed themselves in old clothing, put rags on themselves as a shift. It was all only rags that they put on themselves.

And also some were selected from among us men—those who were strong, those soon grown to manhood, and those of whom later as young men they would make messengers, who would be their messengers, those known as *tlamacazque*. Of some they then burned [branded] the cheeks; of some they painted the cheeks; of some they painted the lips.

And when the shields were laid down, when we fell, it was in the year count Three House; and in the day count it was One Serpent.

And when Quauhtemoc went to give himself up, then they took him to Acachinanco, when already it was night. And upon the next day, when already there was a little sun, once again the Spaniards came. There were indeed many. They likewise came still spent. They came in battle array,

[with] iron cuirasses, iron helmets, but not their iron swords, and not their shields. Only all of them pressed against their noses with fine white cloths; the dead sickened them—they already smelled offensive; they already stank.

26

The Assault on Peru

Francisco Pizarro, the illegitimate and illiterate son of an infantry colonel, convinced the king of Spain to grant him permission to enter the west coast of South America. Along with Diego de Almagro and Hernando de Soto (later explorer of Florida), the fifty-eight-year-old adventurer led an absurdly small force of sixty-seven horsemen and 110 foot soldiers into the heart of Inca territory during 1532. He learned that the land was torn by civil war between Atahualpa and Huascar, sons of the late Inca Huaina Capac, who had divided his possessions between the two, giving the northern kingdom of Quito to the former and the southern area around Cuzco to the latter (Document 38). When the Spanish arrived, Atahualpa had succeeded in reuniting the land and imprisoning his half-brother.

"hurling themselves like thunderbolts at the Indian squadrons. . . ."

Exactly what Atahualpa thought of the newcomers or why he invited them to visit Cajamarca, where he resided with his enormous army, has never been made clear. The lack of resistance to the march inland and Atahualpa's apparently trusting reception might be attributed to a lack of fear, interest in meeting unusual strangers, or the traditional hospitality extended to self-proclaimed ambassadors.

The capture of the ruler, discussed in the following selection, was not that much different than the taking of Moctezuma in Mexico twenty years before. While in captivity, Anahualpa may have ordered his allies to murder his half-brother, so that Huascar might not take advantage of the situation. This was the primary offense the Spanish charged against the ruler in the mock trial, which ended in his execution. The original conquerors did not reap much benefit from this. Pizarro settled a dispute with Diego de Almagro by executing him, and in turn Almagro's supporters conspired to assassinate Pizarro.

The rapid capitulation of the country after the death of their ruler might be explained by its political structure. Like the Aztecs, the Peruvians were military conquerors whose empire was no more than a century old when it was toppled. To keep peace within the empire, the rulers evacuated conquered populations and replaced them with other peoples. Scrambling populations this way deprived them of independent leadership. The populace had also been trained into submission under a paternalistic regime that provided for all material needs under constant regulation and supervision. Whatever its drawbacks, the system of social services was more humane than anything later put in its place, and the Spanish could not claim that the Incas sacrificed humans, as did the Aztecs. The only lasting resistance to the Spanish was centered on Quito, outside the borders, and in the Andean mountains, which were suitable for guerrillas.

This selection was written by the son of a Spanish captain and an Inca princess. He chose to emphasize his Andean heritage in a history of the ruling family that brought its achievements, such as skilled building in massive stone, an enormous road system, and a deeply caring government, to the attention of Spanish intellectuals. The noble speeches attributed to Atahualpa demonstrate both the writer's celebration of his people's dignity and the willingness of Renaissance historians to present what should have been said, even if the words did not take that exact form in reality. The Inca leader's confused response to admonitions delivered to him by a priest demonstrate how little the Amerindians understood the Christian and European-state formulas in the Requirement (Document 28), even when translated.

When the emissaries arrived back among their own, they described the marvelous things they had seen in the Inca's palace, and the exquisite courtesy that had been shown them. Then they made equal division of the Inca's presents, with which everybody was delighted. But, like all good soldiers, they nevertheless did not neglect to prepare their weapons and their horses for the morrow, in order to be able to fight like Spaniards worthy of the name, despite the crushing superiority of Atahualpa's forces. When day dawned, they divided their cavalry, which only numbered sixty, into three groups of twenty men, commanded respectively by Ferdinand Pizarro, Ferdinand de Soto, and Sebastian de Belalcazar; then each one of these groups went and hid behind a wall, while waiting for the moment to swoop down on the Indians, thus increasing tenfold the effect of terror to which their appearance would give rise. The governor, Don Francisco Pizarro, took command of the infantry, which was composed of hardly more than one hundred men, and went to await King Atahualpa at one end of the main square.

Meanwhile, Atahualpa was advancing on a golden litter carried on the

SOURCE *The Incas. The Royal Commentaries of the Inca Garcilaso de la Vega, 1531–1616*, trans. Maria Jolas from the French ed. of Alain Gheerbrant, introduction by Alain Gheerbrant (New York: The Orion Press, 1961), pp. 329–365, passim. Footnotes removed.

shoulders of his men, accompanied by his entire household and his court, and with a degree of magnificence that displayed as much pomp and majesty as it did military power. The litters were preceded by a multitude of servants, who cleared the ground, removing all stones and pebbles and even bits of straw, from the road over which the king was to travel. The military escort was composed of four squadrons, each one comprising eight thousand men. The first preceded the king, two more surrounded him, and the fourth closed the ranks, in the role of rear guard; all of these troops were commanded by General Rumiñaui. There was a distance of one league between the king's camp and the main square of the city, where the Spaniards were waiting for him; however, with all his pomp, it took him more than four hours to cover it. As we shall see later, it was not Atahualpa's intention to fight, but only to listen to the communications from the Pope and the Emperor that had been brought him by the Spaniards. The latter had been described to him as people who were so weak that they could not even climb a hill on their own feet: "That is why they have horses," people said, "some of them ride on their backs while others have to be pulled, hanging on to the horse's tail or to its girth; they are incapable of running as we do, nor can they carry anything heavy."

So all of this information, added to the fact that he considered the Spaniards to be divine beings, made Atahualpa quite unable to suspect the kind of reception that these people had been planning for him.

He entered the square with his three first squadrons, the fourth remaining outside. When he saw the handful of Spanish infantrymen awaiting him, in tightly serried ranks, as though filled with fear, the king said: "These people are messengers from God. See that no harm is done them, but, on the contrary, treat them respectfully and courteously."

Upon which, a Dominican friar approached the Inca, cross in hand, to speak to him in the name of the Emperor. This was Friar Vincente de Valverde.

Everything in the aspect of this man was calculated to excite the Inca's curiosity, for he had never seen anyone like him. He wore a beard, the tonsure, and the frock of his order; in one hand he held a wooden cross, and in the other, a book which, according to certain chroniclers was *The Summum*, by Sylvester, unless it was the breviary or the Bible.

"What is this Spaniard's estate?" asked the Inca. "Is he the superior, inferior, or equal of the others?"

One of the three dignitaries who had been attached to the Spaniards since their arrival in Cajamarca replied: "Inca, all I know is that he is a captain, a guide who speaks (by which he meant preacher), and a minister and messenger of the supreme God, Pachacamac [one of two supreme Inca deities], which makes him different from the others." . . .

King Atahualpa understood from the priest's peroration that the Pope had ordered, and that the Emperor [Charles V] desired him to give up his kingdoms willy-nilly: that he would be compelled to do so by fire, sword, and bloodshed; and that, like Pharaoh, he would be exterminated with all his army. From this he concluded that these guests whom he and his people called Viracochas [one of two supreme Inca deities], considering them as gods, had been transformed into mortal enemies of his people and of his line, since they had nothing but these cruel, pitiless things to say to him. And he felt so sad and so distressed that he could not refrain from uttering out loud the word *"Atac!"* which means, alas! Finally, rising above his sorrow, and restraining as best he could the passions that racked his soul, he, in turn, took the floor and spoke as follows:

"Despite the fact that you have refused me all the other things I asked of your emissaries, it would at least have given me great pleasure if you had consented to speak to me through a more learned, more accurate, more experienced interpreter than the one you have; because you must know the incomparable value that words take on for anyone who wants to learn about the customs and the civil and political life of another people; indeed, you might be endowed with the greatest virtues, and it would be difficult for me to appreciate this through what I can see and understand, so long as you do not express yourselves. And how much more pressing still this necessity becomes when the encounter takes place between persons who come from regions that are so remote from one another as ours are. In reality, if such persons attempt to speak and negotiate through the intermediary of interpreters who know neither language, then they might as well choose a four-footed go-between, among their own cattle! I say this, man of God, because I surmise that your words are quite different from those spoken by this Indian; indeed the very reason for our meeting is evidence of this fact.

"We are here to discuss peace, friendship, and permanent brotherhood, even an alliance between our two bloods, as was stated by your first emissaries when they came to call on me. And these words have a different sound from those your interpreter has just spoken; for he only speaks of war and death, of fire and sword, of banishment and destruction, of extinction of the royal blood of the Incas, of alienation of my kingdom, and, whether I will or no, of my vassalage to someone whom I do not even know. From all of this, I can only conclude two things: either your prince and you yourselves are but tyrants who go about ravaging and destroying everything they encounter in the world, appropriating by force kingdoms to which they have no right, killing, robbing, despoiling those who owe them nothing and have done them no harm; or else you are the ministers of God, whom we call Pachacamac, and He has designated you to punish and destroy us. If this be so, my vassals and I accept death and whatever else you may choose to do with us, not at all through fear inspired by your weapons or your threats, but in order that the last wishes of my father, Huaina Capac, may be fulfilled; for he commanded us, on his deathbed, to serve and honor the bearded men, like yourselves, who would come to this land after he had left it. For many years he had known that these men were cruising in their ships along the coast of our Empire; and he told us that their laws and their customs, their science, and their bravery were greater than our own. This is why we called you Viracochas, meaning by this that you were the messengers of the great god Viracocha: his will and his indignation could not be other than just, and who could resist the power of his arms? But he is also full of pity and mercy, and therefore you, who are his messengers and ministers, you who are not human, but divine, you cannot allow a repetition of the crimes, the robberies, and all the other cruelty that was perpetrated in Tumbez and in the other regions you came through.

"In addition to this, your herald spoke to me of five well-known men, whom I should know about. The first is the god three and one which make four [a garbled version of the Trinity], whom you call the creator of the universe; no doubt he is the same as the one we call Pachacamac and Viracocha. The second [Adam] is the one whom you say is the father of the human species, upon whom all other men have laid their sins. You call the third one Jesus Christ, who did not burden his fellow men with his sins, as all other men did, but who was killed. The fourth, you call the Pope, and the fifth, Charles.

"Without taking the others into consideration, you call this latter the all-powerful sovereign of the universe and say that he is above everybody else. But then, if this Charles is the prince and lord of the entire world, how is it that the Pope should have had to grant him permission to make war upon me and usurp my kingdoms? And if this was necessary, this means that the Pope is a greater, more powerful lord than he is, and therefore the prince of the entire universe. I am surprised that I should have to pay tribute to Charles and not to the others; you give no reason for this, and I myself do not see any that would oblige me to do so. Because, if I were obliged, quite frankly, to pay service and tribute to someone, it seems to me that it would rather be to God who, as you say, created us all, and to that first man who was the father of all other men, and to Jesus Christ, who never burdened others with his sins, and, lastly, to the Pope, who can dispose of my person and of my kingdom, to assign them to others.

"But if you say that I owe nothing to any one of these three, it seems to me that I owe even less to Charles, who was never lord of this land, and has never even seen it. And even if we were to admit that, having received the Pope's blessing, he really had some rights over me, would it not be just and fair that you should tell me this, before proclaiming threats of war, bloodshed, and death? I am neither so foolish nor so unreasonable as not to know how to obey him who exerts authority over me by rights, and justly and reasonably; but how am I to comply with the Pope's desires without knowing what they are?

"Lastly, to come back to that eminent man, Jesus Christ, who refused to burden others with his sins, I should like to know how he died: was it from sickness, or at the hands of his enemies? And was he set among the gods before or after his death? I should like to know whether or not you consider as gods these five men whom you hold up to me, and whom you so venerate. For if this be the case, then you have more gods than we have, for we worship no god other than Pachacamac, who is our supreme God, after whom we worship the Sun, whose bride and sister is the Moon. . . ."

In making his reply, the Inca reckoned with the awkwardness of the interpreter, Felipe. He pronounced his sentences slowly, breaking them up into short phrases, so as to give him ample time to understand. And, above all, instead of speaking the language of Cuzco, he chose that of Chinchasuyu, which the Indian understood much better. Despite these precautions, however, the king's thought was nevertheless quite imperfectly and barbarously translated, while the royal historians noted it faithfully on their *quipus* [knotted cords], in order that it might remain in their archives.

But the Spaniards, who had grown impatient during this long speech, suddenly sprang from their hiding places and attacked the Indians in order to rob them of their handsome gold jewels encrusted with precious stones which they were wearing for this solemn occasion. Other Spaniards climbed up a small tower, on top of which was an idol covered with gold and silver plate enhanced with precious stones. Soon there was immense confusion, the Spaniards struggling to take possession of these treasures, and the Indians to defend them. . . .

Shall we say, to summarize, that more than five thousand Indians were killed on that day, among whom were more than fifteen hundred old people, women, and children, who had come out of curiosity to be present at this unprecedented meeting. Some were suffocated in the crowd or trampled to death by the Spanish horses, while others—how many no one can say—died entombed under one of the walls of the square, which collapsed under the pressure of those who were trying to escape. And yet, as I said before, there were on hand more than thirty thousand armed Indian fighters, and the Spaniards only numbered one hundred and sixty! But all these Indians were haunted by the famous prediction of the Inca Viracocha, and they asked themselves if the moment had not arrived when, not only the Empire and its laws, but also their religion and its rites were about to disappear like so much smoke. For this reason, they neither dared to defend themselves, nor to offend the Spaniards whom they considered as gods and the messengers of Viracocha. Spanish historians themselves confirm the fact that Atahualpa forbade his troops to fight. . . .

The Spanish cavalrymen left their hiding places, hurling themselves like thunderbolts at the Indian squadrons, their lances in rest; and they transpierced as many as they could without encountering any resistance. Don Pizarro and his wildly impatient infantrymen had succeeded, meanwhile, in forcing their way to Atahualpa, because at the very idea of so rich a catch they already saw themselves the masters of all the treasures in Peru. The Indians crowded about the royal litter, ready to defend with their own bodies the Inca's sacred person. They were massacred one by one, however, without having made the slightest gesture of defense. Then Don Francisco, who had finally come up close to the king, seized the latter's clothing and, together, they were soon wrestling on the ground.

And thus it was that King Atahualpa became prisoner of the Spaniards, which fact, when the Indians realized it, made them flee in the greatest disorder. Being unable to leave by the only gate of the city, which was in the hands of the cavalry, they hurled themselves with such fury against one of the enclosing walls that they opened up a breach more than one hundred feet wide, through which they were able to escape to the plain. One author wrote that, on this occasion, by yielding to death-hunted men, this stone wall showed more tenderness and pity than the hearts of the Spaniards. Indeed, according to historians, the Spaniards were so angry when they saw the Indians escape, that they dashed across the plain in their pursuit and massacred a large number with their lances, until nightfall forced them to stop. They then pillaged the Inca's camp, where they amassed a considerable amount of booty. . . .

Meanwhile, the Inca Atahualpa, finding himself a prisoner, with his feet in irons, had offered to fill with gold the room he was kept in—which was a fine large room—in order to obtain his freedom.

"When he saw that the Spaniards shrugged their shoulders at this proposal, and turned their backs on him, as though they did not consider this possible," wrote Francisco López de Gómara, "he touched the wall of his room, as high as he could raise his arms and, at this height, drew a red line that ran around the entire room.

"The gold and silver of my ransom will make a pile that high," he said, "on condition that you neither break nor smelt any of the objects that I shall have brought, until this limit will have been reached."

A date of payment was set, and once the deal was concluded, gold and silver began to flow into Cajamarca. But such immense quantities were needed that it seemed as though all Peru's resources would not be sufficient, and the time set came and went. Then the Spaniards began to grumble, saying that the Inca was poking fun at them, and that his envoys, instead of collecting gold and silver, were quite simply levying troops to come and free him. . . .

Atahualpa's trial was a solemn one and it lasted a long time. The court was presided over by Don Francisco Pizarro, with Don Diego de Almagro acting as assessor; Sancho de Cuéllar filled the role of clerk, another, that of prosecuting attorney, another, that of defense lawyer, to plead Atahualpa's case. Then there were two attorney generals, named by each one of the parties; two investigators, who collected the testimony and presented it to the court, and two barristers, who were simply there to give their opinions. Although I knew several of these men personally, I prefer not to name them. . . .

Ten witnesses were heard. Seven of them had been chosen among the servants of the Spaniards, and three from the outside, in order that they should not all be domestics. As Gómara writes, they said everything that the interpreter, Felipe, wanted to make them say. One of the non-domestic witnesses, named Quespe, who was captain of a company, and the last to be examined, replied each time with one single word, saying *i*, which means yes, or *manam*, which means no. And, in order that the judges might understand him and that the interpreter should not betray him, he raised and lowered his head two or three times when he said yes, and nodded it from left to right, in addition to a gesture with his right hand, when he wanted to say no; and the judges and ministers greatly admired the sagacity of this Indian.

But in spite of all that, they were not afraid to condemn to death so great and powerful a king as Atahualpa, and he was notified of his sentence, as we explained. Many of the Spaniards protested vehemently when they heard the sentence, not only among Pizarro's companions, but also among those of Almagro, because these latter were men with generous hearts, capable of feeling pity. . . .

In fact, things came to such a pass that they would have hurled themselves at one another and all been killed, if God had not stopped it by making others, who were less impassioned than they, intervene between the two groups, and thus succeed in appeasing the Inca's defenders, by telling them to consider the necessities that their own lives and the king's service rendered imperative; that it was not right for quarrels over infidels to divide Christians; and that, lastly, there were only fifty persons sharing their point of view, whereas more than three hundred upheld the point of view of the court; and that, if they should come to blows, they would have nothing to gain from it, but on the contrary, would only destroy themselves as well as such a rich kingdom as this one, which was theirs for all time, if they put its king to death.

These threats—or these good reasons—finally calmed Atahualpa's protectors, and they consented to his execution, which the others carried out.

Once the two kings, Huascar Inca and Atahualpa, who were brothers as well as enemies, were dead, the Spaniards remained supreme masters of both Peruvian kingdoms, there being no one left to oppose or even contradict them, because all the Indians, whether they belonged to [the area of] Quito or to [the area of] Cuzco, had remained, after their kings were gone, like sheep without a shepherd.

QUESTIONS

1. Do the stories told by Cortés and the Aztec informants match in all particulars?
2. What did Cortés, coming from a European Christian background, find reprehensible in Aztec life?

3. How does Cortés absolve himself of blame when taking Moctezuma captive and at the time of his death?
4. What, according to Cortés, was the major cause of the loss of life when taking the city of Tenochtitlán?
5. Why were Pizarro and his men able to capture Atahualpa in the midst of his army and his empire?
6. How much of the translated speech about Christian faith and Spanish imperial dominion did the Inca leader understand?
7. How reliable, from the viewpoint of providing accurate assessments of military matters, are the accounts?

THE JUSTIFICATION FOR CONQUEST

Papal Recognition

By the thirteenth century, the papacy lost its leading role in crusading to the secular states. As the Iberian occupation of island chains in the near Atlantic proceeded, the establishment of missionary activity signaled papal acquiescence in the conquests. Because both the Portuguese and the Spanish claimed spreading the faith as their initial justification, it was inevitable that the papacy would be brought in to settle conflicts.

> *"to bring under your sway the said mainlands and islands . . ."*

Which kingdom would have exclusive responsibility to Christianize the peoples in its zone was proclaimed in a series of papal bulls. A *bull* is an important papal letter on parchment, opening with the pope's name and the formula "bishop, servant of the servants of God." It takes its name from a papal insignia seal, which was impressed by a machine called a *bulla* on red wax or on a lead pellet wrapped around a ribbon or cord attached to the document. Each such letter, written in Latin in the third person, is identified by the first two words after the salutation.

Columbus's return in 1493 created new tensions between Spain and Portugal that could be resolved only by treaty, so an appeal was made to Alexander VI. It was not important that the pope came from Ferdinand's Aragón, or that he was obligated to him for previous support, since the long tradition was merely that popes restated the facts presented to them. One controversial aspect of the bull *Inter Caetera* is that it seemingly divided the world between the Spanish and the Portuguese along the imaginary boundary line it describes. The papal intent in giving each power an ecclesiastical jurisdiction was to uphold its role in evangelization and to keep the countries from going to war.

The bull quickly was treated as formal title to the lands, however, despite challenge from Iberian scholars and the French and English crowns that it did no such thing. It is up to the reader to determine if in fact the document, presented here in its entirety, gives secular dominion over the land to the Spanish. Papal lawyers carefully avoided denying that the land was originally under native dominion. Further, since Columbus described the people he met as simple and kindly, they had to be protected by some agent, in this case the crown, from exploitation.

Neglecting the offices of the pope at a two-kingdom conference, the Portuguese and Spanish crowns negotiated the Treaty of Tordesillas in 1494.

In exchange for recognizing Castilian holdings in the Caribbean, the Portuguese king, not wishing to be cut entirely out of the Southwest Atlantic, asked to change the globe-encircling demarcation line from 100 leagues beyond the Azores or Cape Verde Islands to a line 370 leagues further west. This shift placed Brazil, whose existence was apparently unsuspected at the time, outside Castilian rule. Does this mean that the Portuguese monarch had some hint about that land, even before Álvarez de Cabral landed there by chance, blown by winds, during 1500?

A lexander, bishop, servant of the servants of God, to the illustrious sovereigns, our very dear son in Christ, Ferdinand, king, and our very dear daughter in Christ, Isabella, queen of Castile, León, Aragón, Sicily, and Granada, health and apostolic benediction.

Among other works well pleasing to the Divine Majesty and cherished of our heart, this assuredly ranks highest, that in our times especially the Catholic faith and the Christian religion be exalted and be everywhere increased and spread, that the health of souls be cared for and that barbarous nations be overthrown and brought to the faith itself.

Wherefore inasmuch as by the favor of divine clemency, we, though of insufficient merits, have been called to this Holy See of Peter, recognizing that as true Catholic kings and princes, such as we have known you always to be, and as your illustrious deeds already known to almost the whole world declare, you not only eagerly desire but with every effort, zeal, and diligence, without regard to hardships, expenses, dangers, with the shedding even of your blood, are laboring to that end; recognizing also that you have long since dedicated to this purpose your whole soul and all your endeavors—as witnessed in these times with so much glory to the Divine Name in your recovery of the kingdom of Granada from the yoke of the Saracens [Muslims]—we therefore are rightly led, and hold it as our duty, to grant you even of our own accord and in your favor those things whereby with effort each day more hearty you may be enabled for the honor of God himself and the spread of the Christian rule to carry forward your holy and praiseworthy purpose so pleasing to immortal God.

We have indeed learned that you, who for a long time had intended to seek out and discover certain islands and mainlands remote and unknown and not hitherto discovered by others, to the end that you might bring to the worship of our Redeemer and the profession of the Catholic faith their residents and inhabitants, having been up to the present time greatly engaged in the siege and recovery of the kingdom itself of Granada were unable to accomplish this holy and praiseworthy purpose; but the said kingdom

SOURCE The papal bull *Inter Caetera,* in *European Treaties Bearing on the History of the United States and Its Dependencies to 1648,* ed. F. G. Davenport, 4 vols. (Washington, D.C., 1917–1937), vol. I, pp. 75–78.

having at length been regained, as was pleasing to the Lord, you, with the wish to fulfill your desire, chose our beloved son, Christopher Columbus, a man assuredly worthy and of the highest recommendations and fitted for so great an undertaking, whom you furnished with ships and men equipped for like designs, not without the greatest hardships, dangers, and expenses, to make diligent quest for these remote and unknown mainlands and islands through the sea, where hitherto no one had sailed; and they at length, with divine aid and with the utmost diligence sailing in the ocean sea, discovered certain very remote islands and even mainlands that hitherto had not been discovered by others; wherein dwell very many peoples living in peace, and, as reported, going unclothed, and not eating flesh.

Moreover, as your aforesaid envoys are of opinion, these very peoples living in the said islands and countries believe in one God, the Creator in heaven, and seem sufficiently disposed to embrace the Catholic faith and be trained in good morals. And it is hoped that, were they instructed, the name of the Savior, our Lord Jesus Christ, would easily be introduced into the said countries and islands. Also, on one of the chief of these aforesaid islands the said Christopher has already caused to be put together and built a fortress fairly equipped, wherein he has stationed as garrison certain Christians, companions of his, who are to make search for other remote and unknown islands and mainlands. In the islands and countries already discovered are found gold, spices, and very many other precious things of divers kinds and qualities.

Wherefore, as becomes Catholic kings and princes, after earnest consideration of all matters, especially of the rise and spread of the Catholic faith, as was the fashion of your ancestors, kings of renowned memory, you have purposed with the favor of divine clemency to bring under your sway the said mainlands and islands with their residents and inhabitants and to bring them to the Catholic faith.

Hence, heartily commending in the Lord this your holy and praiseworthy purpose, and desirous that it be duly accomplished, and that the name of our Savior be carried into those regions, we exhort you very earnestly in the Lord and by your reception of holy baptism, whereby you are bound to our apostolic commands, and by the bowels of the mercy of our Lord Jesus Christ, enjoin strictly, that inasmuch as with eager zeal for the true faith you design to equip and dispatch this expedition, your purpose also, as is your duty, to lead the peoples dwelling in those islands and countries to embrace the Christian religion; nor at any time let dangers or hardships deter you therefrom, with the stout hope and trust in your hearts that Almighty God will further your undertakings.

And, in order that you may enter upon so great an undertaking with greater readiness and heartiness endowed with the benefit of our apostolic favor, we, of our own accord, not at your insistence nor the request of anyone else in your regard, but of our own sole largess and certain knowledge and out of the fullness of our apostolic power, by the authority of

Almighty God conferred upon us in blessed Peter and of the vicarship of Jesus Christ, which we hold on earth, do by tenor of these presents, should any of said islands have been found by your envoys and captains, give, grant, and assign to you and your heirs and successors, kings of Castile and León, forever, together with all their dominions, cities, camps, places, and villages, and all rights, jurisdictions, and appurtenances, all islands and mainlands found and to be found, discovered and to be discovered towards the west and south, by drawing and establishing a line from the Arctic pole, namely the north, to the Antarctic pole, namely the south, no matter whether the said mainlands and islands are found and to be found in the direction of India or towards any other quarter, the said line to be distant one hundred leagues towards the west and south from any of the islands commonly known as the Azores and Cape Verde.

With this proviso however that none of the islands and mainlands, found and to be found, discovered and to be discovered, beyond that said line towards the west and south, be in the actual possession of any Christian king or prince up to the birthday of our Lord Jesus Christ just past from which the present year one thousand four hundred and ninety-three begins.

28

The Requirement

The mentality of sixteenth-century European peoples tended toward a careful observation of legal niceties. Since it was thought insufficient to claim that might alone makes right, a committee of jurists and theologians met in Valladolid, Spain, during 1513 to draw up a manifesto that would base the conquest of the New World on what they considered to be the unassailable truths of the Bible, the medieval theory of Just War, and European ideas concerning national sovereignty. The document that they issued was intended to be read aloud to natives so that they would have the opportunity to peacefully abandon their religions in favor of Christianity before hostilities ensued. The Spanish had been given express ecclesiastical jurisdiction over the mainlands and islands by papal decree (Document 27). Having the Requirement announced before fighting began signified Spanish intent to carry out their religious obligation to spread the Gospel.

> *"the deaths and losses which shall accrue from this are your fault, . . ."*

Critics have always been cynical about the lack of provision for translating the document into native languages. Even the principal author of the document, Juan López Palacio Rubios, admitted to being amused when he heard how it was shouted out as boats approached clearings, and mumbled to trees or empty huts. It should be noted, however, that much more is expected from the hearers than a change of religion. The obvious incomprehensibility to non-Europeans of the document's key concept of a papal dominion over the universe that had been transferred to the monarchs of Spain did not trouble the conscience of soldiers.

The Requirement was incorporated into the basic law of the land in 1526. By 1573 that law was superseded by a general ordinance, issued by King Philip II, that condemned the use of force and expressly rejected using "conquest" to describe Spanish activities in the New World.

On the part of the King, don Fernando [Ferdinand], and of doña Juana, his daughter, Queen of Castile and León, subduers of the barbarous nations, we their servants notify and make known to you, as best we can, that the Lord our God, Living and Eternal, created the Heaven and the Earth, and one man and one woman, of whom you and I, and all the men of the world, were and are descendants, and all those who come after us. But, on account of the multitude which has sprung from this man and woman in the five thousand years since the world was created, it was necessary that some men should go one way and some another, and that they should be divided into many kingdoms and provinces, for in one alone they could not be sustained.

Of all these nations God our Lord gave charge to one man, called St. Peter, that he should be Lord and Superior of all the men in the world, that all should obey him, and that he should be head of the whole human race, wherever men should live, and under whatever law, sect, or belief they should be; and he gave him the world for his kingdom and jurisdiction.

And he commanded him to place his seat in Rome, as the spot most fitting to rule the world from; but also he permitted him to have his seat in any other part of the world, and to judge and govern all Christians, Moors, Jews, Gentiles, and all other sects. This man was called Pope, as if to say, Admirable Great Father and Governor of men. The men who lived in that time obeyed that St. Peter, and took him for Lord, King, and Superior of the universe; so also have they regarded the others who after him have been elected to the Pontificate, and so it has been continued even until now, and will continue until the end of the world.

One of these Pontiffs, who succeeded that St. Peter as Lord of the world, in the dignity and seat which I have before mentioned, made donation of these isles and *terra firme* [mainland] to the aforesaid King and Queen and to their successors, our lords, with all that there are in these territories, as is

SOURCE Arthur Helps, *The Spanish Conquest in America and Its Relation to the History of Slavery and to the Government of the Colonies* (London: J. W. Parker & Sons, 1855–1861), vol. I, pp. 264–267. Text revised.

contained in certain writings which passed upon the subject as aforesaid, which you can see if you wish.

So their Highnesses are kings and lords of these islands and land of *terra firme* by virtue of this donation; and some islands, and indeed almost all those to whom this has been notified, have received and served their Highnesses, as lords and kings, in the way that subjects ought to do, with good will, without any resistance, immediately, without delay, when they were informed of the aforesaid facts. And also they received and obeyed the priests whom their Highnesses sent to preach to them and to teach them our Holy Faith; and all these, of their own free will, without any reward or condition, have become Christians, and are so, and their Highnesses have joyfully and benignantly received them, and also have commanded them to be treated as their subjects and vassals; and you too are held and obliged to do the same. Wherefore as best we can, we ask and require you that you consider what we have said to you, and that you take the time that shall be necessary to understand and deliberate upon it, and that you acknowledge the Church as the Ruler and Superior of the whole world and the high priest called Pope, and in his name the King and Queen doña Juana our lords, in his place, as superiors and lords and kings of these islands and this *terra firme* by virtue of the said donation, and that you consent and give place that these religious fathers should declare and preach to you the aforesaid.

If you do so, you will do well, and that which you are obliged to do to their Highnesses, and we in their name shall receive you in all love and charity, and shall leave you your wives, and your children, and your lands, free without servitude, that you may do with them and with yourselves freely that which you like and think best, and they shall not compel you to turn Christians, unless you yourselves, when informed of the truth, should wish to be converted to our Holy Catholic Faith, as almost all the inhabitants of the rest of the islands have done. And besides this, their Highnesses award you many privileges and exceptions and will grant you many benefits.

But if you do not do this, and wickedly and intentionally delay to do so, I certify to you that, with the help of God, we shall forcibly enter into your country and shall make war against you in all ways and manners that we can, and shall subject you to the yoke and obedience of the Church and of their Highnesses; we shall take you and your wives and your children, and shall make slaves of them, and as such shall sell and dispose of them as their Highnesses may command; and we shall take away your goods, and shall do all the harm and damage that we can, as to vassals who do not obey, and refuse to receive their lord, and resist and contradict him; and we protest that the deaths and losses which shall accrue from this are your fault, and not that of their Highnesses, or ours, nor of these gentlemen who come with us. And that we have said this to you and made this Requirement, we request the notary here present to give us his testimony in writing, and we ask the rest who are present that they should be witnesses of this Requirement.

Vitoria

The Dominican scholar Francisco de Vitoria began classes each year that he was professor of Sacred Theology at the University of Salamanca, Spain, with a public lecture on an important world problem. The published notes from these lectures, which he gave starting in 1532, are the basis of his reputation for formulating certain key principles of international law. This selection is a summary, a condensation of points made in his *De Indis* . . . , published posthumously in 1559, wherein he put to rigorous questioning the stated and unstated principles that were the basis for his country's domination of the Indies.

> *"the aborigines undoubtedly had true dominion in both public and private matters, . . ."*

Vitoria was well aware of the interests of bureaucrats, clerics, intellectuals, lawyers, and soldiers in the legitimacy, or lack thereof, of the conquests. He focused on the issue of dominion. Some theorists had proposed that a single world government under one ruler, such as Charles V, king of Spain and Holy Roman Emperor, was desirable. If this were so, the degree to which outsiders could be coerced to enter this universal dominion was a vital question. If the Amerindians properly possessed their land, under what circumstances, if any, might the emperor deprive them of it?

It was also unclear if a sinner, an infidel, a Jew, or a Muslim could be deprived of possession. Vitoria had to estimate the degree to which the pope had a right to grant the Americas, or any part of the world, to Spain or another Christian government. An equally thorny matter involved the jurisdiction, if any, that the pope had over non-Christians, especially when these non-Christians violated so-called natural law, alleged by Europeans to be binding on all human beings, with acts of cannibalism, human sacrifice, or incest.

Vitoria never visited the New World and at the time of his lectures, firsthand information about the different peoples was lacking. He lumped all groups together, not knowing about the high cultural and organizational level reached by certain states, and not realizing that customs were entirely different from area to area. Despite weaknesses in his factual base, the conclusions he reached were sufficiently disturbing to the government that government officials voiced strong objections to Vitoria's superiors. Clearly, public figures in Spain and its empire felt free to debate major ethical issues, despite censorship and the Inquisition.

Summary of the First Section

1. How a person in doubt on any matter, to obtain safety of conscience, should consult those whose business it is to give instruction in such matters.
2. After one in doubt has taken such advice he ought to follow what the wise have laid down, else he will not be safe.
3. Whether one in doubt ought, consistently with safety of conscience, to follow the advice given by the wise in a doubtful matter when they lay down that to be now lawful which in other circumstances is unlawful.
4. Whether the Indian aborigines before the arrival of the Spaniards were true owners in public and in private law; and whether there were among them any true princes and overlords.
5. Examination of the error of those who assert that persons living in mortal sin cannot have ownership of anything at all.
6. Mortal sin does not preclude civil ownership of the true kind.
7. Whether ownership is lost by reason of unbelief.
8. The divine law does not make heresy a cause of forfeiture of the heretic's property.
9. Whether heresy causes loss of ownership by human law.
10. A heretic incurs the penalty of confiscation of his property as from the date of the commission of his offence.
11. But although the heretic's offence is patent, the fisc [state treasury] may not seize his property before condemnation.
12. Even though condemnation issues after the heretic's death, confiscation of property dates back to the time of the commission of the offence, no matter who is vested with the property.
13. Sales, gifts, and all other modes of alienation by a heretic are void as from the date of the commission of the offence, etc.
14. Whether a heretic before condemnation is the owner of his property in the forum of conscience.
15. A heretic may lawfully live on his own property.
16. A heretic may make a gratuitous conveyance of his property, as by way of gift.
17. A heretic whose offence has rendered him liable to process may not convey his property for value, as by way of sale or dowry.
18. In what case a heretic may lawfully alienate his property for value.
19. Barbarians are not precluded by the sin of unbelief or by any other mortal sins from being true owners alike in public and in private law.

Source *The Spanish Origin of International Law. Francisco De Vitoria and His Law of Nations*, pp. ix–xl, by J. S. Brown, Carnegie Endowment Classics of International Law, 1934. Reprinted by permission of Oxford University Press.

20. Whether the use of reason is a prerequisite of capacity for ownership.
21. Whether a boy can be an owner before he has the use of reason.
22. Whether a person of unsound mind can be an owner.
23. Inasmuch as the Indian aborigines were not of unsound mind, they are not precluded from being true owners on the pretext of unsoundness of mind.
24. These aborigines were true owners alike in public and in private law before the advent of the Spaniards among them.

T wenty-fourth*. The upshot of all the preceding is, then, that the aborigines undoubtedly had true dominion in both public and private matters, just like Christians, and that neither their princes nor private persons could be despoiled of their property on the ground of their not being true owners. It would be harsh to deny to those, who have never done any wrong, what we grant to [Muslims] and Jews, who are the persistent enemies of Christianity. We do not deny that these latter peoples are true owners of their property, if they have not seized lands elsewhere belonging to Christians.

It remains to reply to the argument of the opposite side to the effect that the aborigines in question seem to be slaves by nature because of their incapability of self-government. My answer to this is that Aristotle certainly did not mean to say that such as are not over-strong mentally are by nature subject to another's power and incapable of dominion alike over themselves and other things; for this is civil and legal slavery, wherein none are slaves by nature. Nor does the Philosopher [Aristotle] mean that, if any by nature are of weak mind, it is permissible to seize their patrimony and enslave them and put them up for sale; but what he means is that by defect of their nature they need to be ruled and governed by others and that it is good for them to be subject to others, just as sons need to be subject to their parents until of full age, and a wife to her husband. And that this is the Philosopher's intent is clear from his corresponding remark that some are by nature masters, those, namely, who are of strong intelligence. Now, it is clear that he does not mean hereby that such persons can arrogate to themselves a sway over others in virtue of their superior wisdom, but that nature has given them capacity for rule and government. Accordingly, even if we admit that the aborigines in question are as inept and stupid as is alleged, still dominion cannot be denied to them, nor are they to be classed with the slaves of civil law. True, some right to reduce them to subjection can be based on this reason and title, as we shall show below. Meanwhile the conclusion stands sure, that the aborigines in question were true owners, before the Spaniards came among them, both from the public and the private point of view.

*The editor has eliminated discussions of the first twenty-three items.

Summary of the Second Section

On the illegitimate titles for the reduction of the aborigines of the New World into the power of the Spaniards

1. The Emperor [Charles V] is not the lord of the whole world.
2. Even if the Emperor were the lord of the world, that would not entitle him to seize the provinces of the Indian aborigines and to erect new lords and put down the former lords or to levy taxes.
3. The Pope is not civil or temporal lord of the whole world, in the proper sense of civil lordship and power.
4. Even if the Supreme Pontiff had secular power over the world, he could not give that power to secular princes.
5. The Pope has temporal power, but only so far as it subserves things spiritual.
6. The Pope has no temporal power over the Indian aborigines or over other unbelievers.
7. A refusal by these aborigines to recognize any dominion of the Pope is no reason for making war on them and for seizing their goods.
8. Whether these aborigines were guilty of the sin of unbelief, in that they did not believe in Christ, before they heard anything of Christianity.
9. What is required in order that ignorance may be imputed to a person as, and be, sin, that is, vincible ignorance. And what about invincible ignorance?
10. Whether the aborigines are bound to hearken to the first messengers of Christianity so as to commit mortal sin in not believing Christ's Gospel merely on its simple announcement to them.
11. If the faith were simply announced and proposed to them and they will not straight-way receive it, this is no ground for the Spaniards to make war on them or to proceed against them under the law of war.
12. How the aborigines, if they refuse when asked and counselled to hear peaceably the preachers of religion, cannot be excused from mortal sin.
13. When the aborigines would be bound to receive Christianity under penalty of mortal sin.
14. In the author's view it is not sufficiently clear whether Christianity has been so proposed and announced to these aborigines that they are bound to believe it under the penalty of fresh sin.
15. Even when Christianity has been proposed to them with never so much sufficiency of proof and they will not accept it, this does not render it lawful to make war on them and despoil them of their possessions.
16. Christian princes cannot, even on the authority of the Pope, restrain these aborigines from sins against the law of nature or punish them therefor.

194

... For some (I know not who) assert that the Lord by His especial judgment condemned all the barbarians in question to perdition because of their abominations and delivered them into the hands of the Spaniards, just as of old He delivered the Canaanites into the hands of the Jews. I am loath to dispute hereon at any length, for it would be hazardous to give credence to one who asserts a prophecy against the common law and against the rules of Scripture, unless his doctrine were confirmed by miracles. Now, no such are adduced by prophets of this type. Further, even assuming that it is true that the Lord had determined to bring the barbarians to perdition [damnation], it would not follow, therefore, that he who wrought their ruin would be blameless, any more than the Kings of Babylon who led their army against Jerusalem and carried away the children of Israel into captivity were blameless, although in actual fact all of this was by the especial providence of God, as had often been foretold to them.

Nor was Jeroboam right in drawing Israel away from Rehoboam, although this was done by God's design, as the Lord had also threatened by his prophet. And, would that, apart from the sin of unbelief, there might be no greater sins in morals among certain Christians than there are among those barbarians! It is also written (I *St. John*, ch. 4): "Believe not every spirit, but try the spirits whether they be of God"; and as St. Thomas [Aquinas] says (*Prima Secundae*, qu. 68), "Gifts are given by the Holy Spirit for the perfecting of virtues." Accordingly, where faith or authority or providence shows what ought to be done, recourse should not be had to gifts.

Let this suffice about false and inadequate titles to seize the lands of the Indians. But it is to be noted that I have seen nothing written on this question and have never been present at any discussion or council on this matter. Hence it may be that others may found a title and base the justice of this business and overlordship on some of the passages cited and not lack reason in so doing. I, however, have up to now been unable to form any other opinion than what I have written. And so, if there be no other titles than those which I have discussed, it would certainly be of ill omen for the safety of our princes, or rather of those who are charged with the discovery of these matters; for princes follow advice given by others, being unable to examine into these matters for themselves. "What is a man advantaged," so saith the Lord, "if he gain the whole world and lose himself, or be cast away?" (*St. Matthew*, ch. 16; *St. Mark*, ch. 8; *St. Luke*, ch. 9.)

Summary of the Third Section

On the lawful titles whereby the aborigines of America could have come into the power of Spain

1. How the aborigines might have come into the power of the Spaniards on the ground of natural society and fellowship.

2. The Spaniards have a right to travel to the lands of the Indians and to sojourn there so long as they do no harm, and they cannot be prevented by the Indians.

3. The Spaniards may carry on trade among the Indian aborigines, so long as they do no harm to their own country, by importing the goods which the aborigines lack, and taking away gold and silver and other articles in which the Indians abound; and the princes of the Indians cannot prevent their subjects from trading with the Spaniards. . . .

4. The Indians cannot prevent the Spaniards from a communication and participation in those things which they treat as common alike to natives and to strangers.

5. Any children born to Spanish parents domiciled in those parts who wish to become citizens thereof cannot be excluded from citizenship or from the advantages enjoyed by other citizens.

6. What course ought to be adopted if the aborigines desire to prevent the Spaniards trading with them.

7. If the Spaniards, after resort to all moderate measures, cannot attain security among the aborigines or Indians save by seizing their cities and reducing them to subjection, whether they can lawfully do this.

8. When and in what case the Spaniards can resort to severe measures against the Indians, treating them as faithless foes, and employ all the rights of war against them and take away their property and even reduce them to captivity, aye, and depose their former lords also and set up new lords.

9. Whether the Indians could have come under the sway of the Spaniards, in the interest of the spread of Christianity. Christians have a right to preach and publish the Gospel in the lands of barbarians.

10. The Pope could entrust to the Spaniards alone the task of converting the Indian aborigines and could forbid to all others not only preaching, but trade too, if the propagation of Christianity would thus be furthered.

11. The Indians are not to be warred into subjection or despoiled of their property, if they give the Spaniards unhindered freedom to preach the Gospel, and this whether they accept the faith or not.

12. How the aborigines who hinder the spread of the Gospel, whether it be their lords or the populace, may be coerced by the Spaniards, so long as no scandal is caused. And what is to be said of those who, while admitting preaching, prevent conversion, either by killing or punishing or terrorizing those who have been converted to Christianity?

13. How the Indians might have come under the sway of the Spaniards by the fact that, when they had been converted and become Christians, their princes desired to bring them back to idolatry by force or by fear, and so they were taken into the protection and guardianship of the Spaniards.

14. The Indians might have come under the sway of the Spaniards by the fact that, after the conversion of a large part of them to Christianity, the

Pope, either with or without a request on their part, might on reasonable grounds have given them a Christian prince, such as the King of Spain, and driven out their infidel lords.

15. Whether the Indians could have come under the sway of the Spaniards because of the tyranny of their lords or because of tyrannical laws which injured innocent folk.

16. The Indian aborigines could have come under the sway of the Spaniards through true and voluntary choice.

17. The Indians might have come under the sway of the Spaniards by a title of alliance and friendship.

18. Whether the Spaniards could have reduced the Indians into their power, if it were certainly clear that they were of defective intelligence.

18.* There is another title which can indeed not be asserted, but brought up for discussion, and some think it a lawful one. I dare not affirm it at all, nor do I entirely condemn it. It is this: Although the aborigines in question are (as has been said above) not wholly unintelligent, yet they are little short of that condition, and so are unfit to found or administer a lawful State up to the standard required by human and civil claims. Accordingly they have no proper laws nor magistrates, and are not even capable of controlling their family affairs; they are without any literature or arts, not only the liberal arts, but the mechanical arts also; they have no careful agriculture and no artisans; and they lack many other conveniences, yea necessaries, of human life.

It might, therefore, be maintained that in their own interests the sovereigns of Spain might undertake the administration of their country, providing them with prefects and governors for their towns, and might even give them new lords, so long as this was clearly for their benefit. I say there would be some force in this contention; for if they were all wanting in intelligence, there is no doubt that this would not only be a permissible, but also a highly proper, course to take; nay, our sovereigns would be bound to take it, just as if the natives were infants. The same principle seems to apply here to them as to people of defective intelligence; and indeed they are no whit or little better than such so far as self-government is concerned, or even than the wild beasts, for their food is not more pleasant and hardly better than that of beasts. Therefore their governance should in the same way be entrusted to people of intelligence. There is clear confirmation hereof, for if by some accident of fortune all their adults were to perish and there were to be left boys and youths in enjoyment, indeed, of a certain amount of reason, but of tender years and under the age of puberty, our sovereigns would certainly be justified in taking charge of them and governing them so long as they were in that condition.

*The editor has eliminated discussions for the first 17 items.

Now, this being admitted, it appears undeniable that the same could be done in the case of their barbarian parents, if they be supposed to be of that dullness of mind which is attributed to them by those who have been among them and which is reported to be more marked among them than even among the boys and youths of other nations. And surely this might be founded on the precept of charity, they being our neighbours and we being bound to look after their welfare. Let this, however, as I have already said, be put forward without dogmatism and subject also to the limitation that any such interposition be for the welfare and in the interests of the Indians and not merely for the profit of the Spaniards. For this is the respect in which all the danger to soul and salvation lies.

QUESTIONS

1. What is a papal bull?
2. Why did Spain and Portugal go to the papacy when their monarchs wished to share the globe?
3. If Alexander VI's bulls did in fact "give" the New World to the Spanish, why did he do this?
4. Summarize the views of sacred and secular history presented in the Requirement.
5. How does the Inca leader Atahualpa's reply to Friar Vincente de Valverde in Document 26 show how little might have been understood by local populations concerning the ideas of the Requirement?
6. At first glance, the Requirement may strike the modern reader as being hypocritical. How might its writers have defended its wording and use?
7. What are the principal arguments Vitoria outlines against despoiling original owners of their property, forcing aboriginal populations to become Christian, and replacing native government with European rule?
8. Vitoria's sentiments seem at first totally opposite to the ideas in the Requirement. Is there anything in common between them, in practical terms?

THE "BLACK LEGEND" OF SPAIN

30

The Dominican Advent Sermons

The rapid decline in the number of islanders and the chaotic collapse of their governmental structures led to fears that the same would happen elsewhere in the New World. The Dominicans, who came to Hispaniola in 1510 under the leadership of Pedro de Córdoba, began to protest in private. More significant and public action had to be taken. In December 1511, Father Antón Montesino preached two sermons in Hispaniola that signaled the start of a long struggle on the part of missionaries to protect their flocks. The Dominicans did not protest the right of the Spanish to dominate the natives, but just the colonists' abuse of their position. Even this little amount of protest was enough to arouse Alonso de Loaysa, the Dominican provincial, to warn

> *"Tell me, what right have you to enslave them!"*

Montesino that "you have given in your sermon occasion for all this to be lost; everything might have been disturbed, and, on account of your sermon, all of the Indies might have rebelled so that neither you nor any other Christians would have been able to remain."

The Dominican order was founded in Spain during the thirteenth century by Domingo de Guzmán. His Order of Preachers, also known as the Black Friars, were exhorted by their founder to tramp the roads barefoot and in poverty, preaching against heresy. In this role as enemies of heretics, they came to direct both the medieval Papal Inquisition and the later Spanish Royal Inquisition. They were also energetic missionaries who followed in the worldwide expansion by the Spanish, Portuguese, and French. By the seventeenth century, the order was established in China, Japan, and the Philippines.

T he Dominican friars had already pondered on the sad life and harsh captivity suffered by the natives on the island and had noticed the Spanish lack of concern for their fate except as a business loss which brought about no softening of their oppression. There were two kinds of Spaniards, one very cruel and pitiless, whose goal was to squeeze the last drop of Indian blood in order to get rich, and one less cruel, who must have felt sorry for the Indians; but in each case they placed their own interests

SOURCE Bartolomé de Las Casas, *History of the Indies*, trans. and ed. Andrée Collard (New York: Harper & Row, 1971), Book III, Chs. 3–5, pp. 181–187, passim. Reprinted by permission.

above the health and salvation of those poor people. Of all those who used Indians, I knew only one man, Pedro de Rentería—of whom there will be much to say later, if God so wills—who was pious toward them. The friars, then, weighed these matters as well as the innocence, the inestimable patience and the gentleness of Indians, and deliberated on the following points among themselves. Weren't these people human beings? Wasn't justice and charity owed them? Had they no right to their own territory, their own kingdoms? Have they offended us? Aren't we under obligation to preach to them the Christian religion and work diligently toward their conversion? How is it that in fifteen or sixteen years their number has so decreased, since they tell us how crowded it was when they first came here? . . .

The most scholarly among them [the Dominicans] composed the first sermon on the subject by order of their superior, fray Pedro de Córdoba, and they all signed it to show that it represented common sentiment and not that of the preacher alone. They gave it to their most important preacher, fray Antón Montesino, who was the second of three preachers the Order had sent here. Fray Antón Montesino's talent lay in a certain sternness when reproaching faults and a certain way of reading sermons both choleric and efficient, which was thought to reap great results. So then, as a very animated speaker, they gave him that first sermon on such a new theme; the novelty consisting in saying that killing a man is more serious than killing a beetle. They set aside the fourth week of Advent for the sermon, since the Gospel according to St. John that week is "The Pharisees asked St. John the Baptist who he was and he said: *Ego vox clamantis in deserto.*" ["I am a voice crying in the wilderness."] The whole city of Santo Domingo was to be there, including the admiral Diego Columbus, and all the jurists and royal officials, who had been notified each and every one individually to come and hear a sermon of great importance. They accepted readily, some out of respect for the virtue of the friars; others, out of curiosity to hear what was to be said that concerned them so much, though had they known, they would have refused to come and would have censured the sermon as well.

At the appointed time fray Antón Montesino went to the pulpit and announced the theme of the sermon: *Ego vox clamantis in deserto.* After the introductory words on Advent, he compared the sterility of the desert to the conscience of the Spaniards who lived on Hispaniola in a state of blindness, a danger of damnation, sunk deep in the waters of insensitivity and drowning without being aware of it. Then he said: "I have come here in order to declare it unto you, I the voice of Christ in the desert of this island. Open your hearts and your senses, all of you, for this voice will speak new things harshly, and will be frightening." For a good while the voice spoke in such punitive terms that the congregation trembled as if facing Judgment Day. "This voice," he continued, "says that you are living in deadly sin for the atrocities you tyrannically impose on these innocent people. Tell me, what right have you to enslave them? What authority did you use to make war against them who lived at peace on their territories, killing them cruelly with methods never before heard of? How can you oppress them and not care to feed or cure them, and work them to death to satisfy your greed? And why don't you look after their spiritual health, so that they should come to know God, that they should be baptized, and that they should hear Mass and keep the holy days? Aren't they human beings? Have they no rational soul? Aren't you obliged to love them as you love yourselves? Don't you understand? How can you live in such a lethargical dream? You may rest assured that you are in no better state of salvation than the Moors or the Turks who reject the Christian Faith." The voice had astounded them all; some reacted as if they had lost their senses, some were petrified and others showed signs of repentance, but not one was really convinced. After his sermon, he descended from the pulpit holding his head straight, as if un-afraid—he wasn't the kind of man to show fear—for much was at stake in displeasing the audience by speaking what had to be said, and he went on to his thin cabbage soup and the straw house of his Order accompanied by a friend.

When he had left, the congregation began such whispering that I believe they could not finish the Mass. You can imagine they didn't sit around reading ... after dinner that day, and they can't have enjoyed the meal either since presently they all met at the admiral's house, that is, Diego Colum-bus, the discoverer's son. They decided to reprehend and frighten the preacher and his companions, to punish him as a scandalmaker and originator of a new doctrine that condemned them against the King's au-thority by stating they could not use the Indians the King had given them, which was a most serious and unpardonable matter. They called at the friars' house, the porter opened the door, they asked for the superior, and the venerable father fray Pedro de Córdoba came alone to meet them. Imperi-ously they demanded to see the preacher; he answered prudently saying that as a prelate he could speak for all his friars. They insisted but he evaded the issue by using grave and modest words, as he was wont to do, with an air of prudence and authority. Finally, the reverence of his person prevailed upon the admiral and other royal officials to change their tone; they softened and begged him to please bring the friar to them because they wanted to ques-tion him about the basis of a sermon that had preached such new and prejudicial things in disservice of the King and damage to the residents of the island. . . .

They decided then, each one for his own reasons, to demand a retraction on the following Sunday, and blindness drove them to the point of threaten-ing to send the friars back to Spain if they should not comply. The superior answered that, "Surely, this could be easily done," and this was true, for, besides their habits of coarse frieze, they owned nothing but a rough blanket for the night. They slept on straw pads held up by X-shaped supports; as for the articles of Mass and their scant library, that would easily fit in two trunks. When they realized that threats brought no results, they softened again and asked them to consider another sermon which in some way would satisfy a scandalized town. The friars, in order to put an end to their frivolous importunities and get rid of them, conceded that the same fray Montesino would preach the following Sunday and do his best to satisfy them and elucidate things, and once this was agreed upon, they went home happily.

The news of the friar's recantation to be made the following Sunday spread so rapidly that, come Sunday, no invitation was needed to draw the whole town to church. Fray Antón Montesino went to the pulpit and read a theme from Job 36: "From the beginning I shall repeat my knowledge and my truth and I will show my words of last Sunday, that so embittered you, to be true." They were quick to sense the tenor of the sermon and sat there itching to restrain him. The friar backed up his sermon with supporting authorities and gave more reasons to condemn the tyranny of Spanish oppression as illegal, while stressing the point that in no way could a Spaniard save his soul if he persisted in that state. He asked them to mend their ways and said that his Order would refuse to confess anyone except those who moved from place to place. They could publicize this; they could write to anyone they pleased in Castile; for their part, the friars knew for certain this was the only way to serve both God and the King. After he left, they grumbled in indignation, frustrated in their hopes that the friar would deny what he had said, as if a disavowal could change the law of God which they violated by oppressing Indians. . . .

To return to the subject: they left the church in a state of rage and again salted their meal that day with bitterness. Not bothering with the friars, since conversation with them had proved useless, they decided to tell the King [Ferdinand] on the first occasion that the Dominicans had scandalized the world by spreading a new doctrine that condemned them all to Hell because they used Indians in the mines, a doctrine that went against the orders of His Highness and aimed at nothing else but to deprive him of both power and a source of income. The King required an interview with the Castilian provincial of the Order—the friars of Hispaniola had not yet been granted a charter—and complained to him about his choice of friars, who had done him a great disservice by preaching against the state and causing disturbances all over the world. The King ordered him to correct this by threatening to take action. You see how easy it is to deceive a King, how ruinous to a kingdom it is to heed misinformation, and how oppression thrives where truth is not allowed a voice.

31

Las Casas

In April 1493, the eighteen-year-old Bartolomé de Las Casas saw Columbus pass through Seville on his return from the first voyage. That year his father and two uncles sailed on Columbus's second voyage. Las Casas traveled to the New World with the Spanish governor Nicolás de Ovando in 1502. He became a Dominican Friar in 1523, after condemning his colonial way of life and his former compatriots' treatment of the natives.

> *"all the violence and tyranny that the Christians have practised . . ."*

He published his *Brief Relation of the Destruction of the Indies* in Seville in 1522. Other books followed, as he became the foremost propagandist for his cause. Las Casas had advantages over his opponents: friends at the royal court and diverse contact with many Amerindian groups, for he crossed the Atlantic ten times.

Spanish patriots have condemned him for helping to add to a "black legend" about exceptional Spanish cruelty. Other elements of this accusation are the tortures of the Inquisition, the expulsion of Jews and Muslims, and the brutal military activities of its army in the Low Countries and Italy. Las Casas proved useful to enemies of the Spanish empire when the English published a translation of the *Brief Relation*, as they were about to seize Jamaica. Another edition was issued by Washington during the Spanish-American War to justify the U.S. conquest of Cuba, Puerto Rico, and the Philippines.

Las Casas has always been applauded by proponents of human rights. However, despite his reputation as "defender of the Indians" and his warm sympathies for them, Las Casas argued from unexamined premises. The first premise was that Christianity is the true religion, which all Amerindians should accept, and the second was that the Spanish sovereigns exercised a proper political jurisdiction over the Indies. To give him credit, it is doubtful he would ever have been heard if he had not clung to these views. Today's scholars join in the attack on Las Casas because he shaped the truth as he wished it to be. He wrote about places he never saw and made up statistics to fit his case. It is up to the reader to decide if his virtues outweigh his sins.

God has created all these numberless people to be quite the simplest, without malice or duplicity, most obedient, most faithful to their natural Lords, and to the Christians, whom they serve; the most humble, most patient, most peaceful, and calm, without strife nor tumults; not wrangling, nor querulous, as free from uproar, hate and desire of revenge, as any in the world.

They are likewise the most delicate people, weak and of feeble constitution, and less than any other can they bear fatigue, and they very easily die of whatsoever infirmity; so much so, that not even the sons of our Princes and of nobles, brought up in royal and gentle life, are more delicate than they; although there are among them such as are of the peasant class. They are also a very poor people, who of worldly goods possess little, nor wish to possess: and they are therefore neither proud, nor ambitious, nor avaricious.

Their food is so poor, that it would seem that of the Holy Fathers in the desert was not scantier nor less pleasing. Their way of dressing is usually to go naked, covering the private parts; and at most they cover themselves with a cotton cover, which would be about equal to one and a half or two ells square of cloth. Their beds are of matting, and they mostly sleep in certain things like hanging nets, called in the language of Hispaniola *hamacas*.

They are likewise of a clean, unspoiled, and vivacious intellect, very capable, and receptive to every good doctrine; most prompt to accept our Holy Catholic Faith, to be endowed with virtuous customs; and they have as little difficulty with such things as any people created by God in the world.

Once they have begun to learn of matters pertaining to faith, they are so importunate to know them, and in frequenting the sacraments and divine service of the Church, that to tell the truth, the clergy have need to be endowed of God with the gift of preeminent patience to bear with them: and finally, I have heard many lay Spaniards frequently say many years ago, (unable to deny the goodness of those they saw) certainly these people were the most blessed of the earth, had they only knowledge of God.

Among these gentle sheep, gifted by their Maker with the above qualities, the Spaniards entered as soon as they knew them, like wolves, tigers, and lions which had been starving for many days, and since forty years they have done nothing else; nor do they otherwise at the present day, than outrage, slay, afflict, torment, and destroy them with strange and new, and divers kinds of cruelty, never before seen, nor heard of, nor read of, of which some few will be told below. . . .

SOURCE *Very Brief Account of the Destruction of the Indies,* trans. F. A. MacNutt, *Bartolomé de Las Casas* . . . [Cleveland: The Arthur H. Clark Co., 1909], pp. 312–319, passim. Paragraph numbers removed.

Of the Island of Hispaniola

The Christians, with their horses and swords and lances, began to slaughter and practise strange cruelty among them. They penetrated into the country and spared neither children nor the aged, nor pregnant women, nor those in child labour, all of whom they ran through the body and lacerated, as though they were assaulting so many lambs herded in their sheepfold.

They made bets as to who would slit a man in two, or cut off his head at one blow: or they opened up his bowels. They tore the babes from their mothers' breast by the feet, and dashed their heads against the rocks. Others they seized by the shoulders and threw into the rivers, laughing and joking, and when they fell into the water they exclaimed: "boil body of so and so!" They spitted the bodies of other babes, together with their mothers and all who were before them, on their swords.

They made a gallows just high enough for the feet to nearly touch the ground, and by thirteens, in honour and reverence of our Redeemer and the twelve Apostles, they put wood underneath and, with fire, they burned the Indians alive.

They wrapped the bodies of others entirely in dry straw, binding them in it and setting fire to it; and so they burned them. They cut off the hands of all they wished to take alive, made them carry them fastened on to them, and said: "Go and carry letters": that is; take the news to those who have fled to the mountains.

They generally killed the lords and nobles in the following way. They made wooden gridirons of stakes, bound them upon them, and made a slow fire beneath: thus the victims gave up the spirit by degrees, emitting cries of despair in their torture.

I once saw that they had four or five of the chief lords stretched on the gridirons to burn them, and I think also there were two or three pairs of gridirons, where they were burning others; and because they cried aloud and annoyed the captain or prevented him sleeping, he commanded that they should strangle them: the officer who was burning them was worse than a hangman and did not wish to suffocate them, but with his own hands he gagged them, so that they should not make themselves heard, and he stirred up the fire, until they roasted slowly, according to his pleasure. I know his name, and knew also his relations in Seville. I saw all the above things and numberless others.

And because all the people who could flee, hid among the mountains and climbed the crags to escape from men so deprived of humanity, so wicked, such wild beasts, exterminators and capital enemies of all the human race, the Spaniards taught and trained the fiercest boar-hounds to tear an Indian to pieces as soon as they saw him, so that they more willingly attacked and ate one, than if he had been a boar. These hounds made great havoc and slaughter.

And because sometimes, though rarely, the Indians killed a few Christians for just cause, they made a law among themselves, that for one Christian whom the Indians killed, the Christians should kill a hundred Indians. . . .

Of New Spain

New Spain [Mexico] was discovered in the year 1517. And the discoverers gave serious offence to the Indians in that discovery, and committed several homicides. In the year 1518 men calling themselves Christians went there to ravage and to kill; although they say that they go to populate. And from the said year 1518, till the present day (and we are in 1542) all the iniquity, all the injustice, all the violence and tyranny that the Christians have practised in the Indies have reached the limit and overflowed: because they have entirely lost all fear of God and the King, they have forgotten themselves as well. So many and such are the massacres and cruelty, the murder and destruction, the pillage and theft, the violence and tyranny throughout the numerous kingdoms of the great continent, that everything told by me till now is nothing compared to what was practised here. . . .

Among other massacres there was one took place in a town of more than thirty thousand inhabitants called Cholula; all the lords of the land, and its surroundings, and above all the priests, with the high priest came out in procession to meet the Christians, with great submission and reverence, and conducted them in their midst to lodge in the town in the dwelling houses of the prince, or principal lords; the Spaniards determined on a massacre here or, as they say, a chastisement to sow terror and the fame of their valour throughout that country, because in all the lands the Spaniards have invaded, their aim has always been to make themselves feared of those meek lambs, by a cruel and signal slaughter.

To accomplish this, they first sent to summon all the lords and nobles of the town and of all its dependencies, together with the principal lord; and when they came, and began to speak to the captain of the Spaniards, they were promptly captured, without any one who could give the alarm, noticing it.

They had asked for five or six thousand Indians to carry their baggage, all of whom immediately came and were confined in the courtyards of the houses. To see these Indians when they prepared themselves to carry the loads of the Spaniards, was a thing to excite great compassion for they come naked, with only the private parts covered, and with some little nets on their shoulders containing their meagre food; they all sit down on their heels, like so many meek lambs.

Being all collected and assembled in the courtyard, with other people who were there, some armed Spaniards were stationed at the gates of the courtyard to guard them: thereupon all the others seized their swords and lances, and butchered all those lambs, not even one escaping.

Two or three days later, many Indians who had hidden, and saved themselves under the dead bodies (so many were they) came out alive covered with blood, and they went before the Spaniards, weeping and asking for mercy, that they should not kill them: no mercy, nor any compassion was shown them; on the contrary, as they came out, the Spaniards cut them to pieces.

More than one hundred of the lords whom they had bound, the captain commanded to be burned, and impaled alive on stakes stuck in the ground. One lord however, perhaps the chief and king of that country, managed to free himself, and with twenty or thirty or forty other men, he escaped to the great temple, which was like a fortress and was called *Quu*, where they defended themselves during a great part of the day.

But the Spaniards, from whom nothing is safe, especially among these people destitute of weapons, set fire to the temple and burned them, they crying out: "wretched men! what have we done unto you? why do you kill us? go then! in Mexico you will find our universal lord Moctezuma who will take vengeance upon you for us." It is said, that while those five, or six thousand men were being put to the sword in the courtyard, the captain of the Spaniards stood singing. . . .

Of the Province and Kingdom of Guatemala

Let us again speak of the great tyrant captain [Pedro de Alvarado], who went to the kingdom of Guatemala, who, as has been said, surpassed all past and equalled all present tyrants. The provinces surrounding Mexico are, by the route he took (according to what he himself writes in a letter to his chief who sent him), four hundred leagues distant from the kingdom of Guatemala: he advanced killing, ravaging, burning, robbing and destroying all the country wherever he came, under the above mentioned pretext, namely, that the Indians should subject themselves to such inhuman, unjust, and cruel men, in the name of the unknown King of Spain, of whom they had never heard and whom they considered to be much more unjust and cruel than his representatives. He also gave them no time to deliberate but would fall upon them, killing and burning almost at the same instant that his envoy arrived.

When he reached this kingdom, he began with a great massacre. Nevertheless the principal lord, accompanied by many other lords of Ultatlan, the chief town of all the kingdom went forth with trumpets, tambourines and great festivity to receive him with litters; they served him with all that they possessed, and especially by giving him ample food and everything else they could.

The Spaniards lodged outside the town that night because it seemed to them to be strong, and that they might run some risk inside it. The following day, the captain called the principal lord and many others, and when they came like tame lambs, he seized them and demanded so many loads of gold. They replied that they had none, because that country does not produce it. Guiltless of other fault and without trial or sentence, he immediately ordered them to be burned alive.

When the rulers throughout all those provinces saw that the Spaniards had burnt that one and all those chief lords, only because they gave them no gold, they all fled from their towns and hid in the mountains; they commanded all their people to go to the Spaniards and serve them as their lords, but that they should not, however, reveal to them their hiding place.

All the inhabitants came to offer themselves to his men and to serve them as their lords. This compassionate captain replied that he would not receive them; on the contrary, he would kill them all, if they did not disclose the whereabouts of their chiefs. The Indians answered that they knew nothing about them but that the Spaniards should make use of them, of their wives and children whom they would find in their houses, where they could kill them or do with them what they wished. And this the Indians declared and offered many times.

Stupefying to relate, the Spaniards went to the houses where they found the poor people working in safety at their occupations with their wives and children, and there they wounded them with their lances and cut them to pieces. They also went to a quiet, large and important town, where the people were ignorant of what had happened to the others and were safe in their innocence; within barely two hours they destroyed it, putting women, children, and the aged to the sword, and killing all who did not save themselves by flight.

Seeing that with such humility, submission, patience and suffering they could not break nor soften hearts so inhuman and brutal, and that they were thus cut to pieces contrary to every show or shadow of right, and that they must inevitably perish, the Indians determined to summon all their people together and to die fighting, avenging themselves as best they could on such cruel and infernal enemies; they well knew, however, that being not only unarmed but also naked and on foot, they could not prevail against such fierce people, mounted and so well armed, but must in the end be destroyed.

They constructed some pits in the middle of the streets, covered over with broken boughs of trees and grass, completely concealing them: they were filled with sharp stakes hardened by fire which would be driven into the horses' bellies if they fell into the pits. Once, or twice, did some horses fall in but not often, because the Spaniards knew how to avoid them. In revenge, the Spaniards made a law, that all Indians of whatsoever rank and age whom they captured alive, they would throw into the pits. And so they threw in pregnant and confined women, children, old men and as many as they could capture who were left stuck on the stakes, until the pits were filled: It excited great compassion to see them, particularly the women with their children.

They killed all the others with lances and knives; they threw them to savage dogs, that tore them to pieces and ate them; and when they came across some lord, they accorded him the honour of burning in live flames. This butchery lasted about seven years from 1524 to 1531. From this may be judged what numbers of people they destroyed.

32

Motolinía

The traditional rivalry and often bitter hostility among the Church's major orders of friars shows up in this attack by a Franciscan upon a Dominican. Friar Toribio de Motolinía, who rose to a high rank in his order, was one of the "Franciscan Twelve" who began the mission to America. He became a serious scholar of Nahua culture, and changed his name from Benavente to Motolinía, the Nahuatl word meaning "one who is poor or afflicted," in keeping with his vow of poverty.

> *"the Indians have been well treated, looked after and defended; . . ."*

Motolinía wrote to the emperor of Spain, Charles V, in 1555 because he was thoroughly exasperated by Las Casas's campaign against the Spanish presence in the Indies. The Franciscan was a spokesman for the ordinary Spanish settler, who fervently believed it was God's will that Mexico was conquered, and that evil practices such as human sacrifice were ended. He was proud of the careful instruction of his flock, the reduction of tribute demanded from the natives, the comfort extended to the dying, and the role of his order in the spread of the faith to Florida. The full version of the letter rambles, much like a symphony with several false climaxes, because each time he was ready to bring it to an end, he was infuriated by yet another publication by the prolific Dominican.

S acred Caesarean Catholic Majesty: Grace and mercy and peace *a Deo patre nostro et Domino Jesu Christo.* Three things principally move me to write your majesty [Charles V] this letter, which I believe will be enough to remove some of the scruples of conscience that this Las Casas has proposed to your majesty and the members of your councils, all the more in the things he is now writing

SOURCE *Letters and Peoples of the Spanish Indies: Sixteenth Century,* pp. 220–240, passim, trans. and ed. by James Lockhart and Enrique Otte. Copyright © 1976. Reprinted with the permission of Cambridge University Press.

and having printed. First I must tell your majesty that when the Spaniards entered New Spain here, it had not been ruled for very long from Mexico City, nor by the Mexica [Aztecs], and the Mexica themselves had won and usurped dominion through war. . . .

Your majesty, when the Marqués del Valle [Cortés] entered this land, God our Lord was very offended with it; people suffered the cruelest of deaths, and our adversary the demon was very pleased with the greatest idolatries and most cruel homicides there ever were, because the predecessor of Moctezuma, lord of Mexico, called Ahuitzotzin, offered to the idols in a single temple and in one sacrifice that lasted three or four days, 80,400 men, whom they brought along four streets, in four lines, until they reached the sacrificial block before the idols. And at the time when the Christians entered New Spain, more than ever before there was sacrificing and killing of men before the idols in all the towns and provinces. . . .

. . . [A]bout five or six years ago I was ordered by your majesty and your Council of the Indies to collect certain confessionals that Las Casas left here in New Spain, handwritten, among the friars. I sought out all those to be found among the Franciscans and gave them to don Antonio de Mendoza, your viceroy, and he burned them, because they contained false and scandalous statements. Now, in the last ships to reach New Spain, there have arrived the same confessionals in print, which has caused a great outcry and scandal throughout the land, because many times he gives the conquerors, encomenderos and merchants the names of tyrants, robbers, violaters, ravishers and thieves. He says that always and every day they are oppressing the Indians; he also says that all the tributes from the Indians have been and are being taken evilly, unjustly and tyrannically. If that were so, a fine state your majesty's conscience would be in, since your majesty draws from half or more of the most important towns and provinces of New Spain, and the encomenderos and conquerors have only what your majesty orders them to be given.

And as far as the Indians receiving moderate tribute quotas, and being well treated and looked after, through the goodness of God today they almost all are; and as to justice and religion being administered to them, that is what is being done. Even so, this Las Casas maintains what he has said, and more; his principal insult or insults are to your majesty, and he condemns the learned men of your councils, often calling them unjust and tyrannical. And he also insults and condemns all the men of the law that there are and have been in all New Spain, whether ecclesiastic or secular, and your majesty's Audiencias and their regents. Certainly the Marqués del Valle, and Bishop don Sebastián Ramírez, and don Antonio de Mendoza, and don Luis de Velasco, who governs now with the Audiencia judges, have ruled and governed both commonwealths, Spaniards and Indians, very well, and continue to. Surely, for the bit of canon law that Las Casas studied, he dares too much; his confusion appears great, his humility small. He thinks that all err and he alone is right, because he also makes this statement, which follows word for word: "All the conquerors have been robbers and ravishers, the most qualified in evil and cruelty that there ever have been, as is manifest to the whole world." All of the conquerors, he says, without making a single exception. Your majesty already knows the instructions and orders that those who go to new conquests carry and have carried, and how they work to observe them, and are of as good life and conscience as Las Casas, and have a more upright and holy zeal.

. . . I am amazed that your majesty and those of your councils have been able to bear for so long with a man so vexatious, unquiet, importunate, argumentative and litigious, in a friar's habit, so restless, so poorly bred, insulting, prejudicial and troublemaking. For fifteen years I have known Las Casas, since before he came to this country. He was going to Peru, and not being able to stay there, he was in Nicaragua, and was not calm there for long, and after that he was among the people of Oaxaca, where he felt as little repose as in the other places. After he came to Mexico City he was in the Dominican monastery, but he soon had enough there too and went back to wandering and going about with his tumult and unrest, always writing indictments of other people, seeking out the crimes and bad things that the Spaniards had committed through this whole land, to exaggerate and make worse the evils and sins that have occurred. In this he seemed to do the work of our adversary [Satan], though he thought himself more zealous and more just than the other Christians, including the friars; but he had hardly anything to do with religion here. . . .

As to the overseers, tribute-collectors and miners, he calls them executioners, soulless, inhuman and cruel. And granted that some have been greedy and of ill repute, certainly there are many others who are good Christians, pious and charitable, many of them married and of good life. . . .

I would like to see Las Casas persevere for fifteen or twenty years in confessing ten or twelve sick, ailing Indians daily, and an equal number of healthy old ones who never confessed before, and see to many other things, many of them spiritual, concerning the Indians. A fine thing it is that there in Spain, to show his zeal, he says to your majesty and those of your councils: So-and-so is no friend of the Indians, he is a friend of the Spaniards; do not believe him. . . .

Since for the past ten years there has been great mortality and pestilence among the Indians, there are far fewer of them; even where there has been the least loss, two thirds are gone, in other places four fifths, in others seven eighths. For this reason there are excess lands in many places, aside from the uncultivated land and the war grounds that they left unplanted. . . .

During the last ten years the natives of this land have diminished greatly in number. The reason for it has not been bad treatment, because for many years now the Indians have been well treated, looked after and defended; rather the cause has been the great diseases and plagues that New Spain has had, so that the natives continue to decrease each day. God knows the cause; his judgments are many and hidden from us. Whether or not the great sins and idolatries that took place in this land cause it, I do not know. . . .

As to the cause of that destruction, or that of this country and the islands, God knows it. Your majesty and the Catholic Monarchs [Ferdinand and Isabella] of holy memory have ordered all the measures and remedies humanly possible, but human council and human power have not been enough to remedy it. It is a great thing that so many souls should have been saved, as they continue to be, and that so many evils, idolatries, homicides and great offenses against God should have been halted and prevented. What is very important at present is that your majesty should provide stability for this land, for as it now is, it suffers greatly.

QUESTIONS

1. What impelled the first Dominican missionaries to propose that one of their number preach a sermon they knew would not be well received by the colonists?
2. What was the content of preacher Antón Montesino's Advent sermons?
3. What action did the colonists take in response to the sermons?
4. What, according to Las Casas, typified Spanish treatment of the natives?
5. How trustworthy are these accounts by Las Casas?
6. Does Toribio de Motolinía successfully refute the charges brought by Las Casas?
7. Do the intimate observations of the Dominican's abrasive personality and questionable activities strengthen the Franciscan's case that the Dominican's observations about cruelty to natives are not to be trusted?
8. Who makes the best case concerning the cause or causes of depopulation—Las Casas or Motolinía?

SPANISH DEBATE OVER THE JUSTICE OF THE CONQUEST

33

Sepúlveda

Few conquerors have argued that their right to rule over a defeated people was based simply on limitless greed, the joys of naked aggression, or the desire to exercise power for personal pleasure. Certainly, as the Spanish dominion in the New World proceeded at a rapid pace, its apologists rushed to provide more sophisticated justifications.

> *"War against these barbarians can be justified . . ."*

Juan Ginés de Sepúlveda was a distinguished scholar of the works of the ancient Greek philosopher Aristotle and a master of Latin style. He was also an ardent nationalist much impressed by his compatriots' achievements. To him, the Spanish were champions of an advanced civilization against ignorant barbarism. He sincerely believed that the aboriginal peoples of America were similar to the primitive foes of Greece or Rome—none of these "barbarians" had the quality of mind and spirit possessed by classical civilization or their European successor Christian societies.

Never having visited the territories under question, he cannot be faulted for having a personal or fiscal stake in the matter. On the other hand, he had no direct knowledge of native life or customs and relied for information on hostile or uncomprehending critics of alien ways of life. He treated the peoples in the Western Hemisphere as if they were all on a par with the least advanced of their fellows. With this bias, he followed the same line of thought as Aristotle, who believed it natural that "higher" forms of created life had domination over all "lower" forms, and that "civilized" societies had a duty to direct the destiny of "barbarians."

Sepúlveda issued his dialogue *Demócrates Alter*, of which a segment is reprinted here, during 1547, when conflicting opinions about the correctness of Spanish activities were agitating the royal court. In this dialogue, Demócrates argues with a German Lutheran who initially believes the conquest to be unjust, but is finally convinced that the king of Spain is obliged to wage war against the natives. Sepúlveda's position was popular with colonists. His proposal that natives be trained by Spanish lords in "virtuous and humane customs," in return for which "just and prudent Spaniards" should get the free use of their labor, seemed to support the controversial new *encomienda* system, which entrusted laborers to settlers who were to protect and convert them. The municipal council of Mexico City sent him a letter of congratulations and thanks.

The man rules over the woman, the adult over the child, the father over his children. That is to say, the most powerful and most perfect rule over the weakest and most imperfect. This same relationship exists among men, there being some who by nature are masters and others who by nature are slaves. Those who surpass the rest in prudence and intelligence, although not in physical strength, are by nature the masters. On the other hand, those who are dim-witted and mentally lazy, although they may be physically strong enough to fulfill all the necessary tasks, are by nature slaves. It is just and useful that it be this way. We even see it sanctioned in divine law itself, for it is written in the Book of Proverbs: "He who is stupid will serve the wise man." And so it is with the barbarous and inhumane peoples [the Indians] who have no civil life and peaceful customs. It will always be just and in conformity with natural law that such people submit to the rule of more cultured and humane princes and nations. Thanks to their virtues and the practical wisdom of their laws, the latter can destroy barbarism and educate these [inferior] people to a more humane and virtuous life. And if the latter reject such rule, it can be imposed upon them by force of arms. Such a war will be just according to natural law. . . .

One may believe as certain and undeniable, since it is affirmed by the wisest authors, that it is just and natural that prudent, upright, and humane men should rule over those who are not. On this basis the Romans established their legitimate and just rule over many nations, according to St. Augustine in several passages of his work, *The City of God*, which St. Thomas [Aquinas] collected and cited in his work, *De regimine principum*. Such being the case, you can well understand . . . if you know the customs and nature of the two peoples, that with perfect right the Spaniards rule over these barbarians of the New World and the adjacent islands, who in wisdom, intelligence, virtue, and [understanding] are as inferior to the Spaniards as infants to adults and women to men. There is as much difference between them as there is between cruel, wild peoples and the most merciful of peoples, between the most monstrously intemperate peoples and those who are temperate and moderate in their pleasures, that is to say, between apes and men.

You do not expect me to make a lengthy commemoration of the judgment and talent of the Spaniards. . . . And who can ignore the other virtues of our people, their fortitude, their humanity, their love of justice and religion? I speak only of our princes and those who by their energy and industriousness have shown that they are worthy of administering the commonwealth. I refer in general terms only to those Spaniards who have received a liberal education. If some of them are wicked and unjust, that is no reason to denigrate the glory of their race, which should be judged by the

SOURCE "Demócrates alter de justis belli causis apud Indios," pp. 47–52, from *Latin American History: Select Problems*, by Frederick B. Pike, trans. by J. L. Phelan, copyright © 1969 by Harcourt, Brace Jovanovich, Inc., reprinted by permission of the publisher.

actions of its cultivated and noble men and by its customs and public institutions, rather than by the actions of depraved persons who are similar to
slaves. More than any other country, this country [Spain] hates and detests
depraved individuals, even those who have certain of the virtues that are
common to nearly all classes of our people, like courage and the martial
spirit for which the Spanish legions have always provided examples that
exceed all human credibility. . . . And I would like to emphasize the absence
of gluttony and lasciviousness among the Spaniards. Is there any nation in
Europe that can compare with Spain in frugality and sobriety? . . .

Now compare these natural qualities of judgment, talent, magnanimity,
temperance, humanity, and religion with those of these pitiful men [the
Indians], in whom you will scarcely find any vestiges of humanness. These
people possess neither science nor even an alphabet, nor do they preserve
any monuments of their history except for some obscure and vague rem-
iniscences depicted in certain paintings, nor do they have written laws, but
barbarous institutions and customs. In regard to their virtues, how much
restraint or gentleness are you to expect of men who are devoted to all kinds
of intemperate acts and abominable lewdness, including the eating of human flesh? And you must realize that prior to the arrival of the Christians,
they did not live in that peaceful kingdom of Saturn [the Golden Age] that
the poets imagine, but on the contrary they made war against one another
continually and fiercely, with such fury that victory was of no meaning
if they did not satiate their monstrous hunger with the flesh of their
enemies. . . . These Indians are so cowardly and timid that they could
scarcely resist the mere presence of our soldiers. Many times thousands
upon thousands of them scattered, fleeing like women before a very few
Spaniards, who amounted to fewer than a hundred. . . .

In regard to those [of the Aztec and other Indian civilizations] who in-
habit New Spain and the province of Mexico, I have already said that they
consider themselves the most civilized people [in the New World]. They
boast of their political and social institutions, because they have rationally
planned cities and nonhereditary kings who are elected by popular suffrage,
and they carry on commerce among themselves in the manner of civilized
people. But . . . I dissent from such an opinion. On the contrary, in those
same institutions there is proof of the coarseness, barbarism, and innate
servility of these men. Natural necessity encourages the building of houses,
some rational manner of life, and some sort of commerce. Such an argument
merely proves that they are neither bears nor monkeys and that they are not
totally irrational.

But on the other hand, they have established their commonwealth in
such a manner that no one individually owns anything, neither a house nor
a field that one may dispose of or leave to his heirs in his will, because
everything is controlled by their lords, who are incorrectly called kings.
They live more at the mercy of their king's will than of their own. They are
the slaves of his will and caprice, and they are not the masters of their fate.

The fact that this condition is not the result of coercion but is voluntary and spontaneous is a certain sign of the servile and base spirit of these barbarians. They had distributed their fields and farms in such a way that one third belonged to the king, another third belonged to the religious cult, and only a third part was reserved for the benefit of everyone; but all of this they did in such a way that they themselves cultivated the royal and religous lands. They lived as servants of the king and at his mercy, paying extremely large tributes. When a father died, all his inheritance, if the king did not decide otherwise, passed in its entirety to the oldest son, with the result that many of the younger sons would either die of starvation or subject themselves to an even more rigorous servitude. They would turn to the petty kings for help and would ask them for a field on the condition that they not only pay feudal tribute but also promise themselves as slave labor when it was necessary. And if this kind of servitude and barbaric commonwealth had not been suitable to their temperament and nature, it would have been easy for them to take advantage of the death of a king, since the monarchy was not hereditary, in order to establish a state that was freer and more favorable to their interests. Their failure to do so confirms that they were born for servitude and not for the civil and liberal life. . . .

Such are, in short, the character and customs of these barbarous, uncultivated, and inhumane little men. We know that they were thus before the coming of the Spaniards. Until now we have not mentioned their impious religion and their abominable sacrifices, in which they worship the Devil as God, to whom they thought of offering no better tribute than human hearts. . . . Interpreting their religion in an ignorant and barbarous manner, they sacrificed human victims by removing the hearts from the chests. They placed these hearts on their abominable altars. With this ritual they believed that they had appeased their gods. They also ate the flesh of the sacrificed men. . . .

How are we to doubt that these people, so uncultivated, so barbarous, and so contaminated with such impiety and lewdness, have not been justly conquered by so excellent, pious, and supremely just a king as Ferdinand the Catholic was and the Emperor Charles [V] now is, the kings of a most humane and excellent nation rich in all varieties of virtue? . . .

War against these barbarians can be justified not only on the basis of their paganism but even more so because of their abominable licentiousness, their prodigious sacrifice of human victims, the extreme harm that they inflicted on innocent persons, their horrible banquets of human flesh, and the impious cult of their idols. Since the evangelical law of the New Testament is more perfect and more gentle than the Mosaic law of the Old Testament (for the latter was a law of fear and the former is a law of grace, gentleness, and clemency), so also [since the birth of Christ] wars are now waged with more mercy and clemency. Their purpose is not so much to punish as to correct evils. What is more appropriate and beneficial for these barbarians than to become subject to the rule of those whose wisdom, virtue, and religion have converted them from barbarians into civilized men (insofar as they are capable of becoming so), from being torpid and licentious to becoming upright and moral, from being impious servants of the Devil to becoming believers in the true God? They have already begun to receive the Christian religion, thanks to the prudent diligence of the Emperor Charles, an excellent and religious prince. They have already been provided with teachers learned in both the sciences and letters and, what is more important, with teachers of religion and good customs.

For numerous and grave reasons these barbarians are obligated to accept the rule of the Spaniards according to natural law. For them it ought to be even more advantageous than for the Spaniards, since virtue, humanity, and the true religion are more valuable than gold or silver. And if they refuse our rule, they may be compelled by force of arms to accept it. Such a war will be just according to natural law. . . . Such a war would be far more just than even the war that the Romans waged against all the nations of the world in order to force them to submit to their rule [for the following reasons]. The Christian religion is better and truer than the religion of the Romans. In addition, the genius, wisdom, humanity, fortitude, courage, and virtue of the Spaniards are as superior to those same qualities among those pitiful little men [the Indians] as were those of the Romans vis-à-vis the peoples whom they conquered. And the justice of this war becomes even more evident when you consider that the Sovereign Pontiff, who represents Christ, has authorized it.

34

Las Casas

The greatest spokesman for the protection of the Amerindians was the Dominican friar Bartolomé de Las Casas. He tirelessly lobbied King Charles V and the Council of the Indies that, until the issue of the propriety of the invasions was settled, licenses of all expeditions should be revoked and no new ones issued. The council advised the king on 3 July 1549 that the dangers both to the bodies of the Amerindians and the souls of Christians was so great that a learned committee should discuss "how conquests might be conducted justly and with security of conscience."

"poisons disguised with honey."

Remarkably, Charles V, the Holy Roman Emperor who was the richest ruler in Europe, ordered in 1550 that conquests in his name cease until the Council of the Indies should meet to decide upon the justness of Spanish conduct. A committee of fourteen officials, scholars, and theologians was formed to advise the council. Juan Ginés de Sepúlveda appeared several times before this committee, whose sessions began in 1550, then reconvened the following year for a vote. Sepúlveda reiterated the arguments from his book (Document 33) that the conquests were just, and he focused on his interpretation of the bulls of Alexander VI (Document 27), which he claimed gave Spain authority over the Indies.

The committee next heard a three-hour summary by Las Casas of his chief arguments against those positions. Starting the second day of his appearance, he read word for word from an enormous manuscript. This went on for five days, until the committee could bear to hear no more, at least according to his opponent. Las Casas wore his audience down by endlessly amplifying and constantly reiterating a few arguments. One of the committee members condensed the long argument and submitted it to Sepúlveda, who replied to each of the twelve major points made by the Dominican. The two contenders never debated face to face, which makes the confrontation somewhat less dramatic than it is sometimes portrayed.

Both Las Casas and Sepúlveda drew upon an immense store of arguments from the Bible, the writing of the Church fathers, the pagan philosophers, and records of the conquests. Sepúlveda gained his principal knowledge of Amerindian cultures from Gonzalo Fernández de Oviedo (Documents 23 and 41), whom Las Casas damned for "a preconceived attitude against the Indians because he held Indians as slaves." The proceedings proved inconclusive, since the committee never produced a final report. In a sense Las Casas "won," however, because Sepúlveda was prohibited from publishing his book.

In the last quarter of the sixteenth century, the view of the crown coincided to some extent with Las Casas because it wished to keep the incorporation of new territories peaceful and orderly. Kings and their ministers wanted clear and legal title to fend off land claims by colonizers, and to keep new subjects from becoming the slaves of the conquistadores. In 1573 the Council of the Indies drew up the *Ordenanzas sobre descubrimientos*, after reviewing Las Casas's manuscripts. The ordinances substituted the word *pacification* for *conquest* to ensure peaceful methods, although it did not entirely prohibit the use of force. By laying down strict conditions for granting new licenses for expeditions, the crown disowned the ruthless methods of the conquistadores. Although we now know from hindsight that most of the conquests were over, who then could say if rich new kingdoms might yet be found? The advocates for Las Casas struggled to right what they saw as hideous wrongs, a position that the modern observer may wish to judge not only by concrete results, but also by the passion with which the participants fought for their ideals.

I llustrious Prince [Philip II]:

It is right that matters which concern the safety and peace of the great empire placed in your keeping by the divine goodness be reported to you, for you rule Spain and that marvelous New World in the name of the great Charles [V], your father, and you strive for immortal glory, not just with the imperial power but especially with the generous spirit and with the wisdom implanted in you by Christ. Therefore I have thought it advisable to bring to the attention of Your Highness that there has come into my hands a certain brief synopsis in Spanish of a work that Ginés de Sepúlveda is reported to have written in Latin. In it he gives four reasons, each of which, in his opinion, proves beyond refutation that war against the Indians is justified, provided that it be waged properly and the laws of war be observed, just as, up to the present, the kings of Spain have commanded that it be waged and carried out.

I hear that it is this man's intention to demonstrate the title by which the Kings of Spain possess the empire of the Indies and to bolster his position with arguments and laws, so that from now on no one will be able to slander you even tacitly on this point. I have read and reread this work carefully. And it is said that Sepúlveda drives home various other points at greater length in his Latin work (which I have not yet had the chance to see). What impression it has made on others I do not know. I certainly have detected in it poisons disguised with honey. Under pretext of pleasing his prince, a man who is a theologian offers honey-coated poison. In place of bread, he offers a stone. Great Prince, unless this deadly poison is stopped by your wisdom, so that it will not become widespread, it will infect the minds of readers, deceive the unwary, and arm and incite tyrants to injustice. Believe me, that little book will bring ruin to the minds of many. . . .

First, I shall refute Sepúlveda's opinion claiming that war against the Indians is justified because they are barbarous, uncivilized, unteachable, and lacking civil government.

Second, I shall show that, to the most definite ruin of his own soul, Sepúlveda is wrong when he teaches that war against the Indians is justified as punishment for their crimes against the natural law, especially the crimes of idolatry and human sacrifice.

Third, we shall attack his third argument, on the basis of which Sepúlveda teaches that war can be waged unconditionally and indiscriminately against those peoples in order to free the innocent.

Fourth, I shall discuss how foreign to the teaching of the gospel and Christian mercy is his fourth proposition, maintaining that war against the

SOURCE Selections from Bartolomé de Las Casas, *In Defense of the Indians. The Defense of the Most Reverend Lord, Don Fray Bartolomé de Las Casas, of the Order of Preachers, Late Bishop of Chiapa, Against the Persecution and Slanders of the Peoples of the New World Discovered Across the Sea.* Translated, edited and annotated by Stafford Poole. © 1974 by Northern Illinois University Press. Used with permission of the publisher.

Indians is justified as a means of extending the boundaries of the Christian religion and of opening the way for those who proclaim and preach the gospel. . . .

They who teach, either in word or in writing, that the natives of the New World, whom we commonly call Indians, ought to be conquered and subjugated by war before the gospel is proclaimed and preached to them so that, after they have finally been subjugated, they may be instructed and hear the word of God, make two disgraceful mistakes. First, in connection with divine and human law they abuse God's words and do violence to the Scriptures, to papal decrees, and to the teaching handed down from the holy fathers. And they go wrong again by quoting histories that are nothing but sheer fables and shameless nonsense. By means of these, men who are totally hostile to the poor Indians and who are their utterly deceitful enemies betray them. Second, they mistake the meaning of the decree or bull [Document 27] of the Supreme Pontiff Alexander VI, whose words they corrupt and twist in support of their opinions, as will be clear from all that follows. . . .

The second argument by which Sepúlveda justifies war against the Indians is as punishment for the crimes of idolatry and human sacrifice by which these people offend God. Here, as in his other arguments, Sepúlveda is completely wrong because of some mistaken suppositions and expressions.

To make the matter clearer, we have to suppose that we can punish the sins of unbelievers or that they can punish ours, either when we are their subjects or when they are ours or come under our authority. Now this can happen for four reasons. The first is dwelling or habitation; for example, if they should live among Christians. Or [second] it can be by reason of origin or by reason of a person whose case, or that of his parents, is under litigation. Third, a person is considered our subject if he is a vassal and has taken an oath of fealty [loyalty] to us according to proper form, that is, by means of some feudal right by which he owes us service. The fourth reason is a crime committed in someone's jurisdiction, either against the ruler himself or against the property or persons of his subjects. Similarly, one gains competence by reason of a contract or by reason of property, for example, if an alien acquires ownership of an apple orchard within the jurisdiction of some ruler. By reason of that property, the owner is considered to be within the ruler's competence. None of these persons are subjects properly so called but only under certain aspects: by reason of property or contract they can be summoned by the judge from whose jurisdiction they are exempt by law. . . .

Now the fact that one must refrain from war, and even tolerate the death of a few innocent persons, is proved by arguments and many authorities.

The first argument is this: According to the rule of right reason when we are confronted by two choices that are evil both as to moral guilt and punishment and we cannot avoid both of them, we ought to choose the lesser evil. For in comparison with the greater evil, the choice of the lesser evil has the quality of a good. This is what the Philosopher [Aristotle] teaches. Now the death of a small number of innocent persons is a lesser evil than the eternal damnation of countless numbers of persons killed in the fury of war.

Again, the death of the innocent is better or less evil than the complete destruction of entire kingdoms, cities, and strongholds. For not all of them eat the flesh of the innocent but only the rulers or priests, who do the sacrificing, whereas war brings the destruction of countless innocent persons who do not deserve any such thing. Therefore if those evils cannot be removed in any other way than by waging war, one must refrain from it and evils of this kind must be tolerated.

Furthermore, it is incomparably less disastrous that a few innocent persons die than that Christ's holy name be blasphemed by unbelievers and that the Christian religion be brought into ill repute and be hated by those peoples and by others to whom word of this flies, when they hear how many women, children, and aged people of their nation have been killed by the Christians without cause, as will unavoidably happen, and indeed has happened, in the fury of war. What, I ask, will be the result, if not a perpetual barrier to their salvation, so that there will be no further hope for their conversion? Therefore when there is a question of war over a cause of this kind it is better to let a few innocent persons be oppressed or suffer an unjust death. In fact it would be a very great sin, and against the natural law [which Nature sets for all creatures], to wage war on these unbelievers for this reason. This is proved in the following way.

According to right reason, and therefore the natural law, it is evident that in every case and in every matter that concerns two evils, especially those involving moral guilt, one must choose that which is less harmful or is thought to be less harmful. Therefore to seek to free innocent persons in the case proposed, within their territories, as has been proposed, would be against the natural law and a sin, which, although not mortal, is very serious indeed. This is evident because the greater the damage sin inflicts, the more serious it is, according to St. Thomas [Aquinas]. And this is true even if that damage is not intended or foreseen, since everything that necessarily follows upon a sin belongs in some way to the very species of the sin. From such a war a countless number of innocent persons of both sexes and all ages will unavoidably perish, and the other evils that have been mentioned will necessarily follow upon that war. Therefore anyone who would try to free those who suffer evils of this type by means of war would commit a very serious mortal sin. . . .

At this point we shall refute Sepúlveda's fourth argument or cause [for war], in which he says that war can be waged against the Indians so that, once the path has been totally cleared for the preachers of the gospel, the Christian religion may be spread. Indeed, I cannot cease being astonished by Sepúlveda. For what spirit leads a theologian, mature and well versed in humane letters, to set these poisons before the world so that the far-flung Indian empires, contrary to the law of Christ, would be prey for most savage thieves? In the same way, and to this very moment, the greed of the Spanish people has led to such crimes among those peoples as—according to history—have never been committed by any other nation, no matter how fierce it may have been. In fact, Sepúlveda tries with all his might to increase these crimes, until the last nation in that world will finally be wiped out, when the just and upright God, provoked by these actions, will perhaps pour forth the fury of his anger and lay hold of all of Spain sooner than he had decreed.

And so Sepúlveda first cites what Augustine [early Christian writer] writes in his letter to the heretic Donatus. Sepúlveda claims that Augustine teaches that peoples during the first period of the nascent Church were to be led to the faith of Christ courteously and gently, whereas later, when the powers of the Church had increased, they could be forced to enter Christ's sheepfold, as in the parable of the wedding feast. Surely Sepúlveda speaks wickedly and commits many errors to the destruction of his soul, especially on three points.

The first is that he says the decrees of the Church against heretics, published by the Pope and the Emperors, should be observed even against unbelievers [in general]. He fails to distinguish the four kinds of unbelievers. Some are unbelieving Moors and Jews who live under the rule of Christians. Others are apostates and heretics. Others are Turks and Moors who persecute us by war. Others are idolatrous unbelievers who live in very remote provinces.

The second error is that Sepúlveda gives a distorted interpretation of the parable of the wedding feast. . . . [C]ertainly that gospel parable does not in any way prove what Sepúlveda would have it prove. He tries to prove that Christ wanted the Church, once it had been strengthened by resources and rulers, to force men to embrace the truth of the gospel, not by forcibly baptizing them but by uprooting the worship of idols and crushing their power, so that they could not obstruct the preaching of the gospel. Above all, I would gladly learn from Sepúlveda why God should want force to be used on unbelievers by the Church and Christian rulers rather than by angels, by whose ministry God frequently leads unbelievers to knowledge of himself. . . .

. . . [T]he words of the Pope [Alexander VI], saying that he hoped for nothing more than to see the barbarians vanquished, referred to the Moors of Granada, who were barbarians—as I have said before—and in comparison with other barbarians were most dangerous enemies of the Christian state. Therefore those words of the bull do nothing toward strengthening Sepúlveda's wicked opinion. For how could the Roman Pontiff approve what is so far from Christ's teaching, as has been sufficiently argued above?

I have preached these things, in keeping with the measure of grace granted me, in defense of this lengthy and holy cause, bound as it is by Christian piety. As for the rest, I exhort and advise by Jesus Christ, Sepúlveda, my brother and colleague in Christ, and the other enemies of the

Indians to obey the words, to heed and respect the traditions of the holy Fathers, and to fear God, who punishes perverse undertakings.

QUESTIONS

1. What proof does Sepúlveda present to show that the Spanish should, by right, rule over the population of the New World?
2. How compelling a case does Sepúlveda make when contrasting the alleged virtues of the Spanish with the alleged vices of the natives?
3. How does Sepúlveda justify war against the native populations, and in what way does Las Casas refute him?
4. Where do both men stand regarding the controversial and alleged donation by the bull of Alexander VI (Document 27) of much of the New World to the Spanish?
5. What was the point of the arguments traded by the two contenders regarding the merit, or lack thereof, of forced conversion?
6. On which major points does Las Casas get the better of Sepúlveda, and vice versa?

OTHER COLONIZERS

35

Raleigh

Despite the efforts of Spain and Portugal to keep interlopers out of what they regarded as their private domain, a common mercantile capitalism and shared naval and military technologies inspired other kingdoms to break the monopoly. At the center of the European continent, an armed attack by one sovereign was sure to provoke counterattacks. Rarely could a ruler conquer sufficient territory to pay for the armed conflict, much less generate new revenue. Only by staking out a maritime empire against an underequipped foe would armed aggression pay dividends. What is remarkable about the New World is not that others wanted to reap profits there, but just how long the Spanish were able to keep rivals at bay.

> *"it was a very impatient work to keep the baser sort from despoiling and stealing, . . ."*

Elizabeth I's England, limited to the resources generated by half an island, looked to a form of piracy and some large-scale assaults on port towns to stay in the game. Sir Walter Raleigh propagandized for the establishment of land bases in the New World from which to best England's rival. He was that versatile type of individual once called a "Renaissance man": poet, explorer, seaman, soldier, courtier, and historian. In the middle of his career, after winning fame and vast estates in Ireland, he resided at court, where he agitated for further colonial expansion. Although Raleigh himself never set foot in North America, he did much to establish a colony on what is now the coast of North Carolina, naming the country Virginia, in honor of Elizabeth the Virgin Queen.

During 1594 he received permission from the queen to discover and conquer lands not possessed by any Christian prince, with an eye to "offend and enfeeble" the king of Spain. Raleigh's main, if rather implausible, personal goal was to find *El Dorado*, the mythical "Golden Man" who was allegedly anointed every day by his subjects with oil and rolled in gold dust. He hoped to locate an as-yet-undiscovered civilization the equal of Mexico or Peru in the extensive forests between the Amazon and Orinoco rivers. Unfortunately for him, the expedition was turned back by bad weather.

His pamphlet proposing a new expedition, excerpted in the next document, failed to sway the queen into committing money or troops, despite his best effort to demonstrate how rich the domains were, how hated the Spanish were, and how noble, by comparison, were the Englishmen. Not one to give up easily, he tried again in 1617, during the reign of a later sovereign, with thirteen ships and about 1,000 men. This too was a fiasco, ending with the death of his son, Walter, and the suicide of his trusted lieutenant. He arrived home in disgrace and was beheaded two years later on an old, trumped-up charge of conspiring with the Spanish.

The empire of Guiana is directly east from Peru towards the sea, and lies under the equinoctial line, and it has more abundance of gold than any part of Peru, and as many or more great cities than ever Peru had when it flourished most: I have been assured by such of the Spaniards as have seen Manoa the imperial city of Guiana, which the Spaniards call El Dorado, that for the greatness, for the riches and for the excellent seat, it far exceeds any of the world.

Although these reports may seem strange, yet if we consider the many millions [in silver] which are daily brought out of Peru into Spain, we may easily believe the same: for we find that by the abundant treasure of that country the Spanish King vexes all the princes of Europe, and is become, in a few years, from a poor King of Castile, the greatest monarch of this part of the world. . . .

The great river of Orinoco has nine branches which fall out on the north side of his own main mouth: on the south side it has seven other fallings into the sea, so it discharges by sixteen arms in all, between islands and broken ground, but the islands are very great, many of them as big as the Isle of Wight. The river's mouth is 300 miles wide at his entrance into the sea. . . .

On both sides of this river, we passed the most beautiful country that ever mine eyes beheld: and whereas all that we had seen before was nothing but woods, prickles, bushes, and thorns, here we beheld plains of twenty miles in length, the grass short and green, and in various parts groves of trees by themselves. In the meanwhile our companies in the galley thought we had been all lost (for we promised to return before night), and sent the *Lions Whelp*'s boat with Captain Whiddon to follow us up the river; but the next day, after we had rowed up and down some fourscore miles, we returned, and went on our way up the great river; Captain Gifford being before the galley and the rest of the boats, seeking out some place to land upon the banks to make fire, spied four canoes coming down the river; after a while two of the four gave over, and ran themselves ashore, every man taking himself to the fastness of the woods. Those canoes that were taken were laden with bread: but in the lesser [canoes] there were three Spaniards, who having heard of the defeat of their governor in Trinidad, and that we purposed to enter Guiana, came away in those canoes: one of them was a gentleman, another a soldier, and the third a refiner.

SOURCE "The Voyage of Sir Walter Raleigh (1595) to Trinidad and Guiana," Richard Hakluyt, *Voyages*, 8 vols. (London: Everyman's Library, 1907, reprinted 1962), vol. VII, pp. 314–349, passim. Language modernized.

In the meantime, nothing on the earth could have been more welcome to us, next to gold, than the great store of very excellent bread which we found in these canoes; for now our men cried, "Let us go on, we care not how far." I took my barge, and went to the bank's side with a dozen shot, where the canoes first ran themselves ashore and landed there: as I was creeping through the bushes, I saw an Indian basket hidden, which was the refiner's basket; for I found in it his quick-silver, saltpetre, and various things for the trial of metals and also the dust of such ore as he had refined, but in those canoes which had escaped there was a good quantity of ore and gold. I then landed more men, and offered five hundred pounds to what soldier soever could take one of those three Spaniards that we thought were landed. But our labors were in vain; for they put themselves into one of the small canoes: and so while the greater canoes were in taking they escaped. But seeking after the Spaniards, we found the Arawaks hidden in the woods, which were pilots for the Spaniards, and rowed their canoes; of which I kept the chiefest for a pilot, and carried him with me to Guiana, by whom I understood where and in what areas the Spaniards had labored for gold. . . .

The Arawakan pilot with the rest, feared that we would have eaten them, or otherwise have put them to some cruel death (for the Spaniards, to the end that none of the people in the passage towards Guiana or in Guiana itself might come to talk with us, persuaded all the nations, that we were cannibals) but when the poor men and women had seen us, and that we gave them food, and to every one something or other, which was rare and strange to them, they began to conceive the deceit and purpose of the Spaniards, who indeed (as they confessed) took from them both their wives and daughters daily, and used them for the satisfying of their own lusts, especially such as they took in this manner by strength. But I protest before the Majesty of the living God, that I neither know nor believe, that any of our company one or other, by violence or otherwise, ever knew [sexually] any of their women, and yet we saw many hundreds, and had many in our power, and of those very young, and excellently favored, which came among us without deceit, stark naked.

Nothing got us more love among them than this usage: for I suffered not any man to take from any of the nations [natives] so much as a pineapple, or a potato root, without giving them payment, nor any man so much as to offer to touch any of their wives or daughters: which course so contrary to the Spaniards (who tyrannize over them in all things) drew them to admire her Majesty [Elizabeth I] whose commandment I told them it was, and also wonderfully to honor our nation.

But I confess it was a very impatient work to keep the baser sort from despoiling and stealing, when we came to their houses: which because in all I could not prevent, I caused my Indian interpreter at every place when we departed, to know of the loss or wrong done, and if ought were stolen or taken by violence, either the same was restored, and the perpetrator punished in their sight, or else was payed [sic] for to their uttermost demand. . . .

Guiana is a country that has yet her maidenhead [virginity], never sacked, turned, nor wrought, the face of the earth has not been torn, nor the virtue and salt of the soil spent by manurance, the graves have not been opened for gold, the mines not broken with sledges, nor their images pulled down out of their temples. It was never entered by any army of strength, and never conquered by any Christian prince. . . .

The West Indies were first offered Her Majesty's grandfather [Henry VII] by Columbus a stranger, in whom there might be doubt of deceit, and besides it was then thought incredible that there were such and so many lands and regions never written of before. This empire [Guiana] is made known to Her Majesty by her own vassal, and by him that owes to her more duty than an ordinary subject, so that it shall ill sort with the many graces and benefits which I have received to abuse Her Highness, either with fables or imaginations. The country is already discovered, many nations won to Her Majesty's love and obedience, and those Spaniards which have latest and longest labored about the conquest, beaten out, discouraged and disgraced, which among these nations [natives] were thought invincible. Her Majesty may in this enterprise employ all those soldiers and gentlemen that are younger brothers, and all captains and chieftains that lack employment, and the charge will be only the first setting out in feeding and arming them: for after the first or second year I doubt not but to see in London a Contraction House of more income for Guiana, than there is now in Seville [Spain] for the West Indies.

I am resolved that if there were but a small army a foot in Guiana, marching towards Manoa the chief city of Inca, he would yield to her Majesty by agreement so many hundred thousand pounds yearly, as should both defend all enemies abroad, and defray all expenses at home, and that he would besides pay a garrison of three or four thousand soldiers very royally to defend him against other nations.

For whatsoever prince shall possess it, shall be greatest, and if the King of Spain shall enjoy it, he will become unresistible. Her Majesty hereby shall confirm and strengthen the opinions of all nations, as touching her great and princely actions.

I trust in God, this being true, will suffice, and that he which is King of all Kings and Lord of Lords, will put it into her heart which is Lady of Ladies to possess it.

36

The French and the English

The English, French, and Dutch can hardly be said to differ greatly from the Spanish in their relations with the natives in the New World. Major distinctions in behavior and attitude do not arise from flaws in "national character," whatever that may be, but from the differing situations in which the Europeans found themselves with respect to aboriginal populations. Whenever Europeans met sedentary peoples with a gradation of elites and masses of peasants, they generally killed the upper elites and turned the next class of elites into mediators and tribute collectors to keep the farmers at work. When Europeans met semisedentary or wandering tribal peoples, they drove them away, killed as many as they could, or placed them on reservations. All Europeans treated Amerindians and Africans harshly in mines, salt pans, and on plantations, but these peoples were treated less harshly when they were organized by extensive agricultural communities dominated by village economies.

"the peaceful or forceful transfer of ownership of those lands. . . ."

The next reading selection discusses how the French experience on the mainland of North America differed from the English as well as from the Spanish. Its author considers the issue of whether the French deserve any praise, in contrast to the scorn often directed toward the other colonizers.

A lthough the French and English approached exploration and settlement with visions of Spanish achievement shimmering before their eyes, the natural resources and, more important, the native societies they encountered in the areas they settled precluded a duplication of Spanish success. As soon as extensive exploration by both nations began, their policy makers and settlers alike quickly discovered the lack of mineral resources in their respective areas of colonization. Moreover, the French found little land suitable for farming in the St. Lawrence Valley, and so they turned to the fur trade as the only valuable resource other than the fishing banks off the coast of Canada. In the fur trade, the French and Native Americans formed a symbiotic relationship that did not require the French

SOURCE R. F. Berkhofer, Jr., *The White Man's Indian. Images of the American Indian from Columbus to the Present* (Vintage Books, Random House, 1979), pp. 127–134, passim. Author's footnotes eliminated. Reprinted by permission.

to occupy much land or to exercise obvious political control. In the valley of the St. Lawrence, where the French made the only extensive settlement in mainland Canada, the land had been mostly abandoned by native tribes on the eve of White settlement in the seventeenth century. Furthermore, the peculiarities of topography and the lack of French *habitants* confined White occupation to thin lines along the sides of the river. Some pressure for conversion was exerted by priests in the field or on the few reserves founded by *réligieux* along the St. Lawrence.

The policy of *Francization,* or converting the Indians to French civilization as well as religion, so much the aim of secular authorities and religious leaders alike in the beginning of the colony, proved a failure without containment upon a reserve, and even here many questioned the results. Even after the abandonment of the policy of *Francization,* some efforts were made to bring the Indians into full-fledged legal and social equality in New France [Canada], but the achievement of such an aim still depended as much as ever upon the ability of the French priests and politicians to control the life of a tribe or its members individually. De facto sovereignty unlike de jure sovereignty depended upon actual control rather than theoretical jurisdiction, and so the high ideals of integrating the inhabitants of the Franco-American colony into one people hinged as much upon concrete power as upon good intentions. Integration still presumed acculturation and French dominance, and discrimination underlay Franco-Indian relations as actually practiced.

In the end, the success often attributed to French Indian policy must be ascribed to the failure of Canada as a colony when judged by Spanish and English achievement. French settlement seemed compatible with Indian occupancy because the French settled and farmed so little of mainland Canada and that principally where the natives had vacated. The fur trade required minuscule portions of land and rested primarily upon a reciprocal economic relationship beneficial to both sides in contact. Even though the fur trade can be described as the least destructive of the White methods of exploiting native resources, still it promoted profound changes in Native American societies. These transformations, however, came as much in response to the desires of native peoples as at the behest of Whites. Under these circumstances, the pressures for assimilation to White ways remained as minimal as the French desire for extensive native lands. Wherever the French attempted the type of agricultural settlement pursued by the English, however, they encountered similar native resistance and engaged in the same kind of warfare.

If in general the French during the seventeenth century did not need native labor as the Spanish employed it, the English needed but could not use native labor, given the nature of tribal social and political organization they encountered in the areas of mainland North America they settled. Although both nations' settlers came upon the same type of stateless bands and tribes, the French fur trade needed no higher level of social organization for its exploitation, but English agriculture, especially in the southern colonies, could have used a captive labor force of the kind employed by the

Spanish in central Mexico. Like the French, the English also turned to fish and furs at first, but their permanent settlements soon came to depend upon agriculture and the trade associated with it as the main support of their economy. The English fur trade appeared as compatible with native lifestyles as that conducted by the French. English political jurisdiction and land claims as represented by the fur trade impinged as lightly upon native title and ways as those carried into the forest by voyageur and priest. English farming, however, whether of the southern or northern variety, depended upon the extensive and exclusive use of the land and so demanded, at the same time that it promoted, the rapid expansion of White settlement upon native territory. Virginia alone had a larger population in 1650 than all of New France in 1700, and Massachusetts counted almost as large a population at mid-century as Canada did fifty years later.

Moreover, English agricultural practices presumed exclusive White usage of the land, thereby precluding any sharing of resources with Red neighbors, and English tenure and legal jurisdiction recognized this approach to territorial control. White uses of the land destroyed Indian subsistence from hunting as well as native horticulture and forced each tribe to contest White destruction of its economy, or to convert to White ways and methods, or to remove further into the frontier and encroach upon another tribe's territory. As a result of this conflict between native and English economies as well as cultures, the history of the mainland English colonies in the seventeenth century (and later) consists primarily of the expansion of White settlement onto native lands and the peaceful or forceful transfer of ownership of those lands from Red to White hands.

After the initial years of English settlement, this transfer of title took place through two main means of cession. Although the early English explorers claimed vast territory in the name of the monarch, who in turn granted portions to the various agents or agencies empowered to settle America, the colonists acquired actual possession and completed title to the land by slower but more certain means. The English in Virginia gained a foothold through a combination of methods: permission from some chiefs who lived there, the claim of sovereignty symbolized in Powhatan's coronation ceremony, and outright seizure. Certainly of all the native societies encountered by the English on the east coast of what was to become the United States, the so-called Powhatan Confederacy possessed the greatest potential for exploitation along Spanish lines. Since Powhatan was apparently establishing a nascent conquest state through which he received tribute, the English could have asserted a feudal overlordship consistent with the Spanish practice of receiving tribute and labor service. Such a possibility never came to pass, however, as the initial gentlemen adventurers gave way to tobacco-raising settlers. Pilgrims and Puritans located their first settlements upon lands temporarily depopulated by what the pious considered providential plagues and therefore they claimed title by virtue of *vacuum domicilium*.

Subsequent land possession and title were obtained north and south through native cession by purchase or warfare. Apparently colonial leaders thought the practice of buying tracts of land from the natives as a means of quieting Indian title claims cheaper than forceful seizure in warfare and equally effective in theory—even though cajolery and coercion often entered into the actual negotiations. Scholars debate just when cessions through formal and recorded purchase started in New England, but the practice became general throughout the colonies after the 1630s. As the seventeenth century progressed, colony after colony adopted legislation restricting the right of purchase from Indians to the official agents of the government. By thus placing the right of preemption in the hands of official colonial representatives, the legislatures hoped to avoid the conflict between individual Whites and Indians over the legitimacy of various cessions and purchases. The other source of cession resulted from White victories over native tribes in warfare. Under the impression that Indians should recompense the colonists for conquering them, White leaders demanded substantial land cessions from hostile tribes as the price of renewed peace—if any tribespeople survived warfare.

Whether obtained in war or through purchase, whether recorded in deed and treaty or by informal arrangement, the English demanded and received title and possession of tract after tract from the tribes they encountered in their expansion westward. By this gradual process of cession, the colonists brought their actual control of native resources and populations into line with the exorbitant territorial claims made by the early explorers for the English crown. . . .

Scholars have assigned many reasons for the failure of the English missions as compared to Spanish and French achievements: Protestant apathy versus Catholic zeal; Catholic, especially Jesuit, flexibility versus Protestant rigidity in the field; the ceremonialism of Catholicism versus the dull services of the Protestants; and even Latin racial sentiment versus Anglo-Saxon prejudices. Without minimizing the importance of these and other factors in explaining the differences in the missionary results achieved by the various colonizing powers, one must still place these factors into the larger context of each European nation's overall relationships with Native Americans for the perspective necessary in understanding the diverse outcomes. The English missionaries, like their French colleagues, found no hierarchical and centralized native political administrations that they could use as the Spanish missionaries had in the Aztec empire to gain nominal mass conversion. In fact, the Spanish friars ran into the same kind of problems as the English and French missionaries when they entered tribes with the same type of stateless and "democratic" organization faced by their northern peers. Neither could the English missionaries operate under the permissive contact conditions associated with the fur trade because of the rapid expansion of agriculture by their fellow colonists and the resultant hostilities. . . .

Thus the propagation of the faith, like the other White uses of the Indian, ultimately depended upon the compatibility of White aims and methods of exploitation with native social organization and natural resources. If Spanish and French missionary success is measured by complete conversion to the Roman Catholic religion rather than nominal allegiance to form and syncretic practice, then perhaps the discrepancy between English and Latin achievements diminishes considerably. In the end, the religious toilers of all three nations faced tribespeople, no matter how little or much organized politically and socially, who preferred their own beliefs and practices to those of the foreign invaders.

If the European powers did not get all they wanted from the Indians, they accomplished their basic goals of transforming many natives into colonial subjects in their own homelands, transferred title in theory and often in fact from native inhabitants to crown and settlers, and exploited native resources in ways consonant with European economies and tribal organization. Toward these ends, policy makers used the image of the Indian to justify the necessity as well as to prove the desirability of their policies. They also used the image of the Indian as the base line for measuring how far they had succeeded in their efforts to convert Native Americans to White civilization and religion.

37

Civilizing the Wilderness

Words have a reality all their own. Call a person a "heretic," a "gook," or a "dirty Jew," and he or she is made less than human. In the process of being conquered, highly refined native populations in the Western Hemisphere lost everything, including their identities, becoming "barbarians" and "savages" to their new rulers. This terminology was highly useful to sixteenth-century theorists, who rested their argument for the subjugation of native populations on the claim that the Amerindian peoples were identical with the earlier "barbarians," described by the ancient philosopher Aristotle. He had declared the earlier "barbarians" to be "natural slaves," who deserved to be subordinated to the obviously superior Greeks. Aristotle's view

> *"the myths created by the cant of conquest endure . . ."*

helped diffuse the challenge posed to early modern Europe by the entirely different cultural assumptions that governed life in the Americas. Such variations in human behavior could thereby be written off as proof of inferior status.

At the deepest level of the popular culture the United States inherited from Europe, its citizens find reminders of the cherished national myth that "civilized" white men, beginning with Columbus, won this land from Indian "savages." Myth mongering was important in the United States because federal officials vacillated in their policy between paternalism and neglect toward natives, and private enterprise and local governments, using stereotypes to ease their way with citizens and voters, found justification for their acquisition of natives' assets.

The conquerors of America glorified the devastation they wrought in visions of righteousness, and their descendants have been reluctant to peer through the aura. Decent men with pigmentless skins no longer overtly espouse delusions of peculiar grandeur, but the myths created by the cant of conquest endure in many forms to mask the terrible tragedy that was Europe's glory. Although the ideologists of conquest can no longer evoke admiration for holy wars or pseudobiology, they have yet one great and powerful system of myth among their resources. In it the Christian Caucasians of Europe are not only holy and white but also *civilized*, while the pigmented heathens of distant lands are not only idolatrous and dark but *savage*. Thus the absolutes of predator and prey have been preserved, and the grandeur of invasion and massacre has kept its sanguinary radiance.

From very ancient times self-consciously "civilized" people have favorably compared themselves with their neighbors. The Greeks invented the term *barbarian* to apply to outsiders—even such as Egyptians and Persians—and the Romans were not slow to adopt the idea. As W. R. Jones has remarked, "The antithesis which opposed civilization to barbarism was a highly useful cliché, and one which served equally well as a means of self-congratulation and as a rationalization for aggression." Barbarism's definition varied from century to century, sometimes stressing linguistic or cultural differences, sometimes denoting little more than heathenism in religion, but always retaining a core meaning of inferiority in moral worth. In Jones's words, "The image of the 'barbarian,' whatever its specific historical context and to whomever applied, was the invention of civilized man who thereby expressed his own strong sense of cultural and moral superiority."

Sometimes the factual difference between civilization and savagery was very slight indeed. In 1395 Richard II of England excoriated the "wild" Irish who maintained independence of his rule. "Wild Irishman" is a humorous phrase nowadays, but Richard was not making jokes, and neither were his officials in Ireland who used the term repeatedly and who hanged those

Source *The Invasion of America: Indians, Colonialism and the Cant of Conquest,* by Francis Jennings. © The University of North Carolina Press. Published for the Institute of Early American History and Culture, Williamsburg, VA. Reprinted by permission.

Irishmen when they caught them. "Wild Irish" is really a translation from the Norman-French used by the conquest aristocracy. The words actually written by Richard were *"irrois savages, nos enemis"*—literally "savage Irish, our enemies." In an era of linguistic mixing, the words "wild" and "savage" were used interchangeably not only to identify Irish people but also to describe the Scots of the highlands and the islands, contrasting them with the anglicized inhabitants of the lowlands. Ironically, Richard was attacking the Irish as savages at just the moment that England was plunging into the Wars of the Roses.

It may be worth our trouble to examine how fine a line actually distinguished the societies of England and Ireland at that time. Both countries were Christian and Catholic, although the independence of the Irish monastic movement kept rankling the bureaucratic hierarchy of the bishops and thus influenced the papacy to give its support to England. Both countries were fully agricultural, with flocks and herds as well as tillage. Both were haphazardly literate, and the Irish had their own alphabet as well as literature. Both had metals and masonry and weaving. Both had towns and ships and commerce with other countries; the Irish were, on the whole, a more rural people than the English, but England was by no means an urbanized country even by the standards of that day. A contemporary Italian would have laughed at the thought.

The difference was political and no more. What made Irishmen morally inferior to Englishmen, and thus imposed a duty on England's kings to conquer the "other island," was the government of most of Ireland by independent tribes and clans instead of subject vassal lords. One might say that Ireland was fit to be conquered simply because it was there, but wars require more elaborate justification than mountain climbing. With no substantial difference between the two societies except tribal government on the one hand and a feudal state on the other, the Norman-French kings of England set themselves up as carriers of civilization to a savage people.

At other times and on other occasions powers bent on conquest have been able to point to more substantial differences between their own cultures, always deemed as civilization, and the uncivilized societies of their opponents. Most frequently, perhaps, the difference has been one of religion. At other times it might have been nomadic instead of sedentary habitation or one mode of subsistence versus another: communities without agriculture—or those possessing horticulture but lacking animal husbandry—were barbarous or savage. Some social scientists have tried to bring validity and precision to these conceptions by making literacy the criterion of civilization. All of these floundering attempts at explanation only serve to obscure the essential fact that the civilized-uncivilized distinction is a moral sanction rather than any given combination of social traits susceptible to objective definition. It is a weapon of attack rather than a standard of measurement. There are other ways of using these terms, to be sure, although the taint of historical usage makes difficult any attempt to purify them. . . .

Whatever efforts are made to objectify its definition, *civilization* necessarily implies not only technical but moral superiority over the stages assumed to be lower on the evolutionary scale. Civilization is rarely conceived of in terms of empirical data, and although its phenomena might vary as widely as those of ancient Sparta and Victorian England, its essence is always its status on the top of the evolutionary ladder. That constant can be preserved through an infinity of empirical transformations.

There are, of course, many meanings that can be given to the word *civilization*. In its mythical sense it is an absolute quality that cannot be grammatically pluralized. This sense must be distinguished from the relative use of the term, as when Greek civilization is compared to medieval European civilization or Chinese civilization or even North American Indian civilization. In modern usage one may refer to different sorts of civilization in a way that makes the term interchangeable with the anthropological term *culture*. The ambiguity between absolute and relative meanings for the same term has created great confusion. . . .

The alternative to the historian of frontier semantics and mythology is the ethnohistorian. In the lexicon of the ethnohistorian the opposing absolutes of evil savagery and good civilization become morally neutral and relatively comparable as "societies" and "cultures." Instead of assuming an impassable chasm between societies, the ethnohistorian postulates their capacity to exchange cultural traits in processes of cooperation as well as conflict, and he sets himself the task of describing those processes, to which he gives the inclusive neutral name of *acculturation*. The word's equality of application must be noted carefully. "Acculturation" has been used improperly by some writers to mean merely something that happened to natives to make them more like Europeans; thus used, it becomes merely a synonym for "civilizing."

As the ethnohistorian holds the anthropologist's respect for theory, he analyzes events for their demonstration of known cultural processes; as he holds the historian's methodological respect for fact, he tests the theory of abstract processes by their fit on unique and unalterable events. Thus, in examining the American past, an ethnohistorian finds, not the triumph of civilization over savagery, but an acculturation of Europeans and Indians that was marked by the interchange or diffusion of cultural traits and the emergence of social and cultural dominance by the Europeans in a large society marked by a submerged Indian subculture. Cultural origination was encouraged in both of the interacting societies by the acculturation situation. Dramatic demographic changes in both quantity and location of populations took place. Ecological balance was crucially changed by social alteration of geographical environment, and symbiosis continued between Europeans and Indians for a long time during which a certain amount of social assimilation occurred. Cultural conflict induced episodic efforts for the extermination of one population by the other, and finally the dominant groups in both societies asserted cultural identities independent of each other in conception though not in reality, emphasizing their differences in nativistic or nationalistic movements. These movements influenced the development of mythologies in both cultures, antipodal in form but sprung from the same historical womb.

This is a different world of discourse from that of civilization versus savagery, and it leads to the discovery of a different world of facts. To affirm that European-Indian interaction has produced cultural origination and trait diffusion is to identify something different in form and substance from "the continuous rebirth of society" of the frontier historian. The latter conception assumes the true existence, in ideal form, of only one society; it is properly to be compared, as a phenomenon of culture conflict, with the revelations of Indian nativist prophets. There is no need, however, to impose a specialized scientific terminology on every description of events; plain English will serve the same end if it avoids the specialized terminology, conceptions, and purposes of myth.

The historian cannot wholly free himself from the outlook of his own cultural tradition. In perceiving and reflecting upon the interaction of two cultures, he necessarily adopts a viewpoint somewhere in his own. The idea of a neutral ethnohistory is itself a product of the scientific tradition of European culture. Because of this inescapable bias of outlook, reinforced by the historian's dependence for source materials on the literate Europeans' corpus of documents, it seems desirable to make a special effort of imagination to see things as Indians might. A modern historian has remarked that he had not, "for the most part, attempted to account for the actions and reactions of the natives." He took this approach, he said, "by necessity, as well as by inclination." An ethnohistorian, I think, should not accept such a necessity or share such an inclination. When "natives" are regarded as rational human beings rather than mythical creatures, their actions and reactions do not seem so difficult to infer from both circumstances and the available documentary evidence. The same statement, it may be added, holds true for persons whose ancestors were natives of Europe.

European explorers and invaders discovered an inhabited land. Had it been pristine wilderness then, it would possibly be so still today, for neither the technology nor the social organization of Europe in the sixteenth and seventeenth centuries had the capacity to maintain, of its own resources, outpost colonies thousands of miles from home. Incapable of conquering true wilderness, the Europeans were highly competent in the skill of conquering other people, and that is what they did. They did not settle a virgin land. They invaded and displaced a resident population.

This is so simple a fact that it seems self-evident. All historians of the European colonies in America begin by describing the natives' reception of the newcomers. Yet, paradoxically, most of the same historians also repeat identical mythical phrases purporting that the land-starved people of Europe had found magnificent opportunity to pioneer in a savage wilderness and to bring civilization to it. As rationalization for the invasion and conquest of unoffending peoples, such phrases function to smother retroactive moral scruples that have been dismissed as irrelevant to objective history. Unfortunately, however, the price of repressing scruples has been the suppression of facts.

The basic conquest myth postulates that America was virgin land, or wilderness, inhabited by nonpeople called savages; that these savages were creatures sometimes defined as demons, sometimes as beasts "in the shape of men"; that their mode of existence and cast of mind were such as to make them incapable of civilization and therefore of full humanity; that civilization was required by divine sanction or the imperative of progress to conquer the wilderness and make it a garden; that the savage creatures of the wilderness, being unable to adapt to any environment other than the wild, stubbornly and viciously resisted God or fate, and thereby incurred their suicidal extermination; that civilization and its bearers were refined and ennobled in their contest with the dark powers of the wilderness; and that it all was inevitable.

Allowing for reasonable qualification and modification, the grand myth is fallacious because there never were such absolutes as "savagery" and "civilization" (considered as savagery's antithesis) that play the myth's active roles; there was accordingly no triumph of civilization and no death of savagery; there was nothing in the product of the events to make their survivors inherently superior to mankind elsewhere; and only the events unwilled by human agency were inevitable. Historians have now begun to examine and analyze the origins of the myth.

QUESTIONS

1. Raleigh contrasts his treatment of the natives and the behavior of the Spanish toward them. How believable is his account?
2. What benefits would Queen Elizabeth I receive if England were to compete with the Spanish in Guiana?
3. Can it be said that any European colonizing power had a better record than any other in the treatment of native populations?
4. In what ways might different exploitation of New World natural resources explain the varieties of relations whites had with the Amerindians?
5. What, in early English history, prepared its people to apply harsh terms to conquered peoples?
6. Why should Europeans have referred to their colonies as "pristine wilderness" if this description was not accurate?
7. How does an ethnohistorian deal with explosive terms like *civilized* and *savage*?

Photograph Portfolio B

Figure B–1
A Cannibal Feast

Cannibals fascinated readers. A sure way to sell a pamphlet, broadside, or book was to include a description of a bloody feast. Amerigo Vespucci described a 1499 visit to the island of Trinidad in a published letter:

> They do not eat one another among themselves, but they sail in certain vessels which they call canoes and with these canoes they drag their prey from the islands or mainland from tribes which are their enemies or are not allied with them. They do not eat any women, except those they possess for slaves. And these things we verified in many places where we found such people, because we often saw the bones and skulls of some that they had devoured, and they did not deny it; the more they boasted of it, the more their enemies stood in fear of them.

FIGURE B–1

How convincing is this description? Does he say he actually saw anyone eaten?

The illustration was done in the sixteenth century by an artist who had never visited the New World. It combines the two exciting themes of cannibalism and nudity. Some of the details are accurately rendered, although the exact location of these specific natives is not established in the text. The picture accompanies an account of the travels of a Milanese adventurer, Gerolamo Benzoni. Leaving Italy for Spain in 1541, he continued on to the colonies. He returned home in 1556, delighted to have seen "so many novelties, so much of the world and so many strange countries."

The huts are similar to longhouses in North America, but the roasting rack resembles those used in South America for preparing small animals. Is the depiction of the meal realistic? How many humans had to be killed to prepare it? The natives are shown standing for their meal. Does it strike you as a comfortable or likely way to eat? Amerindians, like many peoples of the world, normally sit on the ground when eating. Would roasted flesh from man or beast look like what is shown here being consumed? The illustrator did not take into account the changes in meat made by roasting. Why is the picture deliberately inaccurate?

The depiction of the natives varies. Most of the men seem to be encased in feathers or some form of skin. Not only are the men bald or with shaved heads, but so, it appears, is the little boy. How realistic is the depiction of the natives? Is it typical of Amerindians to have light-colored hair? Facial hair is rare among Amerindians. The bearded man in the rear is a shipwrecked European observing the scene. What overall message does the illustration as a whole deliver about its subject? What opinion would it leave in viewers' minds about Amerindians?

Figure B–2
Death in Hispaniola

Within fifty years of Columbus's arrival in the Caribbean, the Taínos were almost exterminated. The great majority died from European diseases new to them. Father Las Casas, a missionary who knew the area, claimed that 3 million natives perished on Hispaniola between 1494 and 1508! The dreadful health conditions were exacerbated by the harsh and careless treatment natives received at the hands of the conquerors. In their helpless condition, some natives starved, let their children die, or committed suicide. Pregnant women aborted when they stopped eating. These tragic stories provided anti-Spanish propaganda that was disseminated throughout Europe, some by the pictures of Theodor de Bry, of which this is one. Figure B–5, also by de Bry, offers another example of his propaganda. What similarities do you notice in the messages?

The artist was born into a rich Protestant family. He fled France because of persecution and settled in a German town, where he supported himself selling books and art. Eventually, he became an engraver, illustrating six travel books about the New World. From the safety of his Protestant base, he assailed Catholic Spain's reputation in books that were sent to all parts of Europe. After his death, his son continued the series.

The figures in the forefront of the illustration are variously eating a poisonous plant, and piercing their flesh with a spear or a knife. To the rear, parents drown their children. One is being clubbed to death. How sympathetically are the natives treated? Some hang from trees, and five figures are shown leaping to their deaths from a hill. Could anti-Spanish sentiment be stirred by this picture? Is it effective, even though no Spanish are shown?

The figures do not resemble the actual natives of the island. Would their depiction in the guise of Europeans, posed in conventional positions copied from Renaissance art, decrease or increase empathy in the viewer of the day? Does the illustration get its message across?

FIGURE B–2

Figure B–3
An Outing in Brazil

The broad, if uncritical, European interest in the New World is demonstrated by the enthusiastic reception of travelers' accounts, no matter how ill-informed the narrator. André Thévet, whose illustration appears here, was a Franciscan friar who went on an expedition to Brazil with fellow Frenchmen. The landing party at Guanabalda on the Río de Janeiro was led by Nicholas Durnand de Villegegron. Father Thévet immediately fell ill. Within two months he returned home, so the book he published three years later was largely hearsay. In it, he insists that he also spent twenty days in Canada.

The illustration presents seven Tupinambá residents in Brazil. Is it a more favorable view of Amerindians than that presented in Figure B–1? In what activities are these natives engaging? What physical objects do they carry? As in the previous illustrations, the body types are European rather than Amerindian. This is surprising because the author had firsthand knowledge of the natives.

FIGURE B–3

One figure is shown starting a fire by turning a hard stick in a soft log. His radial feather crown is accurately rendered. A young boy feeds tinder into the fire. The lead figure in the group would catch a viewer's interest because he is smoking a thick wad of tobacco leaves. The first reference to this habit was made by Luis de Torres and Rodrigo de Jerez, sent ashore by Columbus on his first voyage. They reported that the natives "drank smoke." Rodrigo was imprisoned by the Inquisition in 1518 for bringing back to Spain this "devilish habit."

To the rear of the illustration are two women with bundled leaves on their backs. One carries a string of fish. Europeans were impressed by the abundance of food in the New World, and so foodstuffs appear in many pictures. In general, what would a viewer of the day find attractive or unattractive about the way of life presented here?

Figure B–4
Encounter with the Inca

Native pictures present quite a different view of their way of life than that seen in the previous illustrations. This drawing was made by Felipe Guaman Poma de Ayala, a half-Spanish, half-Peruvian writer. It is one of many in a multivolume book, dedicated to King Philip III, that trace the history of the Peruvian people through the domination of the Inca to Spanish rule.

The specific event depicted here is the initial meeting in 1532 between the ruling Inca lord and the conquistadores. The heading reads: "Atahualpa Inca is in the city of Cajamarca on his royal throne." The Inca is surrounded by his soldiers. Is the Inca sympathetically portrayed? Do the Peruvians appear to be a formidable fighting force?

The two Spanish commanders kneel at the throne, Francisco Pizarro to the front, and behind him, Diego de Almagro. On the other side, the Franciscan friar Vicente de Valverde stands clutching a holy book. The individual with a ring in his nose is Felipe, a native interpreter. Who dominates the pictorial space—the conquistadores, the Inca, or the priest?

The events of the meeting, as described in the accompanying text, are that the Spanish "ambassadors" came to kneel before the emperor. What would be the symbolic importance of this act to both groups? The priest made a long speech about the Incas' obligations to the Christian God and the Spanish king, but the interpreter badly mangled the meaning. The Inca replied with dignity and majesty that he understood little and, although he wished their friendship, he would worship no deity but the sun. The friar next handed the Inca his book (either a breviary or the Bible). Never before having encountered such an object, the Inca put it to his ear. "This does not speak to me," he said and threw it to the ground. At that, the priest called for an assault: "Assist me *caballeros!* At these gentile Indians who are

FIGURE B–4

against our faith!" Other, more contemporary versions of the battle omit discussion of long speeches and any insult to a holy book, focusing instead on the Spanish leaders, who gave the signal to attack as soon as they were close enough to seize the ruler. Which account is the most likely? The truth is difficult to determine.

How does this portrayal of Amerindians drawn by a Peruvian differ from others done by Europeans? What impression of the Inca nation does Waman Puma wish to give his intended audience at the Spanish court?

Figure B–5
Work in the Mines

When the population of the New World had diminished, slaves from West Africa were brought in to replace them. By the 1560s, more blacks than whites lived in the Spanish possessions. There were always far more blacks in the southern continent and islands than in the northern continent.

In this illustration, slaves are shown working a mine. Note the heavy

FIGURE B–5

wooden props used to hold up the entrance to the shafts. What safety equipment, if any, are the workers wearing? What implements are they using to dig out the wealth? Are the working conditions degrading to the miners?

The wealth the Spanish extracted from the New World was remarkable, even by modern standards. Between 1500 and 1650, American gold totaled close to 200 tons, worth at least $3 billion today. Yet silver far overshadowed gold. In the first fifty years alone, over $3.3 billion in today's currency was recorded as legally entering Spain, and this does not include the vast amount smuggled into the country. By 1600, the amount of precious metals in Europe increased eight times over what had circulated before Columbus set sail.

The greatest source of specie was the "silver mountain" of Postosí in Bolivia. During the first fifty years of its operation, some 6,000 African slaves were brought in to supplement the "free" Amerindians working in forced-labor gangs. By 1650, the city around the mine was the largest in the New World, with a population of at least 160,000.

This picture showing a small mine is meant to be symbolic rather than realistic. How are the Spanish presented? The illustrator was a French Protestant, who disliked the Catholic Spanish. The standing soldiers are holding long pikes, still the weapon commonly used in military formations in the sixteenth century. One man rests a firearm on his shoulder. The seated gentleman with the elegant hat holds a baton, symbolic of executive power since Roman times. How is the relationship between the Spanish and the workers expressed in the illustration? Is it difficult to tell who is in charge?

Figure B-6
A Portrait Gallery

The unusual European passion to catalogue the whole world led to encyclopedic books by the eighteenth century. This page mixes together Amerindians from Florida, Virginia (the east coast of today's North Carolina), and Brazil. Even at this comparatively late date, how accurate is the depiction of peoples? The figures represent less the actual dark-skinned residents of the Americas than idealized Greeks or Romans dressed in New World costumes. Are the figures more, or less, noble than the ones displayed in Figure B-1?

Continental intellectuals during the so-called Enlightenment were bent on abolishing what they saw as artificial conventions of their society. They became fascinated with the myth of the Noble Savage. This idealized individual, although "uncivilized," put to shame the pretensions of "civilized" but corrupt Christians. The Noble Savage lived without laws, but in such an upright way that he outdid in virtue the decadent European.

Note that all these individuals are modestly covered. The warriors carrying a bow (portrait 1) or a Brazilian war club (portrait 3) are wearing fig leafs,

FIGURE B–6

a puritanical artistic convention that was a result of the Reformation and Counter Reformation, which put an end to the nudity of High Renaissance art. Compare this picture with the other illustrations. Some of the types portrayed are a "king" and a "queen" (portrait 4), and a matron and a mother (portrait 5). What do the costumes have in common?

What would contemporary viewers have noticed about the infant the mother is carrying? It was common in Europe for women to swaddle the young, that is, to wrap cloth tightly around the infant's entire body. It was believed that keeping a child still was a health measure that increased its chances for survival. Visitors to the New World were astonished at how much freedom children had to move about and to play unsupervised.

Note portrait 2. He is an "Ewaiphema," from an imaginary race mentioned in medieval travel literature as living somewhere in distant Asia. After the first encounter with the New World, their home was moved there to fit new circumstances. Sir Walter Raleigh, returning from Guiana in 1595, wrote:

> . . . [A] nation of people, whose heads appear not above their shoulders; . . . they are reported to have their eyes in their shoulders, and their mouths in the middle of their breasts, and that a long train of hair grows backward between their shoulders. . . . for my part I saw them not, but I believe that so many people (who did see them) did not plan together or cooperate to make their report.

How believable is his account? Everyone likes to repeat whoppers. In Shakespeare's *Othello*, the well-traveled Moor of Venice considered various tales with which to woo Desdemona. "And of the cannibals that each other eat . . . and men whose heads do grow beneath their shoulders, this to hear would Desdemona seriously incline?" Why would anyone believe these stories, either in the sixteenth or the eighteenth centuries? Perhaps the fascination compares to that attached to the UFO sightings chronicled in today's tabloids. Since the New World is no longer a source of wonders, the locale has been changed to outer space.

PART THREE

ENCOUNTER

MERINDIANS VIEW THE WHITES

38

Premonitions

The Western Hemisphere was populated by a vast assortment of peoples with social organizations ranging from the rudimentary to the highly sophisticated. Few reasonable generalizations can be made for such a diverse group. Although several peoples are grouped together in this and the next reading to bring out similarities in the way they approached the coming of the Europeans, it is best to recall that they are vastly different in every other respect.

> *"everything shall become a desert because other men are coming to the earth."*

The Taínos of the island of Hispaniola, whose views are presented in the first selection, are discussed in the introductions to Documents 22 and 23. The people of Michoacán, later designated by the name Tarascan, spoke a language unrelated to their neighbors in Mesoamerica. These Tarascans, featured in the second selection, lived in Western Mexico around Lake Pátzcuaro. They were in independent kingdoms during pre-Hispanic times, until they were brought into a union during the fifteenth century by a line of aggressive leaders who fought off the Aztecs.

The background of the Aztecs is discussed in the introduction to Document 25. They believed that a legendary god, the Toltec chieftain Quetzalcóatl, would return from out of the east to reclaim his dominion during a One-Reed year, which recurred every fifty-second year in the sacred calendar. The Aztec story is presented in the third selection. By a remarkable coincidence, the Spanish adventurer Cortés arrived on the coast in 1519, a One-Reed year. He thus may have had the preliminary advantage of cautious treatment by the Great Speaker Moctezuma.

Humans have lived in Peru since at least 8,000 B.C. Advanced cultures developed in different parts, but they were not unified until the Incas set out from Cuzco on a path of conquest, which in fifty years brought under their control the area of present-day Peru, Bolivia, northern Argentina, Chile, and Ecuador. The population was heavily concentrated in the high valleys between the mountain ranges and at a few locations on the Pacific coastal plains, near mountain streams. The prediction in the final selection, made by the last Inca who led an undivided realm, was as influential in its own way as the one in the Aztec reading.

Many Amerindian groups have in common these melancholy presentiments about the coming of the white man, but it is, of course, open to question if such defeatist sentiments came before or after the fact. Predictions created to suit events are a way to fit new phenomena into old patterns. If all was foretold, then the blow of the unexpected is softened and ancient ways rejustified.

The Taínos of Hispaniola

The natives of Hispaniola were much impressed by the arrival of the Spaniards. Formerly two *caciques* [chiefs], of whom one was the father of Guarionex, fasted for fifteen days in order to consult the *cemes* [images] about the future. This fast having disposed the *cemes* in their favour, they answered that within a few years a race of men wearing clothes would land in the island and would overthrow their religious rites and ceremonies, massacre their children, and make them slaves. This prophecy had been taken by the younger generation to apply to the cannibals; and thus whenever it became known that the cannibals had landed anywhere, the people took flight without even attempting any resistance. But when the Spaniards landed, the islanders then referred the prophecy to them, as being the people whose coming was announced. And in this they were not wrong, for they are all under the dominion of the Christians, and those who resisted have been killed. . . .

The Tarascan of Mexico

These people say that during the four years before the Spaniards came to the land, their temples were burned from top to bottom, that they closed them and they would be burned again, and that the rock walls fell as their temples were made of flagstones. They did not know the cause of this except that they held it to be an augury. Likewise, they saw two large comets in the sky and thought that their gods were to conquer or destroy a village and that they were to do it for them. These people imitate parts of their dreams and do as much of what they dreamed as they can. They report their dreams to the chief priest, who in turn conveys the information to the Cazonci [Chief Tzíntzícha Tangaxoan]. They say that the poor who bring in wood and sacrifice their ears dream about their gods who are reported as having told them that they would be given food and that they should marry such and such Christian girls. If this were a kind of omen they dared not tell it to the Cazonci.

A priest related that, before the Spaniards came, he had dreamed that people would come bringing strange animals which turned out to be the horses which he had not known. In this dream these people entered the houses of the chief priests and slept there with their horses. They also

SOURCE *De Orbe Novo. The Eight Decades of Peter Martyr D'Anghera*, trans. F. A. MacNutt (New York: G. P. Putnam's Sons, 1912), p. 176.
SOURCE *The Chronicles of Michoacán*, pp. 53–57, trans. and ed. by Eugene R. Craine and Reginald C. Reindorp. Copyright © 1970 by the University of Oklahoma Press.

brought many chickens that soiled the temples. He said he dreamed this two or three times in considerable fear for he did not know what it was until the Spaniards came to this province. When the Spaniards reached the city, they lodged in the houses of the chief priests with their horses where they held their prayer and kept their vigil. Before the Spaniards arrived they [the Spaniards] all had smallpox and measles, from which large numbers of people died, along with many lords and high families. All the Spaniards of the time are unanimous in that this disease was general throughout New Spain, for which reason it is to be given credence. The people are in accord in that measles and smallpox were unknown until the Spaniards brought them to the land.

The priest also indicated that the priests of the mother of Cueraváperi [goddess of agriculture and fertility], who were in a village called Cinapecuaro, had come to the father of the dead Cazonci and reported the following dream or revelation prophesying the destruction of the house of their gods, an event which actually happened in Ucareo: the lord of the village of Ucareo, whose name was Vigen [Vigel], had a concubine among his other women, and the Goddess Cueraváperi, mother of all the earthly gods, came and took that woman from her own house. These people say that all their gods frequently enter their houses and take people to be sacrificed to them. The goddess, without leaving the village, took the woman first a little way toward the road to Mexico City and then directed her to go out of the village on the road to Araro. Then putting the woman down the goddess untied a gourd dish shaped like a bowl, which was tied to her skirt, and after washing it in water, prepared a beverage made of water and something like a white seed. She gave this beverage to the woman who, upon drinking it, grew faint, and the goddess told her to walk on alone, saying: "I am not to take you; there is one, all dressed up, who is to take you; I shall neither harm you nor sacrifice you, nor will he who is to take you. You will be taken where there is a council and you will hear all that is said in that council. Then you shall report it all to the King Zangua [Zuangua], who is over all of us."

The woman walked along the road and soon met a white eagle, whistling and bristling his feathers, and with a great wart over large eyes which indicated that he was the God Curicaveri. The eagle greeted her, telling her that she was welcome, and she returned the greeting, saying, "Lord, may you have good fortune." The eagle replied, "Climb up on my wings and do not be afraid of falling." As soon as the woman was seated, the eagle, whistling, rose with her and took her through a forest where there was a spring heated by brimstone and as dawn was breaking placed her on the top of a very high mountain called Xanoatajacanzio [Xanoato Huacío]. . . .

To the woman it seemed that they were all in a very large house and the eagle told her to be seated and she would hear everything that was said.

By this time the sun had risen and the God Curitacaheri was washing his head with soap. He had removed his braid, but he usually wore a wreath of colors on his head, some wooden ear ornaments, miniature earthen jugs around his neck and was covered with a thin blanket. His brother, called

Tiripanienquarencha, was with him and they looked very handsome. All the other gods greeted them and extended a welcome to which Curitacaheri replied: "Well, you have all arrived, be sure that no one has been forgotten or was not called." They replied that they were all present and they began asking among themselves, "Have the Gods of the Left Hand arrived too?" The answer was that all were present, and again Curitacaheri urged them to be sure that they had not forgotten to call someone. Once more they assured him that everyone was there. Then he said, "Let my brother tell you what has to be said, and I do not want to go into the house." Then spoke Tiripanienquarencha, saying: "Come close, you Gods of the Left Hand and of the Right. My brother has told me what to tell you. . . .

'You First-born Gods and you, Gods of the Left Hand, gird yourselves for suffering and let it be as it was determined by the gods. How can we contradict what has been established? We do not know what this is about. In fact, was it not decided and ordered in the beginning, that no two of us gods should be together before the light came so that we should not kill ourselves nor lose our deity? It was ordered then that the earth should become calm at once and make two revolutions; that they were to be thus forever, and this which all we gods had agreed upon was not to change before the light came.' Now, we do not know what these words are. The gods tried to contradict this change but under no circumstances were they allowed to speak. Let it be as the gods will it. You First-born Gods and you Gods of the Left Hand, go all of you to your houses and do not bring back that wine you have.

"Break all those jugs for it shall not be from here on as it has been up to now when we were very prosperous. Break all the wine tubs everywhere, leave off the sacrifice of men and bring no more offerings with you because from now on it is not to be that way. No more kettledrums are to be sounded, split them all asunder. There will be no more temples or fireplaces, nor will any more smoke rise, everything shall become a desert because other men are coming to the earth. They will spare no end of the earth, to the Left Hand and to the Right, and everywhere all the way to the edge of the sea and beyond. The singing will be all one for there will not be as many songs as we had but only one throughout the land. And you, woman, who are here pretending not to hear us, publish this and make it known to Zuangua the King, who is in charge of all of us." All the gods of the council replied, saying it would be so and began to wipe the tears from their eyes. The council broke up and that vision was seen no more.

The Aztec of Mexico

 When night came and everyone was asleep the king [Moctezuma] went to a terrace on the roof. Having watched there until midnight

SOURCE Diego de Durán, *The Aztecs: The History of the Indies of New Spain*, trans. Doris Heyden and Fernanda Horcasitas (New York: Orion Press, 1964), pp. 247–271, passim. Footnotes eliminated.

he saw the comet appear with its brilliant tail, whereupon he was astonished. Then he remembered what Nezahualpilli had said, and he was so filled with fear that he thought his death would arrive within the hour.

The next day Moctezuma called in the priests, sorcerers, soothsayers, diviners and astrologers and consulted them, but they claimed that they had not seen any signs in the sky, for which the king had them jailed.

Then Moctezuma asked the king of Texcoco to tell him what it meant. "O lord," responded Nezahualpilli, "your vassals, the astrologers, soothsayers and diviners, have been careless! That sign in the heavens has been there for some time and yet you describe it to me now as if it were a new thing. I thought that you had already discovered it and that your astrologers had explained it to you. Since you now tell me you have seen it I will answer you that that brilliant star appeared in the heavens many days ago. It is an ill omen for our kingdoms; terrible, frightful things will come upon them. In all our lands and provinces there will be great calamities and misfortunes, not a thing will be left standing. Death will dominate the land! All our dominions will be lost and all of this will be done with the permission of the Lord of the Heights, of the Day and the Night and of the Wind. You will be witness to these things since it will all happen in your time. For as soon as I depart from the city of Mexico I go to die. You will never behold me again; this is the last visit in which we will see each other in this life. I long to hide, to flee from the labor and afflictions which await you. Do not be faint, do not feel anguish or despair! Make your heart wide, strengthen your spirit and manly chest against these predestined troubles!"

Moctezuma then wept bitterly, saying, "O Lord of All Created Things! O mighty gods who give life or death! Why have you decreed that many kings shall have reigned proudly but that my fate is to witness the unhappy destruction of Mexico? Why should I be the one to see the death of my wives and children and the loss of my powerful kingdoms and dominions and of all that the Aztecs have conquered with their mighty arms and strength of their chests? What shall I do? Where shall I hide? Where shall I conceal myself? Alas, if only I could turn into stone, wood, or some other earthly matter rather than suffer that which I so dread! But what can I do, O powerful monarch, but await that which you have predicted? For this reason I kiss your hands and thank you. Alas, I cannot at this moment become a bird in order to fly into the woods and hide in their depths." With these words, says the *Chronicle*, the two kings said farewell to each other with great sadness. . . .

Moctezuma was so disturbed that he was half desirous that the events which had been predicted take place immediately. In the midst of his preoccupation he called the chieftains of the wards, asking them if they had dreamed anything regarding the arrival of the strangers whose coming he so feared. He told them to reveal these dreams even though they might be contrary to his desires, since he wished to know the truth in this much-talked-of matter.

The heads of the wards told him that they had dreamed nothing nor had they seen or heard anything about this affair. He answered, "Then I beg you, my friends, to tell all the old men and women of the wards to inform me of whatever dreams they may have had, be they in my favor or against me. Also, tell the priests to reveal any visions they may see, such as ghosts or other phantoms that appear at night in the woods and dark places. Let them ask these apparitions about things to come. It will also be good to give this advice to those who wander about in the late hours; if they encounter the woman who roams the streets weeping and moaning, let them ask her why she weeps and moans."

Soon Moctezuma was notified that certain old people had dreamed strange things and they were brought before him. Said one old man, "Powerful lord, we do not wish to offend your ears or fill your heart with anxiety to make you ill. However, we are forced to obey you and we will describe our dreams to you. Know then, that these last nights the Lords of Sleep have shown us the temple of Huitzilopochtli [patron god of war] burning with frightful flames, the stones falling one by one until it was totally destroyed. We also saw Huitzilopochtli himself fallen, cast down upon the floor! This is what we have dreamed!"

Moctezuma then asked the old women and received the following answer, "My son, do not be troubled in your heart for what we are about to tell you, although it has frightened us much. In our dreams we, your mothers, saw a mighty river enter the doors of your royal palace, smashing the walls in its fury. It ripped up the walls from their foundation, carrying beams and stones with it until nothing was left standing. We saw it reach the temple and this too was demolished. We saw the great chieftains and lords filled with fright, abandoning the city and fleeing toward the hills. This is what we have dreamed!"

Moctezuma listened attentively to what the old men and women had described. When he saw that it was not in his favor but that it confirmed the earlier ill omens he ordered that the dreamers be cast in jail. There they were to be given food in small measures until they starved to death. After this no one wished to tell his dreams to Moctezuma. . . .

Moctezuma became even more worried and attempted to discover what kind of people had come to his land, their place of origin, lineage and, above all, whether they planned to return. For this reason he called Teoctlamacazqui and conversed with him in private. He said that he wanted to know more about those who had just departed and that he wished to have a painting made of them. He wished the picture to be drawn in his presence but said that it must be done secretly.

Teoctlamacazqui answered that he was willing to have this picture made, whereupon he ordered that the best artist of Mexico, an old man, be brought. Moctezuma told this man that he should not reveal anything that might happen, under pain of death. The painter was cowed, exclaiming that he was not a man to uncover secrets of such a great and mighty lord. His paints were brought to him and Teoctlamacazqui began to tell him what he should depict. The artist drew a picture of the ship in the way it had been seen, showing the Spaniards with their long beards and white faces. He painted their clothing in different colors, their hats upon their heads and their swords in their belts. When Moctezuma saw this he marveled and gazed upon the painting for a long time. Having looked, he said to Teoctlamacazqui, "Were these things as they have been painted here?" The answer was, "Yes, O lord, they are exactly so; I have not lied or added anything!"

Moctezuma paid the artist for his work, saying, "Brother, I beg you to answer me this question: by any chance do you know anything about what you have painted? Did your ancestors leave you a drawing or description of these men who were to arrive in this land?" The painter answered, "Powerful lord, I will not lie to you or deceive you—you are the image of the god. Therefore I will tell you that I and my ancestors never were occupied with any arts save those of painting pictures and other symbols. My ancestors were merely the artists of past kings and they depicted what they were ordered. Therefore, I know nothing of that which you ask me; if I tried to answer your question my answer would be a lie."

Moctezuma then ordered him to question the other artisans of his profession, asking if they possessed some picture coming down from their ancestors regarding those who might come to this land and possess it. The artist agreed to do so and for several days he inquired. But the painter was unable to find out anything certain and therefore returned to Moctezuma and told him that he had discovered nothing exact regarding these things. . . .

Moctezuma was about to call the painters of books from Xochimilco, but the noble Tlillancalqui Teoctlamacazqui said to him, "Powerful lord, do not tire yourself or waste time in questioning so many men. None of them will be able to tell you what you desire to know as clearly as an ancient man from Xochimilco whom I know well. His name is Quilaztli and he is well informed in all matters which concern ancient history and painted books. If you wish I will bring him to you; I will tell him what you wish to know and he will produce his antique paintings." The king thanked him, commanding him to bring the old man immediately. When the latter appeared he brought with him his painted manuscripts. He appeared before Moctezuma, Angry Lord, who received him well because he was a venerable old man and of fine appearance.

Said Quilaztli to the sovereign, "O mighty lord, if because I tell you the truth I am to die, nevertheless I am here in your presence and you may do what you wish to me!" Before showing him the papers, he narrated that mounted men would come to this land in a great wooden house. This structure was to lodge many men, serving them as a home; within it they would eat and sleep. On the surface of this house they would cook their food, walk and play as if they were on firm land. They were to be white, bearded men, dressed in different colors and on their heads they would wear round coverings. Other human beings were to arrive with them, mounted on beasts similar to deer and others on eagles which would fly like the wind. These men were to possess the country, settle in all its cities, multiply in great numbers and be owners of gold, silver and precious stones.

"So that you may see," continued Quilaztli, "that what I say is the truth, behold it drawn here! This painting was bequeathed to me by my ancestors." He then took out an ancient picture on which were depicted the ship and the men dressed in the same manner as those which the king already knew through his painting. There he also saw other men mounted on horses or on flying eagles, all of them dressed in different colors, wearing their hats and swords.

Moctezuma, seeing the similarity between what the old man described and what appeared upon his painting, almost lost his senses and began to weep and to show anguish. Uncovering his chest to the elder, he cried out, "O brother Quilaztli, I now see that your ancestors were verily wise and well informed. Only a few days ago the men that you have shown me on your painting arrived in this land from the east. They came in the wooden house that you have described, dressed in the same colors and manner that appear in your drawing. I will show you how I ordered that they be painted: behold them here! However, one thing consoles me; I have sent them a present and begged them to go away in peace. They have obeyed me, departed, and I doubt if they will return."

"It is possible, O mighty prince," exclaimed Quilaztli, "that they came and went away again! Listen to the words I will say to you, and if I lie I am willing to have you annihilate me, my children and my descendants! Behold, before two years have passed, or at the most three, the strangers will return to these lands. Their coming was meant only to find a convenient way to return. Even though they said to you that they were returning to their native country, do not believe them! They will not go that far but will turn back when they have gone half way!"

Three years later, when Moctezuma had almost forgotten these things, news came from the sea that a hill was moving to and fro upon the waters again.

The Incas of Peru

O ne day, as Huaina Capac [twelfth sovereign of Peru, 1493–1527] was coming out of a lake in which he had just bathed, near Quito, he was suddenly seized with a sensation of chill, which was followed by one of intense heat. His condition [smallpox from Europeans?] grew

SOURCE *The Incas. The Royal Commentaries of the Inca Garcilaso de la Vega, 1539–1616,* trans. Maria Jolas from French ed. by Alain Gheerbrant, intro. by Alain Gheerbrant (New York: The Orion Press, 1961), pp. 287–288.

worse and worse and, after a few days, he realized that the predictions concerning his death were about to come true.

Further signs had appeared in the sky, amongst which was a huge green comet; lightning had struck in his own house; and the *amautas* [philosophers] had for several years agreed with the soothsayers in predicting his approaching end which, according to what they said, would constitute the prelude to an avalanche of calamities from which neither the Empire nor the royal line of the Incas would be able to recover. And Huaina Capac knew all that, although these sinister predictions continued to be hidden from the people, out of fear lest the entire nation should pine away of despair.

The king, therefore, summoned his sons, his relatives, and all the governors and captains who could reach the palace in time, and he spoke to them as follows:

"Know ye," he said, "that the moment has come when I must go and rest beside our father the Sun. Already, a long time ago, he made it known to me that he would call me from a lake or from a river. The indisposition with which I was seized upon leaving the water is therefore a sign which I cannot mistake. When I am dead, cut my body open; take my heart and my entrails and bury them in the city of Quito that I have so dearly cherished; then take my body to Cuzco, to lie beside those of my forefathers. I commend to you my beloved son, Atahualpa. May he reign in my stead over the kingdom of Quito and over all the lands that he succeeds in conquering; and you, captains of my army, you shall serve him with the love and loyalty that you owe to your king; obey him in all things, because all that he will ask of you, it is I who shall have revealed it to him, on orders from our father the Sun."

These were the last words that Huaina Capac addressed to his sons and relatives. He then had all his other captains and *curacas* [officials] summoned, all those who were not of royal blood. After making the same recommendations to them, he concluded as follows:

"Our father the Sun disclosed to us a long time ago that we should be twelve Incas, his own sons, to reign on this earth; and that then, new, hitherto unknown people would arrive; that they would obtain victory and subject all of our kingdoms to their Empire, as well as many other lands. I think that the people who came recently by sea to our own shores are the ones referred to. They are strong, powerful men, who will outstrip you in everything. The reign of the twelve Incas ends with me. I can therefore certify to you that these people will return shortly after I shall have left you, and that they will accomplish what our father the Sun predicted they would: they will conquer our Empire, and they will become its only lords. I order you to obey and serve them, as one should serve those who are superior in every way; because their law will be better than ours, and their weapons will be more powerful and invincible than yours. Dwell in peace; my father the Sun is calling me, I shall go to rest at his side."

Initial Impressions

Unfortunately, no record survives telling what the Caribbean natives thought of Columbus and his men. No doubt it was something like later records of European contact with the New World. Aztec accounts of the fall of their empire were written as early as 1528, only seven years after the collapse. The shock and surprise expressed in the first selection may have given the invaders an initial advantage, although that did not last long. European technical superiority was not clear-cut because Cortés's men had few swords, pikes, or knives. His firearms numbered a mere thirteen muskets, four light cannon, and ten bronze cannon. Besides, the powder for these arms was damp most of the time. The Spanish did not lack adaptability, however; when their impressive iron suits proved a liability in the climate, they abandoned them in favor of the local quilted cotton armor.

> *"they were very different from us, in face and costume, . . ."*

The Aztec lords had made religion almost a private cult, excluding commoners. The high born were godlike, according to their rites, so it is not surprising that the same status was at first granted the Spanish. Since the principal Aztec deities were nourished by blood-letting ceremonies, it was logical for the emissaries to pour that sacred fluid over gift offerings of food, should the Spanish actually have turned out to be gods.

The Tarascan account in the second selection was compiled by a Franciscan about 1540, on the basis of earlier narratives. It gives an accurate sense of the complexity of the impressions made on the inhabitants of western Mexico by the Spanish. The text also demonstrates the natives' effort to locate parallels within their own lives that would help them make sense of the behavior of the newcomers.

The third selection presents the views of the Incas of Peru about the outsiders. It again points out the initial response by a native group that the white men might be gods. A fourteenth-century ruler had been encouraged in the major victory of Inca expansion by the god Viracochas, in whose name he then developed a cult. The Inca rulers were themselves treated as gods—children of the sun—so it was not unreasonable to think the foreigners, although obviously in the form of men, could in some sense be divine. They too were called Viracochas.

An Aztec Account

Seventh Chapter, in which is related the account by which the messengers who had gone to see the boats reported to Moctezuma.

And when this was done, they thereupon reported to Moctezuma; so they told him how they had gone marveling, and they showed him what [the Spaniards'] food was like.

And when he had so heard what the messengers reported, he was terrified, he was astounded. And much did he marvel at their food.

Especially did it cause him to faint away when he heard how the gun, at [the Spaniards'] command, discharged [the shot]; how it resounded as if it thundered when it went off. It indeed bereft one of strength; it shut off one's ears. And when it discharged, something like a round pebble came forth from within. Fire went showering forth; sparks went blazing forth. And its smoke smelled very foul; it had a fetid odor which verily wounded the head. And when [the shot] struck a mountain, it was as if it were destroyed, dissolved. And a tree was pulverized; it was as if it vanished; it was as if someone blew it away.

All iron was their war array. In iron they clothed themselves. With iron they covered their heads. Iron were their swords. Iron were their crossbows. Iron were their shields. Iron were their lances.

And those which bore them upon their backs, their deer [horses], were as tall as roof terraces.

And their bodies were everywhere covered; only their faces appeared. They were very white; they had chalky faces; they had yellow hair, though the hair of some was black. Long were their beards; they also were yellow. They were yellow-bearded. [The Negroes' hair] was kinky, it was curly.

And their food was like fasting food [ordinary human food]—very large, white; not heavy like [tortillas]; like maize stalks, good-tasting as if of maize stalk flour; a little sweet, a little honeyed. It was honeyed to eat; it was sweet to eat.

And their dogs were very large. They had ears folded over; great dragging jowls. They had fiery eyes—blazing eyes; they had yellow eyes—fiery yellow eyes. They had thin flanks—flanks with ribs showing. They had gaunt stomachs. They were very tall. They were nervous; they went about panting, with tongues hanging. They were spotted like ocelots; they were varicolored.

And when Moctezuma so heard, he was much terrified. It was as if he fainted away. His heart saddened; his heart failed him. . . .

SOURCE Bernardino de Sahagún, *Florentine Codex: General History of the Things of New Spain*, trans. A. J. O. Anderson and C. E. Dibble (Salt Lake City: School of American Research and University of Utah, 1950–1982), *Book XIII: The Conquest of Mexico*, Chaps. XVI, XVII, XXIII, pp. 44–66. Reprinted by permission.

Then at that time Moctezuma sent emissaries. He sent all evil men—soothsayers, magicians. And he sent the elders, the hardy [warriors], the brave [warriors] to secure [for the Spaniards] all the food they would need: turkey hens, eggs, white tortillas, and what they might desire. And in order that their hearts might be well satisfied, they were to look to them well. He sent captives so that they might be prepared: perchance [the Spaniards] would drink their blood. And thus did the messengers do.

But when [the Spaniards] beheld this, much were they nauseated. They spat; they closed their eyes tight, they shut their eyes; they shook their heads. And [the emissaries] had soaked the food in blood, they had covered it with blood. Much did it revolt them; it nauseated them. For strongly did it reek of blood.

And Moctezuma had acted thus because he thought them gods, he took them to be gods, he worshipped them as gods. They were called, they were named "gods come from heaven." . . .

A Tarascan Account

When the Indians first saw the Spaniards, they marveled at such strange people who did not eat the same kind of food or get drunk as the Indians did. They called the Spanish *Tucupacha*, which means gods, and *Teparacha*, which means big men and is also used to mean gods, and *Acacecha*, meaning people who wear caps and hats. As time passed they began to call them Christians and to believe that they had come from heaven. They were sure that the Spaniards' clothes were the skins of men such as the Indians themselves used on feast occasions. Some called the horses deer, others *tuycen*, which were something like horses which the Indians made from pigweed bread for use in the feast of *Cuingo* and to which they fastened manes of false hair. The Indians who first saw the horses told the *Cazonci* [Chief Tzíntzícha Tangaxoan] that the horses talked, that when the Spaniards were on horseback they told the horses where they were to go as they pulled on the reins. They also said that Mother Cueravaperi [goddess of agriculture and fertility] had given them the wheat, seeds, and wine they brought when they came to the land. When they saw the religious so poorly dressed, wearing their crowns and not wanting either gold or silver, they were astonished. Since the priests had no women, the Indians thought they were priests of a god who had come to the land and called them *Curitiecha* as they did their own priests who wore fiber wreaths on their heads and some false temples. They were amazed that the priests did not dress as the other Spaniards, and they said how fortunate are these who want nothing.

As time went by some of their priests and witches made the Indians

SOURCE *The Chronicles of Michoacán*, pp. 87–89, trans. and ed. by Eugene R. Craine and Reginald C. Reindorp. Copyright © 1970 by the University of Oklahoma Press.

believe that the religious were dead men, that the habits they wore were shrouds, that, in their houses at night they shed their forms, become skeletons, go to the Inferno where they have their women, and return by morning. This tale lasted a long time, until they began to understand more. The witches also said that the Spaniards did not die, that they were immortal, that the baptismal water which was sprinkled on their heads was blood, and that the Spaniards split open the heads of their children. For these reasons they dared not baptize their children for they did not want them to die. The Indians called the crosses Holy Mary, because they did not know the doctrine and they thought the crosses were gods like those they had.

When they were told that they were to go to heaven, they did not believe it, saying that they had never seen anyone go. They would not believe anything the religious told them nor did they trust them. They said the Spaniards were all as one and they were sure that the Monks had been born with their habits on and had never been children. These beliefs also were long lived and even now they still do not believe that the Monks had mothers. When the religious said mass, the Indians thought that they could see the present and the future by looking in the holy water. They did not trust those witches [Catholic priests] and would not tell the truth in confession for fear they would be killed. Should an Indian go to confession, all the others would spy on him to see how he did it, and the more so if it were a woman. Afterward they wanted to know what the priest had asked and said, and they told everyone all about it.

The Castilian women were called *Cuchahecha* which means ladies and goddesses. They thought that the letters which they were sent to deliver could talk so they dared not lie at any time. They marveled at every new thing they saw, for they are greatly interested in novelties. They called horseshoes "coats of mail" and "iron shoes" for horses. In Taxcala [Tlaxcala] they brought rations of chickens for the horses as well as for the Spaniards. They were astonished to hear what the priests preached to them and called them witches who knew everything they did at home, or they knew it because somebody told on them, or because they had confessed to them.

An Inca Account

T hey said they had seen beings quite different from us landing in their country, different as much by their conduct as by their clothing. They resembled the Viracochas [one of two chief deities], that name by which we referred, in times gone by, to the Creator of all things. Thus they named them, first because they were very different from us, in

SOURCE Titu Cusi Yupangui (Diego de Castro), *Relación de la Conquista del Perú y Hechos del Inca Manco II* [1570], *Colección de libros y documentos referentes a la Historia del Perú*, 1st series, vol. II, Lima, 1916, pp. 8–9, in Nathan Wachtel, *The Vision of the Vanquished. The Spanish Conquest of Peru Through Indian Eyes, 1530–1570* (New York: The Harvester Press, 1977), p. 45.

face and costume, second because they saw them riding on the backs of huge animals with silver feet (this from the sparks struck out by the iron shoes). Another reason was that they saw the strange beings converse with one another, silently, by means of pieces of white cloth, just as easily as one man speaks to another by word of mouth (this from their reading of letters and books). Then again, they called them Viracochas, because of their remarkable appearance. There were great differences of feature between them; some had black beards, some red. They saw them eat from silver plates. Furthermore, they possessed *Yllapas*, the name we give to thunderbolts (this was because of their armament, which they thought to be bolts from heaven).

QUESTIONS

1. Locate the common themes in the various Amerindian premonitions or prophesies about the coming of the white man.
2. What were the principal signs, in atmospheric disturbances and in dreams, that something tragic was about to happen?
3. What in Aztec myths or about their history predisposed the Aztec leader Moctezuma to think the arrival of the strangers on the coast was expected?
4. How much would the old gods in the various societies help in dealing with anticipated threats to the survival of their peoples?
5. What did Amerindians find most astonishing about the technology, appearance, or way of life of the Spanish?
6. What was hateful or distasteful to native groups about the white man? What was worthy of admiration?

HITES VIEW THE AMERINDIANS

Cannibalism

The New World was named after Amerigo Vespucci because a German cartographer decided that he, not Columbus, was the first to stumble onto the southern continent and realize that it was not Asia. Vespucci, a native of Florence, Italy, became an intimate friend of Columbus and was held in sufficient confidence by the Spanish crown to be named their chief pilot for coordinating aspects of exploration from Seville.

> *"a device to make conquest and exploitation morally legitimate."*

Numerous narratives circulating throughout Europe were claimed to have been written by Vespucci. The printed version of a letter dated 1500, which is the first selection, stands a good chance of being just that. He may have made four voyages to the Western Hemisphere, starting in 1497, although scholars are willing to accept only two along the shores of the southern continent, the last as far as Brazil in 1501. Among many things mentioned in the letter is his belief that the natives of Trinidad relished a form of food prohibited to Europeans.

Michel Eyquem de Montaigne succeeded to the family estate at Pérogord, France, in 1571, and thereafter lived the life of a country gentleman, disturbed only by a few trips abroad and election, both times against his wishes, to the office of mayor of Bordeaux. He preferred to stay at home, in a quiet, cork-lined room of a tower, writing the *Essais*, which gave him his literary reputation. He pioneered the personal essay form, fearlessly criticizing his own thoughts in a highly original style that shows the broadest sympathy for all the varieties of human ways. Even cannibalism, if such a thing existed, had to be brought into his range of understanding, since nothing human was alien to him. The great personalities of his country, including its king, made the pilgrimage to his home to learn about his idiosyncratic ideas. Few of his contemporaries—or successors, for that matter—were as able as he, in the second selection, to escape the ethnocentric bias that what we eat is the only proper food for a human being.

The third selection is by a modern writer who places the issue of cannibalism into a historical context, which demonstrates that stories of cannibals long predate the first visit to the New World and never required hard evidence to be believed. Man-eaters showed up in the fantastic adventures of Sir John Mandeville (Document 6), where it is clear that his cannibals were as much a fantasy as was his island filled with Amazons. The issue of where and when—if ever—humans regularly ate other humans for the nutritional value remains unsettled because even alleged eyewitness accounts are open to question.

Vespucci

Let me say that after we turned our course toward the north, the first land that we found to be inhabited was an island [Trinidad] ten degrees from the equator. When we came up with it we saw a great multitude along the shore who stood staring at the wonderful sight. We rode at anchor about a mile from the land and manned the boats and went ashore with twenty-two men well armed. When the people saw us leaping ashore and discerned that we were of a different nature—because they have no beard or clothing, the men, like the women, appearing just as they issued from the wombs of their mothers, without covering any shame, and because of the difference of color, they being grayish and brownish yellow and we white—they had fear of us and betook themselves to the woods. With great difficulty, by means of signs, we reassured them and negotiated with them.

We discovered that they were of the breed called cannibals and that the majority of them lived on human flesh. Your Excellency may hold this for certain, that they do not eat one another among themselves, but they sail in certain vessels which they call "canoes," and with these canoes they drag their prey from the islands or mainland, from tribes which are their enemies or are not allied with them. They do not eat any women, except those they possess as slaves. And these things we verified in many places where we found such people, because we often saw the bones and skulls of some that they had devoured, and they did not deny it; the more they boasted of it, the more their enemies stood in fear of them. They are people of affable comprehension and of beautiful physique. They go entirely naked. The weapons they carry are bows and arrows and small shields. They are religious people of great courage, and very excellent bowmen. In conclusion, we had dealings with them, and they conducted us to one of their villages that lay two leagues inland. They gave us breakfast and everything we asked of them, but they gave more through fear than affection. And after we had stopped with them all one day, we returned to the ships, remaining friendly with them.

We sailed along the coast of this island and saw the inhabitants of other large villages along the seashore. We landed in a skiff and found them waiting for us, all loaded with provisions, and they gave us the wherewithal for a very good breakfast of their native dishes. Seeing they were such kind people, who treated us so well, we did not resort to seizure of anything of theirs.

SOURCE Letter from Seville, 1500, to Lorenzo di Pier-Francesco de Medici in F. J. Pohl, *Amerigo Vespucci: Pilot Mayor,* 1945, pp. 81–82, passim. Used with permission of the translator, Mr. J. Frederick Pohl.

Montaigne

We all call barbarism that which does not fit in with our usages. And indeed we have no other level of truth and reason but the example and model of the opinions and usages of the country we live in. There we always see the perfect religion, the perfect government, the perfect and accomplished manner of doing all things. . . .

. . . Each man [among the cannibals] brings back as a trophy the head of the enemy he has slain, and fixes it over the entrance of this dwelling. After treating his prisoner well for a considerable time, and giving him all that hospitality can devise, his captor convokes a great gathering of his acquaintance. He ties a cord to one of his prisoner's arms, holding him at some distance for fear of being hurt, and gives the other arm to be held in the same way by his best friend; and these two, in presence of the whole assembly, dispatch him with their swords. This done, they roast and eat him in common, and send bits of him to their absent friends. Not, as one might suppose, for nourishment, as the ancient Scythians used to do, but to signify an extreme revenge.

And that it is so, may be seen from this: having perceived that the Portuguese, who had allied themselves with their adversaries, inflicted a different kind of death on their prisoners, which was to bury them up to the waist, shoot the upper part of the bodies full of arrows, and afterwards to hang them; they imagined that these people of another world (seeing that they had sown the knowledge of a great many vices among their neighbours, and were much greater masters than themselves in every kind of wickedness) had some reason for adopting this kind of vengeance, and that it must be more painful than their own; wherefore they began to give up their old method, and followed this one.

I am not so much concerned that we should remark on the horrible barbarity of such acts, as that, whilst rightly judging their errors, we should be so blind to our own. I think there is more barbarity in eating a live than a dead man, in tearing on the rack and torturing the body of a man still full of feeling, in roasting him piecemeal and giving him to be bitten and mangled by dogs and swine (as we have not only read, but seen within fresh memory, not between old enemies, but between neighbours and fellow citizens, and, what is worse, under the cloak of piety and religion), than in roasting and eating him after he is dead. . . .

Three men of this [Amerindian] nation, not knowing how dear, in tranquillity and happiness, it will one day cost them to know the corruptions of this side of the world, and that this intercourse will be the cause of their ruin, which indeed I imagine is already advanced (poor wretches, to be allured by the desire to see new things and to leave their own serene sky to

SOURCE *The Essays of Montaigne*, trans. E. J. Trechmann, 2 vols. (London: Oxford University Press, 1927), vol. I, pp. 205–215, passim. Reprinted with permission.

come and see ours!), were at Rouen at a time when the late King Charles the Ninth was there. The King had a long talk with them. They were shown our ways, our pomp, the form of a fine city. After that somebody asked their opinion, desiring to know what they most wondered at. They mentioned three things, the third of which I am sorry to have forgotten, but I still remember two. They said that in the first place they thought it very strange that so many big men with beards, strong and armed, who were about the King (they were probably thinking of the Swiss who formed his guard) should submit to obey a child, and that they did not rather choose one of their own number to command them. Secondly (they have a way of speaking of men as if they were halves of one another), that they had observed that there were men amongst us, full and gorged with all kinds of good things, and that their halves were begging at their doors, emaciated with hunger and poverty; and they thought it strange how these necessitous halves could suffer such injustice, and that they did not seize the others by the throat, or set fire to their houses.

I had a long talk with one of them; but I had an interpreter who followed my meaning so badly, and was at such a loss, in his stupidity, to take in my ideas, that I could get little satisfaction out of him. When I asked the native, "What he gained from his superior position among his people?" (for he was a captain, and our sailors called him a king), he said it was "to march foremost in war." How many men did he lead? He pointed to a piece of ground, to signify as many as that space could hold: it might be four or five thousand men. Did all his authority lapse with the war? He said "that this remained, that, when he visited the villages that were dependent on him, they made paths through their thickets, by which he might pass at his ease." All this does not sound too ill; but hold! they don't wear trousers.

A Modern Reassessment

T he European interest in man-eating amounts almost to an obsession. Anthropophagi, as they were called before the discovery of America, have played their role in the description of non-European cultures ever since the first Greeks ventured out into the western Mediterranean. Polyphemus and the Laestrygones, who fed off Odysseus's crew (and whom Peter Martyr identified with the unfortunate Arawak), the Achaeans and the Heniochi, who lived on the shores of the Black Sea, the Massagetae and the Padeans (in fact the Birhors) of India, the famed anthropophagi of Pliny, even the ancient Irish and the "Scots," whose behaviour St Jerome recounted in careful detail—all these races, to name only a few, were thought to possess an insatiable craving for human flesh. All, of course, were in one sense or another outsiders to those who described them; all

SOURCE *The Fall of Natural Man. The American Indian and the Origins of Comparative Ethnology*, pp. 80–84 passim, by Anthony Pagden. Copyright © 1982. Reprinted with the permission of Cambridge University Press.

lived far beyond the limits of the inhabitable world. And so, too, of course, did the Indians.

Classical accounts of man-eating were popularised by Christian ency-clopaedists such as St Isidore of Seville and Tertullian and extended to include other races (Tartars, Thracians, Mongols), so that by the end of the fifteenth century the anthropophagi had become a regular part of the topog-raphy of exotic lands. When Columbus entered unknown water in 1492 he inevitably made inquiries into the existence of such peoples, just as he asked after the Amazons and the giants which Pierre d'Ailly had led him to believe he would find in the southern latitudes.

On 4 November he was told by a group of obliging Arawak [Taínos] that on an island to the south there lived a race called the "Caribs"—hence the term cannibalism—"who eat men." In addition to a passion for human flesh the Caribs were also, Columbus learnt from his informants (with whom, however, he had no common language), the men who, once a year, "had intercourse with the women of Matinino . . . where there is no man!" Columbus had thus successfully located both the anthropophagi and the Amazons. Only the giants still eluded him; but later explorers unfamiliar with mammoth bones would make good his failure.

Accusations of cannibalism contributed to the de-humanisation of the outsider, for men who ate other men were never thought to be quite human. In the minds of many who claimed to have encountered them they were neither culturally, nor indeed physically, like others of their species. Co-lumbus was surprised to find that the Caribs had not been deformed by their foul diet. The English settlers in the short-lived Sagadahoc colony in New England were convinced that their supposedly cannibal neighbours were equipped with a special set of canine teeth three inches long and the Arab merchants of the Sudan described the Azande—the most famous of the African cannibals—as having dog-faces, dog-teeth and dog-tails. The associ-ation with dogs as symbols of unselective eating habits is a commonplace. Columbus, for instance, claimed that his Arawak informant described the Caribs as having "dogs' noses," although the Indian could never have seen a dog.

Man-eating was not only thought to be a cause of physical transforma-tions in the consumer, it was also believed to create an insatiable craving for human flesh. Once hooked on the meat of his own kind, the cannibal would be satisfied by no other. This belief, like so many other aspects of the cannibal myth, occurs in a number of cultures—in Azande accounts of man-eating, for instance, and in Iroquois creation myths—so we may as-sume it to be the result of inference rather than observation.

Nearly all supposedly eyewitness accounts of Amerindian cannibal ritu-als follow closely an established pattern. The link with human sacrifice, the propitiatory rites to placate the gods, the orgiastic wine-sodden "mingling of males with females," the total collapse of an in any case fragile social order so that the proper distinction between the social categories male/female, young/old, kin/non-kin dissolves in a tumble of bodies "devoid of any sentiment of modesty" and finally in the frenzied consumption of the sacrificial victim, all, or most, of these—details of [the ancient Roman] Livy's account of the Bacchanalia—may be found, *mutatis mutandis,* in most European accounts of Indian cannibal festivities. . . .

The most famous of the Amerindian cannibals were, of course, the Mexica [Aztecs], whose spectacular bouts of human sacrifice were assumed to have been followed by orgiastic feasts on the flesh of the victims. But there were many others. The nomadic Xixime and Chichimeca of northern Mexico, the Guarani of Paraguay and the Maya of the Yucatán were all, at one time or another, accused of being cannibals. So, too, were the Tupinamba of Brazil, who, thanks to the lurid account of a German castaway called Hans Standen, earned themselves a fearsome reputation as frenzied man-eaters, prepared, as one Spaniard put it, to "eat their victims down to the last fingernail." The Jesuit Manuel da Nóbrega, who lived among them for many years and even wrote a treatise denouncing cannibalism (although he never once pretended to have witnessed the gruesome meals he described), claimed that the Tupinamba's whole existence depended on two things: the possession of women and the killing of their enemies. "And these," he wrote, "they inherited from the first and the second man and learnt from him who lived at the beginning of the world when all was homicide." Because of their closeness to the unrestrained violence of the animal world of Cain, the Tupi, claimed Nóbrega, ate not only men, "but also fleas and lice and every form of filth." The link between sexual excess and cannibalism in these claims is a commonplace; so, too, is the association between the eating of human flesh and the eating of filth. Both, as we shall see, form part of a comprehensive evaluation of the significance of the man-eating act.

But why did Indians and other barbarians eat men? It is very likely that, except for survival cannibalism and acts of extreme revenge, the Amerindians at least did not. From the perspective of four hundred years it is easy enough to explain away accusations of cannibalism by "primitive" peoples as a device to make conquest and exploitation morally legitimate. But everyone in the sixteenth century, even men like Las Casas, seems to have believed these stories of Indian cannibalism. And for them some immediate explanation of the motives behind such anti-social behaviour was urgently required. Two related theories were offered. The first was the supposedly universal human desire for revenge. Eating one's enemies as the ultimate expression of hostility was not an unfamiliar occurrence even in Europe. . . .

The second motive was the cannibal's supposed need, in the absence of any native livestock, to make good a protein deficiency. Human flesh was merely food. The protein argument (which still appeals to Professor Marvin Harris) conjured up in the sixteenth-century mind the image of human butchers' shops among the Arawak and the Maya, even among the supposedly Christian "Ethiopians." Sober-minded royal officials like Tomás López Mendel were fully convinced that the Mexica and the Maya cut up and weighed the limbs of their victims for all the world as if they were "sheep or pigs or some other animal, because it is meat which they desire and they eat it with pleasure." And in 1534 the Castilian crown urged Cortés to step up the importation of cattle into Mexico, "so that they [the Indians] may have meat to eat and with which to support themselves." . . .

QUESTIONS

1. What evidence does Vespucci offer that the Trinidad islanders engaged in cannibalism?
2. Does Vespucci find anything to admire about the islanders?
3. Does Montaigne successfully excuse the roasting of dead captives by comparing this alleged New World practice to even more brutal treatment accorded live prisoners by Europeans?
4. In what way does Montaigne use the visit of the three natives to the king of France to belabor the faults of his own society?
5. What literary and historical accounts circulated long before the encounter with the New World predisposed Europeans to believe man-eating was often to be found in distant locations?
6. How strong a case does Pagden make that cannibalism was almost entirely a figment of the collective European imagination?
7. Why would it be useful for European colonizers to allege that Amerindians were cannibals?

41

Varieties of Sexual Practice

A popular device to grant credibility to the earliest sensational writings about the New World was to attribute authorship to Amerigo Vespucci (Document 40). The first selection, which was circulated widely throughout Europe as a pamphlet, concerns an alleged voyage of his in 1497. It is filled with details about the sexual practices of mainland natives, described in a lurid manner sure to entice readers.

> *"libidinous beyond measure, . . ."*

The second selection, by Michele de Cuneo to a fellow Genoese, is an excerpt from a 1495 letter in which he discusses his part in Columbus's second voyage. The Admiral handed to his crew nubile women with little regard for native feelings. The sexual lives of sailors have been marked traditionally by a reliance upon prostitutes, so it is not unusual that Cuneo boasts about this brutal episode in "locker room" style. Island women seem to have been accustomed to a rather free sexual life, in which many engaged for personal pleasure. Since overt female sexuality outside of prostitution was extremely upsetting to European crews, they encouraged the women to ask for bribes and gifts.

Gonzalo Fernández de Oviedo y Valdés was a nobleman with years of experience in the Spanish wars with France, which raged throughout Italy. He also ranked high in the civil service of Valencia and Aragón. In 1514 he went to the Western Hemisphere with the expedition of Pedrarias Dávila. While there, he served as supervisor of gold smelting, charged with destroying native artifacts for the sake of the precious metal. His writing shows little aesthetic sensibility toward non-European art. Because his many volumes constituted the first "official" histories of the New World and were in Castilian, not Latin, they were extremely influential in conveying to a large audience his beliefs and prejudices concerning the native populations. Oviedo's views on homosexuality, presented in the third selection, have to be taken with caution. Although he was an eyewitness, his post as a government official and his exploitation of Amerindians might have caused him to portray the peoples he oversaw in the worst possible light.

European attitudes toward homosexuality have varied over time and from country to country. Differences from prescribed sexual norms were accorded some measure of toleration until the High Middle Ages, when crusading fervor and repression made life difficult for homosexuals, Jews, and religious dissidents. The traditional punishment for homosexuality was burning at the stake, but this horrible torture was applied with less rigor in some societies than in others. The conquistadores had few compunctions about punishing Amerindians for what was called "crimes against nature," including having helpless offenders torn to bits by dogs. If many natives were homosexuals, this would be yet another evil that had to be eradicated. Father Las Casas, the self-appointed "defender of the Indians" whose views are presented in the final selection, differs considerably from Oviedo; however, he is not necessarily more accurate because he typically presents natives as innocent lambs.

Vespucci

They do not practise marriage amongst themselves. Each one takes all the wives he pleases; and when he desires to repudiate them, he does repudiate them without it being considered a wrong on his part or a disgrace to the woman; for in this the woman has as much liberty as the man. They are not very jealous, and are libidinous beyond measure, and the women far more than the men; for I refrain out of decency from

SOURCE Amerigo Vespucci, *Letter to Piero Soderini, Gonfaloniere,* trans. and ed. G. T. Northup (Princeton, N.J.: Princeton University Press, 1916), pp. 7–10, passim.

telling you the trick which they play to satisfy their immoderate lust. They are very fertile women, and in their pregnancies avoid no toil. Their parturitions are so easy that one day after giving birth they go out everywhere, and especially to bathe in the rivers; and they are sound as fish. They are so heartless and cruel that, if they become angry with their husbands, they immediately resort to a trick whereby they kill the child within the womb, and a miscarriage is brought about, and for this reason they kill a great many babies. They are women of pleasing person, very well proportioned, so that one does not see on their bodies any ill-formed feature or limb. And although they go about utterly naked, they are fleshy women, and that part of their privies which he who has not seen them would think to see is invisible; for they cover all with their thighs, save that part [for] which nature made no provision, and which is modestly speaking, the *mons veneris*. In short they are no more ashamed [of their shameful parts] than we are in displaying the nose and mouth. Only exceptionally will you see a woman with drooping breasts, or with belly shrunken through frequent parturition, or with other wrinkles; for all look as though they had never given birth. They showed themselves very desirous of copulating with us Christians. . . .

. . . They are so [liberal] in giving that it is the exception when they deny you anything; and, on the other hand, [they are free] in begging, when they show themselves to be your friends. But the greatest token of friendship which they show you is that they give you their wives and daughters; and when a father or a mother brings you the daughter, although she be a virgin, and you sleep with her, they esteem themselves highly honored; and in this way they practise the full extreme of hospitality.

Michele de Cuneo

While I was in the boat I captured a very beautiful Carib woman, whom the said Lord Admiral [Columbus] gave to me, and with whom, having taken her into my cabin, she being naked according to their custom, I conceived desire to take pleasure. I wanted to put my desire into execution but she did not want it and treated me with her finger nails in such a manner that I wished I had never begun. But seeing that, (to tell you the end of it all), I took a rope and thrashed her well, for which she raised such unheard of screams that you would not have believed your ears. Finally we came to an agreement in such manner that I can tell you that she seemed to have been brought up in a school of harlots. . . .

SOURCE Michele de Cuneo's Letter on the Second Voyage, 28 October 1495, in *Journals and Other Documents in the Life and Voyages of Christopher Columbus*, trans. and ed. S. E. Morison (New York: The Heritage Press, 1963), p. 212. Reprinted by permission.

Oviedo

Thus, what I have said of the people on this island and its neighbors is very well known, and applies also to the mainland, where many of these Indian men and women were sodomites [homosexuals], and it is known that many of them are [still]. Observe the degree to which they take pride in this sin: just as other people are accustomed to wearing jewels or precious stones around their necks, in some parts of these Indies they wear a jewel made of gold, representing one man on top of another in that base and diabolical act of Sodom. I saw one of these jewels of the devil that weighed twenty pesos of gold, cast in a mold and hollow inside, which was acquired at the port of Santa Marta on the coast of the mainland in the year 1514, when the Armada that the Catholic King sent to Castilla del Oro with His Captain General Pedrarias Dávila touched there. And since it was brought to the heap of gold that was taken there, and they subsequently brought it to be smelted before me as a royal official and overseer of gold smelting, I broke it with a hammer and pounded it up with my own hands on an anvil in the smelting house in the city of Darien.

Thus it may be seen that if one takes pride in and adorns oneself with such ornaments, he will also indulge in those sinful practices, and that in a land where they wear such ornaments, those practices will not be a new custom, but rather one that is common and ordinary among them. You should know that the man who consents and takes the burden of being the woman in that bestial and perverse act takes on the status *(oficio)* of a woman and wears *naguas*. And when at some point I mention a word that is foreign to our Castilian language, to satisfy the reader I would like to explain it before continuing on. For this purpose I will say that *naguas* are pieces *(mantas)* of cotton that the women of this island wear from the waist to half way down the leg, all the way around, in order to cover their shameful parts, and the most important women wear *naguas* that go down to their ankles. The girls who are virgins, as I said in another place, do not wear anything over their shameful parts, nor do the men, since not knowing what shame is, they do not employ any defense for it.

Returning to the subject of this abominable and unnatural sin: It was commonly practiced among the Indians of this island, but it was hateful to the women, more out of their interest than for scruples of conscience, though in fact there were some women who practiced good conduct on an island that had the most shameless and lustful women that have been seen in these Indies. . . .

SOURCE Gonzalo Fernández de Oviedo, *História general y natural de las Indias*, trans. J. H. Parry and R. G. Keith, 5 vols., *New Iberian World* (New York: Times Books, 1984), vol. I, pp. 13–14, passim. Reprinted by permission.

Las Casas

T he people of these four islands, Hispaniola, Cuba, Puerto Rico, and Jamaica, and those of the Lucayos, did not eat human flesh, nor did they sin against nature [sodomy], or steal and other evil habits. On the first nobody has even been in doubt until today, about the second, none of those who dealt with and knew these people did, except [Gonzalo Fernández de] Oviedo, who pretended to write the history of things he never saw or knew, or witnessed any one of these, accused them of the abominable vice saying they were all sodomites, as easily and imprudently as if he were saying that their color was a bit dark or more brownish than those of Spain.

What I say here is true because in many years in this island [Cuba] I saw and knew the people there and dealt with the Spaniards and with the friars and the Spaniards who came with the First Admiral [Columbus] the first time they arrived, and with my own father, who then came with him, and I never heard, or suspected of those in Spain who are our own; on the contrary, I heard sometimes the Spaniards themselves, who oppressed and killed them to say "oh, how blessed were these people if they were Christians" knowing the natural kindness they had and their lack of vices, and afterwards, searching on purpose into it and asking those persons who might know or suspect something about it, if it existed, I was told that no memory or suspicion ever existed [of homosexuality]. And among several people there was an old woman, Indian chief or lady, who had been married to a Spaniard, one of the first in the island [Cuba], while I was taking her confession, I looked into this and asked her whether before the arrival of the Spaniards in the island had been among the men any habit or blemish of this vice [sodomy], and she replied to me: "No father, because if it existed among the Indians, the women would eat them in bites, and no man could remain alive."

QUESTIONS

1. What might sixteenth-century Europeans regard as the most sensational aspects in Vespucci's accounts of alleged native sexual practices?
2. What deep-seated attitudes about female sexuality lurk in Vespucci's letter?
3. Discuss the masculine point of view that justifies a brutal rape by claiming that the woman is a "Prostitute."
4. Does Oviedo offer much evidence to prove the widespread acceptance of homosexuality among the mainland natives?
5. How strong a case does Las Casas make that the Cubans were never homosexual?
6. Why should Oviedo and Las Casas have taken such opposing attitudes about this issue?

SOURCE Bartolomé de Las Casas, *Historia de las Indias*, 3 vols. (Mexico: Fondo de Cultura Economica, 1951), vol. III, ch. 23, pp. 517–518. Editor's translation.

ULTURAL CONDITIONING

42

Reception of the New World in the Old

The handful of Europeans aware of Columbus's findings were at first unsure what to make of his voyage, since the prospect of his having circumnavigated the globe in so short a trip appeared to them unlikely. Columbus did, however, bring back parrots and certain plants that suggested he might actually have reached "the Indies." In 1494 an Italian resident at the court of Ferdinand and Isabella came up with an astute observation about the lands visited so far: "When treating of this country one must speak of a New World, so distant is it and so devoid of civilization and religion."

> *"prejudice, curiosity, and caution."*

This article notes that it was exactly through the twin lenses of civilization (classical or contemporary) and religion (Judeo-Christian) that intellectual Europeans viewed life in the Western Hemisphere. They could not approach new findings with an innocent eye, although in time this intellectual background provided a way to assimilate the unusual experiences.

It is asking a good deal of any society to take to heart the lessons which may be learnt from foreigners, especially when it has defeated and subjugated them. Perhaps cultural receptivity on any major scale can be expected only in a well-integrated society confident of its own identity (like medieval Islamic society when confronted with the learning of the Greeks) or else in a society which becomes forcibly aware of its own relative deficiencies, like nineteenth-century Japan. Renaissance Europe was neither so self-confident as to borrow from others on an extensive scale, nor so vulnerable and insecure as to require the mass importation of ideas and techniques. Instead, it approached the outer world with a combination of prejudice, curiosity, and caution. It was perhaps more genuinely interested in the workings of this alien world than it had shown itself to be when confronted by medieval Islam, but less interested than its twentieth-century successor in the life-styles and achievements of non-European societies. There is, for instance, a striking contrast between the solitary labours of the fifteenth-century Spanish scholar Juan de Segovia, desperately scouring

SOURCE Fredi Chiapelli, ed. *First Images of America*, vol. I, pp. 12–21, and vol. II, 879–880.

289

Europe for someone with a knowledge of Arabic to assist him in translating the Koran, and the activities of a whole group of sixteenth-century Spaniards dedicated to studying the language and customs of Amerindian societies. No doubt Western attitudes to Islam fluctuated over the centuries, with a greater readiness at some moments than at others to inquire into its ways. No doubt, too, the local situation in America—not least the opportunity and necessity for mass conversion of non-Christian peoples— goes a long way towards explaining the reasons for the contrast. But there are also indications of a greater willingness in the sixteenth century, if only in restricted circles, to come to terms intellectually with the realities of an alien world. However untypical, it is at least noteworthy that Bernardino de Sahagún, that great Franciscan ethnographer, should have committed himself to the statement that the allegedly barbarous peoples of Mexico were in some respects superior to other peoples with a greater presumption of civility.

Obviously, late fifteenth- and early sixteenth-century Christendom was unlikely to respond except by violently rejecting the strange native religions which were revealed to its startled gaze. But if we pitch our expectations rather lower, and attempt to identify those areas where some kind of positive response seems possible, the following would appear acceptable candidates: (1) geographical lore and learning; (2) Europe's conception of mankind; (3) its views on the past and present organization of the family, the polity, and society in general; (4) aesthetic attitudes and the arts and crafts. . . .

Rather than pointing Europe in totally new directions, the discovery of America emphasized and strengthened certain elements in European civilization at the expense of others. This happened because the Judeo-Christian and classical traditions were themselves so rich and varied that they made it possible both to interpret and absorb a substantial part of what America had to offer without provoking a seismic shock in the European system.

The shock was perhaps greatest in the most specifically circumscribed area—Europe's inherited geographical knowledge and experience. Although the classical geographical tradition, as interpreted by fifteenth-century cosmographers, provided an inspiration and a springboard for overseas voyages of exploration, this tradition was itself the first and most decisive casualty of the voyages. Personal inquiry and investigation confronted myths with facts. Again and again that wonderful chronicler of the Indies, Gonzalo Fernández de Oviedo [Document 41], insists, not without satisfaction, that traditional cosmography has been discredited: "What I have said cannot be learnt in Salamanca, Bologna, or Paris. . . ." The ancients had got it wrong: personal experience proved to have more authority than Authority itself; or, in the words of Sir Humphrey Gilbert: "These moderne experiences cannot be impugned." But the emphasis on personal observation was no sixteenth-century novelty, and was itself justified by Authority—in this instance, the authority of Quintilian: "For there are no subjects in which, as a rule, practice is not more valuable than precept." Even here, then, there was a kind of resilience within Europe's cultural inheritance which helped to cushion the shock of what at first sight appeared a devastating refutation of long-cherished beliefs. If Authority weighed heavily on Renaissance Europe, experience also had its proper place.

The absence in the European tradition of complete exclusiveness, of a total commitment to one set of values at the expense of another, was equally important in enabling the inhabitants of Christendom to come to terms with the existence of new peoples as well as new lands. Trained to think in terms of global conversion to the Christian faith, Europeans naturally looked upon the inhabitants of the Indies primarily as souls to be saved. . . .

Europeans still possessed within their own cultural tradition the mental equipment necessary for perceiving and recognizing alien societies. As trained by Renaissance humanism, it made them especially well suited to deal with the cultural consequences of overseas discovery. Here, after all, was a generation acutely conscious of a civilization that was not its own—that of Greek and Roman antiquity—and one which was now far removed in time. This newly acquired sense of temporal perspective must have helped it to come to terms also with civilizations far removed in space.

If classical antiquity provided Europeans with an alternative image—the existence of which alone makes it possible to develop some sense of perspective—it also gave them the basic tools of inquiry for the investigation of other lands and peoples. Fernández de Oviedo confessedly follows the model of Pliny [ancient Roman naturalist] in expounding the marvels and mysteries of the Indies. Even where the lack of written records threatened to impede an inquiry into the history and customs of alien populations, classical antiquity could again be brought to the rescue. Had not Herodotus [ancient Greek historian], after all, grappled with just such problems? No doubt in many instances the histories came first and the adducing of precedents followed, but in an age so deeply imbued with reverence for authority, the existence of Authority was itself a comforting vindication of pioneering enterprise. The Herodotean revival of the sixteenth century may have been, at least in part, a response from within the European tradition to the novel problems of historical method posed by the discoveries. . . .

Once it was accepted that peoples passed through different stages of development, there was no valid reason for excluding Europeans from the same historical process. If, in Montaigne's words, the New World was "so new and infantine, that he is yet to learne his A.B.C.," presumably the Old World too had once been illiterate. The presence of primitive peoples in the newly-discovered lands made it easier to envisage what these untutored Europeans must have been like; and the fact that John White's drawings of North American Indians in 1585 were used as the basis for imaginative representation of ancient Picts and Britons shows that there were some who took the point.

UNIVERSALE DESCRITTIONE DI TUTTA LA TERRA CONOSCIUTA FIN QUI

As soon as the process of comparison got under way—and it began in a relatively unrefined form when Europeans first set eyes on the Caribbean islanders—Europe had the opportunity to see itself in new perspectives. It had already learnt, by the late fifteenth century, to see itself in relation to the old world of Greece and Rome. Now it could also look at itself in relation to the new world of America. For there was always something narcissistic in Europe's approach both to antiquity and to America. In observing America it was, in the first instance, observing itself—and observing itself in one of two mirrors, each of which distorted as it revealed. It could see in America its own ideal past—a world still uncontaminated by greed and vice, where men lived in felicity and prelapsarian innocence. Or, as occurred increasingly with the advance of the sixteenth century, it could see in America its actual past—a time when Europe's rude inhabitants were as yet untouched by civil manners or by Christianity. . . .

. . . Clearly, Christianity took absolute precedence in any area of potential conflict between the religious and aesthetic. Where no such conflict arose, appreciation was easier, but it was naturally an appreciation inspired by contemporary European aesthetic attitudes. The rarity of the materials, the strangeness of the object, the cunning of the craftsmen—it was these which impressed sixteenth-century Europeans when they looked at Amerindian artifacts. When Bernal Díaz [Document 43] compared Indian craftsmen in Mexico City to Berruguete and Michelangelo, it was the skill and cunning of their workmanship that moved him. Verisimilitude to nature, technical skill, proportion, and perspective were the qualities which sixteenth-century Europeans looked for in works of art, and both pre-Conquest and post-Conquest native work was judged in accordance with these criteria.

I would suggest, therefore, that across the range of experience, from its vision of the world to its vision of art and aesthetics, Europe passed America through a selective screening process, which enabled it to reject images that were too far out of alignment with its own preconceptions. These preconceptions derived from the fusion of classical and Christian values and beliefs, and were now in many instances being filtered through the lens of Renaissance humanism. But the values and beliefs were themselves sufficiently rich, diversified, and sometimes self-contradictory to leave space for the partial and relatively painless incorporation of new facts and impressions into an image of the world and of mankind that was neither entirely rigid nor entirely exclusive. Moreover, the twin ideals of Christianity and

---

PAOLO FORIANI, WORLD MAP (1565) [left] *The engraver has reconciled Ptolemy's ancient map with reports of new discoveries. Africa, East India, Southeast Asia, and South America are quite close to their respective shapes. However, Antarctica (with its own unicorn) fills up too much of the Southern Hemisphere. The image of North America is based on a 1546 view by Gastaldi, shown as an extension of China.*

classical antiquity—the desire to convert and the desire to know—happened to be unusually alive and potent in Europe at the moment of America's discovery, and their vitality helped to ensure that the immediate response of Christendom to the newly discovered lands and peoples was more generous than restrictive, more positive than negative.

Certain dangers to European values and attitudes were implicit in this initially positive response. But these dangers were reduced by the built-in screening mechanism to which I have referred—a mechanism which operated to limit the range and extent of cultural shock. In this respect—and leaving aside the sheer technical problems which attended the dissemination of information in Early Modern Europe—I believe that it is reasonable to talk about the blunted impact of the discovery of America on the sixteenth-century European consciousness. But the bluntness of the impact can itself be explained by the unique resilience and diversity of the society that received it. Whatever may have been true of America, Renaissance Europe was tailor-made for a soft landing. And, paradoxically, the softness of the landing was itself the necessary precondition for the slow, erratic but nevertheless persistent process by which the Old World adjusted itself to the forces released by its conquest of the New.

43

Díaz

Bernal Díaz del Castillo, born in 1492, died on his estates in Guatemala at age eighty-nine, the last of the survivors of the subjugation of Mexico. He had joined Cortés on the march to the capital city of the Aztecs with no misgivings about the rightness of his cause or the severity of the penalties his comrades inflicted on those pagans "who sat in darkness," indulging in human sacrifice on a massive scale.

"they could not distinguish him from an Indian, . . ."

The old warrior wrote his history to ensure that his heirs secured the financial recognition from the crown he believed they deserved for his contribution to the expansion of the empire. He was goaded into recording the heroic activities of the captains and soldiers because they were neglected by Cortés, who seldom mentioned anybody but himself (Document 25); by historians with whom he took issue; and by Las Casas, who condemned the conquerors for their cruelty and brutality. Díaz was no scholar, but he wrote in a blunt style that has stood the test of time longer than his rivals because it remains vivid.

During the exploration of the Yucatan coast under Francisco Hernandez de Córdoba, Díaz first learned that some shipwrecked Castilians had fallen into the hands of native chiefs. At the time he did not make much of this, but two years later, in 1519 under Cortés's prompting, an effort was made to locate them. One captive left but the other stayed behind. The issue of the pull of a different way of life on some Europeans is brought to life by this episode. Strangers were often incorporated into the tribes in kinship ceremonies, when they were given full rights. The attractiveness of marriage to native women could be strong, as is indicated by Document 49. Cortés was right to be disturbed that the second Castilian refused to return, for he eventually was to lead his new people in battle against his old people.

In his diligence, Cortés sent for me [Bernal Días] and a Basque called Martin Ramos, to ask us what we thought about the Campeche Indians' cries of *"castilan, castilan!"* that I mentioned in my account of our expedition under Francisco Hernandez de Cordóba. When we had carefully described the incident once more, Cortés said that he had often thought about it, and wondered whether there might not be some Spaniards living in that country. "I think it would be a good thing," he said, "to ask these chiefs of Cozumel if they know anything about them."

So through Melchior (the man from Cape Catoche, who now understood a little Spanish and knew the language of Cozumel very well), all the chiefs were questioned, and each one of them answered that they knew of certain Spaniards, whom they described. They said that some *caciques* [chiefs] who lived two days' journey inland held them as slaves, and that here in Cozumel were some Indian traders who had spoken to them only two days before. We were all delighted with this news, and Cortés told the chiefs that letters—which in their language they call *amales*—must be sent to them at once to summon them to the island. He gave beads to the chiefs and to the Indians who carried the letters, and spoke kindly to them, telling them that when they returned he would give them some more beads. The *cacique* advised Cortés to send a ransom to their owners, so that they might let them come; and this Cortés did, giving the messengers various sorts of beads. Then he ordered the two smallest ships to be got ready. These he sent to the coast near Cape Catoche, where the larger ship was to wait for eight days, which allowed enough time for the letters to be taken and for a reply to arrive; and when it did so the smaller vessel was to bring Cortés immediate news. Cape Catoche is only twelve miles from Cozumel, and within sight of it.

In his letter Cortés said: "Gentlemen and brothers, here in Cozumel I

SOURCE *The Conquest of New Spain*, pp. 59–65, passim, by Bernal Díaz, translated by J. M. Cohen (Penguin Classics, 1963), copyright © J. M. Cohen, 1963. Reproduced by permission of Penguin Books Ltd.

have heard that you are captives in the hands of a *cacique*. I beg you to come to this place at once, and for this purpose have sent a ship with soldiers, in case you need them, also a ransom to be given to those Indians with whom you are living. The ship will wait for you eight days. Come as quickly as you can, and you will be welcomed and looked after by me. I am staying at this island with five hundred soldiers, and eleven ships in which I am going, please God, to a town called Tabasco or Champoton."

The two vessels were soon dispatched with the two Indian traders of Cozumel, who carried the letter on board, and in three hours they had crossed the straits. The messengers were then landed with their letters and the ransom, and in two days these were delivered to a Spaniard called Jeronimo de Aguilar. For this we discovered to be his name, and I shall call him by it henceforth. When he had read the letter and received the ransom, he carried the beads delightedly to his master the *cacique* and begged leave to depart. The *cacique* gave him permission to go wherever he wished, and Aguilar set out for the place some fifteen miles away where his comrade, Gonzalo Guerrero, was living. But on hearing the contents of the letter Gonzalo answered: "Brother Aguilar, I am married and have three children, and they look on me as a *cacique* here, and a captain in time of war. Go, and God's blessing be with you. But my face is tattooed and my ears are pierced. What would the Spaniards say if they saw me like this? And look how handsome these children of mine are! Please give me some of those beads you have brought, and I will tell them that my brothers have sent them from my own country." And Gonzalo's Indian wife spoke to Aguilar very angrily in her own language: "Why has this slave come here to call my husband away? Go off with you, and let us have no more of your talk."

Then Aguilar spoke to Gonzalo again, reminding him that he was a Christian and should not destroy his soul for the sake of an Indian woman. Besides, if he did not wish to desert his wife and children, he could take them with him. But neither words nor warnings could persuade Gonzalo to come. I believe he was a sailor and hailed from Palos.

When Jeronimo de Aguilar saw that Gonzalo would not come, he at once went with the two Indian messengers to the place where their ship had been waiting for him. But when he arrived he could see no ship. For the eight days that Ordaz had been ordered to stay had expired; and after giving him one more day, he had returned to Cozumel without news of the Spanish captives. On finding no ship, Aguilar returned sadly to his master in the town where he had been living. . . .

When the Spaniard Aguilar learnt that we had returned to Cozumel with the ships, he was very joyful and gave thanks to God. He then came in all haste with the two Indians who had carried the letters and the ransom, and embarked in a canoe. Since he could pay well with the green beads we had sent him, he had soon hired one with six Indian oarsmen, who rowed so hard that, meeting no head wind, they quickly crossed the twelve-mile strait between the island and the mainland.

When they reached the coast of Cozumel and were disembarking, some soldiers who had gone out hunting—for there were wild pigs on the island—reported to Cortés that a large canoe had come from the direction of Cape Catoche and had beached near the town. Cortés sent Andres de Tapia and two other soldiers to see what was happening, since it was something new for Indians to come fearlessly into our neighbourhood in large canoes. So they set out. As soon as the Indians who had brought Aguilar saw the Spaniards, they took fright, and wanted to get back in their canoe and put out to sea. But Aguilar told them in their own language not to be afraid, for these men were his brothers. When Andres de Tapia saw that they were Indians—for Aguilar looked exactly like one—he immediately sent to tell Cortés that there were seven Cozumel Indians in the canoe. As he leapt ashore, however, Aguilar exclaimed in inarticulate and clumsy Spanish: "God and the blessed Mary of Seville!" Then Tapia went to embrace him, and the soldier who was beside him, seeing that he was a Spaniard, ran hurriedly to Cortes to beg a reward for being the first with the news. We were all delighted when we heard it.

Tapia quickly brought the Spaniard to the place where Cortés was, but before they got there some soldiers asked Tapia: "Where is this Spaniard?" Although they were close beside him, they could not distinguish him from an Indian, for he was naturally dark, and had his hair untidily cut like an Indian slave. He carried a paddle on his shoulder and had an old sandal on one foot, the other sandal being tied to his belt. He wore a very ragged old cloak, and a tattered loincloth to cover his private parts; and in his cloak was tied an object which proved to be a very old prayer-book.

When Cortés saw him in this condition he was as much deceived as the others, and asked Tapia where this Spaniard was. When Aguilar heard his question, he squatted down in Indian fashion and answered: "I am he." Cortés at once ordered him to be given a shirt and doublet and breeches, a cloak and some sandals, for he had no other clothes. Cortés asked him his name and history and when he had come to that country. The man answered, pronouncing with difficulty, that his name was Jeronimo de Aguilar, that he came from Ecija and was in holy orders. He said that eight years ago he had been wrecked with fifteen other men and two women on a voyage from Darien to the island of Santo Domingo, where he had some differences at law with a certain Enciso y Valdivia. They were carrying with them ten thousand gold pesos and the documents of the case, when the ship in which they were travelling struck the Alacranes and could not be floated off. He, his companions, and the two women had then got into the ship's boat, thinking strong that they were thrown ashore in this country, where the *calachiones* [chiefs] of the district had divided them up, sacrificing many of his companions to their idols. Some too had died of disease, and the two women only recently of overwork, for they had been made to grind corn. The Indians had intended to sacrifice him, but one night he had escaped and fled to that *cacique* with whom he had been living ever since.

Now, he said, the only survivors were himself and a certain Gonzalo Guerrero, whom he had gone to summon but who had refused to come.

Aguilar thanked God for his deliverance, and Cortés promised that he would be well looked after and compensated. He then asked him about the country and the towns. Aguilar answered that, having been a slave, he only knew about hewing wood and drawing water and working in the maize-fields, and that he had only once made a journey of some twelve miles when he was sent with a load, under which he had collapsed, for it was heavier than he could carry. He understood, however, that there were many towns. When questioned about Gonzalo Guerrero, he said that he was married and had three children, that he was tattooed, and that his ears and lower lip were pierced, that he was a seaman and a native of Palos, and that the Indians considered him very brave. Aguilar also related how a little more than a year ago, when a captain and three ships arrived at Cape Catoche—this must have been our expedition under Francisco Hernandez de Cordóba—it had been at Guerrero's suggestion that the Indians had attacked them, and that he had been there himself in the company of that *cacique* of a great town, about whom I spoke when describing that expedition. When Cortés heard this he exclaimed: "I wish I could get my hands on him. For it will never do to leave him here."

QUESTIONS

1. Why was it difficult for the first Europeans in the New World to see the Amerindians clearly, with an innocent eye?
2. In what ways did the Judeo-Christian tradition and the enthusiasm for classical antiquity eventually assist European intellectuals to incorporate the New World discoveries into their mental framework?
3. Why did Gonzalo Guerrero decide to stay with his captors, whereas Jeronimo de Aguilar struggled to return to his people?
4. What attractions did native society offer Guerrero?
5. Why was Cortés upset that he had to leave a Spaniard behind with the natives?

44

Adaptation

The state of Oaxaca, south of Mexico City, is today poor and isolated. In pre-Hispanic times, its peoples maintained contact with the Aztec empire of the northwest and, to the east, had relations with the Mayans. Far from being isolated, the valley of Oaxaca formed the central part of ancient Mexico. In 500 B.C. it gave rise to Mesoamerica's first true city: Monte Alban. From A.D. 450 to A.D. 700, this terraced city on three hilltops reached a peak population of nearly 25,000 people, which diminished until the city was abandoned at last after 1,700 years of continuous occupation.

> *"learning all they could from the Spaniards."*

In the first years of the Spanish invasion, the predominant linguistic groups of the area had varied social organizations. The great kingdom of the Zapotecs of the valley kept many towns under their control and maintained a highly stratified society, in which an inbred ruling group relied upon religion to exercise rigid control over its peasants. By contrast, the Zapotecs of the northern mountains, as well as the Chantes and the Mixtecs, were more egalitarian and thus politically fractured. All the groups maintained a contact beyond their immediate locales based upon commerce in cocoa beans, obsidian glass, cotton, and products from the sea. This communication network rapidly spread the news that the Spanish had arrived and led to the ultimate accommodation with the strangers.

The reading selection addresses the perplexing question of why the best organized and most highly stratified societies offered the least resistance to the newcomers. It raises doubts about the traditional presumption that the Spanish occupied the whole of Mesoamerica with such dazzling speed entirely due to superior Iberian military skills, fatalism on the part of native leaders, and the spread of European diseases. What this old triad of reasons leaves out is the possibility of enlightened self-interest on the part of local elites and other sectors of the population, who decided the Spanish way was an attractive alternative to their previous life.

It should be pointed out that a vast number of people in the Western Hemisphere today speak an imported language, are fervent Catholics, and embrace the culture of Iberia. Many celebrate Hispanic ideals of courage, individualism, and the *dignidad*—a word that has no adequate English equivalent but can be loosely translated as every person's potential endowment of dignity, honor, and integrity that merits respect from others.

The Spaniards arrived in Oaxaca the same year they disembarked from the Gulf Coast. This one was merely an initial entry. The real Spanish penetration would initiate two years later, in 1521. But those two years were sufficient for the dissemination of the extraordinary news of the presence of those men. The news of the destruction of the city of Mexico (Tenochtitlán) must have been decisive. Several early documents indicate that the Mixtec lords and the Zapotec lords of the valley regarded the Spaniards as successors to the Aztecs. They were now to obey them and pay them tribute. The Spaniards knew how to make good use of this situation, although the recognition that the natives offered them was not mechanical. Some natives seemed not to have put up any resistance to them. Others tested their strength in initial battles. Others resisted during various decades. But this does not prevent us from noticing that the most sophisticated and highly politically centralized groups were those that offered the least durable resistance. . . .

The years of anarchy ended between 1530 and 1535. In the years that followed, the Spaniards themselves tried to establish order. They regulated the tributes, named authorities in charge of imparting justice, and the evangelizing began. The construction of houses for the friars began and the city of Oaxaca was founded.

While the Spaniards reorganized their empire, the Indians, in a more serene atmosphere, began to show an unusual interest in learning all they could from the Spaniards. The first years, despite the alterations that were suffered, had permitted the Indians to learn about the wheat and fruits of Castile, the hydraulic mills, and all the objects that the Spaniards brought, from velvet capes to scissors and wine. By 1540, the natives already participated in the activities taken from the Spanish culture such as the raising of sheeps and goats, the cultivation of wheat and barley, the raising of fowl from Castile, and the care of the silkworm. Many of these products were sold in the cities of New Spain. The Indians transported silk thread, salted meat, skins, and wool; they sold in the interior markets what they produced and with the money they obtained, they acquired the European articles they desired.

Various native regions of New Spain showed interest in these occupations. In Oaxaca, the Mixtecs and the Zapotecs of the valley stood out. The Mixtec kingdoms developed a great commerce in livestock. The realms of the Upper Mixtec region came to have herds whose number reached 300,000. The Mixtecs contracted Spanish teachers to teach them how to take care of the smaller livestock—how to shear them, castrate them, or wean the young. They learned to salt the meat, prepare the skins, and weave the wool. They also learned how to care for the silkworm and how to weave the thread. In the valley, the Indians established iron forges to make their own tools.

SOURCE Unpublished paper, "Oaxaca in the Sixteenth Century," by María de las Angeles Romero, delivered at "The Encounter of Cultures: Sixteenth Century Mexico" talk presented at the Instituto Nacional de Antropología e Historia, Mexico City and Oaxaca, July 10–August 11, 1989. Reprinted with permission.

We find ourselves before a native society that, far from remaining passive and in a position of domination, participated vigorously in the economy of those years. Toward 1560, the economy of the first years based on tributes already lacked importance. In its place was installed a mercantile economy in which the natives participated. Until around 1580 at least, that native commerce prospered, despite the impact of the conquest and of the epidemics the Spaniards introduced. In Oaxaca, precisely those towns that had offered the least resistance to the Spaniards were the ones that were the most productive economically.

The years that followed were to be different. The natives were being displaced from the economy because of the consolidation of the Spanish economic interest and the effects of the epidemics. The care of smaller livestock continued to be of importance, but silk production fell, and the Indians generally lost the possibility of trading their products or participating in other branches of production, such as the transformation of their raw materials into elaborate products (wool and cotton into cloth; the skin into shoes, saddles, etc.).

While the years of prosperity lasted, they brought to the Mixtec region and the valley a new and luxurious style of life. Toward 1560, the Mixtec lords wore capes from Castile and velvet suits. They possessed paintings and gold images of the Virgin and of the saints. For new Catholic temples, the towns spent the thousands of *reales* that they earned from livestock and sericulture. They bought linen tablecloths to cover the altars, brocade ornaments for the priest, and gold chalices. On their land, they built magnificent Renaissance style monasteries. Much of what they earned was used to buy wine from Castile and food, which they distributed among the people in their sacred festivals dedicated now to the Catholic saints. Some of the principal expenditures of the towns in the sixteenth century were dedicated to the upkeeping of the Catholic religion and the festivals of the saints.

Native participation was basic and indispensable to the economy of those years. From the middle of the sixteenth century, in the north of New Spain [today's Mexico], important silver deposits had been found. From then on, the principal export from New Spain was silver; imported articles were paid for with it, especially wine and Dutch and French cloth. Silver, at the same time, was necessary for the European economy. It was needed as coin and to finance the growing commerce with the Orient. But all of that was made possible by those who consumed the products that arrived from Europe in exchange for the silver. The Spanish population that could consume those articles was not very large; even in the mid-seventeenth century, it barely constituted 13 percent of the population of New Spain, and, of course, not all the Spaniards were wealthy. Many of them were poor. What fueled the transatlantic trade in those years was the native people's consumption, not only in Oaxaca but also in other Indian regions of New Spain. . . .

Many questions can be asked about those years. The most obvious, and the one that many historians have formulated, is: How was it possible that such a small group of Spaniards, although well armed, could subdue so many native kingdoms, kingdoms that were not inhabited by poor farmers like the towns of today, but by "men of war," by individuals who at the same time as they cultivated their plots of land were ready to fight when their lord required it? How was it possible that in less than ten years after the arrival of the Spaniards, the greater part of the Mixtec kingdoms were paying tribute to the Spaniards? How could that be, when twenty years later, in 1550, the same Spaniards were still afraid that the Indians would rise up in arms and all that had been gained would be lost? . . .

Despite all the surprises, the subjection of the natives was not something mechanical. There were armed encounters. The natives tried to establish alliances with the Spaniards and tried to take advantage of their presence within their needs and conflicts. After the first encounter, they tried to make alliances with the newly arrived Spaniards. They tried to incorporate all those new elements of Spanish life into their own framework. Thus the Zapotec lord of Tehuantepec offered his friendship to the Spaniards in exchange for horses to subdue his enemies.

In these attempts to establish alliances, we see that not everything hinged on the violence of the Spaniards. On various occasions when the conquerors arrived in an Indian kingdom, the native lord received them in his palace and offered them food. Immediately an exchange of presents took place between the natives and the Spaniards. The Indians gave gold jewelry, and the Spaniards gave European clothes and other objects of everyday use. Exchange was an essential concept in the indigenous culture. It was present in many aspects of their lives, and implied respect and mutual obligation. Even the tribute that the Indians gave to their lords was conceived as a collective effort that they gave over in exchange for protection and sacred intercession. Thus, when they established that exchange with the Spaniards, for the natives it signified giving recognition to the Spanish, with the stipulation that the Indians would receive support against their enemies and maybe other things. But the Spaniards regarded it in mercantile terms. They were interested in gold and slaves for the power these would confer upon them, the wealth, and the upward social mobility.

In the exchanges, the differences of interests between the two cultures became clear: the mercantile interest of the Spaniards and the desire of the natives to possess the Spanish objects. The attitude of the Spaniards may be easier to understand because it is closer to our way of thinking, and that of the natives may require more explanation. The jewels that they gave to the Spaniards had been part of the luxurious and sacred store of the lords. No common person had possessed such jewels before. This fact alone signified a recognition of the Spaniards equal to that given to their lords, at least during those first years.

Moreover, the interest of the natives to possess the articles brought by the Spaniards stands out. If luxurious consumption had once served to reinforce the power of the lords, one can now understand that the native lords wanted to adopt the external elements and wealth of the Spanish culture as a way to reinforce their own power.

From the first, the acceptance on the part of the natives, especially by the nobles, of the Spaniards and their desire to acquire everything introduced by them facilitated the conquest. If the lords gave the Spaniards recognition, the common people, who for generations were accustomed to give almost limitless obedience, gave that much more. The power of the Spaniards was consolidated because of the cooperation of the native lords. The latter saw in the Spaniards a threat to their power, and unfortunately tried to diffuse it by making an alliance with the Spaniards and accepting their external forms of culture.

QUESTIONS

1. After the fall of the Aztecs, why did the politically centralized societies in central Mesoamerica offer less resistance to the Spanish than the more loosely organized ones?
2. What did the Oaxacans admire in Spanish civilization?
3. Why did a new prosperity flourish for the natives, at least until around 1580?
4. How did the native elite attempt to use the Spanish to reinforce its own power over the peasantry?

45

Incomplete Conversion

Bernardino de Sahagún collected ancient manuscripts and interviewed elders because he, along with other clerics in sixteenth-century Mexico, had become skeptical about the claim that everyone truly had converted to Christianity. The Franciscan was a pioneer ethnographer in the sense that he did not simply reject past practices as "abominable pagan heresies," but strove for a half-century to understand his informants' conception of their world. However much Father Sahagún came to admire the high ethical standards of the Aztec culture, his ultimate aim to develop an awareness in Christian confessors about disguised remnants of earlier religious practice remained; hence his assault in the first selection against apparently orthodox local shrines.

> "*a conspiracy of silence existed . . .*"

The shrine of the Virgin of Guadalupe, patron saint of Mexico's Catholics, is located near what was in pre-Hispanic times a temple dedicated to a mother goddess. The site's present religious importance is due to purported appearances during December 1531 of the Virgin Mary to an Amerindian, baptised Juan Diego. The bishop of Mexico City did not at first believe him, but was convinced when Diego presented to him out-of-season roses, wrapped in his tunic. When Diego unfolded his tunic, an image of the Virgin was found miraculously imprinted on the coarse cactus-fiber cloth. She appears as a crowned, light-skinned Amerindian maiden standing on a sliver of moon that rests on the head of a small angel. The angel holds the hem of her red-brocade dress in his left hand, her star-filled cape in his right. Thousands of pilgrims flock to the shrine to gain a glimpse of the image or to make special vows or requests.

Since 1933, Robert Ricard's La "conquête spirituelle" du Mexique has convinced scholars that the spread of Christianity in this area was a rapid and virtually total success. J. Jorge Klor de Alva, the author of the second selection, argues instead that natives covertly resisted indoctrination, borrowing from the new religion whatever public show was necessary for safety. This argument supports Father Sahagún's conclusion in the opening selection. Ancient rituals attached to Christian ones included a sweeping ceremony that accompanied the bringing of the Eucharist to the sick, the lighting of fires on the eve of the Nativity, the extreme use of self-flagellation, the burning of a traditional incense (copalli) before images of saints, dedicating strings of ears of corn to the Virgin, and so forth. Such mixed rites upset the Christian clergy, but the rites were so ingrained that they could not be eradicated. How un-Christian all this was remains an open question.

Sahagún

Near the mountains, there are three or four places where they [Aztecs] were accustomed to perform very solemn sacrifices and they came to them from very distant lands. One of these is here in Mexico where there is a small mountain they call Tepeyacac. The Spaniards call it Tepeaquilla; now it is called Nuestra Señora de Guadalupe. At this place they had a temple dedicated to the mother of the gods whom they called Tonantzin, which means Our Mother. There they performed many sacrifices in honor of this goddess. And they came to them from more than twenty leagues away, from all the border regions of Mexico, and they brought many offerings. Men and women, youths and maidens came to these feasts. There was a great conflux of people on these days, and they all said: "We are going to the feast of Tonantzin."

And now that a church of Our Lady of Guadalupe is built there, they also

SOURCE A History of Ancient Mexico, pp. 90–91, by Bernardino de Sahagún, translated by F. R. Bondelier, 1932. Reprinted by permission of Fisk University Press.

call her Tonantzin, being motivated by the preachers who called Our Lady, the Mother of God, Tonantzin. It is not known for certain where the beginning of this Tonantzin may have originated, but this we know for certain, that, from its first usage, the word means that ancient Tonantzin. And it is something that should be remedied, for the correct [native] name of the Mother of God, Holy Mary, is not Tonantzin but rather Dios inantzin. It appears to be a Satanic invention to cloak idolatry under the confusion of this name, Tonantzin. And they now come to visit this Tonantzin from very far away, as far away as before, which is also suspicious, because everywhere there are many churches of Our Lady and they do not go to them. They come from distant lands to this Tonantzin as in olden times.

The second place where there were anciently many sacrifices, to which they came from distant lands, is near the mountain range of Tlaxcalla where there was a temple which was called Toci, where a great multitude of people met at the celebration of this feast. Toci means Our Grandmother, and by another name she was called Tzapotlan tenan, which means the goddess of sweatbaths and medicines. And subsequently they built a Church of Santa Ana there where there is now a monastery with monks of Our Father Saint Francis. And the natives call her Toci and people from over forty leagues away attend the feast of Toci. And they name Santa Ana [St. Ann] in this manner, being motivated by the preachers who say that, since Santa Ana is the grandmother of Jesus Christ she is also our grandmother, [grandmother] of all Christians. And so they have called her and call her Toci at the pulpit, which means our grandmother. And all the people who come, as in times past, to the feast of Toci, come on the pretext of Saint Ann. But since the word is ambiguous, and they respect the olden ways, it is believable that they come more for the ancient than for the modern. And thus, also in this place, idolatry appears to be cloaked because so many people come from such distant lands without Saint Ann's ever having performed any miracles there. It is more apparent that it is the ancient Toci rather than Saint Ann. In this year of 1576 the plague which prevails began there and, they say, there are no people there now. It seems mysterious for the punishment to have started there where the transgression of cloaking idolatry under the name of Saint Ann started.

The third place where there were anciently many sacrifices, to which they came from distant lands, is at the foot of the volcano, in a village of Calpa, which is called Tianquizmanalco San Juan. At this place they performed a great feast in honor of the god they called Telpochtli which is Tezcatlipoca. And as they heard the preachers say that Saint John the Evangelist was a virgin, and such in their language is called *telpochtli*, they took occasion to perform that feast as they were accustomed to perform it in times past, cloaked under the name of San Juan Telpochtli as it appears on the surface but [performed] in honor of the old Telpochtli, which is Tezcatlipoca. Since Saint John has performed no miracles there, neither is there reason to meet there rather than any other place where he has a church.

A Recent View

A mple evidence suggests that numerous Spaniards who were not priests were skeptical of the alleged Indian conversions; Mendieta himself felt compelled to answer the widespread charge that the Indians "are not truly Christians" by pointing out how devout the natives were toward the ceremonies of the church, "whereby one can deduce that in effect they are truly Christians and not [merely] in jest, as some believe." Torquemada was also moved to answer the charge that the natives easily accepted any faith, whether good or bad, and consequently, just as easily abandoned it. In his *Advertencias para los confessores* (1600) the Franciscan Juan Bautista explains that the many superstitions of the natives are not sufficient reason to accuse them of being idolaters as many people do, since the Spaniards have many superstitions themselves. However, in a letter signed in 1544, Gonzalo de Aranda advises the monarch that among the Indians, "though there are many who appear to be good Christians, there are many more who are not [and who] do not fear God nor know Him because they neither concern themselves with truths nor do they speak it, concerning themselves solely with stealing and deceiving."

There are good reasons to believe that many priests shared similar doubts about the sincerity of the natives. The reservations of Sahagún and Diego Durán are well known but worthy of special attention. Both of these friars worked closely with the Aztecs for many years, and their ethnographic bent compelled them to become well versed in their *antiguallas* ("ancient ways"). The overwhelming mass of documentation on the subject from the colonial era confirms their worst suspicions, including Sahagún's frank and penetrating admission late in the sixteenth century: "now it is almost impossible to remedy [the idolatry]. . . ."

In a voice filled with rage against the Mendicant Orders, whose negligence he attacked, Archbishop Montúfar records in the second half of the sixteenth century that in Mexico "where the Indians ought to be better Christians, they are the worst."

One hundred years later Jacinto de la Serna in his *Manual de ministros de indios* points out that the city of Mexico is where the "ministers of Satan" celebrate their many rites with the greatest immunity, cleverly disguising under Christian forms their various idolatries, "and I know for a fact, to our greater shame and confusion, that everyone within and outside the City [of Mexico], and throughout the kingdom is corrupted passively and actively: some because they practice all the . . . superstitions . . . ; and others passively, consenting to others making and using these. . . ."

SOURCE J. J. Klor de Alva, "Spiritual Conflict and Accommodation in New Spain: Towards a Typology of Aztec Responses to Christianity," *The Inca and Aztec States, 1400–1800. Anthropology and History*, ed. G. A. Collier, R. I. Rosaldo, J. D. Wirth (New York: Academic Press, 1982), pp. 358–363, passim. Author's citations eliminated. Reprinted by permission.

As the Inquisition records amply attest, the great number and variety of indigenous spiritual leaders—called diviners, witches, enchanters, and healers by the Christian priests—enjoyed a large following and a substantial income. They were accused of perpetuating the ancient beliefs by instigating the celebration of native rites and by preaching against Christianity. These self-styled Indian clerics and healers, who succeeded the precontact priests in tending to the spiritual and physical needs of the recalcitrant Aztecs, are examples of those who actively resisted the Christian faith or, less likely, those who completely abandoned the new faith after an initial acceptance. The penitents to whom they catered had either converted only nominally to Christianity or had apostatized; many who had incomplete conversions also made use of their services, particularly as healers. . . .

Sociopolitical and economic expediency, together with the simple lifestyle and general goodwill of the missionaries, made baptism attractive for the Aztecs; Spanish military and administrative power made it a requisite for all but the most marginalized.

However, conversion in any meaningful sense demanded a radical change in values, customs, and world view. The Christian ethos was slowly accepted by some only in the course of several generations and only after the precontact mores had been sufficiently transformed by the newly evolving colonial culture.

Nonetheless, however much the interference of Spaniards and blacks altered the old patterns, many tenaciously adhered to whatever vestiges were available well into the seventeenth century and, as modern ethnography shows, into the present. Sahagún asserted late in the sixteenth century that a conspiracy of silence existed on the part of both the dissimulating Indians and those who wished to keep untainted the memory of the first friars who had supposedly enjoyed overwhelming successes; as a consequence, he added, many were kept from seeing or recounting the failure of the spiritual conquest. By the time the massive campaign against the Andean religions was launched in 1610, the Indian population of New Spain was so badly decimated that few Spaniards troubled themselves any longer with the continuance of native modes of spirituality among the survivors. The various mixed castes were rapidly growing in number and developing fidelity to European values and practices. But among the Aztecs, few were wholeheartedly embracing the vision of the world implied by Christianity, many resisted it passively, most failed to meet the minimal test required of a convert (belief in one God who died to redeem humanity), and almost all mixed the colonial versions of the ancient beliefs with the Christian doctrine.

QUESTIONS

1. What made Father Sahagún suspicious about the newly established shrines dedicated to the Virgin Mary, her mother, St. Ann, and St. John the Evangelist?

2. Is there much evidence that the Mexicans were evading control by missionaries and priests into the seventeenth century?
3. How complete could the "spiritual conquest" of Mexico have been if the masses were giving only lip service to their new-found religion?
4. When did insincere conversions become less pressing to Church authorities?

EXCHANGING DISEASES

46

Epidemics in the New World

The Western Hemisphere, through its isolation from the rest of the globe for thousands of years, provided a testing ground for completely self-contained societies to work out their destinies. There were a range of tightly structured states, stable chiefdoms, and nomadic or semi-nomadic groups. The intrusion of Europeans with new diseases into this aseptic environment was a traumatic shock.

"We were born to die!"

The Cakchiquel, in collaboration or rivalry with the Quiché, formed that branch of the Maya that occupied the present republic of Guatemala. Until the middle of the fifteenth century, the two groups lived with a certain harmony, but serious dynastic rivalries erupted just before the coming of the Spanish. Hernández Arana, who was descended from the last monarch, began to compile these annals when it became clear to him that he would never have to be concerned with state administration. He was about eighteen years old when the Spanish arrived in 1524. In the text, conquistador Pedro de Alvarado is called Tunatiuh ("the sun") because of his blond hair. The terrible burden of forced labor he imposed on the people was eased in 1536 with the arrival of the first governor, Alonso de Maldonado also called President Mantunalo. The epidemic described may have been smallpox, which first hit the islands in 1517 and was introduced to Mexico shortly thereafter.

Arana's rejection of his traditional gods and their images ("the wood and the stone") in favor of missionary Christianity should be evaluated in terms of the argument made in the second selection, which takes a modern long-range view of the impact of disease. The defeats suffered by indigenous peoples always had a religious dimension—the traditional gods seemed to have lost their power to save their worshippers' lives. The argument that these abandoned worshippers then accepted whatever awaited them at the hands of their conquerors is, however, the subject of continuing debate.

Arana

It happened that during the twenty-fifth year [1519] the plague began, oh, my sons! First they became ill of a cough, they suffered from nosebleeds and illness of the bladder. It was truly terrible, the number of dead there were in that period. The prince *Vakaki Ahmak* died then. Little by little heavy shadows and black night enveloped our fathers and grandfathers and us also, oh, my sons! when the plague raged.

On the day 1 Ah [October 3, 1520] ended one cycle and five years after the revolution, while the plague spread.

During this year when the epidemic broke out, our father and grandfather died, *Diego Juan.*

On the day 5 Ah [March 12, 1521] our grandfathers started a war against *Panatacat,* when the plague began to spread. It was in truth terrible, the number of dead among the people. The people could not in any way control the sickness.

Forty days after the epidemic began, our father and grandfather died; on the day 12 Camey [April 14, 1521] the king Hunyg, your great-grandfather, died.

Two days later died also our father, the Ahpop Achí Balam, your grandfather, oh, my sons! Our grandfathers and fathers died together.

Great was the stench of the dead. After our fathers and grandfathers succumbed, half of the people fled to the fields. The dogs and the vultures devoured the bodies. The mortality was terrible. Your grandfathers died, and with them died the son of the king and his brothers and kinsmen. So it was that we became orphans, oh, my sons! So we became when we were young. All of us were thus. We were born to die! . . .

On the day 1 Ganel [February 20, 1524] the Quichés were destroyed by the Spaniards. Their chief, he who was called *Tunatiuh Avilantaro,* conquered all the people. Their faces were not known before that time. Until a short time ago the wood and the stone were worshiped. . . .

On the day 13 Ah [August 12, 1530] ended the thirty-fourth year after the revolution.

During this year heavy tribute was imposed. Gold was contributed to Tunatiuh; four hundred men and four hundred women were delivered to him to be sent to wash gold. All the people extracted the gold. Four hundred men and four hundred women were contributed to work in *Pangán* on the construction of the city, by order of Tunatiuh. All this, all, we ourselves saw, oh, my sons! . . .

During the year, on the day 11 Noh [May 16, 1536], came the President Mantunalo, who came to alleviate the sufferings of the people. Soon there

SOURCE *The Annals of the Cakchiquels*, pp. 115, 119, 129–133, 143–144. Translated from the Cakchiquel Maya by Adrián Recinos and Delia Goetz. Copyright © 1953, 1981 by the University of Oklahoma Press.

was no more washing of gold; the tribute of boys and girls was suspended. Soon also there was an end to the deaths by fire and hanging, and the highway robberies of the Spaniards ceased. Soon the people could be seen traveling on the roads again as it was before the tribute commenced, when the lord Maldonado came, oh, my sons! . . .

. . . [T]here came to our church the Fathers of St. Dominic, Fray Predro de Angulo and Fray Juan de Torres. They arrived from Mexico on the day 12 Batz [February 10, 1542]. The Fathers of St. Dominic began our instruction. The Doctrine appeared in our language. Our fathers Fray Pedro and Fray Juan were the first who preached the word of God to us. Up to that time we did not know the word nor the commandments of God; we had lived in utter darkness. No one had preached the word of God to us. . . .

In the sixth month after the arrival of the Lord President in *Pangán*, the plague which had lashed the people long ago began here. Little by little it arrived here. In truth a fearful death fell on our heads by the will of our powerful God. Many families [succumbed] to the plague. Now the people were overcome by intense cold and fever, blood came out of their noses, then came a cough growing worse and worse, the neck was twisted, and small and large sores broke out on them. The disease attacked everyone here. On the day of Circumcision [January 1, 1560], a Monday, while I was writing, I was attacked by the epidemic. . . .

One month and five days after Christmas my mother died, and a little later death took my father. We buried my mother, and six days later we buried my father. At the same time, on the day 11 Akbal, doña Catalina, the wife of don Jorge, died.

Seven days after Christmas the epidemic broke out. Truly it was impossible to count the number of men, women and children who died this year. My mother, my father, my younger brother, and my sister, all died. Everyone suffered nosebleeds. . . .

A Modern Overview

Wholesale demoralization and simple surrender of will to live certainly played a large part in the destruction of Amerindian communities. Numerous recorded instances of failure to tend newborn babies so that they died unnecessarily, as well as outright suicide, attest the intensity of Amerindian bewilderment and despair. European military action and harsh treatment of laborers gathered forcibly for some large-scale undertaking also had a role in uprooting and destroying old social structures. But human violence and disregard, however brutal, was not the major

SOURCE *Plagues and Peoples*, pp. 119–209, passim, by W. H. McNeill, 1976. Reprinted by permission of Doubleday, a division of Bantam, Doubleday, Dell Publishing Group, Inc.

313

factor causing Amerindian populations to melt away as they did. After all, it was not in the interest of the Spaniards and other Europeans to allow potential taxpayers and the Indian work force to diminish. The main destructive role was certainly played by epidemic disease.

The first encounter came in 1518 when smallpox reached Hispaniola and attacked the Indian population so virulently that Bartolomé de Las Casas believed only a thousand survived. . . .

From Hispaniola, smallpox traveled to Mexico, arriving with the relief expedition that joined Cortés in 1520. As a result, at the very crisis of the conquest, when Moctezuma had been killed and the Aztecs were girding themselves for an attack on the Spaniards, smallpox raged in Tenochtitlán. The leader of the assault, along with innumerable followers, died within hours of compelling the Spaniards to retreat from their city. Instead of following up on the initial success and harrying the tiny band of Spaniards from the land, therefore, as might have been expected had the smallpox not paralyzed effective action, the Aztecs lapsed into a stunned inactivity. Cortés thus was able to rally his forces, gather allies from among the Aztecs' subject peoples, and return for the final siege and destruction of the capital.

Clearly, if smallpox had not come when it did, the Spanish victory could not have been achieved in Mexico. The same was true of Pizarro's filibuster into Peru. For the smallpox epidemic in Mexico did not confine its ravages to Aztec territory. Instead, it spread to Guatemala, where it appeared in 1520, and continued southward, penetrating the Inca domain in 1525 or 1526. Consequences there were just as drastic as among the Aztecs. The reigning Inca died of the disease while away from his capital on campaign in the North. His designated heir also died, leaving no legitimate successor. Civil war ensued, and it was amid this wreckage of the Inca political structure that Pizarro and his crew of roughnecks made their way to Cuzco and plundered its treasures. He met no serious military resistance at all.

Two points seem particularly worth emphasizing here. First, Spaniards and Indians readily agreed that epidemic disease was a particularly dreadful and unambiguous form of divine punishment. Interpretation of pestilence as a sign of God's displeasure was a part of the Spanish inheritance, enshrined in the Old Testament and in the whole Christian tradition. The Amerindians, lacking all experience of anything remotely like the initial series of lethal epidemics, concurred. Their religious doctrines recognized that superhuman power lodged in deities whose behavior toward men was often angry. It was natural, therefore, for them to assign an unexampled effect to a supernatural cause, quite apart from the Spanish missionary efforts that urged the same interpretation of the catastrophe upon dazed and demoralized converts.

Secondly, the Spaniards were nearly immune from the terrible disease that raged so mercilessly among the Indians. They had almost always been exposed in childhood and so developed effective immunity. Given the interpretation of the cause of pestilence accepted by both parties, such a manifestation of divine partiality for the invaders was conclusive. The gods of the

Aztecs as much as the God of the Christians seemed to agree that the white newcomers had divine approval for all they did. And while God thus seemed to favor the whites, regardless of their mortality and piety or lack thereof, his wrath was visited upon the Indians with an unrelenting harshness that often puzzled and distressed the Christian missionaries who soon took charge of the moral and religious life of their converts along the frontiers of Spain's American dominions. . . .

From the Amerindian point of view, stunned acquiescence in Spanish superiority was the only possible response. No matter how few their numbers or how brutal and squalid their behavior, the Spaniards prevailed. Native authority structures crumbled; the old gods seemed to have abdicated. The situation was ripe for the mass conversions recorded so proudly by Christian missionaries. Docility to the commands of priests, viceroys, landowners, mining entrepreneurs, tax collectors, and anyone else who spoke with a loud voice and had a white skin was another inevitable consequence. When the divine and natural orders were both unambiguous in declaring against native tradition and belief, what ground for resistance remained? The extraordinary ease of Spanish conquests and the success a few hundred men had in securing control of vast areas and millions of persons is unintelligible on any other basis.

47

Syphilis in Europe

The various forms of syphilis are usually transmitted through sexual contact, but also may be passed from mother to fetus. Today's syphilis is relatively benign compared to the epidemic nature of the virulent post-1492 outbreak. Exactly when the disease arrived in the Old World is a matter of dispute. Evidence for its New World origin comes from skeletal remains of ancient Amerindians. The first references made to it in Europe follow the return of Columbus's men to Spain; however, what was called leprosy by Europeans in the Middle Ages seems quite similar in that it was connected with sexual contact, was contagious, and responded to the same mercury therapy as does syphilis. Therefore, cases thought to have been the one may have been the other. The sibilant name for this infection comes from a poem, published in 1530, by Girolamo Fracastoro about a Greek shepherd Syphilus, who was punished for offending the goddess of love, Venus (hence, "venereal" disease, or VD).

"that cursed disease . . ."

O ur problem is whether syphilis virulent, widespread, and abundant enough to affect economic life existed in pre-Columbian America; if so, whether it was brought to Europe from the New World; and whether syphilis of this type existed in the Old World before Columbus returned from his first or second voyage. . . .

[Gonzalo Fernández de] Oviedo, who spent about half of his adult life in America, reared a family on Hispaniola and was benevolently disposed toward Indians and Spaniards (though not toward many public servants) said that not only did syphilis exist in the New World long before white men came but that very few Indians had not had syphilis, "one of the most hopeless of all diseases." Bartolomé de Las Casas, whose admirable friendship with Indians began in 1500, asked natives on many occasions whether there was syphilis in pre-Columbian America and was told that it had been there longer than anyone could remember. Las Casas said it was carried to Europe on the first voyage of Columbus, and Oviedo put it on the second. Dr. Ruy Díaz de Isla, perhaps the first great authority on syphilis in Europe, whose clinical description leaves no doubt that he *knew* it when he saw it, says that at Barcelona—whither the Admiral went by sea to report his success to Ferdinand and Isabella—he treated members of the first crew of Columbus and many other sufferers for syphilis, that it came from Hispaniola, and that it was not known in Spain or discussed in books on medicine before that time. He also said that from Barcelona syphilis spread all over Europe and to all known and accessible parts of the universe.

In 1493 Díaz de Isla was 31 years old. It seems reasonable to assume that for six or seven years he had practiced medicine at Seville, a flourishing river port, to which ocean-going vessels came with crews not noted for chastity. If there had been syphilis in Europe he would have had many cases in Seville and would have remembered them during the ten years between 1495 and 1521 that he spent as a syphilis specialist in the Hospital de Todos los Santos in Lisbon, where he wrote his great monograph on syphilis "from the first letter to the last" while associated with other syphilis specialists. Another distinguished Sevillan physician, Dr. Nicolás Monardes, said that the Indian captives on the first voyage of Columbus were the carriers of syphilis to the Old World, "first of all from Santo Domingo." Still another distinguished Andalusian physician practicing in Mexico said in 1591 that syphilis originated in America, that there was no province or country in the world with as much syphilis as Mexico, and that there was no syphilis in Europe until "that cursed disease went from here."

The extraordinary amount of syphilis in Seville and Lisbon, the gateways to and from America, and the leadership of Spanish and Portuguese physicians in knowledge and therapy of syphilis suggest American origin. So does the fact that there was no name for syphilis in Europe before 1493, while a

Source Fredi Chiapelli, ed. *First Images of America*, vol. I, pp. 12–21, and vol. II 879–880. Copyright © 1976 The Regents of the University of California.

hundred or more Indian nations or tribes in the New World had specific names for it. The lack of literature on syphilis in Europe before 1493 and the sudden flood of it in the next decade or so point in the same direction.

Let us revert to two earlier eyewitnesses of the emergence of syphilis in Europe. Oviedo had lived or traveled in Spain, France, Naples, and Sicily; and he *said* he had been in England, Germany, Holland, and Flanders. It stands to reason that one with eyes and ears so sensitive to news would have remembered and reported syphilis in some of these places, instead of saying there was none in Europe, if it had been there and virulent. And if there, but not virulent, why did it suddenly become so after 1493? In his magnificent history of Italy, written about 1535–40, Guicciardini said that syphilis was unknown "in this hemisphere" until brought from the Indies by Columbus about the time (1495) Charles VIII marched into Naples. It is hard to believe there could have been enough active syphilis in Europe prior to the discovery of America to affect the economy without Guicciardini's finding evidence of it. He characterized syphilis as a calamity of the greatest magnitude and said it killed or permanently crippled many men and women. Writing before 1521, Díaz de Isla ventured the assertion that "there is not a village in all Europe with a hundred inhabitants in which ten persons have not died [of syphilis] and a third of the people have not been infected."

Syphilis from the New World shortened productive lives, reduced the number of days worked in active years, required costly medical treatment, and physically harmed not only the victims but often their children, and sometimes their grandchildren, as well. Next to tobacco, it was the most harmful gift of the New World to the Old.

QUESTIONS

1. What was the impact of repeated waves of Old World epidemic diseases on the Amerindian peoples?
2. In the Mayan record by Arana, what might be the connection, if any, between the high mortality rate and the eager reception by its author of Christianity?
3. Demographic collapse may have induced such disbelief in native gods that, combined with awe for the new Christian god, conversion was a matter of course. If this is true, how does this correlate with Document 45, which indicates that conversions in Mexico were often insincere?
4. What evidence is available to construct a case that syphilis came from the New World?

DEMOGRAPHIC SHIFTS

48

Population Decline

A lively debate has gone on for decades among demographic historians concerning the size of the New World population prior to the coming of Europeans. Estimates for the Antilles and the circum-Caribbean fluctuate. For the island of Hispaniola alone, estimates range from 50,000 to 60,000 (Verlinden), 100,000 (Rosenblat), to a high of 8 million (Cook and Borah), which is not generally accepted. Central Mexico's population was first judged to be 11 million by the "Berkeley School" (Simpson, Cook, and Borah), who later raised their figure to 25 million. Estimates for Peru range from 2 to 3 million (Sheal) to 9 million (Cook). Colombia has had 3 million proposed (Colmenares). The Amazonia area of Brazil might have had 2.4 million (Hemming) or 6.8 million (Denevan). Naturally, the higher the estimate, the more tragic would be the collapse after the arrival of the Spanish, since there is firm agreement on low figures for the population in the seventeenth century.

> *"no blame can be ascribed."*

This document presents the wide range of estimated figures available for the New World's precontact population, without attempting to establish the correctness of any one figure. The reader interested in investigating the sophisticated calculation techniques used for so elusive a subject should look at S. F. Cook and Woodrow Borah, *Essays in Population History: Mexico and the Caribbean*, 2 vols. (1971–1974).

T here are few who would doubt that the indigenous population of the New World suffered a severe decline as a result of the arrival of European conquerors and settlers. How much of a decline, and its causes, remain subjects of controversy. In both cases debate arises from the simple fact that in the absence of reliable historical data, researchers must devise methods of retrospective projections. Beginning with a "known" (e.g., a well-documented census, evaluations of carrying capacity, etc.) demographers multiply by an assumed "constant" (e.g., a depopulation ratio), arriving thereby at an estimated figure for precontact population.

That the resulting estimates vary by as much as 104,153,750 (Table 1) is

SOURCE Donald Joralemon, "New World Depopulation and the Case of Disease," *Journal of Anthropological Research* 38 (Spring 1982), pp. 108–125, passim. Reprinted by permission.

TABLE 1 New World Precontact Population Estimates

Source	Estimate
Alfred Kroeber (1939)	8,400,000
Angel Rosenblat (1954)	13,385,000
Paul Rivet (1924)	40,000,000 to 45,000,000
Karl Sapper (1924)	40,000,000 to 50,000,000
Herbert J. Spinden (1928)	50,000,000 to 75,000,000
Woodrow Borab (1964)	100,000,000
Henry F. Dobyns (1966)	90,000,000 to 112,553,750

due to the use of radically different "knowns" and "constants." But it is more than basic data which causes such wide divergence in estimates. As Dobyns (1966) has suggested, the selection of projection material and the resulting conservative or liberal estimates often stem from uncritical assumptions about what the precontact New World must have looked like. Researchers, like Kroeber (1939), who imagined a sparsely settled hemisphere, would have chosen to leave out of the formula such factors as mortality from epidemics and ethnohistorical accounts of large populations. Given the opposite vision, as I think is true for Dobyns (1966), such evidence would weigh heavily in the calculation.

An excellent example of divergent reasoning resulted in two very different estimates for precontact population in the Andean area of South America. In 1947 John Rowe reasoned from ethnohistorical records giving numbers of taxpayers in five provinces in 1525 (under the Inca) and in 1571 (under the Spanish) to total province figures at both points in time by assuming a 5:1 ratio of actual population to tribute payer. He then calculated a "depopulation ratio" for each province by comparing the total estimates for 1525 to those of 1571. The resulting ratios vary from a high of 25:1 on the coast to a low of 3:2 in the *sierra*. Rowe took the average ratio, 4:1, and applied it to a total Andean figure in 1571 of 1,500,000 persons to arrive at a precontact figure of six million persons living in the area as late as 1520.

In 1966 Henry F. Dobyns chose to rely on what he called a "standard hemispheric depopulation ratio" of 20:1. This ratio suggested itself to him after a brief review of some area figures from various parts of the New World where such a drastic decline appeared to be the usual case. Applying this ratio to what he considered to be low points ("nadir") in area populations, he arrived at estimates for large sections of the two continents. The nadir figure he chose for the Andean area is 1,500,000, which, while the same as that chosen by Rowe, was placed as late as 1650. Multiplying by his depopulation factor of twenty, Dobyns came up with a precontact figure of thirty million.

Thus, the two researchers arrived at figures which differ by a factor of five by accepting different depopulation ratios (their "knowns" being equal). That Rowe chose to average his ratios instead of taking the high coastal figure seems to reflect his conservative bias, just as Dobyns's selection of the highest ratio is reflective of a more liberal viewpoint. Likewise, Rowe's ethnohistorical accounts show less drastic depopulation, for the most part, than do those selected by Dobyns.

More recently other researchers have sought to improve Andean population estimates by using new sources of information, as well as taking into account more geographic and demographic variables. These revisions are at least partially a response to criticisms leveled at anthropologists by demographers, but they have not significantly reduced the numerical variation of estimates. Although focused regional studies clearly improve historic population figures, the choice of mathematical operations in projecting back to periods without direct documentation still reflects subjective criteria.

What is often lost in these numerical calculations of population decline is a sensitivity to the range of precipitating factors. In Latin American demographic research this insensitivity has, in part, grown from a desire to free estimates from the assumed biases of early sources. The example of the well-known Indian advocate Bartolomé de Las Casas is often raised as an indication of the unreliability of the early chroniclers. It is widely assumed that the high mortality figures of Las Casas and others are broad exaggerations, generated to serve the particular vested interests of the author. This has led many researchers to dismiss the reports of the early chroniclers:

> Their characteristic methodology has included depreciation of all historical population figures. They deprecate the departure of historical witnesses from the "truth" for motives they intuitively impute, but which uniformly led said witnesses to overestimate, in their opinion, aboriginal populations.

Unfortunately, not only is a potential first-hand source for numbers dismissed without evaluation for reliability, but also an awareness of the complex interplay of factors behind New World depopulation is lost when the witnesses are refused a hearing. An overconcern for numbers pure and simple has led many to ignore the reality those numbers reflect. A good example is Jehan Vellard's rejection of disease as a major cause of depopulation in Peru after the conquest, an untenable position in the light of firm historical evidence.

Many of the most widely recognized causes of depopulation are included in what has come to be known as the "Black Legend," [Documents 30–32] which records the loss of Indian lives by outright cruel practices on the part of the conquistadores. Early warfare and continued "pacification," mistreatment of Indians enslaved under the *encomienda* system, harsh labor practices, and general culture disruption resulting from the imposition of Spanish rule are all mentioned as contributing factors. Las Casas, who became protector of the Indians in 1515, ranks as the earliest and most eloquent spokesman to decry the conscious slaughter of Indians. While there remain questions as to the accuracy of his mortality figures, as well as to his having largely ignored disease as a causal agent, there is all too much evidence supporting his claim that a large proportion of Indian populations died at the hands of their captors. . . .

For all of the debate over these issues it remains clear that epidemic disease must be considered a central factor in New World depopulation. As will be demonstrated, it is not as easy as some assume to dismiss early accounts that attribute many thousands of deaths to the ravages of a single epidemic. Ashburn's characterization of the interaction between European and African biospheres on one side, and that of the New World on the other, as a biological war is not far from the truth, at least as that truth is reflected in the historical record:

> Smallpox was the captain of the men of death in that war, typhus fever the first lieutenant, and measles the second lieutenant. More terrible than the conquistadores on horseback, more deadly than sword and gunpowder, they made the conquest by the whites a walkover as compared with what it would have been without their aid. They were the forerunners of civilization, the companions of Christianity, the friends of the invader.

Disease and the Historical Record

The most obvious source of evidence on the impact of epidemic disease is the historical record left behind by the earliest generations of conquerors and settlers. For Latin America these records come from a variety of persons, and range from outright histories to collections of letters between Spanish monarchs and the officials they appointed in the New World. The authors include Christian clerics and missionaries (e.g., Las Casas and Father Acuña), as well as companions of the conquerors (e.g., Díaz del Castillo).

Mention has already been made of one limitation of these sources, namely, the bias of the author. It is said that Las Casas ignored disease as a cause of Indian deaths because he wanted to impress the king of Spain with the cruelties being inflicted consciously by the conquistadores. The problems involved in such second guessing of motives, however, are manifold. An example of a mistake resulting from such imputing of motives in the case of disease will clarify this point.

Juan Friede argues for an initial mistrust of all colonial reports mentioning epidemic outbreaks, suggesting that because many Spaniards viewed disease as either a selective mechanism or a result of sin, their reports of epidemics would necessarily be biased. He urges the use of supporting documents in a cross-checking analysis of any such report, claiming that real epidemics would leave many documented traces; one such trace would be a sudden increase in requests by *encomenderos* for more slaves. Applying this method, he demonstrates that a report of Cieza de León on a plague in the province of Cartago in New Granada cannot be trusted.

While cross-checking is absolutely essential to any use of the chronicles, Friede erred when he assumed that *encomenderos* would request large numbers of Indians after an epidemic. A well-documented epidemic occurred in Peru in 1546, but is not reflected in the collection of letters received by then-governor Gonzalo Pizarro. The number of requests for slaves found in the letters appears quite constant, and the only mention of disease in the time span covered by the collection (1532–60) is one in Arequipa, years later. An alternate motive could be suggested: those who owned slaves did not want the governor to know how quickly they were dying. One problem of assigning motives, then, is that far too often the opposite turns out to be just as feasible.

A much more significant limitation of the early chronicles for disease research stems from the dismal state of medical knowledge at the time, and the general inattention to symptom description. Frequently the accounts employ native terms that are difficult to interpret, and describe symptoms that could be attributed to many diseases. An epidemic in Mexico in 1545, for instance, was known by its Nahuatl name *"matlazahuatl,"* while the Spanish simply called it *"peste."* The following description of the 1540 Peruvian epidemic mentioned above is supplied by Herrera and gives a good idea of what an especially good description of symptoms looks like:

> A general plague from which innumerable people died occurred this year (1546) among Indians throughout the Kingdom of Peru, beginning beyond Cuzco and extending through all the land; it was an illness that caused headaches and strong accompanying fever, and later the head pains passed to the left ear, so aggravating the sickness that they died in two or three days.

Even when the description of symptoms is detailed, the diagnosis is often nothing more than guesswork. When Lozano, a Jesuit living in Paraguay in the early 1700s, describes the last throes of an epidemic disease, he mentions an occluded throat and death by suffocation. One reasonable guess is diphtheria but a number of other possibilities, including fulminating smallpox (which shows no rash), might also be suggested. In only a few cases, usually when described symptoms are characteristic of only one disease, can an isolated account yield enough information for a retrospective diagnosis with any degree of certainty. With more than one account of a single disease outbreak the possibilities are far better.

But there is still a useful place for the accounts of early chronicles. No matter how poor their descriptions of symptoms, nor how underexaggerated their figures, they were still written by eyewitnesses, and can therefore supply information not otherwise attainable. Such accounts are useful in pinpointing in space and time occurrences of major epidemics, in generally describing which sectors of society were most seriously struck, and some-

times in providing reliable figures (through censuses, for instance) and helping to reduce to a minimum the number of possible diagnoses. . . .

The utility of medical information and analogous, well-documented
cases in the evaluation of postcontact Latin American epidemics has been
clearly shown. The careful use of all historical accounts, through cross-
checking wherever possible, supplies a base from which to proceed with
external sources of evidence. Analyzing symptoms, combining isolated reports, and evaluating estimates of mortality all become possible through the
use of such material as complements to the early chronicles. It is only by
employing all relevant information that a full and accurate image of epidemic disease and its relation to demographic decline can be achieved.

The result of such a careful analysis is likely to be a rethinking of the
Black Legend. Since the writings of Las Casas there has been a growing
tendency towards the "weren't they awful" syndrome. Vivid accounts of
Spanish brutalities are presented as the basis for self-righteous condemnations, and as sufficient explanation for the loss of many thousands, if not
millions, of Indian lives. Without question the accounts of the activities of
men like Pedro de Ursua and Lope de Aguirre are tragic documents for
humanity to bear.

Nevertheless, we blind ourselves to what is a continuing tragedy if we
seek only to assign responsibility to a particular nation at a particular place
and time. Lewis Hanke clearly demonstrates that the issue is far more
complex, and has to do with humans who are completely foreign to each
other coming to grips with the reality of the other's existence. In the New
World that process was complicated by religious concepts that initially
denied the Indians human status, and by the avaricious dreams of men
confronted for the first time with two whole continents of unknown possibilities. But these are human problems not peculiar to the Spanish of the
fifteenth and sixteenth centuries.

In addition to the fact that all of human history, up to and including the
present, is characterized by repeated failures in the process of coming to
grips with the reality of others, the process has a biological as well as a social
aspect. As this paper has shown, an uninvited third party accompanied the
white man when he first met the natives of the New World. No question of
responsibility is appropriate here; no blame can be ascribed. The tragedy
appears to be a necessary outcome of human interaction across biological
boundaries.

The process of adapting to the reality of others, socially and biologically,
continues in Latin America's ongoing "Indian problem." Recent ethnographic literature is filled with reports of both consciously imposed disruption in Indian communities and high mortality from the ever-present threat
of epidemic disease. If 1492 began the story, the last chapters are being
written today. This is the reality that is missed when we focus our attention
on retrospective condemnations.

49

Spanish Colonial Interbreeding

Spanish officials did everything they could to "domesticate" conquistadores on the mainland, lest the latest possessions be devoured in the manner of the Caribbean. To encourage this, the crown insisted all men be married. The trickle of Spanish women in the first half of the sixteenth century swelled to 28 percent of all migrants by the 1570s. Nevertheless, the continued shortage of women from the home country encouraged intermarriage, the taking of native mistresses, or sexual enslavement. The male children of these unions were known as *mestizos.* When the blacks arrived, their male offspring with whites were known as *mulattoes,* and with Amerindians as *zambos.* Some authorities consider this interbreeding to be the most important and lasting legacy of the encounter between the Old and the New Worlds.

> *"The borders between the categories were fluid, . . ."*

T he Iberian conquest of the New World was biological as well as military. Few of their own women accompanied the conquistadores from Europe. From the time of Columbus's return to Hispaniola on his second voyage the unceasing threnody was to be heard: "They have taken our wives from us." Native women were as much part of the booty as gold and pearls. On the amazing advent of the bearded white men, many gave themselves freely, not only as to the victorious fighting male, but as offerings to beings who were manifestly gods. Chiefs sought to placate the invaders, or to cement alliances with them, by gifts of women which the Spaniards saw no reason to refuse. Moctezuma gave Cortés one of his daughters, and Atahualpa one of his sisters to Francisco Pizarro, who fathered two sons by her before marrying off the princess to one of his pages. Even the common soldiers, if fortune favoured, could accumulate a veritable harem by means of gifts or rapine. The narrative of Ulrich Schmidl, a German serving under Pedro de Mendoza in Paraguay, reads like an inventory of Don Juan at large in Arcadia: "The women are very beautiful and go as naked as their mothers brought them into the world. . . . They are painted very

Source Stephen Clissold, *Latin America. New World, Third World* (New York: Praeger Publishers, 1972), pp. 47–50, passim. Reprinted by permission.

beautifully from their breasts to their privy parts; a painter from Europe could scarcely have made a finer job of it. They are handsome after their fashion and go stark naked; they fall to temptation on occasion. . . . Here I conquered for myself as booty nineteen persons, young men and women. I had no use for the old, but preferred the young." The attraction of the Indian woman could sometimes be strong enough to make the Spaniard turn native. On landing in Mexico, Cortés encountered two such cases. One of them, although he had forgotten all but a few words of Spanish and would squat on his haunches in native fashion, rejoined his countrymen and did useful service as an interpreter. The other sent word that he had married an Indian and fathered three fine sons; besides, the Spaniards would laugh to see his face painted and his ears pierced in Indian fashion. He persisted in his refusal despite Cortés's stern admonition to "remember he was a Christian, and not to lose his soul on account of an Indian woman" [Document 43].

The Indian woman was capable of remarkable devotion to her white mate and an identification with his cause which greatly facilitated the process of the *Conquista*. The most famous case is that of Malinche or Malintzín, who served Cortés as interpreter, adviser, and mistress, and is execrated today in Mexico as a symbol of native collaboration with the alien intruder. The Crown's attitude towards such alliances was ambivalent. Concubinage was formally forbidden under the terms of the conquistadores' Capitulations, but the prohibition was clearly unenforceable. Marriage with native women was at first also forbidden, but after 1514 permitted. For how could conqueror and conquered be more effectively integrated than through miscegenation [mixing of races]? There was, besides, a chronic shortage of Spanish women in the young colonies.

The reason for the rapid growth of a *mestizo* population is clear from contemporary reports. One friar tells us that every conquistador, in addition to his lawful wife, would take an average of three concubines. Paraguay, a happy hunting ground for Schmidl and his like, was a particularly fertile breeding ground. "Here some men have as many as 70 women, and the very poorest does not have less than five or six," wrote the chaplain González Paniagua to the King. No wonder that Asunción became known as "Mahomet's [Mohammed's] Paradise." Within ten years of its foundation in 1537 the little settlement contained 500 *mestizo* children; by 1575 its population consisted of some 5,000 *mestizos* and only 280 Spaniards. Today Paraguay is one of the most homogeneous and fully *mestizo* countries of Latin America, with a bilingual population proud of the strong Guaraní element in its make-up.

Elsewhere the process of miscegenation proceeded more unevenly. Of the population of New Spain, which had sunk to its lowest ebb by 1650, some 1,270,000 were described as Indians, 120,000 as white, and 130,000 as *mestizos*. By the end of the eighteenth century, the latter had increased by more than seventeen times, to reach some 2,270,000, whereas the number of Indians had quadrupled to give a figure of 5,200,000. Since then, the strength of the Indian population has remained at about the same level, whilst the number of *mestizos* has steadily increased to form the overwhelming bulk of the Mexican nation of today. In Bolivia, Peru, and Ecuador, heirs to the old Inca Empire, the process of racial integration was less intensive; at least half their total population can still be reckoned as Indian, most of the remainder as *mestizos*.

In Brazil and the Caribbean islands, where the Indian population was either scanty or in rapid decline, miscegenation developed mainly between whites and negroes. By 1585, the population of Brazil was estimated to be still only 57,000, of whom nearly one quarter were African slaves. By the close of the eighteenth century, before the flood of European immigrants increased the white element, the Africans formed the majority. The stark confrontation of the two races, European and Amerindian, thus gradually evolved, as *Conquista* merged into colonization, into the emergence of the following categories: a smaller dominant group of European-born Spaniards and Portuguese, their white descendants born in America (generally referred to as Creoles), the subject Amerindians and negroes, and the population of mixed blood (known as *castas* or *mestizos*) formed by the interbreeding of white and coloured, or hybrids between the different groups of coloured. These racial categories corresponded broadly to social divisions, the masterclass formed by European and American-born whites, the base of the pyramid by the negro slaves and by Indians who, although nominally free citizens, were in practice generally condemned to servile status, and the intermediate *mestizos* who identified themselves individually as far as they could with the white élite, but more often became a restless, rootless, disinherited fringe-group. The borders between the categories were fluid, social and economic factors being more of a determinant than the purely racial. Thus Indians who learned Spanish, acquired money or possessed estates—and not a few members of the old Aztec and Inca nobility made the transition in this way—could be reckoned amongst the *gente de razón* or "civilized people"; whatever their racial origins, they would no longer rank as Indians. They might even obtain from the authorities a document formally confirming that they should be "considered white."

50

Migration of Peoples

A useful way to study the development of the American continents is to place them firmly into the context of world events. If the masses of humanity are not fitted into a comparative global overview, history otherwise remains little more than a listing of "important" people—usually politicians—and the doings of nations—usually European. Writers of the new global history, such as Wallerstein (Document 2), Braudel (Document 7), McNeill (Document 46), or Crosby (Documents 50 and 52), focus on recurring themes of food, climate, trade, war, disease, colonization, and cultural diffusion. This approach is an effective way to bring all the silent "people without history" into the mainstream of study. The process of enforced or voluntary migration to America from Africa and Europe, set in motion long ago, continues unabated today, swelled by a flow from Asia. As for the Amerindians, their population crash lasted a long time, but where there is any prospect of recovery, an increase is taking place. In certain areas, the recovery proceeds at a rapid rate. With respect to mixing together the population of continents, Columbus deserves the recognition that he initiated the process of making all the world one.

> *"The Columbian exchange has included man, . . ."*

Few, very few, aborigines of the New World have crossed the Atlantic to colonize in the Old World, but aborigines of Europe and Africa have crossed by the tens of millions to found nations in the regions of America where their pioneers had done the heroic work of bringing diseases to destroy or reduce the resistance of the native Americans. Indeed, the Euro- and Afro-Americans now often consider themselves to be the natives of those nations, and the Indians to be the aliens.

The source of the earliest mass migration of Old World peoples to the New World was not Europe, despite the impression that history textbooks give. The mass of African immigrants arrived in America before the mass of Europeans. With perhaps millions of Native Americans succumbing to cold steel, the musketball, whiskey, and disease in the sixteenth, seventeenth,

SOURCE A. W. Crosby, Jr., *Columbian Exchange. Biological and Cultural Consequences of 1492* (Westport, Conn.: Greenwood Press, 1972), pp. 212–219, passim. Reprinted with permission of the publisher.

and eighteenth centuries, especially in the coastal regions, European exploitation of America was slowed by the shortage of servants and slaves. Europeans could not or would not offer themselves in sufficient numbers to make up this shortage, and so the white conquistadors and plantation masters and merchant princes turned to Africa. The shortage of labor was most pressing in the islands and littoral of tropical America, where the swords and maladies of the Old World had made the cleanest sweep of the aborigines and where the profits to be made from the mass production of tobacco, rice, indigo, coffee, and especially sugar were potentially the greatest. Almost 90 percent of the Africans who were torn from their homes to serve as slaves in America were brought to the tropics of the New World, 38 percent to Brazil and 42 percent to the Antilles alone. The total number brought to America probably falls between 8 million and 10.5 million, and almost all of these had arrived by 1850. In 1950 their descendants, both of pure and part African ancestry, numbered at least 47 million, as compared with the entire African population, Caucasians and Asians included, of 198 million.

The migration of masses of aborigines from Europe to America is an event of no more than the last century and a half. The port officials of Seville recorded only 150,000 people embarking for the New World from 1509 to 1740, and, while this is a serious underestimation of the numbers of Spaniards who made that choice, it does suggest that relatively few did. In the seventeenth century only a quarter million left the British Isles for America, and, in the eighteenth century, only a million and a half. Germany sent only 200,000 before 1800, and other European countries even fewer. Despite interbreeding with the Indians and Afro-Americans and despite what were sometimes fantastically high birth rates, these few people would have never filled up the regions vacated by the Indians if they had not been aided by the multitudes that have followed them since.

In the nineteenth century, news that the American settlements were now more than beachheads and that American land was good and cheap spread throughout Europe. The spacious and dependable steamship replaced the cramped and undependable sailing ship. Population pressure in rural Europe made it more and more difficult to obtain even a small plot of ground, and the early industrial revolution made wages low and unemployment frequent in her cities. The greatest transoceanic migration in all human history began, at first a freshet in the 1830s and then a torrent of Englishmen, Scots, Irishmen, Germans, Swedes, Poles, Spaniards, Portuguese, Czechs, Italians, and Russians, Protestants, Catholics, and Jews crossing the Atlantic to fill in the lands left vacant by the Indians or defined as vacant by the ethnocentric immigrants. From 1851 to 1960, over 61 million Europeans migrated to continents other than that of their birth. The great bulk of these men and women, 45 million by 1924, migrated to the Americas. Of these 45 million, the majority, about 34 million, chose the United States of America as their new home. Those who went to Latin

America went chiefly to Argentina and Brazil, the total to Argentina between 1850 and 1940 approaching 7 million and the total to Brazil from 1821 to 1945 about 4.5 million. Non-American recipients of European immigrants, like Australia and South Africa, lagged far behind.

In 1930 about 20 million people born in Europe were living in other continents: nearly 14 million in North America—12 million in the United States and most of the remainder in Canada—and about 5 million in Latin America, chiefly Argentina and Brazil. And the migration to the New World continues. Between 1946 and 1957 Europe lost 5.4 million emigrants and the Americas gained 4.4 million immigrants.

As of the 1950s the population of the United States was over 85 percent of European ancestry, and the corresponding percentage for Brazil was 42, for Chile 46, for Uruguay 96, and for Argentina 99. There are two Europes, as there are two Africas: one on either side of the Atlantic. The European and African in America are the most blatant products of the Columbian exchange.

The effects of the transatlantic crossing of Old World emigrants, along with their agricultures and industries, has been, of course, enormous, and whole legions of historians have devoted their careers to tracing those influences. We will only briefly note a few of those influences.

All the populations of all the continents have increased in the last two hundred years, but Europe's has increased fastest, from 19 or 20 percent of the world's population in 1750 to 23 percent in 1850. In 1960 the proportion was still 21 percent. This relative increase over the last two centuries must have played a role in enabling the expansion of the area of the world settled by Europeans from no more than 22 percent in 1750 to a peak figure of 36 percent in 1950.

Why did Europeans gain in number relative to Asians and Americans? Because they made fuller use of American crops? Probably not. Because of more efficient government, better sanitation, and other advantages? Probably so. Certainly the removal of more than 50 millions across the Atlantic must have done a great deal to lessen population pressure on the resources of the continent of their birth and, thus, to encourage population growth there. And certainly the export of Europeans and Africans to America helped to bring a manifold return on European investments in the New World, and by thus lessening the burden of poverty, to encourage an increase in marriages and births. . . .

. . . The long-range biological effects of the Columbian exchange are not encouraging.

If one values all forms of life and not just the life of one's own species, then one must be concerned with the genetic pool, the total potential of all living things to produce descendants of various shapes, sizes, colors, internal structures, defenses against both multicellular and unicellular enemies, maximum fertility, and, to speak generally, maximum ability to produce offspring with maximum adaptive possibilities. The genetic pool is usually

TABLE 2 Intercontinental Migration, Selected Countries and Periods

Emigration

Country of Emigration	Period	Number of Emigrants
Austria and Hungary	1846–1932	5,196,000
Belgium	1846–1932	193,000
British Isles	1846–1932	18,020,000
Denmark	1846–1932	387,000
Finland	1871–1932	371,000
France	1846–1932	519,000
Germany	1846–1932	4,889,000
Holland	1846–1932	224,000
Italy	1846–1932	10,092,000
Norway	1846–1932	854,000
Poland	1920–1932	642,000
Portugal	1846–1932	1,805,000
Russia	1846–1924	2,253,000
Spain	1846–1932	4,653,000
Sweden	1846–1932	1,203,000
Switzerland	1846–1932	332,000

Immigration

Country of Immigration	Period	Number of Immigrants
Argentina	1856–1932	6,405,000
Australia	1861–1932	2,913,000
Brazil	1821–1932	4,431,000
British West Indies	1836–1932	1,587,000
Canada	1821–1932	5,206,000
Cuba	1901–1932	857,000
Mexico	1911–1931	226,000
New Zealand	1851–1932	594,000
South Africa	1881–1932	852,000
United States	1821–1932	34,244,000
Uruguay	1836–1932	713,000

expanded when continents join. As plants and creatures move into virgin territory, the adaptations to new environments of those who survive the increased competition produce new types and even many new species. Paleontologists and comparative zoologists call the event "explosive evolution," meaning that it often only takes a few million years. This is what normally would have happened and would be happening after the joining of the Old and New Worlds in 1492—but for man.

Not for half a billion years, at least, and probably for long before that, has an extreme or permanent physical change affected the whole earth. The single exception to this generality may be European man and his technologies, agricultural and industrial. He has spread all over the globe, and non-European peoples have adopted his techniques in all but the smallest islets. His effect is comparable to an increase in the influx of cosmic rays or the raising of whole new chains of Andes and Himalayas.

The Columbian exchange has included man, and he has changed the Old and New Worlds sometimes inadvertently, sometimes intentionally, often brutally. It is possible that he and the plants and animals he brings with him have caused the extinction of more species of life forms in the last four hundred years than the usual processes of evolution might kill off in a million. Man kills faster than the pace of evolution: there has been no million years since Columbus for evolution to devise a replacement for the passenger pigeon. No one can remember what the pre-Columbian flora of the Antilles was like, and the trumpeter swan and the buffalo and a hundred other species have been reduced to such small numbers that a mere twitch of a change in ecology or man's wishes can eliminate them. The flora and fauna of the Old and especially of the New World have been reduced and specialized by man. Specialization almost always narrows the possibilities for future changes: for the sake of present convenience, we loot the future.

The Columbian exchange has left us with not a richer but a more impoverished genetic pool. We, all of the life on this planet, are the less for Columbus, and the impoverishment will increase.

QUESTIONS

1. Why is it difficult to establish accurate figures for the New World population prior to 1492?
2. What total population figure seems to be the most accurate for the entire Western Hemisphere in 1492?
3. Why would Las Casas (Documents 31 and 34) not have agreed with Joralemon (Document 48) that it is better to assign no blame to any humans for the death of vast numbers of Amerindians?
4. Why were liaisons and intermarriage common in the Iberian possessions?
5. Which areas in South America have the largest *mestizo* population?
6. Had the intermingling of peoples produced color and race equality by the end of the sixteenth century?

LORA AND FAUNA

51

Columbus Observes Nature

It is fortunate that we have Las Casas's edited transcription of Columbus's logbook (Document 15) for the first voyage, since the original has never been uncovered. The logbook, known to and used by few of his contemporaries or early historians, remained unpublished until 1825. Despite the limitations imposed upon what Columbus wrote (he expected it to be read by the queen) and the possibility that Las Casas left out important matters that did not fit his intention to show the Amerindians in the best possible light, it remains a source from which writers continue to draw inspiration. Endless battles in print and at scholarly conferences continue, for example, about just exactly where the first landfall in the New World was, all based on rather skimpy and confusing data. The logbook is far more valuable for historical ecology because so much of the vegetation and the life forms have changed on the islands since the first European set foot there. This selection presents an analysis of the entries, examining not only *what* Columbus saw in the Caribbean but *how* he saw it, based upon his experiences, prejudices, and interests.

> "the rhapsodies fall thick and fast, . . ."

C hristopher Columbus had things other than nature to occupy his mind. His indifference to some of the most astonishing aspects of the Americas, such as the new constellations to be seen in the American heavens, has been remarked on more than once. The flora and fauna of America do, however, immediately attract his attention and even manage to distract him momentarily from the search for gold, producing reactions in him that already contain in microcosm all the later attitudes of the European in America.

It is now more than a century since Humboldt congratulated Columbus on being as shrewd an observer of nature as he was intrepid a sailor; in the Admiral's *Journal* and reports he found already "formulated all the problems that occupied the attention of the scientists in the second half of the fifteenth century and throughout the sixteenth century." Thus it seems all

Source Reprinted from *Nature in the New World: From Christopher Columbus to Gonzalo Fernández de Oviedo*, pp. 12–22, by Antonello Gerbi, translated by Jeremy Moyle, by permission of the University of Pittsburgh Press. Translation © 1985, Jeremy Moyle.

the more curious that Alfonso Reyes should complain that Columbus left us "no real impression of American nature and life," and that Iglesia likewise should insist that "in Columbus there is never any disinterested description," and only an "*alleged* feeling for nature."

The important point, in actual fact, is to remember Columbus's expectations, the disappointments he suffered, and the precise aims with which he was writing. His reactions to American nature are never coldly scientific observations, but genuine "reactions," sometimes emotional and enthusiastic, sometimes full of repressed and disguised disappointment. On the one hand, having failed to find in the Antilles the dreamed-of paradise gleaming with gold, he is overcome with doubts and misgivings that will later provide support for numerous denigrators of the continent. On the other hand, and more importantly, he feels joyfully at one with nature in the tropics, revels in the eternally springlike climate, experiences a sensation of perfect happiness and exhilaration, finds himself at peace with his tormented spirit and the dumbly hostile world, and gives vent to an enthusiasm that will echo down through the centuries, all the way to Humboldt and Jacquemont. The weather is always like May. The beauty of one area persuades him to baptize it *Jardines*, "the gardens." Not only nightingales sing, but a thousand other little birds, and innumerable species of palms sway gently in the breeze. The natives are possibly exempt from Original Sin, pure as Adam. If pearls, as Pliny [ancient Roman naturalist] says, are born from the dew falling into oysters, there must certainly be vast numbers of pearls in the Indies, since the dew is abundant!

Small wonder that subsequent observers, failing to rediscover all these paradisal virtues in the Indies, realistically underlined other shortcomings, which were then used to back up the thesis of the inferiority of the American continent. . . .

On the first island he touched on that fateful day, 12 October 1492, Columbus found "no beast of any sort . . . save parrots." At first sight, America's fauna seems meager in the extreme. Two days later, noting the splendor of the fresh green vegetation, like Castile in April or May (14 October), Columbus settles on the contrast—meager fauna, exuberant flora—that is to be repeated down through the centuries. The comparative formula is then reiterated, with few variations, time and again: the new islands, even in the winter months, are as luxuriant and fruitful as the lands of Europe in the best season.

This initial amazement is followed by a vague feeling that such a climate and such a land must produce creatures and plants of extraordinary powers. Terrestrial creatures may be said to be entirely absent. "I saw no animals on land of any sort, save parrots and lizards. A boy told me that he saw a large snake. I saw no sheep or goats or any other animals. . . . [I]f there had been any I could not have failed to see some" (16 October). The insistent repetition contains a note of wonder: though he looks everywhere about him and listens carefully to the crew's stories, the Admiral can find barely a trace of any animal on land.

But the fish are a constant surprise, "fish so *different* from ours, that it is truly wonderful," muticolored and speckled like cockerels, and of such beautiful colors "that everyone marvels at them and takes great delight in them." Myriads of birds warble overhead and flocks of parrots hide the sun, "birds big and small of so many sorts and so different from ours, that one is left marveling" (21 October).

As for the trees, they are startling in their variety and *newness*. "Many trees very *different* from ours . . . and with branches so varied in shape that it is the most astonishing thing in the world, how great a difference there is between one kind and another" (16 October). Their beauty rivals their novelty; they are as green as Andalusia in May, but "the trees are all as *different* from ours as day is from night: and likewise the fruit and the herbs and the stones and everything else." Even if some trees were "similar in nature to others existing in Castile, yet there was a very great difference, and there were so many other sorts of trees that nobody could enumerate them nor compare them with those of Castile" (17 October).

Faced with such exuberance, Columbus is overcome with three separate emotions: enthusiasm for the *newness* of the flora of the Antilles, admiration for its exceptional beauty, and annoyance at being prevented by lack of time and botanical knowledge from appraising its medicinal powers and nutritional value. From the purely cognitive point of view, American nature is different and surprising, "unlike." From the aesthetic-hedonistic viewpoint, it is beautiful and pleasing, euphoric. From the practical point of view, it *must be* very useful and very good, but Columbus does not know. Before all else, he is in a hurry to find gold: "There may be a lot of things of which I know nothing, because I am reluctant to linger here, being anxious to explore numerous islands with a view to finding gold" (15 October). Moreover he cannot even distinguish among these various generic "trees" and candidly confesses and regrets it. "I believe the islands contain many herbs and many trees which will be worth a great amount in Spain for dyes and as medicinal spices, but I do not recognize them and I much regret that" (19 October). "There are trees of a thousand sorts, all with their various fruits, and all marvelously scented. It makes me the saddest man in the world not to know them, because I am quite certain that all are valuable" (21 October).

Firmly convinced that he has reached the eastern tip of Asia, Columbus—still under the influence of Toscanelli's undiscriminating and glowing prophecies [Document 11]—never doubts that all those trees could be identified with precious plants of the Indies and Moluccas if one had the expert knowledge; but he himself does not dare to state as much—and rightly, because one would search vainly for Asiatic prototypes for many American herbs and plants.

But his glance dwells lovingly on every detail of the islands, whose mere existence is sufficient to realize his lifetime's dream and guarantee his immortal glory, quite apart from the splendor of high offices for himself and his descendants. His pen, at times so dry and energetic, now becomes a brush whose delicate strokes caress the tiny islands, on which fortune would subsequently smile so little. With a sort of lover's awkwardness he seeks to wax poetic, and produces a flood of warbling nightingales, blossoming springtimes, May meadows, and Andalusian nights.

The wonder and surprise continue in the broad and beautiful island of Cuba. There Columbus runs into an absurd natural prodigy, "dogs that never barked," and—the antiphrasis renders the extraordinary contrast very well—"tame wild birds" in the natives' houses, and even "large snails, but tasteless, and *not like those of Spain*" (29 October). A whole fauna completely different from Europe's. The flora too is distinctive: there is much cotton, there are "mames," which "are like carrots, and taste like chestnuts" (but which are, according to Las Casas, actually potatoes) and green beans and kidney beans *"very different from ours."*

As the days pass, however, the eye becomes accustomed, nature becomes more familiar, and the first impression of violent contrast with the animals and plants of Europe gives way to a vague but significant awareness of the affinities and similarities. The sailors find "an animal that looked like

FLYING FISH

a badger" and catch a fish, among many others, "which looked just like a pig" (16 November). The Admiral notices "large mice . . . and huge crabs," and in the sky he sees lots of birds and detects a heady scent of spices (17 November). Instead of the exotic and ill-defined trees, he recognizes "oaks and strawberry trees" and a multitude of noble pines straight as spindles, which he can already see sawn up into planks for caravels or raised as masts "for the largest ships in Spain." The forest becomes a fleet. The virgin timber of the American woods is already raw material , merchandise for the mother country, a source of incalculable riches and naval might. The sovereigns will be able to "build as many vessels as might be wished there" (25 November). Two days later, the vision takes more concrete and specific shape: the king and queen will very easily be able to subjugate the new islands, convert the inhabitants, and build cities and fortresses there; and to ensure their lasting dominion over the islands they would be well advised not to allow "any foreigner, except Catholic Christians, to trade or set foot here" (27 November). The foreigner Columbus had only set foot in America six weeks earlier and he was already jealous—in Spain's interest—of any other "immigrant." The barely discoverd paradise is immediately annexed in spirit to the crown of Castile.

Columbus's attitude to nature, which, as we have seen, is strictly subordinated to his ambitions and his political dream, is now about to be reversed. Nature in the West Indies is no longer radically different from Spain's. It is now similar, now almost identical, and more beautiful.

By the time the source of the precious metal is eventually located in Haiti—the Admiral having abandoned Cuba after a fruitless quest for the mines—the change is finally complete. Haiti is the *isla Española*, the "Spanish Island." It is Spain, it belongs to Spain and resembles Spain in every way. There is no further need to glorify the newness of the plants and animals: the nuggets and the gold-bearing sands are as beautiful a novelty as one could wish. It now becomes preferable to depict the island as a welcoming and familiar dwelling-place, where acclimatization is no problem and where one can live as in the mother country. Columbus reaches the coast of Haiti [Hispaniola] on 5 December, and on 6 December he immediately notes that the trees are smaller than in the other islands (less wild exuberance) "and many of them are similar in nature to those in Spain, such as holm-oaks and strawberry trees and others, and this is also true of the plants." He sails further along the coast and confirms his finding "that the whole of that land is very hilly, but has no large trees, only holm-oaks and strawberry trees, *just like the land of Castile*" (7 December). He sees crops "like barley" growing in the fields and broad valleys and countryside and very high mountains, "all resembling Castile." He tries fishing with nets, "and before he reached the shore a skate, *like those of Spain*, jumped right into the boat. Up until then he had seen no fish which resembled those of Castile." The passage goes on and concludes with a sort of hymn of joy exulting in the refrain "Castile." "The sailors went fishing and caught some more skate, and sole and other fish *like those of Castile.* He went a little way into that country, which is all cultivated, and heard a nightingale sing, and other birds *like those of Castile.* . . . He found myrtle and other trees and plants *like those of Castile,* and the land and the mountains resemble Castile too" (7 December). Even the rain and the cold are *"like October in Castile";* and near the port of San Nicolas there are two very beautiful plateaux "almost *resembling the lands of Castile,* and indeed these are superior, wherefore he named this island Hispaniola, the Spanish Island" (9 December).

And so it goes on. Once the enthusiasm of a headstrong visionary like Columbus is aroused the rhapsodies fall thick and fast, unrestrained by any formula, and the equation, already bold enough, becomes a mere stepping-stone to hyperbole. Haiti is like Castile? No, Haiti is better than Castile. Its waters contain fish like those of Spain (11 and 13 December) and mastic like that which makes Chios rich—although the Haitian mastic stubbornly refuses to set, which the sailors ascribe to the inopportune season or the waters (10 and 11 December)—and "young women as fair of skin as any that could be found in Spain." But there are also lands of such beauty "that the fairest and best lands in Castile could not compare with these," and orchards groaning with fruit, rich meadows and broad good roads, nocturnal melodies of nightingales, fragrant breezes and choruses of crickets and frogs and sweet-smelling spices and cotton; and the as yet unfound gold will be found: "They found no gold but it is not surprising that it was not found in such a short time" (13 December).

The potatoes there are as thick as a man's leg, and the trees "so heavily leaved that their foliage is no longer green, but a verdant dark color." The fields are just waiting to be sown with corn, the pastures to be grazed by any sort of cattle and then "everything in the world that man could desire" will flourish in these gardens, fields, and pastures (16 December). Even the natives are more Spanish than the Spanish, in the Admiral's eyes, and he insists that they be treated absolutely fairly, because "he considers them already Christians and subjects of the sovereigns of Castile, *more than the peoples of Castile"* (21 December). They are gentle and softly spoken and always laugh when they speak (25 December), "not like the others who seem to be threatening when they speak"; and they give away gold and parrots and cotton cloth without a second thought.

When the *Santa María* goes aground they help to salvage the cargo and "not a leather thong or a plank or a nail was missing"—something which would not have happened "anywhere in Castile"—and indeed they do their best to console the Admiral, offering him everything they have (25 and 26 December). True, they daub their bodies black, red, and other colors, but the Admiral learns that "they do this to protect themselves in some degree against the sun (24 December and see also 13 January 1493—a first attempt to provide a rationalistic explanation of the rites and customs of the primitives and the first hint of the savages' delicate constitution, which would later be one of Las Casas's most frequent arguments). In short, there is no comparison with Cuba and the Cubans: "There is as great a difference between them and between that island and this in everything, as there is between night and day" (24 December). Gold itself finally arrives in abundance, indeed is "infinite." The Admiral, smothering his exaltation with impatience, was already on 27 December "thinking to make haste for the return to Castile with all possible dispatch."

The return journey and the subsequent expedition, from which nothing has survived in the way of original reports barring a few letters, produce no new observations in the field of science or natural philosophy. From the ship they see the usual frigate birds and petrels and in the sea tuna fish, a shark, and sargasso [seaweed], almost always mentioned at the end of the daily observations, as a normal occurrence. In the so-called *lettera rarissima* of 7 July 1503, relating to the fourth voyage, Columbus mentions numerous species of animals seen on the mainland, many "and very different from ours": two fierce "pigs," a wild beast "that resembles a marsh cat, except that it is much bigger and has a face like a man's," big woolly chickens, "lions, stags, roebuck," and so forth. But there is no recurrence of that lucid balance between dream and greed, that alternation of enquiry and exploitation which had given free reign to the Admiral's contemplative spirit and tender curiosity when he visited the first islands.

52

Accidents of Geography

The breakup of the once united landmass of earth led to the isolation of each of the hemispheres. Vast changes developed as animals died out and alternative strains of plants developed from place to place. This selection takes a fresh look at the continuing argument over why the Europeans came to dominate the Amerindians, by examining handicaps that the New World suffered in comparison with the Old.

Although based on recent scientific evidence, this article fits into a long tradition, beginning with Columbus, of denigrating the Western Hemisphere. Up through the nineteenth century, writers insisted that the "newness" of the land meant that it lagged behind Eurasia, and that its plants, animals, and humans were inherently weaker and more delicate than the tougher Eurasian counterparts.

> *"the New World limped forward on human muscle power alone, . . ."*

It is useful to attempt to refute these charges by turning to the British expert Arnold Toynbee, whose multivolume *A Study of History* (1934–1961) presents themes normative to the development of civilizations. One

343

of these is "challenge and response"—if the challenge (for example, by the environment) is insufficient, a civilization will not advance, but if the challenge is too great, the civilization stagnates after surmounting the original problem. Thus, natives on tropical islands develop few artifacts because life is easy, whereas residents of the frozen north find ingenious ways to cope, but make no further changes because their solutions work all too well.

Much of the New World was in temperate climes, and while the New World peoples may have lacked what Eurasians had, this did not restrain them from finding alternatives. The Amerindians made up for the lack of large animals by developing sledges to drag goods or by organizing elaborate systems of runners to relay messages. Plows without heavy beasts of burden would have been worthless, so they developed a highly productive agriculture by inserting seeds by hand into prepared holes, rather than the broadcasting done by Europeans, who cast seeds onto open furrows. Bean and squash was planted around corn to protect it and to increase the nutritional yield. Rather than debating which hemisphere's technology was "better," a game that always appeals to the winners, let us learn what we can about the natural and constructed environments of the world, note the differences, and leave it at that.

L ook around you in most locations in the United States and Australia and most of the people you'll see will be of European ancestry. At the same sites 500 years ago everyone without exception would have been an American Indian or an aboriginal Australian. This is an obvious feature of our daily life, and yet it poses a difficult question, one with a far from obvious answer: Why is it that Europeans came to replace most of the native populations of North America and Australia, instead of Indians or native Australians replacing the original population of Europe?

This question can be rephrased to ask, Why was the ancient rate of technological development fastest in Eurasia, slower in the Americas (and in Africa south of the Sahara), and slowest in Australia? If we look at the state of civilization in 1492—a highly significant year for both Europeans and Native Americans—we find that Eurasian peoples used iron tools, had writing and agriculture, and were on the verge of industrialization. People in the Americas had agriculture but no iron tools, only the Mayan and their neighbors had some form of writing, and technology stood a few thousand years behind that of Eurasia. Australians, meanwhile, lacked agriculture and writing altogether, and their stone tools were comparable to Eurasian tools made more than 10,000 years earlier.

Nineteenth-century Europeans had a simple, racist explanation for such inequality. They concluded that they themselves were inherently more intelligent than their New World counterparts; they also concluded that they

SOURCE "The Accidental Conqueror," by Jared Diamond, *Discover* vol. 10, no. 12 (December, 1989), pp. 71–76, passim. Copyright © 1989 Discover Publications, reprinted with permission.

therefore had a manifest destiny to conquer, displace, or kill these "inferior" peoples. The trouble with this answer is not just that it was loathsome and arrogant but also that it was completely wrong. Obviously people differ enormously in the knowledge they acquire, depending on their circumstances as they grow up. But no convincing evidence of genetic differences in mental ability among peoples has even been found—despite considerable effort. . . .

. . . Europeans' conquest of America and Australia was not due to their better genes but to their worse germs (especially smallpox), more advanced technology (including weapons and ships), information storage through writing, and political organization—all stemming ultimately from continental differences in geography.

Let's start with the differences in domestic animals. By 4000 B.C. western Eurasia already had the "big five" domestic livestock that continue to dominate today: sheep, goats, pigs, cows, and horses. All provided food, power, and clothing. But the horse, in addition, was of incalculable military value, serving as the tank, the truck, and the jeep of warfare until the twentieth century. Why didn't Indians reap similar benefits by domesticating the corresponding native American mammal species: mountain sheep, mountain goats, peccaries, bison, and tapirs? Why didn't Indians mounted on tapirs, and native Australians mounted on kangaroos, invade and terrorize Eurasia?

The answer is simply that most animals don't take kindly to domestication. Even today people have managed to domesticate only a tiny fraction of the world's wild mammal species. Consider all the attempts that have failed. Innumerable species have reached the necessary first step of being kept captive as tame pets. In New Guinea villages you can routinely find tamed opossums and kangaroos, while in Amazonian Indian villages you can see tamed monkeys and weasels. Ancient Egyptians had tamed gazelles, antelopes, even hyenas and possibly giraffes. Romans were terrorized by the tamed African elephants with which Hannibal crossed the Alps (not Asian elephants, the species seen in most circuses today).

But all these incipient efforts were flops. Since the domestication of horses about 4000 B.C. and reindeer a few thousand years later, no large European mammal has been added to our repertoire of successful domesticates. Our few species of domestic mammals were quickly winnowed from hundreds of others that had been tried and abandoned. . . .

. . . The horse is especially interesting in illustrating what seemingly slight differences make one species prized, another useless. Horses belong to the order Perissodactyla, which consists of the hoofed mammals with an odd number of toes: horses, tapirs, and rhinoceroses. Of the 17 living species of Perissodactyla, all four tapirs and all five rhinos plus five of the eight wild horse species have never been domesticated. Africans or Indians mounted on rhinos or tapirs probably would have trampled any European invaders—but the animals never allowed that event to happen.

A sixth wild horse relative, the African wild ass, gave rise to domestic donkeys, which proved splendid as pack animals but useless as military chargers. The seventh wild horse relative, the onager of western Asia, may have been used to pull wagons for some centuries after 3000 B.C. But all accounts of the onager blast its disposition with words like "bad-tempered," "unapproachable," and "inherently intractable." The vicious beasts had to be kept muzzled to prevent them from biting their attendants. When domesticated horses reached the Middle East about 2300 B.C., onagers were finally kicked onto the scrap heap of failed domesticates.

Horses revolutionized warfare in a way that no other animal, not even elephants or camels, ever rivaled. At first, hitched to battle chariots, they became the unstoppable Sherman tanks of ancient war. After the invention of saddles and stirrups, they enabled Attila the Hun to devastate the Roman Empire, Genghis Khan to conquer an empire from the Adriatic to the Pacific coast of China, and military kingdoms to arise in West Africa. A few dozen horses helped Cortés and Pizarro, leading only a few hundred Spaniards each, to overthrow the two most populous and advanced New World states, the Aztec and Incan empires. Not until the futile Polish cavalry charges against Hitler's invading armies in September 1939 did the military importance of this most universally prized of all domestic animals finally come to an end, after 6,000 years.

Ironically, relatives of the horses that Cortés and Pizarro rode had formerly been native to the New World. Had those horses survived, Moctezuma and Atahualpa might have shattered the conquistadores with cavalry charges of their own. But, in a cruel twist of fate, the Americas' horses had become extinct long before that, along with 80 to 90 percent of the other large animal species of the Americas and Australia.

It happened around the time that the first human settlers—ancestors of modern Indians and native Australians—reached those continents. The Americas lost not only their horses but also other potentially domesticatable species (after all, you never know until you try) like large camels, ground sloths, mammoths, and mastodons. Australia lost all its giant kangaroos, giant wombats, and rhinoceroslike diprotodonts. In fact Australia and North America ended up with no domesticatable mammal species at all, unless Indian dogs were derived from North American wolves. South America was left with only the guinea pig (used for food), the alpaca (used for wool), and the llama (used as a pack animal but too small to carry a rider).

Consequently, domestic mammals made little contribution to the protein needs of native Australians and Americans. No native American or Australian mammal ever pulled a plow, cart, or war chariot, ever gave milk or bore a rider. The civilizations of the New World limped forward on human muscle power alone, while those of the Old World ran on the power of animal muscle, wind, and water.

Do similar arguments apply to plants? Some parallels jump out immediately. As is true of animals, only a very few of all wild plant species have proved suitable for domestication. For example, plant species in which a single hermaphroditic individual can pollinate itself (like wheat) were domesticated earlier and more easily than cross-pollinating species (like rye). The reason is that self-pollinating varieties are easier to select and then maintain as true strains, since they're not continually mixing with their wild relatives. Oaks are another example. Although acorns were a major food source in prehistoric Europe and North America, no oak has ever been domesticated. For every domesticated plant that we still use today, many others were domesticated in the past and discarded. (What living American has eaten sumpweed, which Indians in the eastern United States domesticated for its seeds by 2000 B.C.?)

Such considerations certainly help explain the slow rate of technological development in Australia. That continent's relative poverty in wild plants appropriate for domestication undoubtedly contributed to the failure of aboriginal Australians to develop agriculture. But it's not so obvious why agriculture in the Americas lagged behind that in the Old World. After all, many plants now of worldwide importance were domesticated in the New World—potatoes, tomatoes, and squash, to name just a few. To find the solution to this puzzle, we need to take a close look at the New World's most important crop: corn.

Corn is a cereal—that is, a grass with edible starchy seeds, like barley kernels or wheat grains. Cereals still provide most of the calories consumed by the human race. While all civilizations have depended on them, different native cereals have been domesticated by different civilizations: wheat, barley, oats, and rye in the Near East and Europe; rice, foxtail millet, and broomcorn millet in China and southeast Asia; sorghum, pearl millet, and finger millet in sub-Saharan Africa; but only corn in the New World. Soon after Columbus's arrival, corn was brought back to Europe and spread around the globe, and it now covers more of the world's acreage than any other crop except wheat. Today corn is the most important crop in the United States. Why, then, didn't corn enable Indian civilizations to develop as fast as the Old World civilizations fed by wheat and other cereals?

Unfortunately, corn was a much bigger pain in the neck to develop, and it gave an inferior product. The Near East had more than a dozen wild grasses that were easy to domesticate and grow. Their large seeds, required by the highly seasonal climate (a very wet growing season, followed by an intense dry spell), made their value obvious to incipient farmers. They were easy to harvest en masse with a sickle, easy to grind, easy to prepare for cooking, and easy to sow. Another subtle advantage, first recognized by University of Wisconsin botanist Hugh Iltis, was that people didn't have to figure out for themselves that those wild grass seeds could be stored, since wild rodents in the Near East already made caches of up to 60 pounds of them.

The Old World grains were already productive in the wild. You can still harvest up to 700 pounds of grain per acre from wild wheat growing naturally on hillsides in the Near East. In a few weeks a family could harvest enough to feed itself for a year. Hence, even before wheat and barley were domesticated, there were villages in Palestine that had already developed sickles, mortars and pestles, and storage pits, and that were supporting themselves on wild grains.

Domestication of wheat and barley wasn't a conscious act. It wasn't the case that several hunter-gatherers sat down one day, mourned the extinction of big game animals, discussed which particular wheat plants were best, planted the seeds of those plants, and thereby became farmers the next year. Instead, the process we call domestication—the effecting of changes in wild plants under cultivation—was an unintended by-product of people preferring some wild plants over others, and hence accidentally spreading the preferred seeds. In the case of wild cereals, people naturally preferred to harvest ones with big seeds, ones whose seeds were easy to remove from the seed coverings, and ones with firm, nonshattering stalks that held all the seeds together. It took only a few mutations, favored by this unconscious human selection, to produce the large-seeded, nonshattering cereal varieties that we refer to as domesticated.

Archeological evidence from ancient Near Eastern village sites shows that by 8000 B.C. wheat and barley were beginning to show these changes. The development of other domestic varieties and intentional sowing soon followed. Gradually the dependence on wild foods diminished. By 6000 B.C. crop cultivation had been integrated with animal herding into a complete food-production system. For better or worse, people were no longer hunter-gatherers but farmers and herders, en route to being civilized.

Now contrast these relatively straightforward Old World developments with the story in the New World. Mexico, the Andes, and the Amazon—where American farming began—lacked the Near East's type of highly seasonal climate, hence lacked large-seeded grasses that were already productive in the wild. Indians did start to domesticate three small-seeded wild grasses—maygrass, little barley, and a wild millet—but these were eventually displaced by corn. Yet the process was a tortuous one: the ancestor of corn was a Mexican wild grass called teosinte that, although it did have big seeds, in other respects hardly seemed promising at all. . . .

. . . Corn ears had to be harvested individually and by hand, rather than en masse with a sickle; the cobs had to be shucked; the kernels didn't fall off but had to be scraped or bitten off; and the seeds had to be planted individually, rather than scattered by the handful.

And the result was still poorer nutritionally than Old World cereals: lower protein content, deficiencies of important amino acids, and a deficiency of the vitamin niacin (a lack of which tends to cause the disease pellagra). Alkali treatment of the grain was necessary to partially overcome these deficiencies.

In short, characteristics of the New World's staple food crop made its potential value much harder to discern in the wild plant, harder to develop by domestication, and harder to extract even after domestication. Much of the lag between New World and Old World civilization may have been due to the peculiarities of one plant.

In determining what suitable wild animal and plant species would be available for domestication, geography set the pace of Old and New World civilizations. But geography had another major role that deserves mention. Each civilization depended not only on its local domesticated food plants but also on others that arrived after having been domesticated elsewhere. The predominantly north-south axis of the New World made such diffusion of food plants difficult; the predominantly east-west axis of the Old World made it easy. . . .

Plants and animals spread easily within a climate zone to which they're already adapted. To spread farther they have to develop new varieties with different tolerances. A glance at the map of the Old World shows how species could shift long distances without encountering a change of climate. Many of these shifts proved tremendously important in launching farming or herding in new areas or enriching it in old areas. Species moved among China, India, the Near East, and Europe without ever leaving temperate latitudes. "America the Beautiful" may invoke our spacious skies, our amber waves of grain. But in reality the most spacious skies of the Northern Hemisphere were in the Old World, where amber waves of related grains came to stretch for 7,000 miles, from the English Channel to the China Sea.

The Romans were already growing wheat and barley from the Near East, peaches and citrus fruits from China, cucumbers and sesame from India, and hemp and onions from central Asia, along with oats and poppies originating locally in Europe. Horses spread from Russia to West Africa to transform the practice of warfare there, while goats and sheep spread down the highlands of East Africa to launch herding in southern Africa among the Hottentots, who lacked locally domesticated animals of their own. African sorghum and cotton reached India by 2000 B.C., while bananas and yams from tropical southeast Asia crossed the Indian Ocean to enrich agriculture in tropical Africa.

In the New World, however, the temperate zone of North America is isolated from the temperate zone of the Andes and southern South America by thousands of miles of tropics, in which temperate-zone species can't survive. As a result, the llama, alpaca, and guinea pig of the Andes never spread in prehistoric times even as far north as Mexico, which remained without any domestic mammals to carry packs or to produce wool or meat. Likewise, potatoes failed to spread from the Andes to North America, while sunflowers never spread from North America to the Andes.

Many crops that were apparently shared prehistorically between North and South America actually occurred as different varieties or even species in the two continents, suggesting that they were domesticated independently in both areas. This seems true of cotton, lima beans, chili peppers, and tobacco. Corn did spread from Mexico to the rest of the Americas, but it evidently wasn't easy, perhaps because of the time it took to develop varieties suited to other latitudes. Not until A.D. 900—thousands of years after corn had emerged in Mexico—did it become a staple food in the Mississippi Valley.

If the Old and New Worlds had each been tilted, say, 90 or 60 degrees away from their respective axes, the spread of crops and domestic animals would have been slower in the Old World and faster in the New World. The pace of civilization would have been correspondingly different. Who knows whether that difference would have sufficed to let Moctezuma or Atahualpa invade Europe, despite their lack of horses?

Continental differences in civilization, then, weren't an accident caused by a few individual geniuses. Nor were they the result of average differences in inventiveness among whole peoples. Instead, they were determined by geography, which sets ground rules for the biology of all plant and animal species, including our own. In the long run, and on a broad scale, where we live makes us who we are.

53

From Hemisphere to Hemisphere

A pioneering study about the transferal of European plants and animals to the New World, written by James A. Robertson, first editor of the *Hispanic American Historical Review*, depicted the transfer as a peaceful introduction, whereby Amerindians were brought to a realization of the virtue of beef cattle and hardy wheat. Considerably later, Alfred W. Crosby's *The Columbian Exchange: Biological and Cultural Consequences of 1492* (1972) took the position that this transfer was actually marked by violent conflicts between life forms. He points out that a variety of plants indigenous to the New World were pushed aside by vegetation such as "Kentucky" bluegrass, daisies, and dandelions, while domestic animals and the Amerindians themselves were crowded by vast numbers of wild, imported horses, dogs, pigs, and steers. In an excerpt from an essay reprinted here, Crosby looks at the nutritional aspects of the interchange between the hemispheres, which led to profound change in the human condition.

"Columbus was the greatest benefactor of all time . . ."

Because of the isolation provided by the Atlantic and the Pacific oceans, almost entirely different forms of food were cultivated in the Eastern and the Western hemispheres. Contact between the two was followed by a rapid outflow from the New World of its superior plant types: maize (corn), white potatoes, sweet potatoes, manioc (tapioca), and various nutritious beans. Columbus can be remembered for having added more variety to the world's dinner menu.

T he Old and New Worlds had been separate for millions of years before Columbus, except for periodic reconnections in the far north during Ice Ages. In this immense period the biotas [animals and plants] of the Old and New Worlds evolved and diverged. As of 1492, there were many similar species, especially in Eurasia and North America, such as deer and elm, but the differences were impressive. Europe had nothing quite like hummingbirds, rattlesnakes, and hickory and pecan trees. Further south the contrasts between Old and New World biotas were even more amazing. The biggest mammal in Africa was the elephant; in South America, the cow-sized tapir. The native biotas of the Old and New Worlds were decidedly different, and for most of the previous few million years these biotas had not been in competition or even in contact.

The last bout of competition before the arrival of Columbus included the initial migration into America of the Old World's *Homo sapiens* and the spread of that species from the Arctic Sea to Tierra del Fuego, effecting changes as yet only partly understood. After the last Ice Age ended some ten thousand years ago and the continental glaciers melted back, releasing so much water that the land connection between Siberia and Alaska was innundated, the ancestors of the Amerindians were left in complete or nearly complete isolation. They developed autochthonous [indigenous] cultures, domesticated American plants and animals, and adapted to American microlife. In 1492 they were living in equilibrium with each other and with the other tenants of the New World, macro and micro. The homeostasis no doubt wobbled considerably, even violently, in areas with thick settlements of Amerindian farmers, but in all probability it was more stable then than it has been since.

During the same ten-thousand-year period, peoples of the Old World, in adjustment to the biotas of their continents, engendered their cultures and domesticated and bred their crops, beasts, and, unintentionally of course, their own set of pesky and sometimes fatal germs. These humans were also elements in a system that varied constantly but which was, within broad limits, stable. They even had a modus vivendi with the plague, which had reared up in the fourteenth century and killed approximately one-third of the population of western Eurasia and North Africa. By 1500, however, the European population had recovered its pre–Black Death totals and was growing, despite recurrent waves of plague and other deadly diseases.

SOURCE *The Columbian Voyages, The Columbian Exchange, and their Historians*, pp. 7–19 passim, 1987. Reprinted by permission of The American Historical Association and the author, Alfred W. Crosby.

In 1492 these two systems of homeostasis, one of the Old World and the other of the New World, like tightrope walkers with poles dipping and lifting to maintain balance, collided.

The Old World peoples had some distinct advantages in the biological competition that followed. Although their crop plants were not superior to those of the Amerindians per se—wheat, rice, and yams were "better" than maize, potatoes, and cassava in some ways and inferior in others—the Old World advantage in domesticated animals was great. It was a matter of the Old World's horses, cattle, pigs, goats, sheep, and other domesticated species versus the New World's llamas, guinea pigs, domesticated fowl, and dogs. This advantage was not permanent, because Amerindians adopted many of the new livestock, most spectacularly horses in the Great Plains and pampa, where these animals helped the Amerindians to maintain their independence until the last half of the nineteenth century. The greatest influence of Old World plants and animals was probably in making it possible for Old World pastoralists and farmers to live in the American colonies as they had at home or, in most cases, better. Old World livestock, which had evolved in what seemingly had been a rougher league than the New World's, often outfought, outran, or at least out-reproduced American predators. Free of the diseases and pests that had preyed on them at home, the European animals thrived and even went wild, often in amazing numbers, providing mounts, meat, milk, and leather much more cheaply in the New World than in the Old. The most spectacular instances of this were in southern South America. The first Spanish attempt to colonize the pampa failed in the 1530s, and the survivors departed, leaving some livestock behind. When settlers returned in 1580 they found "infinite" herds of horses. In 1587 Hernando Arias left one hundred cattle behind him at Santa Fé de Paraná in Brazil, and when he returned in 1607 he found, according to his testimony, one hundred thousand. These Iberians were speaking colorfully, rather than statistically, but the natural increase in the feral herds of South America was indeed enormous, probably unprecedented in all history. Smaller but comparable explosions in animal populations took place elsewhere in the New World. . . .

"The greatest service which can be rendered any country is to add a useful plant to its culture . . . ," noted Thomas Jefferson. By this standard, Columbus was the greatest benefactor of all time because by bringing the agricultures of the Old and New Worlds into contact, he added many useful plants to each. He enormously increased the number of kinds and quantities of food available to humans by giving them access to all the masterpieces of plant and animal breeders everywhere, and not just those of two or three contiguous continents.

In the last five hundred years food crops and domesticated animals have crossed the Atlantic and Pacific in both directions, enabling people to live in numbers in places where they previously had had only slim means to feed themselves. The Argentine pampa, Kansas, and Saskatchewan, too dry in large areas for Amerindian maize and in the latter case too far north, are now breadbaskets, producing not only enough Eurasian wheat for themselves but much more to export to the world. Eurasia's domesticated animals—cattle, sheep, pigs, goats, and even water buffalo—provide Americans from the Hudson Bay to the Straits of Magellan with the means to do what was only meagerly possible before 1492: to turn grass, which humans cannot eat, into meat and milk. In 1983, according to the Food and Agricultural Organization (FAO) of the United Nations, the New World slaughtered 84 million cattle, 27 million sheep, and 139 million pigs; in 1492 none at all. New World peoples derive all but a fraction of their animal protein, and almost all their wool and leather, from Old World animals.

Conversely, cassava, a root plant of South American origin, provides calories for multitudes of Africans and Asians in areas previously too wet, too dry, or too infertile to support more than sparse populations. Similarly, as the white potato of South America spread across northern Europe, peasants from county Kerry to the Urals found themselves with the means to raise more food in bulk per unit of land than ever before (although ultimately there were dire results in Ireland, where an American pestilence arrived to destroy the American plant in the 1840s). In the Far East the impact of the arrival of the products of Amerindian plant breeders was at least as great as in Europe or Africa. By the late 1930s New World crops amounted to 20 percent of the food produced in China, where approximately one quarter of the human race lived (and lives now). According to Ping-ti Ho, historian of Chinese demography and agriculture: "During the last two centuries, when rice culture was gradually approaching its limit, and encountering the law of diminishing returns, the various dry land food crops introduced from America have contributed most to the increase in national food production and have made possible a continual growth of population."

In 1983 Amerindian maize accounted for over one-sixth of all the grain produced in the world. Not surprisingly, the United States is the world's largest producer, but, perhaps surprisingly, China is the second greatest producer. China also harvests more sweet potatoes, a native American plant that does marvelously well under conditions that would discourage most other crops, than any other nation; sweet potatoes are an old and dependable famine food for the Chinese. Globally, American root crops, of which the most important are white and sweet potatoes and cassava, exceed in quantity of production all others combined. The world produced 557 million metric tons of root crops in 1983, of which those of Amerindian domestication amounted to 524 million metric tons. The world's leading producer of white potatoes is the Soviet Union, which forks up ten times more potatoes in weight than South America, the home continent of the tuber. Africa produces over 48 million metric tons of cassava, dwarfing the 28 million of South America, where the plant was first cultivated.

The significance of Amerindian crops in the future will increase because all the most important ones were first domesticated in the tropics, where many of them still grow best. The developing nations of the world, where human populations are expanding fastest, are mostly in the tropics and in hot, wet lands nearby. The maize production of the developed world in 1983 was 187 million metric tons, and that of the developing world about 30 million less, but a great deal of the former tonnage went to feed livestock while almost all the latter went directly to feed people. The sweet potato production of the developed societies in the same year was 2 million metric tons, and that of the developing societies over 112 million. All of the cassava raised in 1983 about which the FAO has statistics (123 million metric tons) was raised in the developing nations. Compare these figures with those for wheat, the traditional staple since the Neolithic Age in temperate Eurasia: 300 million metric tons were produced by the developed nations, and not quite 200 million by the developing.

Between 1750 and 1986 the population of the world grew from approximately 750 million to 5 billion. The exchange of crops and domesticated animals between the Old and New Worlds cannot be credited with being the sole cause of this awesome increase, any more than the capital produced by Europe's exploitation of America can be said to be the only cause of the Industrial Revolution, but it is hard to see how the colossal effect could have come about without the Columbian exchange.

QUESTIONS

1. How analytical an observer was Columbus of the vegetation in the Caribbean?
2. Did Columbus's initial conclusions that the New World had meager fauna but luxuriant flora influence subsequent writers?
3. In what ways, and for what purposes, did Columbus find the vegetation and inhabitants of the islands more "Spanish" than in Spain?
4. What accidents of geography caused the rate of New World agricultural innovation to diverge from that of the Old World?
5. What animals and plants were found in Eurasia that were not found in the Western Hemisphere?
6. Why did transplanted Old World livestock outstrip their New World competitors?
7. In what ways did Columbus's landing eventually enrich the diet of all humankind?
8. What area of the world will be the major source of new foods in the future?
9. How significant to world cuisine were the New World contributions?

Photograph Credits

PORTFOLIO A

page 115 Theodor de Bry, *India Occidentalis*, Vol. IV (Impression Francofurti, 1590). Reprinted by permission of The Newberry Library. **page 117** Theodor de Bry, *India Occidentalis*, Vol. IX (Impression Francofurti, 1590). Reprinted by permission of The Newberry Library. **page 119** *Nova Reperta* (Antwerp, 1589). Reprinted by permission of The Newberry Library. **page 121** *Theatrum Orbus Terrarum* (Antwerp, 1579). Reprinted by permission of The Newberry Library. **page 122** *European Vision of America*, illustration #93A (Cleveland Museum of Art, 1975). Reprinted by permission of The New York Historical Society. **page 124** Frontispiece, *de Nieuwe en Onberkende weerld* (Amsterdam, 1671). Reprinted by permission of The Newberry Library.

PORTFOLIO B

page 245 Theodor de Bry, *Peregination in Americam* (Frankfurt-am-Main, 1597). Reprinted by permission of the Newberry Library. **page 247** Theodor de Bry, *India Occidentalis*, Vol. XXII (Frankfurt-am-Main, 1590). Reprinted by permission of The Newberry Library. **page 248** André Thévet, *Les singularitez de la France Antarctique, autrement nommée Amérique* (Paris, 1557). Reprinted by permission of The Newberry Library. **page 250** Felipe Guaman Poma de Ayala (Waman Puma), *El premier neuva crónica y buen gobierno* (1583–1615). Ed. J. V. Murra and Rolena Adorno. Tr. J. L. Urioste (Mexico City: Siglo veintiuno editores, 1980). Original: Royal Library of Copenhagen. **page 251** Theodor de Bry, *Peregination in Americam* (Frankfurt-am-Main, 1597). Reprinted by permission of The Newberry Library. **page 253** Joseph-François La Fitau, *Moeurs des Savages Amériquains* (1724), Vol. 17. Reprinted by permission of The Newberry Library.

GENERAL ILLUSTRATIONS

page 38 Ambrosius Aurelius Theodosius Macrobius (c. 400 A.D.) *In somnium Sciponis exposito Saturnalia* (Brescia, 1483). Reprinted by permission of The Newberry Library. **page 48** Girolamo Benzoni, *La historia del Mondo Nuovo* (Venice, 1572). Photo: Ernie Bradford, *Christopher Columbus* (New York: Viking Press, 1973). Original: Cleveland Public Library. **page 72** Ptolemy (Claudius Ptolemaeus), *Cosmographia* (Rome, 1478). Reprinted by permission of The Newberry Library. **page 101** Frontispiece in Néstor Ponce de León y La Guardia, *The Columbus Gallery* (New York: N. Ponce de León, 1893). **page 168** Bernardino de Sahagún, *General History of the Things of New Spain*. Book 12: *The Conquest of Mexico* (Florentine Codex). (Santa Fe, New Mexico: School of American Research & University of Utah, 1955). Photo: A. J. O. Anderson & E. Dibble. Original: unknown. **page 292** *America in Maps: Dating from 1500 to 1856*. Compiled and edited by Egon Klemp. Tr. Margaret and J. C. Stone (New York: Homes & Meier, 1976). Original: unknown. **page 340** Theodor de Bry, *Peregination in Americam*, Vol. IV (Frankfurt-am-Main, 1597). Reprinted by permission of The Newberry Library.